The Zhong-Lü System of Internal Alchemy

by

Livia Kohn

Three Pines Press
www.threepinespress.com

9 8 7 6 5 4 3 2 1

Printed in the United States of America
This edition is printed on acid-free paper that meets the American National Standard Institute Z39.48 Standard.
Distributed in the United States by Three Pines Press.

Cover Art: Zhongli Quan transmitting the Dao to Lan Caihe, one of the Eight Immortals. Painting at the Baxian'an (Eight Immortals' Retreat) temple in Xi'an, built at the site of the tavern where Zhongli Quan first met Lü Dongbin. Photograph by Karine Martin, 19 June 2012.

Library of Congress Cataloging-in-Publication Data

Names: Kohn, Livia, 1956- author.
Title: The Zhong-Lü system of internal alchemy / by Livia Kohn.
Description: St. Petersburg, FL : Three Pines Press, 2020. | Includes bibliographical references and index.
Identifiers: LCCN 2019057946 | ISBN 9781931483445 (paperback)
Subjects: LCSH: Taoism--China--Sources--Early works to 1800. | Taoism--Doctrines--Early works to 1800. | Alchemy--China--Sources. | Immortality--Taoism. | Zhongli, Quan, active 9th century. Zhong Lü chuan dao ji. | Zhongli, Quan, active 9th century. Ling bao bi fa.
Classification: LCC BL1923 .K6858 2020 | DDC 299.5/1442--dc23
LC record available at https://lccn.loc.gov/2019057946

Contents

Discussion

Translation

Acknowledgments

This book was inspired by editorial work on Mark Bartosh's translation of the lectures and practice instructions by Wang Liping (b. 1949), a major figure in internal alchemy in China today as well as the leader of several practice organizations in the West (www.dragongateacademy.com; www.longmen.eu). His work, which was published in 2019 by Three Pines Press under the title *Daoist Internal Mastery*, claims to rely closely on the Zhong-Lü system and repeatedly cites its core texts.

Editing it, I was left with a sense that a better understanding of this tradition would benefit the community of both scholars and practitioners. Thus I began to translate the texts, the *Zhong-Lü chuandao ji* and the *Lingbao bifa*, in due course obtaining earlier translations by Eva Wong (2000) and Farzeen Baldrian-Hussein (1984)—the latter with the generous help of Karine Martin of the French Taoist Association.

Once the translation was complete, I proceeded to write the introductory part, looking into the historical position of the texts as well as examining their cosmology and practice systems. Over the course of a year, the book was revised repeatedly, notably with the generous help of Fabrizio Pregadio, Stephen Eskildsen, and Mark Bartosh, who took out time from their busy schedules to give it a careful reading and point out various errors, inconsistencies, and questionable statements. Fabrizio Pregadio in particular helped to make the translations more accurate and generously provided both references to original sources and copies of his own recent partial translation of the *Chuandao ji*. They all greatly supported my efforts and helped to make the work more accurate and accessible. I am deeply indebted to their support.

Chapter One
Historical Context

Internal alchemy has been the dominant form of Daoist self-cultivation since the Northern Song dynasty (960-1127), when it reached first full maturity as an integrated system.[1] The Song dynasty was a time of great change and transformation on many different levels—technology, economy, politics, culture, life-style, and religion. Society opened to new dimensions of communication and flourishing, enhancing local culture and bringing about renewal in many different areas. In terms of religion, new kinds of practitioners arose in addition to the priesthood, known collectively as ritual masters—including also mendicant preachers and eccentric adepts of various backgrounds.

In this context, the figure of Lü Dongbin, an eccentric master known for his poetry, alchemy, and sword fighting, rose to prominence especially in the southern part of the country. In the 11th century, he came to be associated with a group of documents describing the first full-fledged system of internal alchemy, called Zhong-Lü after himself and his putative teacher, the Han-dynasty immortal Zhongli Quan. First fully documented in the 12th century, it laid the foundation for the teachings of many later schools of internal alchemy, furnishing structures that are still in use today.

The Song Dynasty

The transition from the Tang to the Song dynasty has been described as "the most decisive rupture in the history of imperial China" (Kuhn 2009, 1). After the rebellion of An Lushan 安祿山 in 755, when the Tang court fled to Sichuan, the dynasty never fully recovered its dominance over the empire, which was plagued by official persecutions, rebellious war-lords, and widespread banditry. By 907, when the dynasty officially ended, the country was split up into ten states, run largely by political newcomers such as "landless peasants, robbers, smugglers, and even former slaves" (2009, 18), whose bloody campaigns ravaged the land. Over the next fifty years, five dynasties claimed the official mantle of emperor (see Lorge 2011; Davis 2002), until in 960, the Zhao clan reunited the country and provided a new level of stabil-

[1] See Kohn and Wang 2009; Needham et al. 1983; Pregadio 2012a; 2014a; Robinet 1989a; 1995.

ity, which soon led to "a complete transformation of the social and political landscape" (Mostern 2011, 24).[2]

Restructuring the spatial and administrative organization of the country, they created a new system of jurisdiction, replaced the aristocratic class of governance by a meritocratic civil bureaucracy (2011, 11), standardized the currency, built roads that could support wider carts, expanded the canal network, and created safety for merchants and travelers by providing armed escorts (Kuhn 209, 224-26). This not only opened up the southern part of the country and but also greatly increased commerce and innovation (Yü 2016, 239), to the point where the Song dynasty has been compared to England during the industrial revolution (Edwards 2013; Pomeranz 2000).

Technological innovations in all different fields, from farming through textile production and metal works to transportation, placed the country far ahead in the world and caused the population to triple, which in turn gave new impetus to economic growth and social innovation.[3] A major factor in this context was the invention of printing, first used in the 9th century in a Buddhist environment to facilitate the copying of sutras, considered a highly meritorious activity, especially in large quantities (Goodrich 1925). Made commercially viable in the Song, printing greatly facilitated mass communication, since posters with announcements could be easily placed in villages and city wards. It also inspired an increase in literacy, further supported by the government's efforts to place both private and public schools in all districts of the empire, and led to the commencement of large-scale encyclopedia projects that collected vast amounts of knowledge in more accessible form.[4]

Another major effect of printing was the development of the world's first viable paper currency, expanding the so-called flying money (*feiqian* 飛錢) in the Tang, which involved paper notes redeemable at distant locations (Verellen 2019, 268). Its Song institutionalization was precipitated by the increasing need of the government for iron and copper in manufacturing (Kuhn 2009, 234) as well as by the expanding commerce across ever wider areas. The latter involved increasingly larger sums of money, which made it cumbersome for merchants to carry hard and heavy coins in heavy sacks. Paper currency came in two forms, first letters of credit and later actual bills, created once printing reached a level of quality that made for-

---

[2] For a detailed presentation of political development under the Song, see Twitchett et al. 2010. For social change, see Hymes 1986; Hymes and Schirokauer 1993.

[3] On technological change, see Fairbank 1992, 88; Kuhn 2009, 220-30; also Elvin 1971. For population growth, see Mostern 2011, 11; Deng 2013. On commerce and urbanization, see Gernet 1982; Shiba 1970; Elvin 1973; Glahn 2003.

[4] Kuhn 2009, 40-41; Fairbank 1992, 94; Furth 1999, 61; see also Cherniak 1994; Chia 1996; 2003; Elvin 1971.

geries difficult. To begin, merchants would carry a promissory note or exchange bill that would guarantee them access to funds in far-away places. Gradually formal institutions developed, forerunners of banks that gradually replaced the direct partnerships between merchant houses. Actual paper bills—printed on pulp made from the bark of the mulberry tree and strictly controlled by the government—are first documented from the year 1020 and were fully viable by 1160 (Kuhn 2009, 238).

All of this contributed greatly to the growth of the merchant class, which had three major effects on the religious scene. First, there was a great increase in lay organizations and lay-sponsored temples and practices. Here ordinary people came together to worship specific deities and to perform rites and cultivation practices, sometimes in private homes, sometimes in special community halls. Many localities that were isolated and dependent on their own resources during centuries of political chaos developed unique organizations and deities, which now—with improved communication—started to spread and turn into wider, often commerce-oriented cults (Glahn 2003, 188-90). "New deity cults and revelatory traditions enriched and reshaped the hierarchical, communal, and aristocratic system" of previous dynasties (Skar 2000, 414; see also Hymes 2002).

Second, there emerged a much larger market for practical religious aids to daily life, from talismans for building homes and spells for granting a safe passage to exorcisms for healing, funeral rites (*liandu* 煉渡), and services for the salvation of the dead (*pudu* 普渡), often involving new and local deities (Skar 2000, 413). And third, as more and more people became religiously engaged, they required more direct contact with gods, spirits, and ancestors, notably for purposes of exorcism and healing (Davis 2001, 3). As a result, trance techniques increased manifold, either through spirit-mediums or by automatic writing with the help of the planchette, a kind of Ouija board, and a new level of religious practitioners came to the fore.

Religious Practitioners

Traditionally, Daoist and Buddhist priests occupied the middle ground between imperially sponsored religious activities and so-called popular religion, which was often denigrated by officials for its followers' engagement in shamanic possession, blood sacrifices, licentious cults, and sexual orgies. Peasants and villagers, as documented in numerous writings, were besieged by threats of supernatural danger, such as ghosts, demons, specters, sprites, hobgoblins, poltergeists, revenants, spooks, bogies, and contagions (Harper 1985, 497), not to mention semi-supernatural animals as well as essences of plants and minerals that had to be placated in various ways (Meulenbeld 2015, 101; Kohn 2019, 35). Many valiant officials strove to convert villagers to more sedate and imperially sanctioned practices or managed to kill particular demonic entities that demanded deeds unacceptable to the higher educated.

Organized Daoist cults as they first developed in the 2nd century CE—and Buddhist orders in their wake—were at odds with both, claiming a direct connection to the divine traditionally reserved for the emperor and his delegates, while also insisting on a purer and more refined way of dealing with the demons of popular religion. Occupying senior positions in a bureaucratic spirit world, run like the imperial government by set administrative procedures and formal judgments, priests of organized religions claimed powers over the supernatural world that affected the living as much as the dead.[5] They executed these powers less by means of shamanic trance or blood sacrifices than through systematic prayers and the submission of written petitions that would obligate the spirits to act in certain, preferably nonharmful ways (Harper 1985, 472-73; Nickerson 2000, 273).

This intermediate position is quite obvious in the dietary restrictions documented in the early code of the Celestial Masters (Tianshi 天師) school, *Laojun shuo yibai bashi jie* 老君說一百八十戒 (180 Precepts Spoken by Lord Lao, in DZ 786; trl. Hendrischke and Penny), created under some Buddhist influence and reflecting similar values (Penny 1996). Rejecting the elite tendency to drink heavily and competitively, it prohibits the consumption of alcohol (no. 24). In opposition to mainstream status-seeking through the serving of meat, it outlaws eating the flesh of wild animals specially killed (no. 172, 173). In contrast to popular cults, moreover, the code demands that members abstain from all killing and the performance of blood sacrifices (no. 39, 79), encouraging them instead to live largely on vegetables (no. 176) (Kohn 2017, 176). Exorcistic practices as well as divination and fortune-telling, and even the basic techniques of Chinese medicine were forbidden, "the penitential petitioning of celestial officials being sufficient" (Nickerson 2000, 277).[6]

Throughout the middle ages, the state-sponsored codification of the priesthood, both Daoist and Buddhist, provided a set role for religious practitioners that allowed them to function in this intermediate sphere between official state religion and popular cults. The Tang-Song transition brought the collapse of this system, leading to a different constellation of groups: official agents that included imperial as well as Daoist and Buddhist hierarchies at the top, village spirit-mediums and lesser acolytes at the bottom, plus "a new and expanding group of lay Daoist exorcists called ritual masters (*fashi* 法師)" in the middle (Davis 2001, 7).

---

5 See Harper 1994, 17; Kleeman 1998, 70; Seidel 1987, 46; Yamada in Pregadio 2008, 62.

6 For more on the relationship of Daoists to popular cults, see Miyakawa 1979; Stein 1979; Nickerson 1994; Schipper 1985; 1994b.

Defined as disciples who had mastered a particular tradition or section of the canon, they were "lay practitioners who looked and performed very much like Daoist priests but who were not priests," yet followed the same rules of purity and correct procedure (2001, 50). Socially members of a class of minor officials, they were "spellbinding erudites" (2001, 61): educated and literate, trained in philosophical and cosmological speculation, they were versed in a variety of ritual techniques, notably the increasingly popular thunder rites (*leifa* 雷法; see Skar 1997; 2000, 456-58; Chao 2009: 104-07), but also engaged in personal cultivation, such as the internal guiding of energy and the refinement of spirit—necessary prerequisites to the successful execution of the rites (Chao 2009, 108-11).

They rose to the fore as independent agents because there were no structured organizations to support them. Court subsidies for religious institutions had ceased so that temples declined, patriarchal lineages ceased, and techniques and doctrines were suspended. There were no famous monasteries or established mountain centers to go to, nor were there any officially recognized masters to follow. Budding practitioners were on their own, wandering from one sacred location to the next, connecting with isolated hermits, perchance finding a stash of old texts or discovering certain efficacious techniques by trial and error. Occasionally they even secured the support of a local ruler—who was usually more interested in alchemical ways of making gold than in spiritual pursuits—and proceeded to reconstruct one or another temple center of old.

These practitioners had no financial cushion to fall back on, and thus had to find ways of serving communities for a fee so they could continue their quest. As a result—and coinciding fortuitously with the needs of the growing merchant class—Daoist ritual masters, in competition with wandering Buddhists, tantric ritualists, and local shamans, offered services of fortune-telling, healing, exorcism, and protection.

A case in point is the famous immortal Chen Tuan 陳摶 (d. 989) who wandered through the country from Hunan to Sichuan to pick up various teachings and eventually settled at the foot of Mount Hua 華山, where he set about to restore the Yuntai guan 雲台觀 (Cloud Terrace Monastery) that had fallen into disrepair. He gained prominence as a physiognomist, recognizing the future first emperor of the Song and also, after being called to court, identifying the son best suited for leadership. [7] In addition, he was renowned for his cosmological speculation and credited with the first *Taiji tu* 太極圖 (Diagram of the Great Ultimate; see Wang 2005a) as well as

---

[7] For a study of Chen Tuan, see Knaul 1981; Kohn 2001a. On his physiognomy, see Kohn 1988. On his sleep practice, see Takehiro 1990. For sleep practice today, see Wang and Bartosh 2019, 155-61.

with various methods of internal cultivation, described as a form of "sleep practice," still part of internal alchemy today.

Lü Dongbin

A figure of the same kind who rose to great prominence—and incidentally was linked to Chen Tuan later—is the immortal Lü Dongbin 吕洞賓, best known as the most popular member of the Eight Immortals. Consisting of seven men and one woman who attained immortality, this group appeared first in theater plays of the 13th century, portrayed as an eccentric and happy lot of supernatural heroes who responded to pleas in emergencies and granted favors and protection (Hawkes 1981; Jing 1996). To the present day widely popular and eagerly worshiped, they are usually venerated as a group. The only one with temples of his own is Lü Dongbin, commonly depicted as a Confucian gentleman with aristocratic features and a sword (Wu et al. 2011, 66). He appears frequently in spirit-writing sessions, serving as inspiring sponsor of many Daoist groups and techniques (Mozias 2020, 17; Tsui 1991).

The story goes that he was born in 796 as Lü Yan 吕严. Well educated, he failed to pass the official examination in 836 (although in some versions, he passed in 837). On his way back home from the capital, he spent the night at an inn—today the site of the Baxian'an 八仙庵 (Eight Immortals' Retreat), the major Daoist sanctuary in Xi'an—where he shared a meal with a mysterious stranger. As the millet cooked over the brazier, Lü fell asleep and dreamed:

> He went up again to the capital as a candidate of the imperial examination and passed it at the top of the list. Starting his career as a junior secretary to one of the Boards, he rapidly rose in rank to positions at the Censorate and the Hanlin Academy. Eventually he became a Privy Councilor, after he had occupied, in the course of his unbroken success, all the most sought-after and important official posts.
>
> Twice he was married, he further dreamt, and both wives belonged to families of wealth and position. Children were born to him. His sons soon took themselves wives, and his daughters left the paternal roof for their husbands' homes. All these events happened before he even reached the age of forty.
>
> Next he found himself Prime Minister for a period of ten years, wielding immense power. This corrupted him. Then suddenly, without warning, he was accused of a grave crime. His home and all his possessions were confiscated, his wife and children separated. He himself, a solitary outcast, was wandering toward his place of banishment beyond the mountains. He found his horse brought to a standstill in snowstorm and was no longer able to continue the journey. (Yetts 1916, 790; Kohn 1993, 125)

At this point he woke up, finding that while he went through an entire official career and family life, the millet had not even fully cooked. Realizing that life was but a fleeting dream and supported by the stranger who turned out to be the Han immortal Zhongli Quan 鍾離權, he began training with him in Daoist cultivation on either Mount Hua in the north or Mount Lu 廬山 in the south, depending on which lineage wrote the tale. The legend continues with the story of ten tests he had to undergo to prove his selfless nature and sincere dedication to Dao.

He had to show that he was generous with his possessions and independent of social approval, had courage in the face of death and other threats or enticements, and was willing to sacrifice himself on behalf of weaker beings. For example,

> Once, on returning home from a walk in the country, he found that during his absence thieves had carried away all his goods and chattels, leaving the house bare. Not even then was his equanimity disturbed. He just set himself to earn a livelihood by tilling the ground. One day when at work with his hoe he unearthed gold pieces to the number of several score. Yet he took not a single one, but quickly covered them all up again. (Kohn 1993, 129)

These moral qualities were not required for their own sake or to enhance particular staunchness of character but served to indicate the stamina and determination necessary for the utter overcoming of body and self on the path to otherworldly immortality. Still practiced in the school of Complete Perfection (Quanzhen 全真) today, as vividly documented in the biography of Wang Liping 王立平 (Cleary 1997), they serve the same function as the abuse heaped on aspiring Zen practitioners when they first enter the training monastery. Standing outside the gate, freezing, hungry, and miserable, they inevitably question everything, culminating in, "How much do I *really* want to do this?" Only if the answer is, "More than anything," is the candidate ready (see Wetering 1974).

Eventually approved, Lü Dongbin received many detailed instructions from Zhongli Quan, both in theory and practice, succeeded in refining himself to higher levels and attained the fullness of immortality. Afterwards, both before and after his ascension into heaven, as the story has it, he traveled widely, incognito performing miracles for ordinary people and spreading the Daoist teaching, including also to the other members of the Eight Immortals.[8]

Lü in History

This hagiographic account appears first in rudimentary form in the *Yueyang fengtu ji* 岳陽風土記 (Record of Local Customs in Yueyang) by the official Fan Zhiming 范致明, dated to 1104. Here Lü is described as a native of Hezhong 何中 in Shanxi who trained on Mount Lu in Jiangxi and was later active in Hunan and Hubei. These locations not only show the spread of his cult in the early 12th century but also match his major later sanctuaries, at the Yueyang Tower 岳陽樓 in Yuezhou 岳州 near Lake Dongting 洞庭湖 in Hunan and the Yongle gong 永樂宮 (Palace of Eternal Joy) near Ruicheng 瑞城 in Shanxi. The story emphasizes that he was skilled in sword techniques and the arts of immortality and made a living by selling paper and ink (Katz 1999, 60; Baldrian-Hussein 1985, 160).

The latter reflects a strong connection of his name to calligraphy and poetry. Poetry, already a major way of communication during the middle ages (Kirkova 2016, 140), became even more widespread under the Song. Then it started to function as a significant social medium beyond the aristocracy, either composed at social gatherings or spread like graffiti on city, temple, and tavern walls—"anonymous, gossipy, popular" (Kuhn 2009, 61). Poetry could be allegorical and descriptive, record events and express emo-

---

8 For studies of the Eight Immortals and the story of Lü Dongbin, see Clart 2009; Jing 1996; Lai 1972; Waley 1930, 15; Wu et al. 2011; Yang 1958; Yetts 1916; 1922.

tions, show ideal moral and cosmic ways, express criticism of current politics and circulate positive energy in the world (Hawes 2005, 11-20).

The Palace of Eternal Joy

Preceding the early hagiography and establishing the connection to poetry is the first work that mentions Lü Dongbin by name: the *Qingyi lu* 清異錄 (Record of Pure and Strange Things) by the official Tao Gu 陶穀 (903-970). He records a sign outside a wine shop in Fengyi 豐邑 (Shaanxi), saying, "Soaring aloft I looked back and bade farewell to the king of spring," followed by the character for "wine," and expresses his admiration for the powerful calligraphy, which he attributes to Lü (Katz 1999, 54; Baldrian-Hussein 1986, 137). This shows that already in the mid-10th century, Lü Dongbin was a well-known and impressive character.

The earliest poem supposedly written by him is called *Zhixuan pian* 指玄篇 (Pointers to the Mystery), often cited in later texts on internal alchemy (Baldrian-Hussein in Pregadio 2008, 1278). Further poems as well as stories featuring his alchemical techniques and magical powers appear in the imperial encyclopedia *Taiping huanyu ji* 太平寰宇記 (A Record of the World during the Reign of Great Peace) of the year 980. Collecting various anecdotes about him, this shows just to what degree his exploits were spreading at the time (Katz 1999, 55).

Closely related are various anecdotes about his prowess as a fortune-teller, recorded in Huang Jian's 黃鑑 (fl. 1015) *Yang Wengong tanyuan* 楊文公談苑 (Conversations with Yang Wengong). According to this, Lü traveled widely and interacted frequently with officials, providing veiled predictions at will and supporting their aspirations if they recognized him as an immortal. The text also contains several poems, one describing his travels and his famous sword, the other alluding to alchemical practices.[9]

In the 1040s, Lü's name was linked with an unsuccessful rebellion in Hebei, and the court instituted a nation-wide search for him, which proved fruitless but did not prevent him from becoming ever more popular (Katz 1999, 57). This lead to more poems being attributed to him that appear variously, including in temple inscriptions (1999, 119). The most important among them is the *Qinyuan chun* 沁园春 (Springtime in the Qin Gardens), a set of lyrics dated to the mid-11th century. [10] Another early alchemical poem appears in the *Huandan zhongxian lun* 還丹眾仙論 (Discussions on Reverting the Elixir by the Host of Immortals, DZ 233), by Yang Zai 楊在, dated to 1052 (Baldrian-Hussein in Schipper and Verellen 2004, 856). It says,

> I get the matron lady to move south
> So she can bring forth six yang energies for me.
> I steam jade fluid in the toad [moon] palace
> And refine jasper liquor at the Kan [water] gate.
>
> The food of spirit immortals long gone
> Today comes to me to taste.
> One cup lasts a myriad eons
> As my intention soars far beyond all things. (14b-15a)

While these texts document the increasing connection of Lü Dongbin to internal alchemy rather vaguely, more specific information begins to appear in the second half of the 11th century. Thus, Chen Shidao's 陳師道 (1053-1101) *Houshan tancong* 後山談叢 (Collected Conversations from Houshan) records Lü's training under Zhongli Quan (Katz 1999, 55). The two are also linked in an inscription commemorating the restoration of the Yuntai guan, dated to 1067 and contained in the *Lequan ji* 樂全集 (Collected Works of the Recluse Lequan; see Hervouet 1978, 385) by Zhang Fangping 張方平 (1007-1091), a direct successor of Chen Tuan (Kohn 2001a, 12).

---

9 Katz 1999, 55; Baldrian-Hussein 1986, 140; Ang 1997.

10 It is first described by Liu Fu 劉斧 (1040-ca. 1113) in his *Qingsuo gaoyi* 青瑣高議 (A Lofty View of Literary Sketchbooks; 8.82) as having been revealed by Lü to a scholar named Cui Zhong 崔中 in the city of Yueyang (Baldrian, 1985, 22). It describes the process of internal alchemy, notably seven-based elixir reversion: collect perfect yang at midnight, fuse it with perfect yin to obtain the elixir seed, then refine it through the firing process and accumulate merit to attain transcendence and liberation. Two commentaries survive: one, by Xiao Tingzhi 蕭廷芝 (fl. 1260), is contained in *Xiuzhen shishu* 修真十書 (Ten Books on the Cultivation of Perfection; DZ 263, ch. 13); the other is by Yu Yan 俞琰 (1258-1314), a scholar of the Southern School (DZ 136). See Boltz 1987, 140; Baldrian-Hussein in Schipper and Verellen 2004, 845; in Pregadio 2008, 1178.

Around the same time, Lü's sword techniques featured in various works (see Eskildsen 2008) and he appears in stories relating him to members of the lower classes, notably wine merchants and barbers (see Baldrian-Hussein 1986; Zaccarini 2011).

In the early 12th century, like many other cults and religious figures, Lü was officially recognized by Emperor Huizong (r. 1101–1125), the last ruler of the Northern Song and a great supporter of Daoism (see Bol 2001). He sponsored and collected Daoist art and himself engaged both in Daoist painting and the exegesis of Daoist scriptures, notably the *Daode jing* 道德經 (Book of the Way and Its Virtue), which was highly venerated by Song rulers in general. Huizong also organized Daoist rites for state protection and good fortune, and inspired many Daoists to come forward and present their views and texts (Ebrey 2000; Ebrey and Bickford 2006). In 1116, he bestowed sev eral honorary titles on Lü, notably Miaotong zhenren 妙通真人 (Perfected of Wondrous Pervasion) and Chunyang zhenren 纯陽真人 (Perfected of Pure Yang), elevating him to an official position in the Daoist pantheon and paving the way for his inclusion in the patriarchal lineage of later schools.

Zhongli Quan

Lü Dongbin's immortal teacher Zhongli Quan was similarly honored, receiving the title Zhengyang zhenren 正陽真人 (Perfected of Rightful Yang). The oldest of the Eight Immortals and commonly depicted as a large, stately man with a round pot-belly (Wu et al. 2011, 57), he had the courtesy name Yunfang 雲房 and was also known as Han Zhongli, since he supposedly lived and served under the Later Han dynasty (2nd c.).

According to various hagiographies (see n. 8 above), he came originally from Xianyang 咸陽 near modern Xi'an and rose through the official ranks under the Han, but was later demoted when his opinions contrasted with those of the court. Under Emperor Wudi of the succeeding dynasty of the Western Jin (r. 265-290), he became a military general, but suffered a massive defeat at the hands of Central Asian invaders. Desperate, and with his troops completely vanquished, he fled into the mountains, where he encountered an old man who guided him to the palace of the celestial deity Donghua di-jun 東華帝君 (Imperial Lord of Eastern Florescence). From him he received the talismans, texts, and teachings of the Daoist religion and himself in due course became an immortal.[11]

[11] Yoshikawa in Schipper and Verellen 2004, 1283-84; Zhang 2019, 3.

Another tradition, documented in the preface of the alchemical text translated below, has it that he holed up in the Zhongnan mountains 終南山 and was visited by various divine dignitaries who revealed instructions of internal alchemy to him. Following them to the letter, he worked diligently and eventually attained immortality. Either way, rather than ascending to heaven, Zhongli Quan opted to stay on earth to help others with his immortal powers and thereby make up for his failure in his official duties. However, he did not find people ready and willing to undergo the necessary hardships of spiritual training. Only in the late Tang did he finally find a worthy disciple in the would-be official and sword master Lü Dongbin.

While Lü Dongbin can be described as the archetypal ritual master, erudite and mobile, accomplished in various techniques and connected to different social strata, Zhongli Quan matches a different Song stereotype, that of the martial protector with immense magical powers. The classical model for this is Beidi 北帝, the Northern Emperor, with control over life and death. He appears as a mighty warrior, dressed entirely in black and armed to the teeth, holding the tablets of destiny, and is the sovereign to whom all spirits, ghosts, and demons owe strict obedience (Mollier 1997, 349; Chao 2011, 21-23; Steavu 2019, 70).

In Daoism under the Song, he was particularly honored as the head of the Department of Exorcism (Quxie yuan 驅邪元), a central part of the celestial administration. He was also in charge of the potent thunder rites, popularized especially by the school of the Celestial Heart (Tianxin 天心), "the most significant and innovative Daoist exorcistic lineage of the Song" (Davis 2001, 74).[12]

The Zhong-Lü Tradition

By the late 11th century, the two immortals were linked to a set of texts that purport to present their particular teachings on the attainment of immortality (Pregadio 2012a, 31). In this context, this is best defined with Nathan Sivin as "the resurrection of the integral personality in a new and imperishable body which is nurtured like an embryo by yogic disciplines within the old physique, just as the alchemist brings an elixir to maturity in a matrix of lead" (1968, 30).

Outlining the first systematic presentation of mature internal alchemy, the texts' teachings were later adopted by many Daoist lineages, both Northern and Southern, and laid the foundation for the multiplicity of practices to come. Set partly in dialogue format, Lü asking questions and Zhongli providing answers, they appear first in the *Daoshu* 道樞 (Pivot of the Dao, DZ 1017), a collection by the bibliophile Zeng Cao 曾慥 (fl. 1131-1155).

Originally from Jinjiang 晉江 in Fujian, he was well educated and "enjoyed a conventional career as a government servant," serving as first as undersecretary to the prime minister and later as magistrate of various districts in Jiangxi, Hubei, and Anhui (Boltz 1987, 231). His prime accomplishment is an anthology of citations from literary works from Han through Song, called *Leishuo* 類說 (Classified Sayings). His *Daoshu*, presenting 108 texts in 118 sections, shows similar erudition.[13]

It is otherwise unknown who may have compiled the Zhong-Lü texts, although some of them are linked—either in prefaces or bibliographies—with a certain Shi Jianwu 施肩吾, a poet and recluse of the Western Hills (Xishan 西山) near Nanchang 南昌 in Jiangxi. He himself, the story goes, was the recipient of the immortals' teachings, while his disciple Li Song 李竦, courtesy name Quanmei 全美, recorded them in writing.

There is a well-known Tang poet by the name of Shi Jianwu, courtesy name Xisheng 希聖, also known as Huayang zhenren 華陽真人 (Perfected

---

[12] On the history of Celestial Heart, see Andersen 1996, 145-46; in Pregadio 2008, 821-22 and 989-93; Davis 2001, 21-24; Drexler 1994, 23-25; Skar 2000, 420-21.

[13] Baldrian-Hussein in Schipper and Verellen 2004, 780-81. See also Nienhauser 1986, 172.

of Flowering Yang). Although he lived around the putative lifetime of Lü Dongbin, around 820 to 835, only few scholars such as Yu Yan 俞琰 (1258-1314) link the texts to him. Most Song and later writers, such as Hu Yinglin 胡應麟 (fl. 1590), doubt that they were compiled by a Tang poet and suggest that another, otherwise unknown person of the same name was their compiler, dating them to the 10th century at the earliest and generally leaning toward the 11th.[14]

The most important of the Zhong-Lü documents is the *Zhong-Lü chuandao ji* 鍾呂傳道集 (Transmission of the Dao from Zhongli to Lü), translated below. It appears in abbreviated form in the *Daoshu* (chs. 39-41) and with full text in the *Xiuzhen shishu* 修真十書 (Ten Books on the Cultivation of Perfection, DZ 263, chs. 14-16), from where it was later reprinted in various collections. Referred to by slightly different names in bibliographic sources, it is cited with its present title in the *Zhizhai shulu jieti* 直齋書錄解題 (Commented Library Catalog of the Zhizhai Studio, 12.348), a private bibliography by the book collector Chen Zhensun 陳振孫 (ca. 1183-1262) (Loon 1984, 164). The *Chuandao ji* consists of eighteen chapters that provide a structured outline of the core teachings of the tradition. The first six focus on cosmology, the next six on alchemical practice, and the last six on the overall purpose of the teachings.[15]

Mentioned toward its end is the second major Zhong-Lü document, the *Lingbao bifa* 靈寶畢法 (Conclusive Methods of Numinous Treasure, DZ 1191, *Daoshu* 42). Lü says, "May I please ask that you instruct me exactly in how to apply and use the proper timing of energy conjunction and the right methods of serious practice?" To which Zhongli responds, "For this, I have compiled the *Lingbao bifa*" (ch. 18). The text consists of twelve sections, two of which were collapsed into one, creating a work in ten chapters, also translated below.

The preface, in the voice of Zhongli Quan, claims that he received the base materials for the text in revelation while hiding in a cave in the Zhongnan mountains. They consisted of thirty scrolls in three major works: the *Jin'gao shu* 金誥書 (Book of Golden Declarations), authored by Yuanshi tianzun 元始天尊 (Heavenly Venerable of Primordial Beginning), the creator deity of the Daoist universe; the *Yushu lu* 玉書錄 (Record Written on Jade), produced by Yuanhuang 元皇 (Primordial Sovereign), a major scrip-

[14] For the question of compilation, see Boltz 1987, 139-40; Baldrian-Hussein 10984, 35; in Schipper and Verellen 2004, 801; in Pregadio 2008, 1277-79.

[15] The text also appears in *Daozang jiyao* 157, *Daozang jinghua lu* 59, and *Daozang jinghua* 3. For an earlier translation, see Wong 2000. For discussions, see Needham et al. 1983, 88; Baldrian-Hussein 1984, 46-47; Boltz 1987, 141; Pregadio and Skar 2000, 475; Pregadio 2012a, 11; Komjathy 2014a, 118; Baldrian-Hussein in Schipper and Verellen 2004, 801; in Pregadio 2008, 330, 1279; Zhang 2009, 60.

ture-revealing deity quite possibly identical with Daojun 道君 (Lord of the Dao); and the *Zhenyuan yi* 真源義 (Meaning of Perfect Prime), transmitted by Taishang 太上 (Highest Lord), that is, Laojun 老君 (Lord Lao), the third major Daoist divinity and closest instructor of humanity.[16]

The text is structured along these lines, introducing each section's presentation with these revealed titles. Following them, it presents several passages of explications and explanations, plus—in the *Daozang* version—some rather obscure poems.[17]

First mentioned in Zheng Qiao's 鄭樵 (1104-1162) *Tongzhi* 通志 (Comprehensive Record, dat. 1161; Loon 1984, 164), the *Lingbao bifa* draws on the Yijing 易經 (Book of Changes) and traditional calendar science for descriptions of the cosmos and on medical literature when discussing the human body. It outlines the progress of internal alchemy in three stages, described as the lesser, medium, and greater vehicles. The first works with breath control and healing exercises, laying the foundation; the second focuses on the circulation of *qi* and fluid; and the third centers on meditation and various methods of transcendence.

Further Works

Two further documents, also contained in the *Daoshu*, are linked to the Zhong-Lü tradition. The first is the *Xishan qunxian huizhen ji* 西山群仙會真記 (Record of the Host of Immortals and Assembled Perfected of the Western Hills, DZ 246, *Daoshu* 38),[18] in its preface attributed to Shi Jianwu, but already in the *Zhizhai shulu jieti* (12.348) dated to the Song. Internal evidence places it in the late 10th century, since it mentions Zhang Mengqian 張夢乾 who died in 998 (1.6a). This would make it an early precursor of the system, which is also borne out by its overall style and content, more philosophical than the two major works and full of citations of previous texts, including one entitled *Xishan ji*.

The preface links it to two traditions: twelve saints of the Western Hills plus Zhongli and Lü. In outline, it follows the system of the five phases, dividing into five main chapters of five sections each, making a total of twenty-five. The major chapters deal with recognition of masters and Dao;

---

[16] These are the gods of the Three Caverns, also known as the Three Pure Ones or the Daoist trinity. They represent the major medieval schools of Highest Clarity (Shangqing 上清), Numinous Treasure (Lingbao 靈寶), and Three Sovereigns (Sanhuang 三皇). See Kohn 2001b, 120; Ofuchi 1979.

[17] The *Daoshu* version is translated in Baldrian-Hussein 1984, 197-286. For more on the text, see Baldrian-Hussein 1984, 41-46; in Schipper and Verellen 2004, 801-02; in Pregadio 2008, 330, 669, 785; Boltz 1987, 142; Zheng 2010, 30, 52.

[18] The text is translated in Bertschinger 2018. For discussions of its history, see Baldrian-Hussein in Schipper and Verellen 2004, 804; in Pregadio 2008, 329, 1112-13.

nourishment of the vital principle; reparation of damage due to diminished *qi*; alchemical ingredients such as yin and yang, lead and mercury; as well as the process of transmutation and the perfection of body and spirit.

Like this work a precursor of the full systematization of the teaching in the *Chuandao ji* and the *Lingbao bifa*—more rudimentary in outlook and usage—is the fourth major text of the group: the *Baiwen pian* 百問篇 (One Hundred Questions, *Daoshu* 5.7a-22a, *Daozang jiyao* 8066-70).[19] It is cited with a passage not contained in the transmitted version in the *Huandan zhongxian lun* of the year 1052, the text that also contains the poem ascribed to Lü Dongbin translated above, and may thus go back to the first half of the 11th century. Set in dialogue format, it consists of eighty-one short, rather basic questions about the terminology of internal alchemy and on how the body corresponds to the greater universe. Although often similar it does not quite match the mature system as present by the mid-12th century, which in turn laid the foundation for the adaptation of internal alchemy into both the Northern and Southern schools.

Complete Perfection

Imitating the Chan Buddhist division of the Tang dynasty into a Northern and Southern school (see McRae 1983), Daoist leaders in the early 13th century created a twofold lineage structure as they competed for favors among the newly ascending Mongol rulers (Baldrian-Hussein in Pregadio 2008, 760). The various lineages in the north, in the greater Yellow River area, were duly subsumed under the school of Complete Perfection, founded by Wang Chongyang 王重陽 (1112–1170). The off-spring of a wealthy family, he received a good education but, after the fall of the Northern Song in 1127, only attained a military prefectural degree and ended up serving as a minor official collecting taxes on alcoholic beverages in Ganhe 甘河 township near Xi'an (Katz 1999, 69; Eskildsen 2004, 4).

A heavy drinker, in 1159, he once sat in a local butcher shop imbibing when he had a vision of two spirit beings who transmitted secret instructions to him. Acting increasingly more eccentric, he met the same immortals again in the following year in nearby Liquan 醴泉, again drinking in a public house and receiving more transmissions. The next year, he left his post and set himself up in a tomb-like hermitage in the Zhongnan mountains. In 1163, he moved to the hermit village of Liuqiang 劉蔣 and practiced with several Daoists, notably He Dejin 和德瑾 (d. 1170) and Li Lingyang 李靈陽 (d. 1189)—converted by a miraculous experience and a

[19] Translated in Homann 1976. See Baldrian-Hussein 1984, 48; Boltz 1987, 139. The *Daoshu* also contains several other texts that bear some relation to the Zhong-Lü system, summarized briefly in Baldrian-Hussein 1984, 48-51. For studies of further *Daoshu* materials on internal alchemy, see also Eskildson 2006; 2007.

mysterious stranger, respectively (Komjathy 2014b, 189)—still drinking and becoming ever more eccentric. This led, in 1164, to another encounter with mysterious superior beings, which finally made him stop drinking and get more serious in his self-cultivation (2004, 7-8; Katz 1999, 70; Marsone 2001, 100).

In 1167, he burnt his hut to the ground and set out for Shandong, where his "strange attire, eccentric behavior, and profound utterances" attracted numerous followers (Eskildsen 2004, 8). Eventually he established five religious communities and converted his leading disciples, beginning with four in 1175, then expanding to seven (Komjathy 2014b, 184). All founders of their own lineages, they became duly known as the Seven Perfected (*qizhen* 七真) and were later featured in a popular novel (Wong 1990).

Wang Chongyang's practice was highly ascetic; he was a stern master who administered severe beatings and subjected his trainees to frequent humiliation (Katz 1999, 70). His lay followers had to chant major scriptures from all three traditions, such as the *Xiaojing* 孝徑 (Classic of Filial Piety), *Daode jing*, and *Xinjing* 心經 (Heart Sutra), and work on mental discipline and morality to eliminate desires and resist sensory attractions (Eskildsen 2004, 14, 23). The overall goal was immortality, a state of spiritual refinement that included complete control over the body, the possession of supernatural powers, and compassion for all beings (Katz 1999, 75-76, citing Eskildsen 1989, 7).

After his death in 1170, his disciples observed the three-year mourning period, then set out to establish communities in different parts of the country. By 1187, they had become well known enough for one of them, Wang Chuyi 王處一 (1142-1217), to be summoned to the Jin court, where he taught about immortality and officiated at various healing and funerary rituals (Katz 1999, 71). In 1201, he performed a rite of cosmic renewal (*jiao* 醮) for the ruler, which precipitated the birth of the heir apparent and significantly increased the school's stature. By this time, a large section of the population, people from all walks of life, were Complete Perfection followers.

Soon after, another of the Seven Perfected, Qiu Chuji 丘處機 (1148–1227), best known as the founder of the Dragongate (Longmen 龍門) lineage, was summoned by Genghis Khan to his Central Asian headquarters, undertaking a three-year trek, recorded in the *Xiyou ji* 西遊記 (Journey to the West; trl. Waley 1931). In 1223, the khan appointed him as the leader of all religions of China, causing his followers to be exempt from taxes and labor. This, in one stroke, made Complete Perfection the most powerful and popular religious group in northern China and contributed greatly to the prominence it still enjoys to this day.[20]

---

[20] Katz 1999, 72; see also Yao 2000; Goossaert 2001; Goossaert and Katz 2001.

Internal alchemy as practiced in Complete Perfection "bears considerable affinity to the *neidan* theories and methods of the so-called Zhong-Lü tradition" (Eskildsen 2004, 7), but it is not clear when the connection was first established. The *Chongyang zhenren jinguan yusuo jue* 重陽真人金關玉鎖訣 (Master Chongyang's Instructions on the Golden Gate and Jade Lock, DZ 1156; trl. Komjathy 2007) outlines relevant methods that bear some resemblance to the Zhong-Lü system and are generally consistent with what is known about Wang's practices. The fact, however, that the work "deals so extensively with health and physiology—to a degree far surpassing Wang's other works—has brought forth speculation that it is a fabrication of some later period" (Eskildsen 2004, 60).

The prime Complete Perfection text on internal alchemy, on the other hand, the *Dadan zhizhi* 大丹直指 (Pointers to the Great Elixir, DZ 244; trl. Komjathy 2014a, 115-68), is quite in line with the Zhong-Lü materials, using much of the same terminology and presenting similar stages and practices. Attributed to Qiu Chuji, it is commonly dated to the late 13th century (Eskildsen 2004, 61). The *Zhonghe ji* 中和集 (Collection of Central Harmony, DZ 249), by the Complete Perfection master Li Daochun 李道純 (fl. 1388-1406) (Despeux in Schipper and Verellen 2004, 1174), like the Zhong-Lü texts, applies dialogue structure and presents many matching concepts, yet in overall outlook is more philosophical and psychological, and also places a greater emphasis on the integrataion and harmony of the three teachings (Cleary 2003, 353-487).

Another way to date Zhong-Lü presence in Complete Perfection is by looking at the role of the two immortals in the school. Zhongli Quan and Lü Dongbin were in due course identified as the mysterious spirit beings who instructed Wang Chongyang, in addition to another rather obscure figure by the name of Liu Cao 劉操, courtesy name Haichan 海蟾. Commonly described as a wealthy government official of the state of Yan 燕 (modern Hebei) of the 10th century, he appears as a disciple of Chen Tuan in mid-Song notebook (*biji* 筆記) literature. By the late 12th century, he was associated with Zhongli Quan, who supposedly convinced him through a magic trick that officialdom was highly hazardous. Liu Haichan duly dedicated his life to Dao and, like Lü Dongbin, was trained by the immortal. He attained transcendence and wandered through the world drinking and making merry, appearing as a beggar or in various disguises to perform miracles, write funky poetry, and teach Daoist cultivation.[21]

All three were duly appointed patriarchs of the Complete Perfection school, as is first recorded in the *Jinlian zhengzong ji* 金蓮真宗記 (Record of the Orthodox Lineage of the Golden Lotus, DZ 173) by Qin Zhi'an 秦志安

[21] Goossaert in Pregadio 2008, 686-88; Lu 2009, 73. See also Boltz 1987, 64-65, 173, 219; Katz 1999, 43-44, 69; Yao 2000, 579; Eskildsen 2004, 5.

(1188-1233), which was published in 1241 (Katz 1999, 69, 77). The work also contains an extended hagiography of Lü Dongbin, claiming that he passed the official examination and later met Zhongli Quan while wandering around Mount Lu. The story of the millet-cooking dream was added after that, as were the various tests and trials—shaping Lü's life story into a mythical model for Complete Perfection practice (Katz 1999, 79, 83).

In addition, Lü's poetic works were collected by He Zhiyuan 何志淵—a disciple of Song Defang 宋德方 (1183-1247) who took refuge in a Complete Perfection community to escape from the Mongol invaders. He compiled them into the *Chunyang zhenren huncheng ji* 纯陽真人渾成集 (Collection of Chaos Complete by the Perfected of Pure Yang, DZ 1055), dated to around 1250 (Boltz 187, 141). The Yongle gong, Lü's major northern sanctuary, moreover, became a Complete Perfection site around the same time (Katz 1999, 72), which means that the Zhong-Lü tradition had come to form a firm part of Complete Perfection by the mid-13th century.

The Southern School

The Southern School (Nanzong 南宗), centered on holy mountains south of the Yangtze, was a great deal more amorphous and is much less well documented than Complete Perfection. It was constructed by Bai Yuchan 白玉蟾 (fl. 1194-1229), courtesy name Haiqiongzi 海瓊子 (Master of Ocean Jade), and his disciples in the early 13th century. Its lineage consists of the so-called Five Purple Masters, that is, Daoists with the word "purple" in their religious titles.[22]

The first was Zhang Boduan 张伯端 (987-1082), courtesy name Pingshu 平叔, religious title Ziyang zhenren 紫陽真人 (Perfected of Purple Yang). Not much is known about him, but most sources agree that he came from Zhejiang, passed the official examination, and served as a minor official in various government posts.[23] He is best known as the author of the *Wuzhen pian* 悟真篇 (Awakening to Perfection, DZ 263, ch. 26-30; trl. Cleary 1987; Pregadio 2009), a major classic of internal alchemy with some overlap to Zhong-Lü teachings.[24]

From him the lineage moved on to Shi Tai 石泰 (d. 1158), a native of Changzhou 長周, who served as a minor government official. The story goes that he met Zhang Boduan in Shanxi when the latter was falsely

---

[22] The lineage is outlined in Boltz 1987, 173; Katz 1999, 77; Baldrian-Hussein in Pregadio 2008, 759-61; Zhang 2009, 61-62; Zhang 2019.

[23] For Zhang's life and work, see Boltz 1987, 174; Pregadio and Skar 2000, 470; Skar in Pregadio 2008, 203-06; Zhang 2009, 61.

[24] For more on the history of the text, see Boltz 1987, 174; Pregadio and Skar 2000, 476-78; Baldrian-Hussein in Pregadio 2008, 1081-84.

accused of an official misdemeanor. When Shi Tai came to his rescue in disregard of his own welfare, Zhang judged him fit to receive his teachings (Baldrian-Hussein in Pregadio 2008, 894-95). He duly continued the transmission by passing it on to Xue Daoguang 薛道光 (d. 1191), an ordained Buddhist monk, who connected to Shi Tai in 1106 (Zhang 2009, 61-62). Xue came originally from Yunnan; after enlightenment, he returned to lay life and worked as a tailor like his master (Baldrian-Hussein in Pregadio 2008, 1144-45).

Next in line is Chen Nan 陳楠, courtesy name Niwan 泥丸 (fl. 1213), originally from Guangdong 廣東 and particularly known for his combination of internal alchemy and healing techniques. Also versed in the thunder rites, he transmitted the lineage teachings to Bai Yuchan on Mount Luofu 羅浮山 (Baldrian-Hussein in Pregadio 2008, 254-55).

While this lineage was put together early in the 12th century, the connection to the Zhong-Lü tradition is later. It rests on the story that Zhang Boduan went to Chengdu in 1069 as a staff member of the army commander Lu Shen 陸詵 (1022-1070), courtesy name Longtu 龍圖. There he met a perfected being, from whom he received oral instructions on the concoction of the internal elixir, which eventually led to his compilation of the *Wuzhen pian* (Pregadio 2000, 470).[25]

The mysterious perfected was in due course identified as Liu Haichan, an essential step in grafting Zhang Boduan into the line of the Zhong-Lü tradition. The link is first made in the *Wuzhen pianji* 悟真篇记 (Record of the *Wuzhen pian*), compiled by Lu Sicheng 陆思诚, a grandson of Lu Shen, and dated to between 1161 and 1173 (Baldrian-Hussein in Schipper and Verellen 2004, 822).[26] The text describes the exploits of another minor official called Wang Zhen 王箴 who, "following the advice of his older brother, Master Chongxi 冲熙先生, undertook to study Dao, then met Liu Haichan and from him obtained the arts of the golden elixir." Based on this and other tales, the text asks, "How can the strange perfected master who Zhang studied with in Chengdu be anyone but Liu Haichan?" (Zhang 2019, 5).

All this means is that by the mid-12th century, when Zhongli Quan and Lü Dongbin had been well established as masters of poetry, magical powers, marital arts, and internal alchemy, Liu Haichan was stylized in a similar manner and associated both with Wang Chongyang, the founder of Com-

---

[25] This is recorded in a supposedly personal preface to the *Wuzhen pian* by Zhang himself found in the *Ziyang zhenren Wuzhen pian zhushu* 紫阳真人悟真篇注疏 (Commentary and Supplementary Explanation of the *Wuzhen pian* by the Perfected of Purple Yang, DZ 141), by Weng Baoguang 翁葆光 (fl. 1173). For a more detailed discussion and full translation, see Zhang 2019.

[26] In *Ziyang zhenren Wuzhen pian sanzhu* 紫阳真人悟真篇三注 (Three Commentaries to the *Wuzhen pian* by the Perfected of Purple Yang, DZ 142).

plete Perfection, and Zhang Boduan, the first master of the Southern School. When the two lineages constituted themselves formally in the early 13th century, under the impact of the Mongol invasion, they similarly appointed the three immortals as divine patriarchs, tracing their line further back from them to Donghua dijun and Lord Lao, the divine Laozi and personification of Dao. This provided an impeccable pedigree for the core teachings of internal alchemy they adopted in the course of the 13th century and developed according to their own unique perspectives.

From here, the concepts and practices of the Zhong-Lü tradition laid the foundation of much of internal alchemy to come. While giving rise to a flourishing literature and numerous variations, branches, and local manifestations over the following centuries, in many fundamental respects they have continued to the present day.

Chapter Two

The Workings of the Universe

The Zhong-Lü texts have their particular take on how exactly the universe works. They agree with traditional Daoist cosmology in that all goes back to Dao, formless and vague, and echo the philosophical perspective that the world evolved in stages without the input of an active, conscious creator. They also match the classical notion that the key factors of cosmic unfolding were vital energy and the two forces yin and yang.

Beyond that, the Zhong-Lü texts also integrate the eight trigrams as core energetic factors that lay the foundation of the five phases. They describe the activities of yin and yang through heaven and earth as well as the movements of the sun and the moon as the major factors that give shape to time and space, emphasizing their ongoing dynamic interactions and their importance for human life in terms of both space-time and numerology.

Origins

At the root of all existence is Dao. As the *Lingbao bifa* says, echoing the *Daode jing,*

> The great Dao has no form: you look or listen for it, yet you cannot see or hear it. The great Dao has no name: you measure and count it, yet you cannot fathom or calculate it. Dao generates form, and following form it establishes names. Its name is great: it is heaven and earth. (ch. 1; see also *Chuandao ji* 2)

Matching the *Zhuangzi* 莊子 (Book of Master Zhuang), the texts also assert that Dao is so big it has nothing above it and reaches so far into every minute aspect of life that there is nothing below or within it. "Its beginning has nothing prior to it: you cannot see anything before it. Its end has nothing after it: you cannot see anything beyond it" (*Bifa* 3).

Originally without being, Dao cannot be described; fundamentally without structure, it cannot be imagined (*Bifa* 10). Any way of thinking about it falls far of the mark. Again, the *Lingbao bifa*, "You may think of Dao as being mysterious and subtle, yet ideas of mystery and subtlety never leave the limitations of questions and answers; you may think of it as being invisible and inaudible, yet ideas of the invisible and inaudible never leave the limitations of seeing and hearing" (ch. 10).

Dao, therefore, is original chaos and yet it is not chaos, the generative prime that yet exists in creation. Primordial, it is blurred and indistinct, beyond all sensory perception and language, and shares the power and characteristics of chaos. Existing, it is systematic and ordered, evident in the rhythmic transformations of the world, and definable in temporal and spatial terms.

Dao, then, as already outlined in the *Daode jing* (ch. 42) and also cited in the *Chuandao ji* (ch. 2), "generated the One; the One generated the two, and the two generated the three." The *Huainanzi* 淮南子 (Book of the Master of Huainan), dated to about 150 BCE, provides an interpretation. "Dao begins with oneness. Oneness alone, however, cannot generate. Therefore, it divided into yin and yang. From the harmonious union of yin and yang, the myriad beings were generated."[1]

Other versions of early Daoist cosmogony appear in manuscripts recently excavated from southern China. Thus, the *Fanwu liuxing* 凡物流形 (All Things Flow in Physical Form; trl. Chan 2014; Wang 2015, 87-93), unearthed at Shangbo 上博, describes universal unfolding as beginning with oneness, which generates the two and the three, but from there it proceeds to the mother and eventually leads to the integrated combination of all. The mother, as is well known, is a common Daoist metaphor of cosmic origin, applying the human relationship of mother and children to the universe and the myriad beings (Chen 1974). However, rather than being a metaphor for Dao as it is in the *Daode jing* and thus resting at the very source of existence (chs. 1, 25, 52), here it appears at a later stage, at the brink of ultimate integration, that is, the emergence of the myriad beings (Wang 2015, 85-87).

The *Taiyi shengshui* 太一生水 (Great Oneness Generates Water) was discovered at Guodian in the same cluster of bamboo slips as fragments of the *Daode jing*, dated to around 350 BCE (trl. Wang 2015, 70-72; Cook 2012). The text clearly shows its influence in both its key concepts, "one" and "water," which it expands to great oneness as the core creative factor of the universe. Its emphasis on the notion that "the Dao of heaven values weakness," too, connects to the *Daode jing*, which favors weakness and softness over aggression and competition. While the *Taiyi shengshui* begins with the One, it does not go on to two but has the universe evolve by moving on to water, from which heaven and earth arise. They in turn connect back to great oneness and water. Once these are established, spirit and light emerge, and only then do the two of the *Daode jing* come into play: yin and yang arise together with summer and winter, cold and heat, dampness and dryness, to eventually result in the ongoing cycle of the years (Wang 2015, 74-75).[2]

---

[1] Major et al. 2010, 133; Major 1993; Morgan 1934, 2; Larre et al. 1993, 41. For more on the One in creation, see Robinet 2011, 49-52.

[2] There is a certain similarity of this vision to the teaching of the Baghdad alchemist Jabir (721-817). In his *Book of Clarification* (*Kitab al-idah*), he proposes

A yet different version of early cosmogony appears in the *Hengxian* 恆先 (Constancy Before; trl. Brindley et al. 2013; Cook 2012). The term *heng* means "constant" and appears in the very first line of the *Daode jing*. Constancy is another key characteristic of Dao, indicating the unchanging and invariable nature of the ultimate. In this version, then, the universe begins with constancy. From here, the text says, "space arises. Once there is space, there is vital cosmic energy, *qi* 氣. Once there is *qi*, there is material reality. Once there is material reality, there is a beginning. Once there is a beginning, there is the passage of time." The ultimate is defined as unmoving as well as having no material reality, being instead "simplicity, stillness, and emptiness." No material reality means that there is nothing, that life is in a state of latency, nothingness, or nonbeing, formless and undifferentiated, not yet manifesting in concrete things, often also called "vessels." This gives rise to *qi*, which in turn leads to presence, existence, or being, and eventually initiates entropy and thus the flow of time (Wang 2015, 31-33).

Echoing these early works, the Zhong-Lü texts also describe cosmogony in terms of successive stages:

> When the Great Prime [Dao] first divided, there was great beginning [*taishi* 太始]; in the midst of this, there was great nonbeing [*taiwu* 太無]; in the midst of this, there arose great emptiness [*taixu* 太虛]; from this, there was the great void [*taikong* 太空]; in the midst of this, there was great material reality [*taizhi* 太質]. Great material reality means there was the pure and turbid material nature of heaven and earth. They were like an egg, consisting of dark and yellow colors, a single one being in the great void. (*Bifa* 3)

> After the great beginning, great material reality emerged, serving as the mother of the myriad beings. Following upon this, there was the great immaculate. . . . It served as the ancestor of the five phases and the root of the great Dao. (*Chuandao ji* 11)

The stages mentioned here recoup the traditional Daoist understanding as first described in the *Liezi* 列子 (Book of Master Lie), which begins with great change (*taiyi* 太易), when not even vital energy had yet arisen, then proceeds to great antecedence (*taichu* 太初), which saw its first

---

two fundamental principles based on Aristotle (384-322 BCE). In his *Meteorologica*, the latter "postulated the existence of two 'exhalations' that emanate from the center of the earth: one is dry and smoky, the other is wet and steamy. Underground, these exhalations condense and produce stones and minerals." In the alchemical view, all metals are compounds of these two principles, now "called mercury (moist) and sulfur (dry). They combine in different proportions and degrees of purity to produce various metals," with gold resulting from their perfect combination and processing (Principe 2013, 35). See also Katz 2008, 16.

beginning. From here, the universe evolved to the stage of great beginning (*taishi* 太始), when physical forms first appeared, and eventually reached the great immaculate (*taisu* 太素), which saw the arising of material reality (ch. 1; Graham 1960, 18-19; see also Zheng 2010, 35).

In religious Daoism, these stages are picked up in the 6th-century *Taishang Laojun kaitian jing* 太上老君開天經 (Scripture of the Highest Lord Lao Creating the Universe, DZ 1437). Here Lord Lao as Dao rests in the pre-state of vast prime and gives rise to first great antecedence, when material reality emerges. Next, he guides the universe into great beginning, which sees the creation of the myriad beings, and from there to great immaculate, a time when people were simple and lived long, preceding the evolution of consciousness and culture (Kohn 1993, 36-37; Schafer 1997, 4-7).

All agree that existence goes back to Dao and unfolds gradually through various stages, bringing about vital energy and material reality in the process. The egg-like form of the raw nature of heaven and earth, moreover, is also part of the classical system, mentioned first in the *Zhuangzi* in the myth of Hundun 混沌, the emperor of the center who is "bored to death" by his friends, the emperors of the north and the south. Described as a shapeless lump of flesh, without any sense openings or other signs of order and culture, he is likened in folklore to a leather sack, a calabash, or a dumpling. The image of chaos he represents is, as Norman Girardot points out, that of a watery and embryonic state, a dark, void abyss, and a harmonious, womb-like enclosure (2008, 24). He stands for the world before creation, with its egg-like lack of internal structure, its utter potentiality and powerful nothingness that then divides into two the core powers of yin and yang (Girardot 1985, 69l).

Yin and Yang

The terms *yin* 陰 and *yang* 陽 are not found on the oracle bones, but appear in early Zhou-dynasty classics, both historical and literary, such as the *Shujing* 書經 (Book of History, ca. 800 BCE; trl. Legge 1960) and the *Shijing* 詩經 (Book of Poetry; trl. Legge 1970) (Wang 2012, 22-24). Here they appear as geographical terms, indicating the sunny and shady sides of a hill and expressing the function of the sun in relation to spatio-temporal reality (2012, 25-26).

From there they acquired a series of associations: bright and dark, light and heavy, strong and weak, above and below, and so on, associated in nature with day and night, summer and winter, spring and fall, male and female. They also came to indicate certain actions, such as generation and completion, movement and rest, expansion and contraction, growth and decline. Complementary to the core, neither is "better" than the other but they must retain an overall balance and steady rhythm. In addition, they also furnish a particular kind of logic, connecting all the different aspects of nature into one system.[3]

Neither concrete things, entities, or objects, yin and yang are qualifiers that characterize the nature of structures and help analyze specific functions of reality. However much they express universal principles, in their application they are always particular and depend closely on their relative context. Expressing nothing in themselves, they qualify relationships, matching the concrete circumstances of life as well as the purposes and priorities of the viewer.[4]

As Robin Wang points out (2012, 8-11), yin and yang function in six characteristic relationships. First, they stand in contradiction and opposition (*maodun* 矛盾), tension and difference, a rather dynamic situation where two entities or situations are mutually exclusive and in contrast to each other, yet interact on one or the other level. Second, they work in mutual interdependence (*xiangyi* 相依), functioning in alternating rhythm, closely connected yet relative to each other, like a door opening and closing. As the *Daode jing* describes this, "Long and short contrast each other; high and low distinguish each other" (ch. 2).

Third, yin and yang function by mutual inclusion (*huhan* 互含), one always holding some aspect of the other, as classically shown in the well-known Taiji symbol, where the black (yin) side contains a white (yang) dot, and vice versa (Louis 2003, 186; Cheng 2006b). In this relationship, the two are constantly implicated in one another, functioning in smooth and steady alternation, mutating from one into the next (see Robinet and Wissing 1990).

Fourth, they interact by interchanging resonance (*jiaogan* 交感), influencing and transforming one another in close interaction (see Cheng 2011). As soon as one changes, the other follows in corresponding resonance, making it possible to achieve outcomes by moving in the opposite direction. Again, the *Daode jing*:

> To contract something, first expand it;
> To weaken something, first strengthen it;
> To destroy something, first let it flourish;
> To get hold something, first give it away. (ch. 36)

3 Bodde 1991, 98; Graham 1986; 1989, 319-25; Unschuld 2003; Zheng 2010, 43.

4 Forke 1925, 214; Harrington 2016, 869; Wang 2012, 7.

Thus, the way nonaction works is to place oneself into a position of yin to encourage the rising of yang, while forceful, interfering measures have a tendency to produce a downturn or stagnation.

Fifth, yin and yang also engage in complementarity and mutual support (*hubu* 互補). They work closely together as one integrated whole, consistently supplementing and balancing each other out in sympathetic response (Geiger 2013, 610), never allowing one to become dominant or establishing patterns of submission and control. Sixth, and finally, the two proceed in patterns of change and transformation (*zhuanhua* 轉化), one endlessly turning into the other, rising and sinking, flourishing and declining, passing through states of excess and deficiency. As the *Daode jing* notes, "reversal is the action of Dao" (ch. 40; Robinet 2011, 2) and says,

> Anything high, it brings down;
> Anything low, it raises up.
> Anything excessive, it reduces;
> Anything insufficient, it supplements. (ch. 77)

In each case, yin and yang constitute an ongoing, never ending cycle (*huan* 環), defining particular agents and situations in terms of time (*shi* 時) and position or domain (*wei* 位) as well as of generation (*sheng* 生, originally showing the image of a plant sprouting) and overcoming or control (*ke* 克) (Wang 2005b; Cheng 1996). Their interaction creates a complex system of dynamic unfolding that encompasses both cyclical and linear elements (Needham 1965, 45; 1981, 108), of flowing probabilities and open-ended possibilities. An auto-generative continuous process of integration, it remains free from distinction between reality and appearance as it outlines the "plural relations of particulars" and provides options for "multiple interpretation models" and worldviews (Nelson 2016, 126-27). It is often described with the term *tian* 天, "heaven," the inherent mover of the natural processes.[5]

The goal in human life, then—from governance through agriculture to art and poetry (Munakata 1983)—is to recognize the patterns as they unfold and establish harmony (*he* 和), which can be hierarchical and systematically structured as in music or integrated and sublimely blended as in cooking (Chan 2011; see also Cheng 1989; 2006a). In all cases, the ideal is not static balance or equilibrium but ongoing generation and transformation under the auspices of universal self-organizing complexity. To follow the ongoing growth and decline of yin and yang, then, means to match one's actions closely to the phases of the sun and the moon and find one's particular way

---

5 Chang 2009, 217, 221; Wang 2012, 14. See also Graham 1989, 319; Mote 1989, 15; Schwartz 1985, 351.

within the weft and warp (*gangji* 綱紀) of universal interchange (Wang 2012, 27-28, 41).

This system plays a key role in the Zhong-Lü texts, who rely particularly on its presentation as found in the *Yijing*. Here the universe first progresses from one—called the Great Ultimate (*taiji* 太極)—to two, i. e., yin and yang, described as the two forces (*liangyi* 兩儀) and depicted as two lines: one double (broken, yielding) and one single (unbroken, firm). From here, it moves on to the four images (*sixiang* 四象), representing the various possible combinations of the two forces or lines in set pairs: yin-yin, yang-yang, yang-yin, and yin-yang.[6] In other words, rather than evolving from one to two and three or through stages of varying complexity, the world here develops by division from two into four, and then into eight.

The Eight Trigrams

The eight trigrams (*bagua* 八卦) are graphic representations of the mixing of yin and yang lines in triplets. Claimed to have been discovered by the sage-king Fuxi 伏羲 in prehistory, they represent eight core factors or forces of universal unfolding.[7] Under the Zhou dynasty in the 11th century BCE, they became part of the dominant divination system, in contrast to the oracle-bone divination of the preceding Shang dynasty, moving beyond yes and no and offering guidance and behavioral advice to optimize alignment with the cosmic patterns.

Cast with the help of milfoil or yarrow stalks, the trigrams were interpreted both as whole entities and in terms of individual lines. An early version, called "stalk divination" recently discovered in manuscripts, connects the trigrams as a whole to seasonal patterns and reads them in terms of good or bad fortune (Cook and Zhao 2017). Within the *Yijing* system, on the other hand, emphasis was also placed on individual lines: some were considered "strong," that is, able to change into their opposite, providing dynamic and more nuanced readings. In addition, the trigrams formed the foundation of the sixty-four hexagrams, each consisting of two trigrams or six lines in total. Arranged variously in the course of history, they present symbols of different dimensions of life (Schultz 2011, 641; Bertrand 2019, 45-47). The dynamic power of line change, moreover, allowed the creation of

6 Described in the *Xici* 繫辭 1.11 (Appended Judgments; trl. Sung 1971, 271-337; Wilhelm 1950, 28–355). See also Geiger 2013, 609; Sung 1974, 104; Wang 2012, 63-64; Wilhelm 1950, xlix. The binary system was later adapted in Western thought, notably by the philosopher Gottfried Wilhelm Leibniz (1646-1716). See Cammann 1991, 587; Nelson 2011; Swetz 2003.

7 For discussions of the eight trigrams, see Andersen 1990b; Bertrand 2019, 34; Cammann 1990, 303; 1991, 577; Geiger 2013, 608; Gu 2205, 262-633; Needham et al. 1956, 342; Nielsen 2015, 131.

more than one hexagram—reaching potentially as many as six—as answer to a given question.

Allegedly compiled into a coherent book by Confucius (551-479 BCE), the *Yijing* was increasingly moralized and systematically explicated in a set of commentaries, known as the Ten Wings. Under the Former Han dynasty (206-6 BCE), it was named as one of the Six Classics and became part of literati training. Many used it to gain personal readings on official careers and family concerns; some studied it in more detail and wrote further interpretations.[8]

The vision of the eight trigrams in the Zhong-Lü texts closely reflects their presentation in the *Shuogua* 說卦 (Explaining the Trigrams; trl. Sung 1971, 338-54; Wilhelm 1950, 262-79), the eighth of the Ten Wings. Here they come in pairs that present mirror images in terms of lines and complementary opposites in terms of qualities and functions, each provided with a unique name and representing a core potency of the cosmos (Gu 2005, 264).

First among them are ☰ and ☷. Consisting of three single lines representing yang and three double lines representing yin, they symbolize heaven and earth and are called Qian 乾 (lit., lasting) and Kun 坤 (lit., subordinate). They stand for the fundamental qualities of being creative, strong, and initiating versus receptive, yielding, and accomplishing (Wang 2012, 191; Pregadio 2014c, 470). Their primary dynamic powers are those of governing and sheltering. Among animals, they are associated with the horse, swift and tireless, and the cow, placid and gentle. Furthermore, Qian suggests the idea of ruler, father, circle, metal, and cold, while Kun relates to concepts of follower, mother, cauldron, wagon, and warmth.

Qian and Kun being the father and mother, the remaining six trigrams are their children (Robinet 2011, 5). As in all *Yijing* structures, the lines change from the bottom up. Thus, ☳ and ☴, where the lowest line has changed into its opposite, are their eldest son and daughter. They stand for thunder (yang at the base) and wind (yin as foundation) and are called Zhen 震 (lit., sound of thunder, shock) and Xun 巽 (lit., mild, gentle). They represent the energetic dynamics of movement and dispersal and the qualities of outgoing activation and dense penetration. Among animals, they match the soaring dragon like the sun rising and the crowing rooster, whose voice pierces the stillness of night. In addition, Zhen is linked with the color yellow, the open road, decision-making, and vigor, while Xun relates to the color white, the idea of wood and carpentry as well as to being aloof and fickle.

Next, are ☲ and ☵, the two "sandwiches," with one yin line between two yang lines and vice versa, one yang line between two yin lines. Repre-

[8] For more on *Yijing* history, see Karcher 2002; Hon 2019; Nylan 2014; Redmond and Hon 2014; Smith 2008; 2012.

senting the middle children, they symbolize fire (more yang) and water (more yin), as apparent in nature as the sun and the rain. Their names are Li 離 (lit., bright, separate) and Kan 坎 (lit., a hollow). Their essential qualities are clinging, connecting, and rising versus seeding, germinating, and burrowing, while their core potentials are those of warming and cooling, drying and moisturizing (Robinet 1989b, 313). Among animals, they are connected to the pheasant as a fiery bird and the pig, wallowing in watery mud. Beyond that, Li is associated with openness, turtles, swords, and the sun, while Kan relates to concealment, wheels, bows, and the moon.

The final pair is ☶ and ☱. Here the top line has changed, so that they consist of one line over two others, representing mountain (yang over yin) and lake (yin over yang). They are called Gen 艮 (lit., hard) and Dui 兌 (lit., exchange), and their core qualities are those of stabilization and excitement, also closely associated with rest and pleasure, holding and interacting (Harrington 2016, 864; Schwartz 2018). Among animals, they relate to the guardian dog and the woolly sheep, again reinforcing the contrast between hard and soft, stable and fluid, massive and open. In more concrete terms, Gen suggests the idea of rocks, creeping plants, and strong trees, while Dui is associated with standing water, decline, and low-hanging fruit.

Together, the eight trigrams can be characterized as representing the core qualities of leading and following, rising and sinking, expanding and penetrating, stationary and fluid. They also symbolize key elements of nature, such as heaven and earth, thunder and wind, sunshine and rain, plus mountains and lakes. And they show the dynamic processes of nature and society. Thus, as the *Shuogua* notes, "all things issue from Zhen," the initial mover that signals the beginning of the agricultural year (Sung 1971, 343; Wilhelm 1950, 269). While Xun (wind) dissolves the lingering ice and spreads the seeds, Kan (rain) and Li (sunshine) nurture them to growth. Gen (mountain) stops them when they are ripe, while Dui (lake) provides the pleasure of the harvest. Qian (heaven) keeps the entire proceedings in check, while Kun (earth) provides storage and shelter. Similarly, the ruler emerges under the auspices of Zhen, establishes himself in Xun, sees the people in Li and puts them to work in Kun. "He rejoices in Dui, struggles in Qian, rests in Kan, and completes [the year's work] in Gen" (Sung 1971, 343; Wilhelm 1950, 268).

The Zhong-Lü texts adopt this ancient understanding of the eight trigrams as elemental building blocks of the universe and also integrate their Later Han interpretation as markers of temporal dynamics. In that, they follow Yu Fan 虞翻 (164-233) and the authors of the apocrypha, who placed the trigrams in relation to the movements of the sun and the moon as well as various cyclical signs (Robinet 1989b, 307; Needham et al. 1956, 329-30).

In the Zhong-Lü system, then, the trigrams with their qualities precede the other major structuring system of yin and yang: the five phases.

The Five Phases

Traditional cosmologists describe the ongoing dynamic of yin and yang in five stages: minor yang, major yang, yin/yang, minor yin, and major yin. They describe the cycle as beginning at a low point, gradually rising to a zenith, then again starting small and increasing toward fullness. The pattern never stops: the world is in constant motion, and one stage necessarily follows the other (Henderson 1984; Bodde 1991, 101; Robinet 2011, 3).

Early on, these five stages were linked with certain organic substances—wood, fire, earth, metal, water—that came to be known as the five phases (*wuxing* 五行). They are first documented in the *Shujing*, where they appear as five materials (*wucai* 五才) and are concrete substances, resources used for human livelihood that quite naturally produce each other (*sheng* 生). Thus, water comes about through rainfall. It makes things grow, so that there is lush vegetation and wood arises. Wood dries and becomes fuel for fire, which burns and creates ashes. Ashes become earth, and earth over long periods of consolidation grows metals in its depths. Metals in the depths of mountains, moreover, attract clouds and stimulate rainfall, thus closing the cycle.

At the same time, however, the five materials also serve as a system of mutual control (*ke* 克), keeping things in their proper order. Thus, water extinguishes fire, fire melts metal, metal cuts wood, wood contains earth, earth dams water, and water again extinguishes fire. Here the inherently dynamic nature of the five materials is not used to increase productivity, but to set boundaries and limit potential excesses. In all cases, the early vision emphasizes that although the five materials are substances for human use, they are not merely innate objects but contain dynamic powers that can be turned both to production or control.

In another chapter of the *Shujing*, entitled "Hongfan" 洪範 (The Vast Plan), the five materials are treated in a slightly more abstract manner and associated with qualities and processes. Thus, wood is linked with the qualities of bending and straightness, fire with flaming and rising, earth with planting and harvesting, metal with being pliable and sharp, and water with wetting and sinking (Nylan 1992). Expanding on this, the cosmologist Zou Yan 鄒衍 (4th c. BCE) created the concept of the "five virtues" (*wude* 五德) by focusing on the potency inherent in the materials, such as wood's power to grow and be lush and fire's power to flame and rise. He then correlated these powers with the political dynamics of succeeding dynasties, linking his own Zhou dynasty with fire, and predicted that it would be overcome by a ruling house represented by the symbolic power of water (see Bauer 1956).

Beyond the political sphere, in the early Han dynasty, the five powers became the foundation of the mature five-phases system as formulated in great detail by Dong Zhongshu 董仲舒 (179-104 BCE) in his *Chunqiu fanlu* 春秋繁露 (Variegated Remarks on the Spring and Autumn Annals; see Queen 1996). They were then associated with colors, directions, seasons, musical tones as well as various functions in the human body and closely linked with the agricultural year. In the official sphere, the system was used to explain why certain actions should be undertaken in certain seasons.

For example, as already outlined in the "Yueling" 月令 (Monthly Commandments) chapter of the *Liji* 禮記 (Book of Rites; trl. Legge 1967), since heaven and earth make the myriad creatures blossom in spring, one should in that season sleep and rise early, loosen the hair, relax the body, and allow all beings to live, abstaining from killing. Going along with the seasonal flow, people could maintain alignment with cosmic *qi* and secure health and harmony in body and society. Any actions against the dominant *qi*-flow, on the other hand, would cause harm to the liver, the organ associated with wood and spring, and create chills in the summer. They might also arouse aggression and anger, the corresponding emotions, and make for social upheaval and unhappiness (Needham et al. 1958, 195; Kalinowski 1991).

In other words, the correspondence system of the five phases, like the multilayered interaction of yin and yang it is based on, provides a vision of the universe that is relational and dynamic. It conceives of all social, physical, and psychological occurrences in terms of natural cycles and ongoing patterns. It places human beings in a world that is not, as in modern science, governed by invariable laws, but subject to patterns of interaction that can be either orderly or chaotic. It thereby both limits and empowers people. It limits them by placing them into a natural cycle, which responds to what they do and puts on them the demand of total adaptation for success and fulfillment. Yet it also empowers them because it gives them an active role in the interaction with all things, the power to either support or disturb the natural and political order.

Space-Time

All this happens in an overarching system of space-time (*yuzhou* 宇宙) that determines the right time and position in which to act. In contrast to some Western positions that see time together with change and motion as ultimately unreal, apparently moving forward while space stands still, in the Chinese vision time and space closely coincide, moving equally and forming a single framework of things and events (Chang 2009, 218; Sivin 1976,

521). That is to say, spatial conception is concurrent with temporal transformation, and there is no single, central, or permanent place or time that validates all. Instead, "certain actions undertaken in a given time-and-position can maximize potency," enhance efficacy, and increase power (Chang 2009, 219).

These time-positions, then, are defined in terms of the five phases. As the *Chuandao ji* says,

> After the great Dao divided, heaven and earth split and set up emperors in the five directions. Thus, the Green Emperor of the east is the ruler of spring, when yang arises from yin and the myriad beings are born. The Red Emperor of the south is the ruler of summer, when yang generates yang and the myriad beings grow. The White Emperor of the west is the ruler of fall, when yin arises from yang and the myriad beings reach maturation. The Black Emperor of the north is the ruler of winter, when yin generates yin and the myriad beings die. (ch. 6)

This matches the classic cosmology of the five phases, connecting seasons and direction with colors. The five emperors, moreover, go back to Han-dynasty mythology. Their line starts with Huangdi 黃帝—the Yellow Emperor who created culture and fought the first war—and continues through the superior rulers Zhuanxu 顓頊 and Di Ku 帝嚳 to the Confucian paragons Yao 堯 and Shun 舜. Another version includes Fuxi (creator of the trigrams), Yandi 炎帝 (Fiery Emperor), and Huangdi, followed by the legendary rulers Shaohao 少昊 and Zhuanxu (Kirkova 2016, 162). Originally deities venerated in different localities, they were integrated into one system under the auspices of the five phases, when the empire was unified and various local mythologies and cults needed to be harmonized (see Karlgren 1946).

Spreading five phases over four seasons and four directions leaves the fifth as the odd one out. One way to reconcile this is to identify a fifth season, associated with earth and the color yellow, usually placed between summer and fall. However, the Zhong-Lü texts choose the other option, assigning the last eighteen days of each season to the Yellow Emperor of the center and making him the assistant of the other four.

In addition, the emperors are associated with a group of so-called heraldic animals (*siling* 四零), massive constellations in the cardinal directions that comprise a number of stars not unlike Western zodiac images. Thus, for example, the immense constellation of the green dragon (*qinglong* 青龍), representative of the east, includes stars from Virgo to Scorpio (Pankenier 2013, 45). The vermilion bird (*chiniao* 赤鳥) in the south "extends from lunar mansion Willow (δ Hya) to Chariot Platform (β Crv)" (2013, 196; Schafer 1967, 125; Lo and Wang 2018, 291).

They further include the white tiger (*baihu* 白虎) in the west and the turtle, later combined with a snake and known as the Dark Warrior (*xuanwu* 玄武), in the north, as well as either a yellow dragon, a unicorn (*qilin* 麒麟), or, as mentioned the *Chuandao ji*, a figure called Gouchen 勾陳 (Angular Arranger), the constellation of the center (Major 1993, 81; Lo and Wang 2018, 296).[9]

The cardinal four appear first as mussel shell mosaics in a Neolithic tomb of the Yangshao 仰韶 culture, dating from the late 4th millennium BCE (Pankenier 2013, 337). After this, they are depicted on a dragon basin and mentioned in an oracle-bone inscription of the Shang dynasty (1953-1046 BCE), then appear on a tile from Fengjing 豐京, one of the capitals of the Zhou before they conquered the Shang (2013, 78, 212).

Essential to Han cosmology and calendar science, the four heraldic animals with their changing positions in the course of the year, like various other star-based omens (Sawyer 1993, 53), provided celestial guidance of when to sow and plant in agriculture, when to advance and retreat in warfare. The physical root of the idea of the heavenly mandate (*tianming* 天命), they literally guided the ancients in their most essential undertakings and were responsible for the survival and prosperity of all (Kohn 2019, 43).

The Ten Heavenly Stems

Beyond their supernatural guardian animals, the five emperors in the Zhong-Lü texts also have children, a son and a daughter each that assist them in their great endeavor of running space-time. The *Chuandao ji* has,

> The children of the Green Emperor are Jia and Yi: they belong to the east and the phase wood. The children of the Red Emperor are Bing and Ding: they belong to the south and fire. The children of the Yellow Emperor are Wu and Ji: they belong to the center and earth. The children of the White Emperor are

---

9 For discussions of the four animals, see Staal 1984; Major 1986; Csikszentmihalyi in Pregadio 2008, 908-11; Chao 2011, 15-20; Johnson 2014, 81-85; Karetzky 2015, 72-73l; Wu and Wu 2016, 27-28. In military strategy, they were related to the musical notes of the pitch pipes and thus to divination (Sawyer 1993, 72-73).

> Geng and Xin: they belong to the west and metal. The children of the Black Emperor are Ren and Gui: they belong to the north and water. (ch. 6; *Bifa* 8)

These five pairs are the ten heavenly stems (*tiangan* 天干), celestial agents and divinities of time, reflecting a vision not unlike that of the decans in ancient Eqypt:

> The Egyptians divinized time, not merely in the abstract sense, but in the concrete sense that each moment of the day and night had its god who must be placated as the moment passed. The decans as they came to be called in Hellenistic times, were really Egyptian sidereal gods of time who had become absorbed in Chaldean astrology and affiliated to the zodiac. They all had images, which vary in different lists. . . .
>
> The decans had various aspects. They had definite astrological significance, as horoscopes presiding over the forms of life born within the time periods over which they presided, and they were assimilated to the planets domiciled in their domain, and to the signs of the zodiac, three decans going with each sign as its three 'faces.' But they were also gods, and this side of them was never forgotten. (Yates 1964, 46)

Allegedly created by the Yellow Emperor, the ten heavenly stems in China go back to names for the ten days of the week under the Shang, probably based on varying constellations in the sky (Wu and Wu 2016, 19). Their names have particular meanings, they show up in the oracle bones in specific forms, and they have certain key qualities associated with them. More specifically, they are (2016, 45-91; Needham et al. 1958, 397):

Stem	**Meaning**	**Form**	**Qualities**
Jia 甲	shell	cross	initiating, creative, straight, authoritative
Yi 乙	fish guts	squiggle	flexible, gentle, kind, strong, vital
Bing 丙	fish tail	star	exciting, stimulating, vivacious
Ding 丁	nail	square	inspiring, passionate, adoring, warm
Wu 戊	lance	hooked cross	stable, solid, mature, stubborn
Ji 己	self	twisted rope	humble, faithful, reflective, trustworthy
Geng 庚	change	horned star	sharp, righteous, clear, critical
Xin 辛	pungent	triangle	sensitive, sympathetic, communicative
Ren 壬	burden	straight line	flowing, nourishing, supporting
Gui 癸	measure	diagonal cross	wise, talented, artistic

Well documented in oracle bone inscriptions, they also connect to the ancient myth of the ten suns, resting at night on the Fusang 扶桑 tree of the east and rising in the sky during the day, scorching and burning the earth, until Archer Yi shot them down, all except one (see Birrell 1993). Commonly listed in the order given here, all odd-numbered stems are considered yang and all those with even numbers are qualified as yin, thus becoming the sons and daughters of the five emperors (Bodde 1991, 112). In Daoist ritual practice, they are furthermore venerated as deities with a strong impact on destiny and good fortune.

Adding to the structure as defined through the five phases and ten stems, the Zhong-Lü system further works with the eight trigrams, subdividing the directions into cardinal and intermediate and arranging the seasons according to the eight nodes or right divisions (*bajie* 八節). Each season, associated with a particular direction, thus, starts at the season's beginning and peaks at the solstices and equinoxes. The trigram arrangement used in this context is the so-called pre-creation or "before heaven" (*xiantian* 先天) version[10], fully matured in the Song dynasty. Here Qian and Kun mark the north-south axis plus the summer and winter solstices, while Li and Kan represent east and west plus the spring and fall equinoxes. The remaining trigrams in matching pairs fill in the intermediate positions and signal the beginnings of the seasons (Kim in Pregadio 2008, 201-03).

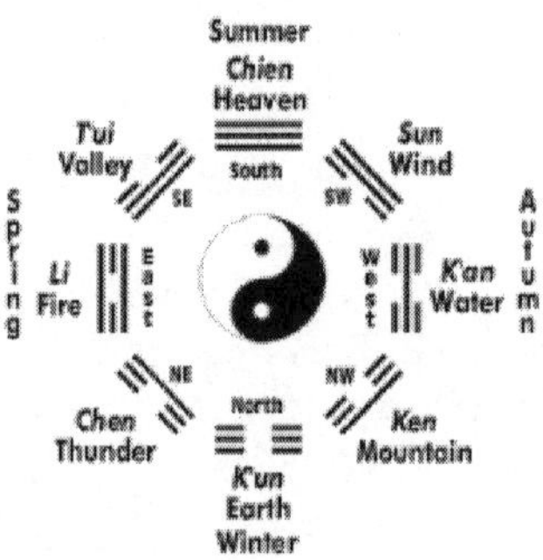

Life Processes

The way life functions within this overall set-up is through the ongoing, continuous movement of yin and yang between heaven and earth, determining cosmic function on the vertical axis (Baldrian-Hussein 1984, 128). The *Chuandao ji* says,

> After the great Dao generated and raised heaven and earth, they took up their separate positions above and below, 84,000 miles apart. After the winter solstice, yang begins to ascend from earth. Each *qi*-period or fifteen days, it ad-

10 The term *xiantian* is also rendered "former heaven" (Mozias 2020, 15,), "prior to the world" (Robinet 2011, 89), or "precelestial" (Pregadio 2013, 7). It indicates the primordial or ancestral dimension of cosmic *qi*, the constant versus the circulating, the one as opposed to the many (2013, 8).

> vances 7,000 miles, and after 180 days arrives in heaven [sky] above. Reaching its great ultimate, it generates yin. (ch. 5)

From here, the process repeats, with yin increasing until the winter solstice, when the entire cycle starts anew (Zheng 2010, 37). As the *Lingbao bifa* says,

> Each year begins at the division of the winter solstice. At this time, yang ascends from earth, and in the course of one *qi*-period or fifteen days, it reaches 7,000 miles. Three *qi*-periods make one division [half season] or forty-five days, during which yang ascends 21,000 miles. Two divisions make one season or ninety days, during which yang ascends 42,000 miles. Reaching the midpoint between heaven and earth, it touches the domain of yin. At this time, yang is halfway in the midst of yin. The weather [*qi*] changes to being warm: the time of the spring equinox has come.
>
> Passing this, yang ascends further and enters the domain of yang. That is, having obtained all the *qi* [of earth], it keeps ascending. Moving as before for forty-five days, it comes to the beginning of summer. After another forty-five days, it reaches the division of the summer solstice, at which point it has passed through the entire 84,000 miles of distance and reached heaven [the sky]. Yang is now in the midst of yang. The weather changes to being hot, and accumulated yang begins to generate yin. (ch. 1)

This reflects the "open universe" (*kaitian* 開天) theory of astronomy, which envisions the earth as a square base covered by a round dome, imitating the shape of a turtle (see Allan 1991). Not unlike a similar understanding in ancient Babylon, it was prominent in China since the 3rd century and gave the distance between the earth and the sky as 80,000 miles (Needham et al. 1958 210-11). The earliest measurements for this appear in the *Huainanzi* based on the application of the gnomon: they came to around 100,000 miles (ch. 3; Major 1993, 147-49; Needham et al. 1958, 225).

In medieval Daoist literature, the numbers tend differ from text to text. For example, the *Tiandi yundu jing* 天地運度經 (Scripture on the Revolutions of Heaven and Earth, DZ 322) has, "Heaven is distant from earth by 90,000 miles" (1a). The *Tianguan jing* 天關經 (Scripture of the Heavenly Pass, DZ 987) states, "Heaven and earth are 48,000 miles apart. Their east and west, north and south ends are 100,005,000 miles from each other" (2ab). The latter number also appears variously in texts cited in the 6th-century polemic *Xiaodao lun* 笑道論 (Laughing at the Dao, T. 2103; trl. Kohn 2008a). The text further adduces the *Wenshi zhuan* 文始傳 (Biography of the Master at the Beginning of the Scripture), the esoteric biography of Yin Xi 尹喜, the first recipient of the *Daode jing*, as saying: "Heaven and earth are 409,000 miles apart." A citation of the same document in the Song encyclopedia *Taiping yulan* 太平御覽 (Imperial Encyclopedia of the Taiping Era), on the other hand, has: "Heaven and earth are 400 million miles from each other" (2.6a; Kohn 2008b, 81).

The number given in the Zhong-Lü texts is of Buddhist origin (Robinet 2011, 67-68). The Buddha Amitabha shed 84,000 forms of illumination, the Buddha Gautama provided 84,000 teachings and possessed 84,000 excellent physical signs, King Ashoka erected 84,000 stupas for the Buddha's relics, and so on (Soothill and Hudous 1937). The *Avatamsaka Sutra* or *Huayan jing* 華嚴經 (Flower Garland Sutra; trl. Cleary 1984) speaks of 84 billion reflections of worlds within worlds, and the Buddhist sutras are said to contain 84 million words. In addition, Buddhist world ages or kalpas were numbered in 84. The smallest consisted of 8.4 million years of growth, followed by 8.4 million years of decline. Twenty regular kalpas made are big kalpa, which lasted for 336 million years, divided into four periods of formation, existence, destruction, and nonexistence (Zürcher 1981, 38-40; Bodde 1991, 124).

The choice of this particular number is not accidental. The number eight refers to the highest and most-encompassing level of consciousness in Buddhism, while four is ubiquitous in Indian thought, apparent in the four directions, the four elements, the four world cycles (*yugas*), the four Vedas, and more. Together, they signify space, while the various zeros added to them indicate the ongoing and never ceasing flow of time. In other words, 84,000 is the classic cosmic number of space-time.

The Zhong-Lü Daoists, as well as related works of the same period, such as the *Hunyuan bajing zhenjing* 混元八景真經 (Perfect Scripture of The Eight Luminants of Chaos Prime, DZ 660; *Daoshu* 17; Schipper in Schipper and Verellen 2004, 824), used the number literally and divided it into appropriate segments, working with a count of seven (Robinet 2011, 68). This is not typically Daoist, either. The first culture to place importance on the number seven was ancient Sumer, whose astronomers identified seven major planets and created the seven-day week we still use today (Belmonte 2010, 2054). From there, it moved into India and came to play a major role in Buddhism and secondarily in China, where memorial services for the dead to the present day work according to a seven-week cycle (see Jordan 1972).

The ongoing movement of yin and yang according to this system, then, provides organization and structure to the world on a vertical basis and creates natural life, establishing weather patterns and giving shape to the agricultural year. Its time divisions are as follows:

Chinese	Literal	Translation	Equivalent	Western
nian 年	Year	year	4 seasons	12 months
shi 時	Time	season	2 half-seasons	3 months
jie 節	Node	division	3 *qi*-periods	6 weeks
yue 月	Moon	month	2 *qi*-periods	30 days
qi 氣	*qi*	*qi*-period	3 base-weeks, half month	15 days
hou 侯	Phase	base-week	5 days	5 days

The Sun and the Moon

Complementing this aspect, and providing structure to the horizontal dimension of life processes, are the movements of the sun and the moon as they move back and forth between the cardinal directions, as already outlined in classical Chinese astronomy (Needham et al. 1958, 392-94; Pregadio 2006a, 214). The *Chuandao ji* says,

> The sun and the moon are the essence of great yang and great yin. They structure the patterns of the interaction of heaven and earth; they support the efforts involved in the generation and maturation of the myriad beings. They rise and set in the east and west to differentiate day and night. They come and go in the south and north to determine heat and cold. (ch. 4)

The *Lingbao bifa* echoes this,

> Rising in the east and setting in the west, the sun follows the way of yang; waxing in the west and waning in the east, the moon follows the way of yin.
>
> In the course of one day, they divide day and night. After the winter solstice, the sun rises from south to north; after the summer solstice, it rises from north to south. (ch. 5)

Both, moreover, match the overall pattern and are said to be 840 miles in diameter and advance in seventy-mile increments across the firmament, but the sun being yang works with the number nine while the moon, yin in quality, works with six.

Moving seventy miles each day, the moon accordingly takes six days to reach 420 miles, that is, the halfway point between the new and full moon, when "the bright section in its dark part is half way and we speak of the first quarter moon" (*Bifa* 5; Zheng 2010, 36). The process continues along these lines to complete one cycle within a month or thirty days. The bright section and dark part of the moon, moreover, are called its spirit and material souls (*hunpo* 魂魄; Pregadio 2013, 14), indicating the dynamic between different internal aspects of yin and yang, while the quarter moon is called a "hanging string" (*xuan* 弦), referring to the sickle-style shape of the waxing or waning moon (Baldrian-Hussein 1984, 120; Robinet 2011, 9-10).

In addition, the sun and the moon in the sky match gold and jade on earth (Needham et al. 1976, 144). As the *Lingbao bifa* notes, "The greatest among the stars and planets are the sun and the moon. The most precious among the soils and stones are gold and jade. Thus, the physical form yin and yang take are the sun and the moon above, gold and jade below" (ch. 4; see also Needham et al. 1976, 144). Both are equally manifestations of the subtlest and most potent forms of *qi,* existing in different spheres but structurally and energetically identical. More specifically,

> In their material reality, gold and jade are hidden in the beautiful *qi* of mountains and rivers. When they float to the surface, their radiance is just as bright as that of the sun and the moon. When grasses and trees receive them, they become auspicious; when birds and beasts take them in, they turn into exceptional species. (ch. 6)

In other words, gold and jade contain the same immediate powers as the sun and the moon, albeit in a denser material form and present on earth. They, moreover, also function according to the same principles.

> The light of the sun and the moon, after they rise, works with the number nine; before they set, it works with the number six. Six and nine are the numbers of Qian and Kun. Similarly, the energies of gold and jade ascend during spring and summer and descend in fall and winter: in moving up and down, they match the timing of heaven and earth. (ch. 7)

The ongoing and never-ceasing rotation of the sun and the moon as well as of gold and jade and all the other expressions of yin and yang constitute the essential power of the universe and manifest its constancy. While Dao in itself is nonbeing, latent, mysterious, and unfathomable, they demonstrate for anyone ready to look and see just how it works. Their unfailing circulation is what connects them to Dao in the most powerful way and guarantees their ongoing existence. As the texts never tire of emphasizing, "Never losing Dao, they can live forever." Essential in this process, moreover, beyond the basic coordinates of space-time is the correct count found in the right numbers and their proper correspondences.

Numbers

The universe proceeds in an orderly fashion, definable through numbers and measurable by count (Bodde 1991, 136). The various beings and entities of the world are classified into distinct categories with the help of numbers—which, as Nathan Sivin notes, are not used "as measures but as a means of ranking phenomena into a qualitative order" (1976, 521). Expressing particular qualities of things, they allow an overall patterning of existence and, through changes in assigned meanings, present possible models of dynamic unfolding (Robinet 2011, 46-47; 1994). "The arithmetic manipulation of numbers was intended to account for the structure of situations and their changes, and thus to make the world understandable" (2011, 48).

The most basic understanding in this cosmic context is that one represents primordial unity, the chaos at the brink of creation, underlying all existence, while two signifies yin and yang, the sun and the moon, gold and jade—the core pair of creative energies in the world that brings forth the myriad beings in all their permutations (2011, 48; 1989b, 313).

Next, all odd numbers are yang in quality, while even numbers are yin. Thus, closely echoing the *Xici* 繫辭 (Appended Judgments; trl. Wilhelm 1950; Sung 1971), an *Yijing* supplement in two parts that makes up the fifth and sixth of the Ten Wings (1.9), the *Chuandao ji* says, "Heaven is one, earth is two, heaven is three, earth is four, heaven is five, earth is six, heaven is seven, earth is eight, heaven is nine, earth is ten" (ch. 13; see also Baldrian-Hussein 1984, 124; Robinet 2011, 62).

If one then takes all the primary odd numbers, they add up to 25, while the primary even numbers add up to 30. Together, they come to 55, the number of the complete process of yin and yang (*Chuandao ji* 13). This, too, goes back to the *Xici:*

> Heaven has five primary numbers, and so does earth. When they are distributed over five positions, each finds its complement. The sum of the heavenly numbers is 25; that of earth is 30. The sum total of both combined is 55. Through them the changes and transformations are effected and ghosts and spirits keep on moving. (1.9; Sung 1971, 291; Wilhelm 1950, 310; see also Baldrian-Hussein 1984, 131; Robinet 2011, 53, 61)

In addition, the key numbers associated with yin and yang are six and nine, the numbers symbolizing space and totality (Robinet 2011, 57-58) as well as the central figures in the *Yijing* divination process. Beginning with a pile of fifty milfoil stalks, one puts one aside to symbolize Dao, then divides the remainder into two random heaps. From here, one takes one stalk and inserts it between the ring and little fingers. Next, one counts off the left-hand heap by fours and inserts whatever stalks are left (0, 1, 2, or 3) between the middle and ring fingers. One repeats this with the right-hand heap and inserts the remainder between the index and middle fingers. As one then takes them off in groups of four, the final result is either two or three. One repeats this whole process twice more to get a total number of six, seven, eight, or nine.

Nine, then, signals a strong or moving yang line, while six represents a strong or moving yin line. Seven is a non-moving yang line, and eight is a non-moving yin line. To get any one hexagram, one has to repeat the entire sequence five more times, building the structure from the bottom up. Each strong line, again moving from the ground up, moreover, changes into its opposite, so that one obtains a sequence of hexagrams, providing ongoing future direction (Wilhelm 1950, lii, 312-13; Cammann 1991, 576; Chen 1972).

The Zhong-Lü texts apply the numbers six and nine in the context of the timing of the year (Baldrian-Hussein 1984, 124). The *Lingbao bifa* notes,

> Counting by six and filling six different positions makes a total of thirty-six: this is the number of the completion of yin. . . . Six by nine makes fifty-four: this is the number of the completion of yang.
>
> One six plus one nine added make fifteen, and fifteen is the number of one *qi*-period. The twenty-four *qi*-periods function according to the eight divisions, matching the proper times of yin and yang ascending and descending.
>
> Also, one six multiplied by one nine is fifty-four, which is divisible by four and thus matches the four seasons and corresponds to them. One season contains ninety days, and four times ninety is 360.
>
> So change based on yang matches the number 216 [4 x 54], while change based on yin matches 144 [4 x 36]. Added together, they make 360, which is the number of one complete heavenly circuit. (ch. 5)

The two latter numbers again go back to the *Yijing*, but are arrived at differently. The hexagram Qian consists of six yang lines, each reached by getting a total of thirty-six stalks, and thirty-six times six equals 216. Similarly the hexagram Kun consists of six yin lines, each gained by getting twenty-four stalks, and twenty-four times six equals 144. The two numbers added make 360, the number of days in the course of a year (Wilhelm 1950, 311-12; see also Robinet 2011, 65).

Another, major way of working with numbers, also closely related to the *Yijing* and important in later Daoism are two charts, supposedly delivered in prehistory directly from heaven via markings on the back of a sacred dragon (yang) and turtle (yin), who emerged from the central rivers of China. Popularized under the Song dynasty, they are known as the *Hetu* 河圖 (River Chart) and *Luoshu* 洛書 (Writ of the Luo).[11] They integrate all cardinal numbers into a square grid to represent the vertical and horizontal aspects of the universe as well as the distribution of forces before and after creation.

---

[11] For discussions of the *Luoshu*, see Bodde 1991, 116; Cammann 1961; 1991, 582-84; Major 1984; Robinet 2011, 62; in Pregadio 2008, 483-85; Saso 1978; Schipper and Wang 1986, 194; Smith 1990; Steavu 2019, 98-100; Wang 2012, 207-11; Wang and Bartosh 2019, 100; Wilhelm 1950, 309-10.

The *Hetu*, the vertical pre-creation chart, looks like a cross and shows three concentric spheres, with the number five in the center, the numbers one through four in the narrow circle, and the higher numbers on the periphery.

		7		
		2		
8	3	5	4	9
		1		
		6		

4	9	2
3	5	7
8	1	6

The *Luoshu*, the horizontal post-creation chart, works with nine squares. It, too, has the number five in the center, but places the odd (yang) numbers into the cardinal directions and the even (yin) numbers in the intermediary positions. Facing south as all traditional Chinese maps do, it has the yin numbers at the bottom (toward the north) representing the cosmic beginning and the yang numbers at the top, showing completion.

Daoists activate these charts by using them in abstract cosmological speculation and numerology and as the basis of the Pace of Yu (*yubu* 禹步), which imitates the mythical sage ruler's wanderings while taming the floods and opens control of the world (Wang and Bartosh 2019, 138). In addition, the magic square is also transposed into the sky, associated with the stars of the Dipper (Robinet 1989b, 172) and used in a practice known as "pacing the heavenly net" (*bugang* 步綱) (Andersen 1990a). Beyond that, it appears in the head in the form of the nine palaces (*jiugong* 九宮), four major and four lesser mansions surrounding the primary Niwan 泥丸 palace in the center. Matching the core area of the brain with its major control centers and ventricles, the nine palaces are engaged in meditation to create a cosmic connection and strong internal control (Réquéna 2012, 149).

Taken together, the workings of the universe as outlined in the Zhong-Lü documents correlate several different dimensions of cosmological speculation and systematization, integrating date based on numerology, astronomy, calendar science, and space-time dynamics into one complex system.

Chapter Three

The Human Condition

Deeply embedded within this system, human beings in their gestation and overall development closely match the unfolding and workings of the universe. In their physical form manifestations of the inherent principles of cosmic functioning, people participate continuously in the greater patterns of heaven and earth, yin and yang. Being microcosmic in scale, their main time frame works dominantly in days and hours in addition to years and months; residents of earth, they actively connect to the twelve earthly branches above and beyond the ten heavenly stems; and living well after creation was complete, their rhythms follow the post-creation rather than pre-creation arrangement of the trigrams.

In addition, being human people have consciousness, free will, desires, and emotions—unlike cosmic yin and yang or the sun and the moon, they are able to deviate from their nature-given course. This results in various forms of difficulties and obstacles to perfection as well as innumerable chances to miss the right path and fail in the great endeavor of ultimate cultivation.

Gestation

Human beings are created in a similar fashion as the greater universe, evolving from the formless and chaotic mingling of yin and yang (Zheng 2010, 39). However, while the universe started out that way, in human beings, this raw condition has to be established first. This is done through the intercourse of the parents and takes the shape of a formless mingling of energies (Needham et al. 1983, 195-96). As the *Chuandao ji* describes it, "Human life comes about when father and mother engage in intercourse, and their two *qi* fuse together. Essence [semen] and blood form a zygote" (ch 1). This is a first stem cell of new life, completely without form, shape, or identity, yet with the potential of a viable living being.

Over ten months, it becomes a replica of the cosmos. Already the *Huainanzi* outlines the gradual emergence of channels, tendons, bones, flesh, and organs until the body is complete (ch. 7; Schipper and Wang 1986, 196), matched amply in later medical sources (Furth 1999, 102-05). A more energy-based description appears in the *Jiudan shanghua taijing zhongji jing* 九丹上化胎精中記 (Central Record of the Nine Elixirs and Their

Supreme Transformation of Embryonic Essence, DZ 1382), a scripture of the Highest Clarity (Shangqing 上清) school. It describes human life as beginning when the energy of the nine heavens descends into the still formless elixir fields and transforms, then outlines the progress month by month:

> In the first month, one receives *qi*; in the second, the life force arrives. In the third, they merge and transform. In the fourth, they coagulate into essence. In the fifth, the skeletal structure and head are complete. In the sixth, one takes on physical form. In the seventh, the body gods [spirit] take their positions. In the eighth, the nine orifices begin to shine. In the ninth, the *qi* of the nine heavens is fully distributed and there is a first sound. In the tenth, the Director of Destiny enters one's name into the ledgers: one receives life-destiny and is born. (1.3a; Pregadio 2006a, 212)

Thus endowed with the core powers of the universe, the human being grows into the most fundamental form of the body, "the boundless organism with infinite boundaries" (*ti* 體) (Sommer 2008). Like a plant, each part of which is interconnected with all others and can propagate and replicate the entire structure, this organic body is an integrated entity of different parts that form one whole yet reaches beyond it (Kohn 2014, 65). The body as boundless organism makes sure human beings are connected to a larger social and cosmic corpus, continuously "consubstantial with the bodies of ancestors and descendants" and "all the people with whom it engages in exchanges of labor and food" (Sommer 2010, 223; Emerson 1996). The organic body is like an extended network: each individual contains many different organisms within and is outwardly bound in with numerous others. "The largest unit of the *ti* is the cosmos itself, a wholeness that can encompass life and death, heaven and earth, and all beings" (Sommer 2010, 224).

This boundless organic body—very much like the cosmos, itself also an organism—during gestation "evolves from the state of great antecedence into that of great material reality" (*Chuandao ji* 1). While essentially imitating the unfolding of the universe, great material reality in this context means the shaping of the human body as physical form (*xing* 形), the natural body everyone receives in the course of gestation. "A discrete, visible shape or mass, whose edges and outlines stand in contrast to the formless" (Sommer 2010, 218), this type of body in the Han dictionary *Shuowen jiezi zhu* 說文解字注 (Annotated Interpretation of Phrases and Explanation of Words) is defined as an image or perceptible manifestation of individualized vital energy.

Cosmologically, physical form marks the beginning of the created world. "Before form, there is the One," says the *Huainanzi* (1.13; Major et al. 2010, 64). Neither circumscribed by cultural norms nor defined through social values, the body as physical form always remains part of the natural world—animals have it as much as human beings. As a living entity, it is the lodge or residence of the spirit (Pregadio 2004, 108), and the more people can keep the spirit whole, retaining innocence and wonder, the more "the physical form stays whole, so that one can live forever" (*Zhuangzi* 11; Billeter 2010, 63; Kohn 2014, 63). Even mutated or mutilated, the physical form is still the residence of the spirit, as shown vividly in stories of hunchbacks and cripples whose virtue or spirit remains strong despite their physical challenges (Sommer 2010, 221-22; Moeller 2015). At one with spirit, moreover, one can allow the physical form to change as it pleases. As Master Yu says in the *Zhuangzi*:

> Let's pretend my left arm changed into a rooster, then I could use it to predict the time of night. Let's assume my right arm turned into a crossbow, then I could use it to shoot an owl for roasting. Let's see: if my butt changed into a wheel and my spirit into a horse, then I could use them to ride around in. What other vehicle would I need? (ch. 6; Kohn 2011, 39)

Animated by spirit and vitalized by the raw vitality of pure life force (*ling* 靈), the physical form is first complete after three hundred days of gestation. The *Chuandao ji* describes it as follows:

> As yin nurtures and yang grows, *qi* transforms in gestation and after three hundred days the physical form is complete. The light of the life force enters the physical organism, and the child is ready to part from the mother. (ch. 1)

> After it develops for three hundred days, the embryo is complete and its *qi* fully viable. When the physical form is ready, spirit arrives, and the infant separates from the mother. Although outside her physical form, they remain energetically fused—their fusion allows one physical form to generate another. (ch. 10)

That is to say, even though gestation is complete and the infant takes birth and appears in a discreet physical form of its own, it never loses its inherent quality of the body as boundless organism and stays in close connection with the mother as well as the cosmos.

Body Cosmology

Daoists express this close connection by describing the human body as a full replica of the universe, complete with heaven and earth, sun and moon, mountains and rivers, and more. As already the *Huainanzi* says (echoed in *Chuandao ji* 6),

> The roundness of the head is an image of heaven, the square of earth is the pattern of earth. Heaven has four seasons, five phases, nine directions, and

> 360 days. Human beings in due correspondence have four limbs, five inner organs, nine orifices, and 360 joints.
>
> Heaven has wind, rain, cold, and heat. Human beings have accordingly the actions of giving, taking, joy, and anger. The gallbladder corresponds to clouds, the lungs to breath, the liver to wind, the kidneys to rain, and the spleen to thunder (ch. 7; Kohn 1991, 227).

This takes up an earlier system outlined in the *Shuogua* that matches the eight trigrams to different parts of the human body: Qian is the head, while Kun forms the abdomen; Li with its brightness and connection to sunlight animates the eyes, while Kan relating to water and sound is present in the ears. Zhen, the power of motion, rests in the feet, while Xun with its energetic dynamics activates the thighs. Gen, the symbol of stability, matches the hands, and Dui, the root of joy, connects to the mouth (ch. 9; Sung 1971, 348).

A slightly more detailed outline appears in the *Chunqiu fanlu* by Dong Zhongshu. According to this, in addition to the features already mentioned, the eyes and ears match the sun and the moon, the various orifices and veins resemble rivers and valleys, the hair is like stars and constellations, breathing is like the wind, and the abdomen with its alternating states of being full and empty relates to the myriad beings. The body also closely connects to time: the four limbs match the seasons, the twelve larger joints imitate the months, and the lesser joints have the same number as the days of the year (ch. 13; Chan 1963, 280-82; Kohn 1991, 229).

In addition, the spine consists of into twenty-four vertebrae, literally "divisions" (*fen* 分), matching the twenty-four solar nodes or fifteen-day *qi*-periods of the year. It has three major sections, divided by passes or barriers (*guan* 關). As the *Lingbao bifa* says,

> The bottom three vertebrae sit right opposite the kidneys. The top three are called the Heavenly Pillar, while the area above them [of the head] is known as the Jade Capital. Below the Heavenly Pillar and above the vertebrae opposite the kidneys, that is, above the Tail Gate, there are eighteen vertebrae. The central among them is called the Double Barrier: there are nine above and nine below it. (ch. 5)

Thus, the spine, which is like a flowing river, contains three major barriers,[1] the Tail Gate (*weilü* 尾閭) at the bottom, the Double Barrier (*shuangguan* 雙關), also known as Narrow Strait (*jiaji* 夾脊), in the middle, and the Heavenly Pillar (*tianzhu* 天柱) or Jade Pillow (*yuzhen* 玉枕) at the top. They

[1] See Baldrian-Hussein 1984, 111; Esposito in Pregadio 2008, 835; Neswald 2009, 42; Mozias 2020, 175; Pregadio 2013, 39.

are shown as gates in the 19th-century *Neijing tu* 內經圖 (Chart of Internal Passageways; Komjathy 2009, 72; Huang 2012, 71-73).

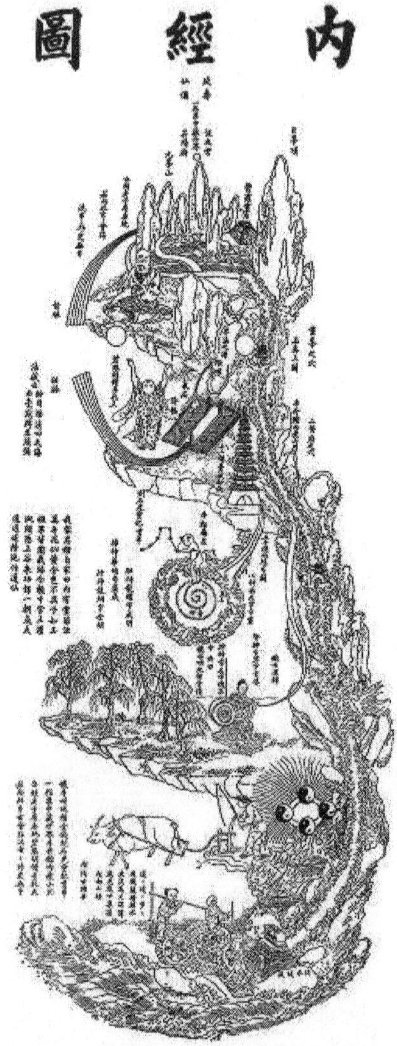

Both medical and Daoist texts describe *qi* in the human body as flowing through a complex system of waterways with the ocean of *qi* in the abdomen, the spine as a mighty river running through the upper torso, smaller tributaries coursing through the four limbs, as well as springs bubbling up from the bottom of the feet (Kohn 2005, 11). The *Chuandao ji* says,

> Water in the human body manifests in the four oceans, five lakes, nine rivers, and three islands. Flowery pond, nephrite pond, phoenix pond, celestial pond, jade pond, chaos pond, primordial pool, lofty garden, spirit water, golden wave, jasper fluid, jade spring, yang cream, white snow—these are some of the many names and appellations for it, too numerous to list. (ch. 7)

The text goes on to define the four oceans as those of blood, *qi*, marrow, and grain; the five lakes as the five organs; and the nine rivers as the twists and bends of the intestines—matching medical literature, notably the *Huangdi neijing lingshu* 黃帝內經零樞 (Inner Classic of the Yellow Emperor, Numinous Pivot; trl. Wu 1993) (Pregadio 2006b, 127). It identifies the three islands as head, heart, and kidneys, then goes on to describe the location of the various other entities. In this, it closely matches information found in earlier Daoist texts that outline the internal landscape and divine palaces of the body, such as the *Huangting jing* 黃庭經 (yellow court Scripture, in DZ 263; trl. Homann 1971; Saso 1995).

The Five Organs

The most important of these palaces and key agents in the Daoist body are the five inner organs, representatives of the five phases that, as already pointed out in the early medical manuscript *Taichan shu* 胎產書 (Book of Gestation; trl. Harper 1998, 377-81), are bestowed upon the fetus during the fourth to eighth months of gestation, thus enabling blood, *qi*, muscles, bones, and skin to form (Unschuld 2003, 84).

As described in great detail in the medical classic *Huangdi neijing suwen* 黃帝內經素問 (Inner Classic of the Yellow Emperor, Simple Questions; trl. Veith 1972; Lu 1987; Ni 1995), the organs are more than mere single entities: inner powers, circles and patterns of *qi*, each of them forms the core of an entire fabric of functions—physical, energetic, mental, and spiritual (Porkert 1974, 117-23). While the organs proper are yin in quality and described as depots or receptacles (*zang* 臟), that is, agents of energy storage, they also come with yang partners, transformative in nature and called offices or viscera (*fu* 腑) (Unschuld 2003, 88). They each correspond to a particular aspect of the body's flesh, its outer appearances, fluids, and secretions. Plus, they each have their own unique orifice, matching particular senses and flavors, as shown in the table below (Wang and Bartosh 2019, 349; see also Baldrian-Hussein 1984, 143-46).

Phase	wood	fire	earth	metal	water
Organ	liver	heart	spleen	lungs	kidneys
Viscera	gall	sm. intestine	stomach	lg. intestine	bladder
Flesh	tendons	arteries	muscles	skin	marrow
Outside	nails	complexion	skin tone	body hair	hair
Fluid	fluid	marrow	essence	blood	urine
Secretion	tears	sweat	mucus	snot	saliva
Orifice	eyes	tongue	mouth	nose	ears
Sense	vision	taste	touch	smelling	hearing
Flavor	sour	bitter	sweet	spicy	salty

In addition, the organs and viscera also work through a set of energy lines or conduits called meridians (*jingluo* 經絡) that establish an organized and tangible connection between the center of the body and the extremities, passing many of the other bodily features in the process.[2] The earth in analogy contains arteries, described and analyzed by Fengshui masters as key lines of energetic interconnection and vibrant functioning. In all cases, they allowed the *qi* to flow as smoothly and as freely as possible.

---

[2] This system is at the core of traditional Chinese medicine and acupuncture. For outlines, see Bensky and O'Connor 1984; Jarrett 2003; Kaptchuk 2000; Kohn 2015; Maciocia 1989; Porkert 1974; Seem 1987; Wiseman 1994.

This energy flow, moreover, follows a particular order, typically beginning with the kidneys, the representatives of earth in contrast to heaven (the heart) as well as the organ matching the phase water and the beginning of the annual cycle at the winter solstice. As the *Chuandao ji* says,

> During gestation, the kidneys generate the spleen, the spleen generates the liver, the liver generates the lungs, the lungs generate the heart, the heart generates the small intestine, the small intestine generates the large intestine, the large intestine generates the gallbladder, the gallbladder generates the stomach, and the stomach generates the bladder.
>
> In this process, yin takes essence and blood and transforms them into physical form, while yang emerges at the moment when life first begins, a single spark of primordial yang settling in the two kidneys. Now, the kidneys are water, which contains fire and ascends as *qi* to move toward the heart. The heart is yang, and yang fuses with yang. When it reaches its great ultimate, it again generates yin. The accumulated *qi* then generates fluid, which naturally descends from the heart and reverts back to the kidneys. (ch. 6)

This is the most fundamental cycle of the phases within the body, centered on the core powers of yin and yang, kidneys and heart, fluid and *qi*. Like yin and yang in the greater universe, they continue to ascend and descend, generating each other in the process. It works like this in all people, established during gestation as part of their intimate connection to heaven and earth.

Beyond this, the five phases—as already determined in the context of the five materials—interact according to either a generating or control cycle. The order of generation is the standard order used in the table above, that is, wood → fire → earth → metal → water. The relationship between the phases and thus the organs in this case is described like that of mother and child. The order of the control cycle is water → fire → metal → wood → earth. The relationship is like that of husband and wife (Robinet 2011, 3).

Taken together, this means that each organ stands in a complex connection to all others. For example, as the *Chuandao ji* points out, "The kidneys are the husband of the heart, the mother of the liver, the wife of the spleen, and the child of the lungs. The liver is the husband of the spleen, the mother of the heart, the wife of the lungs, and the child of the kidneys" (ch. 6), and so on.

Daily Cycles

Following the generative cycle, the *qi* of the organs and viscera runs through the entire physical form in the course of each day, matching the pattern of yin and yang circulating through heaven and earth in the course of a year. The *Chuandao ji* explains this in detail, in fact, its entire chapter 5 is entitled "The Four Levels of Time," referring to time in its human, annual, monthly, and daily dimensions.

To begin, the human life span is 120 years, divided into four segments of thirty each: youth and strength, growth and maturity, old age and infirmity, plus decline and demise. "This is how time works in the human body: it is the first level." Annual time is similarly determined by four segments, that is, the four seasons, which divide into the eight divisions as described earlier. Monthly time, the third level, depends on the moon and works in lunar quarters, each lasting seven to eight days.

Daily time is the most important and also the most alien to Western thinking. As also described in the *Lingbao bifa* (ch. 5), rather than dividing the day into twenty-four hours, the Chinese acknowledge twelve periods, literally "chronograms" (*chen*), commonly called double-hours. Rather than consisting of 120 minutes (*fen*), although the texts use the same term as applied today, each double-hour lasts 500 of these, which I translate "units." In other words, one traditional *fen* or unit lasts 14.4 seconds or is about the length of one quarter minute in the modern system. Similarly, a quarter-hour (*ke*), which I call "segment," rather than fifteen minutes, lasts sixty units, so that eight *ke* plus twenty units make up one double-hour.

Chinese	**Literal**	**Transl.**	**Equivalent**	**Western**
ri 日	sun	day	12 double-hours = 100 segments = 6000 units	1 day
chen 辰	chronogram	double-hour	8 segments 20 units = 500 units	2 hours
ke 刻	quarter-hour	segment	60 units	14.4 minutes
fen 分	part	unit	smallest unit	14.4 seconds

The twelve double-hours, moreover, are named after the twelve earthly branches. Originally stations of the planet Jupiter, which orbits the sun once in twelve years, they go back to particular constellations that form the root of their unique names. In addition, since the 6th century BCE, they have been associated with twelve zodiac animals like sheep, dragon, or dog (Needham et al. 1958, 405) that still dominate the energy of individual years and are actively used in horoscopes.

Each double-hour lasts two Western hours or 120 minutes, is scheduled to begin at an odd hour such as 11 pm, called after a Jupiter station, associated with a zodiac animal, and linked energetically to a particular organ or viscera. To make up the difference in numbers and match the total of ten organs and viscera to twelve double-hours and earthly branches, medical theorists added two further entities. The sixth organ is the pericardium, the sack protecting the heart and thus also known as "heart protector." Its matching yang organ is the "triple heater," a dynamic function that controls the transport, utilization, and excretion of the body's energies. The following table outlines the system, listing time in the 24-hour system (Wu and Wu 2016, 95-167; see also Needham et al. 1958. 402-04).

Time	Branch	Meaning	Animal	Qualities	Organ
23-1	Zi 子	son	Rat	wise, flexible, optimistic	gallbladder
1-3	Chou 丑	ugly	Ox	stable, straight, tough	liver
3-5	Yin 寅	sincere	Tiger	careful, responsible	lungs
5-7	Mao 卯	prosper	Hare	clever, agile, kind	lg. intestine
7-9	Chen 辰	shake	Dragon	powerful, strong, elegant	stomach
9-11	Si 巳	stop	Snake	cautious, intuitive,	spleen
11-13	Wu 午	noon	Horse	enduring, lively, wild	heart
13-15	Wei 未	future	Sheep	tender, gracious	sm. intestine
15-17	Shen 申	lightning	Monkey	flexible, spontaneous	bladder
17-19	You 酉	ferment	Rooster	stylish, alert, humorous	kidneys
19-21	Xu 戌	dismiss	Dog	honest, loyal, stubborn	pericardium
21-23	Hai 亥	roots	Pig	gentle, smart, joyful	triple heater

This understanding forms the backbone of Chinese medicine and provides a foundation of diagnosis. For example, the *Huangdi neijing* says that those who have a disease of the liver are animated and quick-witted in the morning; their spirits are heightened in the evening, and at midnight they are calm and quiet (Temple 1986, 125).

To make matters more complex, traditional calendar masters also added the eight trigrams into the mix, recalibrating the entire system according to the number eight. This means that they had to find equivalents to the eight divisions of the year—solstices, equinoxes, and seasons' beginnings—in the course of the day. They picked the times at the top and bottom of the day plus those in between, that is, midnight and dawn as well as noon and dusk—at the midpoint of certain double-hours—plus 3 and 9 am and pm at the transition point between two periods.

Being part of human life, the trigrams here are used in their post-creation or "after heaven" (*houtian* 後天) arrangement,[3] which developed in the Han dynasty on the basis of the *Shuogua* description that connects them to the agricultural year (Wang 2012, 215; Baldrian-Hussein 1984, 127). The primary factors are no longer heaven and earth, but fire and water, represented by mixed yin-yang lines, symbolizing the energetic muddle of created living.

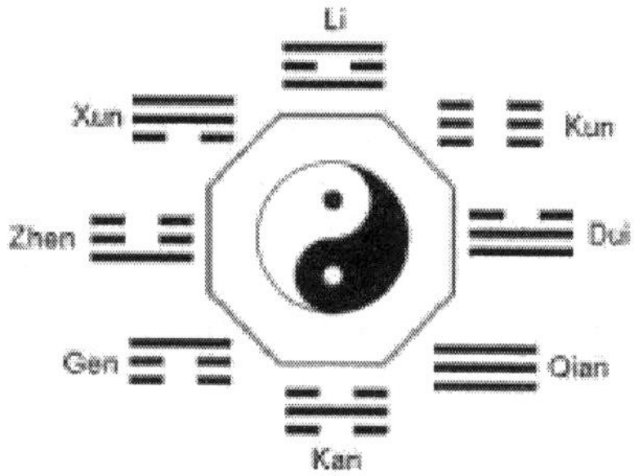

East is marked by Zhen (thunder), the power of movement and initiation, while west is now under the sway of Dui (lake), the sign of joy and marker of a successful harvest. Qian (heaven) and Kun (earth) have each shifted one place toward the western side of the model, while the two intermediate stations on the eastern side are made up by Gen (mountain) and Xun (wind). To move from one trigram to the next in clockwise direction, they all change two lines into their opposite—except Zhen, which changes all three, and Dui, which changes only one (see Cammann 1990). Here is how they connect to time:

Year	**Month**	**Day**	**Double-hour**	**Trigram**
winter solstice	new moon	12 midnight	Zi midpoint	Kan/Water
spring beginning		3 / am	Chou to Yin	Gen/Mountain
spring equinox	first quarter	6 / am	Mao midpoint	Zhen/Thunder
summer beginning		9 / am	Chen to Si	Xun/Wind
summer solstice	full moon	12 noon	Wu midpoint	Li/Fire
fall beginning		3 / pm	Wei to Shen	Kun/Earth
fall equinox	last quarter	6 / pm	You midpoint	Dui/Lake
winter beginning		9 / pm	Xu to Hai	Qian/Heaven

3 The term *houtian* is also translated "later heaven" (Mozias 2020, 41), "posterior to heaven" (Robinet 2011, 90), and "postcelestial" (Pregadio 2013, 7). It designates *qi* after the creation of the universe that circulates continuously. As adepts align and merge with this, they get closer to the primordial or "precelestial" state (2013, 7).

Both Zhong-Lü texts work heavily with the daily cycle and the twelve double-hours, but the *Lingbao bifa* also makes particular use of the trigrams to specify the best periods for certain practices. Time matters, and it is very important to modify and develop the body's energies at the right time, in the right measure, and with the right methods.

Free Will

All these cosmic powers and energetic cycles set up during gestation continue to function throughout human life, but to a different degree, since people overall are subject to rise and decline. The *Chuandao ji* says,

> From the state of great immaculate onward, there are ascent and descent [of *qi*]. Through them, the infant grows like a yellow sprout. After 5,000 days [13.5 years], his *qi* is fully viable and the correct count comes to eight-one.
>
> Reaching the age of fifteen, he is a young man. At this time, his *qi* is half yang within yin, just like the light of the sun rising in the east. From here on, people tend to release and lose primordial yang, waste and scatter perfect *qi*. As their *qi* weakens, they suffer sickness, old age, death, and ultimate destruction. (ch. 1)

That is to say, from the time of pristine purity at birth, the energetic cycles are functioning and cause the physical form to grow. It takes 5,000 days, matching the number of words in the *Daode jing*, to reach puberty, when *qi* has fully developed and is in a state of complete yang, symbolized by the number 81, nine squared. By age fifteen, the child can be considered a young adult, and he or she is halfway through the first stage of life, characterized by youth and strength. From here on, energy may still rise for a few years, but inevitably decline sets in.

The medical classics describe this life cycle in terms of the rise and fall of essence (*jing* 精) or sexual potency—semen in men and menstrual blood in women. Both develop from pure *qi* that sinks down from its center—the ocean of *qi* in the abdomen in men and the cavern of *qi* in the chest in women—and becomes tangible in sexual sensations and fluids. Emitting essence from the body is a major source of *qi*-loss, which can cause physical weakness, lead to diseases, and precipitate early death. But even without excessive loss, vital essence will diminish over a lifetime. Its rise and decline are understood as occurring in an eight-year cycle in males and a seven-year cycle in females (Kohn 2005, 33). As the *Huangdi neijing suwen* says:

> When a girl is 7 years of age, the kidney *qi* [*jing*] becomes abundant. She begins to change her teeth and the hair grows longer. At 14, she begins to menstruate and is able to become pregnant. The movement of the great pulse is strong. The menses come regularly, and the girl is able to give birth.

> At age 21, the energy is steady, the last tooth has come out, and she is fully grown. When she reaches the age of 28, her tendons and bones are strong, her hair has reached its full length, and her body is flourishing and fertile. At 35, her yang brightness pulse begins to slacken, her face begins to wrinkle, her hair starts falling out.
>
> When she reaches the age of 42, the pulse of the three yang regions deteriorates in the upper part of her body, her entire face is wrinkled, and her hair turns gray. At age 49, she can no longer become pregnant, and the circulation of the great pulse is decreased. Her menstruation is exhausted, and the gates of blood are no longer open. Her body declines, and she is no longer able to bear children. (ch. 1)

Above and beyond this natural tendency of rise and decline, people have consciousness and can exercise free will—either allowing the decline to happen, speeding it up by wasting energy in various ways, or counteracting it by taking charge and practicing self-cultivation. As the *Chuandao ji* notes, "Among the myriad beings, the one with the most life force and the noblest is the human. Only human beings can penetrate the principle of the myriad beings and fully explore their own inner nature" (ch. 2). They do so by working with five distinct psychological forces that flow through the five organs and constitute the workings of consciousness.

First among them is spirit (*shen* 神), a pure and rapidly vacillating form of *qi* closely associated with the heart. An active, organizing force, it is without limit or judgment and works with precognition and intuition. In people, it is the main factor that allows consciousness (*shi* 識) and manifests in the mind (*xin* 心), a term that refers both to mental activity in general and also to the internal force responsible for classification and evaluation, desires and emotions. The latter lead to what the Zhong-Lü texts, following Buddhist models, call "mental projections" (*jing* 境), that is, personalized, one-sided visions of reality. Right here is where free will makes its first appearance, because at every instant people have the choice to allow their spirit to flow freely or limit it through mental judgments and sensory affectations.

Next is the spirit soul (*hun* 魂), a directional and individualized aspect of cosmic spirit, which is yang in nature. Physically placed into the liver, linked also with the gallbladder and described as the residence of strategists and judges, it is the origin of all planning, organization, judgments, and decisions—with a tendency to get impatient and aggressive. It pulls people toward heaven, purity, and goodness, enhancing their artistic, intellectual, and spiritual growth, but can also give rise to anger and rage.

Third is the material soul (*po* 魄), yin in nature and connected to the lungs and the large intestine. It represents the physical base of life, manifest in instincts of survival that make sure people get enough food, drink, sleep, and sex (Kohn 1997, 99-101). Driven by instincts, this force may cause people to lose vital energy in sexual passion or dissipate it by hankering after luxury and ease. It may cause fears of deprivation or starvation, bringing forth greed, stinginess, jealousy, and envy, or, if material goals are not forthcoming, may cause people to suffer from sadness, depression, or despair (see also Brashier 1996; Lo and Wang 2018, 296; Yü 1987).

The fourth and fifth psychological forces are will (*zhi* 志) and intention (*yi* 意). The will is the specific direction of effort toward a unique vision of life, both in terms of material and cultural attainments. On its basis, the intention takes care of the concrete steps necessary to move in that particular direction. To even begin internal cultivation according to the Zhong-Lü texts, it is absolutely essential to have "a sincere mind and earnest will" and "persistently apply one's intention."

The will is linked organically with the kidneys, which are closely connected to pre-creation or primordial *qi*. The seat of the root power of personal determination, they can also give rise to insecurity, fear, and anxiety. The intention belongs to the spleen, the storehouse of *qi* and main center of food processing. It has a tendency to overplan or worry, but is also the seat of personal integrity and fundamental honesty.

The Zhong-Lü texts acknowledge the power of these forces and the pitfalls they represent. For example, the *Lingbao bifa* says,

> While still in the womb, their primordial *qi* is full, but soon after, the six desires and seven emotions arise, so that they waste and scatter their primordial yang, release and lose their perfect *qi*. (ch. 1)

The six desires refer to inner urges prompted by sensory experiences through seeing, hearing, smelling, tasting and touching as well as the will to live or the desire to avoid death. The seven emotions are those associated with the five organs—joy, anger, sadness, fear, and worry—plus hatred and greed (Baldrian-Hussein 1984, 204). Together with the five psychological agents they constitute the third level of human physicality in the Daoist system, the personal body (*shen* 身).

Representing the sum total of one's inner life and socially created identity, it develops on the basis of learned conduct and manifests in a physical presence visible to others (Jochim 1998, 47; Jullien 2007, 67). Determined by decision-making, reflection, and set patterns of behavior, this body represents the familial and social personhood of the individual (Sommer 2010, 215-16; Sivin 1995, 14). It is the way people shape themselves as embodied persons; while deeply rooted in nature, it is yet artificial and contrived. The *Daode jing* says that this body is "the reason why I have great afflictions" (ch. 13), referring to apprehensions about winning or losing, being in favor or disgrace (Kohn 2014, 61).

In other words, the personal body is the self-image the heart mind creates on the basis of the five psychological factors, sensory processing, and emotional dispositions. As people grow up, these take on a life of their own and, in a continuous feedback loop with the heart mind, create personality boundaries and a stereotyped vision of life that gets more rigid over time and may lead to restrictive tendencies and increasingly ill health. Daoists work hard to overcome this body in their cultivation practice; internal alchemists incinerate it completely.

The Vicissitudes of Life

The reason why ordinary people never engage in self-cultivation, in a vivid illustration of what it means to have a personal body, is described in the *Chuandao ji* in the first five of a set of nine "hardships" (*nan* 難). First of all, the text says, people are vexed by the procurement of material necessities, such as "clothing for the four seasons and food for three meals each day." Next, they are steeped in social obligations of honoring their elders and otherwise repaying karmic debts, as well as, third, hankered down by feelings for parents, spouses, and children. In addition, they tend to be deluded by visions of grandeur—"wealth accumulating to the tune of ten thousand properties, nobility culminating in the rank of the three dukes"—and afflicted by ailments and diseases, "steeped in darkness and encountering disasters, one's whole life in the world nothing but suffering" (ch. 17). Another passage describes the effects of these hardships:

> People often pass their youth in vain pursuits. Before the rooster has even crowed, they leave their house, anxious that they might be late. When the city's drums are heard widely [at sunset], they return home, complaining that is too soon.
>
> Avarice and madness, competition and eagerness barely pause; foolish imaginings and pervasive worries never stop! Their houses are full of gold and jade, but how does that help them to ward off disease? Their vision is focused on children and grandchildren, but how does that let them exchange rather than lose their *qi*? (ch. 5)

Another dimension of this phenomenon is the fascination with outside reality and sensory pleasures. Again, the *Chuandao ji*:

> Throughout gorgeous mountains and enticing scenery, multi-colored plants exude deluding fragrance; in pavilions perched over rivers and edifices on dangerous cliffs, soft breezes delight the intention. They invite leisurely talks during moonlit nights and drinking with friends during snowbound days.
>
> All these are lascivious pleasures without end that chisel away at our limited time. When one finally thinks to turn the mind back toward Dao, the body is riddled with sickness and disease. (ch. 5)

Disease generally arises, as the *Lingbao bifa* notes, because "yin and yang are out of alignment, typically yang being low and yin overwhelming" (ch 2). The *Chuandao ji* classifies it in three forms, matching the Buddhist division of sickness, old age, and death. Sickness occurs due to varying weather conditions and failure to observe the natural cycles, "going to extremes in labor and leisure, losing all rhythm in hunger and satiation," which leads to chronic ailments and is identified as the "disease of the seasons."

Old age comes from "indulging in emotions and letting the intention run wild, scattering and losing primordial yang, dispersing and diminishing perfect *qi*, with increasing years getting dry and desiccated: this is old age." Death, finally, happens when "the person's *qi* is exhausted and the physical organism is hollow: the spirit soul dissolves and the spirit is drummed out" (ch. 9).

But death is not the end of the story. Rather than "the destruction of the assembled elements of the body, it is the breaking of their union. The change is called death because the body dissolves, but the beings thus dissolved are but transformed" (Yates 1964, 32). In other words, the karmic debts and burdens incurred by self-indulgent and obstructive behavior lead to a less fortunate rebirth in future lives and cause the continuation of a downward spiral. Again, the *Chuandao ji*,

> Once born, they perish again; once gone, they are born again. Cycle after cycle they do not realize this; life after life they keep on sinking lower. Eventually they lose their human form and are born among other species, leak their life force and incarnate in different shells. Their root nature of utmost perfection no longer part of humanity, they are mired in the relentless cycle of reincarnation and rebirth, forever without any chance of liberation. (ch. 1)

The thinking presented here is a mixture of traditional Chinese medical wisdom and Buddhist doctrine. The latter first appeared on the Chinese horizon in the 1st century CE, then underwent several stages of adaptation and modes of translation (Ch'en 1973; Zürcher 1959). By the 5th century, Buddhism had risen to the status of a major religion and Daoist schools adopted its doctrines widely: aspects of worldview, such as ideas of karma, rebirth, and hell; ethics, notably precepts and monastic vows; and philosophical speculation, such as notions of emptiness and the logic of enlightened states (Zürcher 1980).

The process by which one is affected by bad karma is gradual. As the Daoist *Jinjie jing* 禁戒經 (Scripture of Prohibitions and Precepts), an early Tang text found at Dunhuang, points out, people who act morally wrong will first encounter various forms of misfortune, such as "the calamities of water and fire, swords and weapons, capture and prison, many thousands of strokes, evil winds and nasty demons" (l. 71). This will put great stress on their minds and cause increasing madness, while their bodies "will overflow with rot, they will be covered with boils, their hands will be crippled, and their feet deformed" (l. 72). Too sick to live yet not sick enough to die, they are caught in a living hell on earth. Even after death, there is no respite. On the contrary, the real suffering starts in the various depths of hell for kalpas everlasting (Kohn 2004, 26).

Given this dire situation, Daoists developed a keen awareness of different aspects of wrongdoing, distinguishing the bad deed itself, the guilt that accompanied it, and the resulting suffering through disasters and diseases, bad rebirths and the tortures of hell. They created systems for people to keep track how many good and bad deeds they had committed, allowing them to estimate their impact on life expectancy and overall destiny (Kohn 1998a; 1998b).

Suffering from disease in its various forms and learning about long-term karmic consequences often create a strong motivation to practice cultivation. The first step is to look for a cure with medical means:

> Yang in excess and yin in deficiency require a cure through cooling; yin in excess and yang in deficiency require a cure through warming. Old people are cold a lot, while youngsters tend to be hot; obese people have too much saliva, while rich folks have too much accumulation. In males, disease grows from *qi*; in females, afflictions originate in blood.
>
> To cure, one must supplement what is empty, release what is full, protect what is weak, and reduce what is excessive. For minor cases, there are acupuncture and moxibustion; for major ones, there are herbal remedies and drugs. (*Chuandao ji*, ch. 9)

While this may offer a temporary respite and deal with the first level of disease, the ailing body, it does not cure old age or death. Skilled physicians, as the text says, may be able to "irrigate the colon and enhance the flesh" but they typically cannot "smooth out facial wrinkles and restore a youthful complexion" or "preserve the body to remain in the world and attain long life" (ch. 9). For this one must undertake systematic cultivation practice.

Erroneous Ways

However, deciding to undertake Daoist cultivation is only the very first step in a long journey. Once people have made the decision to pursue personal refinement, there are innumerable pitfalls and potential errors. One of them, as the *Chuandao ji* notes as the sixth of the nine hardships, is that people sign up with a fake or useless teacher.

> Seeing that life and death are great affairs, they rush to seek out a teacher, never discriminating between genuine and fake. They may follow a teacher because he makes great arguments and is a proficient speaker or because he has a Daoist mien and hoary appearance. They start out by claiming that they have found a spirit immortal and only after a long time understand that this teacher was in it only for his own fame and profit. (ch. 17)

A closely related problem is that people "use minor, sectarian methods," which may afford some quick results but do not lead to the ultimate goal. Part of the issue is the methods themselves: they are limited and cannot provide lasting effects. The text present a long list of such methods, including "observing the precepts, abstaining from grains, extracting *qi*, swallowing saliva, leaving the family," and so on. It asserts that "the list of minor, sectarian methods is endless; . . . in pursuit of transcendence and liberation, they cause people to put in lots of effort with little to show for, quite possibly inviting an attack of disease" (ch. 2).

Another part of the problem is a deep-seated fickleness in people, "their tendency to desire too much too soon," moving on to yet another fad when the previous technique does not seem to pan out (ch. 2). "One does one thing in the morning and something else at night, sits down to practice then stands up to pursue another idea. One relishes the moment and hates planning long-term, starts out concerned and diligent and ends up lazy and indolent" (ch. 17). A third aspect of the issue of minor methods is the opposite, that is, people tend to get too rigid, "unable to modify and budge from the same practice as long as they live, never changing with the four seasons" (ch. 1).

All this is not for want of trying. The text asserts that many people "start out with a sincere mind and . . . develop an earnest will," but remain unaware of the best methods, the way of the great Dao that matches the inherent workings of the universe.

> Practicing minor methods, they get a lot of strange ideas. Wasting years and months, they never see any real results. In their later years they grow weak and old and eventually fall again into the relentless cycle of reincarnation and rebirth. This causes other [potential] Daoist followers to believe that eternal life is a false idea, that transcendence and liberation are just empty words. . . . Their mind entangled in mental projections, they get involved with things and lose their will. In the end they are unable to escape. (ch. 17)

As a result, there are five different ranks of immortals, that is, practitioners working with various techniques who realize different levels of accomplishment. They are ghost, human, earth, spirit, and celestial, named after the realm of existence they end up as a result of their endeavors. In this form, the distinction is quite unique to the *Chuandao ji*, but it picks up on an earlier division recorded first in Ge Hong's 葛洪 (283-343) *Baopuzi* 抱朴子 (Book of the Master Who Embraces Simplicity, DZ 1185; trl. Ware 1966). He distinguishes earth immortals with an extended life expectancy who prefer to remain on earth from celestial immortals with a spirit body who opt to reside in the heavens or the isles of the blessed (Steavu 2019, 109; Kirkova 2016, 16). A third group in Ge Hong are immortals by deliverance from the corpse (*shijie* 尸解): they transform into celestial entities but have to leave a simulation corpse behind, such as a bamboo staff or a sword (Cedzich 2001; Robinet 1979).

As outlined in the *Chuandao ji*, ghost immortals, at the bottom of the ladder, have escaped the cycle of reincarnation but are stuck in the realm of yin. This happens because "they make their physical form like a withered tree and their mind like dead ashes, keeping their spirit consciousness contained within and their will unified, never letting it scatter. In deep stability [*samadhi*], their yin spirit emerges, so they become ghosts of plain life force rather than immortals of pure yang" (ch. 1). That is to say, according to the Zhong-Lü vision, the Buddhist practice of motionless sitting meditation and complete absorption in deep trance states does not lead anywhere except to a realm of deep darkness.

Human immortals, next, are those who pick one method exclusively:

> With sincere mind and earnest will, they do not budge from it until the end of their days. As a result, the energies of their five phases interact wrongly and go awry, making their physical form and material reality excessively firm. They only manage to become immune to the eight pathogenic influences, allowing them be mostly healthy and rarely ill. (ch 1).

In other words, followers of more medically oriented activities and nourishing life techniques who emphasize health and well-being achieve their goal but do not move toward full liberation.

Earth immortals, third, get to live for a very long time on earth by applying the basic techniques of internal alchemy. They match the energetic cycles of yin and yang as well as the sun and the moon, observe the correct timing to work with *qi*, invert the direction of the five phases, and revert *qi* to the three elixir fields (*dantian* 丹田)—the three energy centers in the head, chest, and abdomen (Pregadio 2006b, 139). Doing so, they achieve a medium level of accomplishment: "They refine their physical form to the point where they can stay in the world and live long without dying."

Moving up the ladder, spirit immortals are earth immortals who take their work to the next level. "Reverting jade fluid to the elixir field, they refine their physical form into *qi*" and create an immortal embryo within. "Their yin all gone, their yang is utterly pure: beyond this body they have yet another body. Liberated from material reality, they ascend to the immortals." Moving even higher, the ultimate and highest level is that of celestial immortals, who serve as officials among the otherworld administration and eventually "reach the realm of emptiness, nonbeing, and spontaneity of the heavens of the Three Clarities" (ch. 1).

Faulty Practice

Striving to ascend along this scale, some people indeed manage to set their mind fully on the great path, find a reliable teacher, pass whatever tests he prescribes, and are moving happily in the right direction. Once at this stage, they yet need to be aware of yet further obstacles to avoid.

The most common is failure to observe the right timing. While the various natural forces and all animals spontaneously flow along with the cycles of life, human beings, given consciousness and free will, have the power to deviate from them and often do so. As the *Lingbao bifa* notes,

> When yang rises to the beginning of spring, moving up from below, within days it gets to be half yang within yin. When yin sinks to the beginning of fall, moving down from above, within days it gets to be half yin within yang. This is the natural way of heaven and earth. Only human beings let their *qi* grow feeble at Gen [3 am], not knowing the right times to nurture it. They let it scatter at Qian [9 pm], not realizing the principles of assembling it. (ch. 2)

This problem is exacerbated by too much reading, reflection, and conscious learning, which leads to a good theoretical understanding of the principles involved, but does not necessarily help with the practice. Thus, "many adepts in the past as much as today, though they may dedicate themselves to cultivation until their hair turns white, only reach a minor level of accomplishment" (ch. 8).

Especially when it comes to the external elixir, the concoction of reverted cinnabar on the basis of chemical compounds such as lead and mercury, they face three reasons for failure. First, they don't rightly know whether the ingredients they gather are genuine or fake and have no clue about the proper firing times. "They take precious ores and scatter them in the flames of the fire, burning them to dust and ashes" (ch. 17). Second, they either know about the ingredients or manage the firing times, but not both. Third, they get both right and succeed in elixir concoction but then are not ready to take the final step and actually ingest it, being afraid of losing their foothold in the human realm.

Beyond all this, practitioners are subject to "ten demonic attacks" (*shimo* 十魔), sometimes also described as the imposition of yin spirits. These are essentially manifestations of emotionally charged states that, as the *Chuandao ji* says, "can happen in waking life, in dreams and sleep, and during [the meditation of] inner observation" (ch. 19). In the wake of the

Zhong-Lü documents, they appear variously in the literature, most prominently in the *Dadan zhizhi* of the 13th century (2.5b-6b; Komjathy 2014, 156-58; Ho 2018, 86-88; see also Eskildsen 2004, 106).

The ten demonic attacks are quite like the visions potentially experienced by the newly deceased according both Daoist materials (Eskildsen 2006) and the *Tibetan Book of the Dead* (Freemantle and Trungpa 1974). Based on previous karma, they conjure up emotionally engaging situations that pull people away from their proper path—be it the track through the bardo to a higher level of rebirth or appropriate cultivation practice. More specifically, they show scenes engaging the six sensory desires and seven emotions, visions of conspicuous wealth and high honors, love and affection, entertainment and pleasure, sexual attraction, and even encounters with fabulous sages and worthies (Baldrian-Hussein 1984, 162; Zheng 2010, 52). On the more negative side, they may also create fear and panic by conjuring up various calamities and difficulties as well as battles and warfare. To give a few examples from the *Chuandao ji* (ch. 17),

> There may be flowery attractions filling the eyes, the music of reeds and pipes filling the ears, the tongue tasting delicious foods, the nose enjoying strange fragrances, emotions and thoughts full of pleasures and delights, intention and will vast and extensive.
>
> There may be immortal ladies and jade maidens, lining up and practicing their arts, their music and singing filling the air, their dance colorful in variegated silks, their services skillful in their red sleeves as they offer wine in golden chalices.
>
> There may be a battle field, full of soldiers, both infantry and cavalry, swords and weapons glittering like frost, spears and axes raised, bows and crossbows drawn, fighting to the death, full of amazing courage and agility.

Whichever they are, as the text insists, "If you encounter any of these, do not engage them but recognize them as a demonic attack." They are easiest to defeat during deep meditation, when one is in a secure environment and restful inner state. If they show up during a dream, one is helpless while the dream is still going on, but upon waking can dismiss them without too much difficulty. It is hardest when they manifest in real life, with their full concrete impact. "Adepts engage with them and get attached, and once they are attached, they are completely hooked. If they never fully attain Dao, it is mostly because of this."

Chapter Four

Stages and Processes

Working hard to move past all these pitfalls and obstacles, practitioners attain the final goal of "transcendence and liberation" (*zhaotuo* 超脫) by passing through three stages. Commonly described as "levels of accomplishment" (*cheng* 成), they come in a minor, medium, and major form, matching the three types of human, earth, and spirit immortals. Each involves different methods of internal alchemy and leads to particular results.

The overall process, moreover, closely matches the system of external or operative alchemy, applied to the energy system of the human body in relation to the greater universe. It imitates the unfolding of the universe and the gestation of the human being, matching the cosmogony in its progression while engineering the "marriage of the internal metals and thereby making a birth possible" (Eliade 1962, 36).[1]

However, while the universe starts with pure yin and yang, and gestation rests with the energies of the parents, adepts of external alchemy must first assemble the raw materials, while internal practitioners need to isolate the core ingredients. That is to say, they begin by working with cosmogonic regression, moving from the tangible to the subtle, then reconstitute the creative process in a new dimension.[2]

The Three Stages

Internal alchemy matches Daoism in general in that it outlines the path toward oneness with Dao in terms of the three stages of health, longevity, and immortality. As the *Chuandao ji* says:

---

[1] Western spiritual alchemy distinguishes four stages, described in terms of colors. The first, nigredo or blackening, involves the search for the *prima materia* and thus a descent into the darkness of the inner world; the second, albedo or whitening, opens the soul to self-awareness in the reflected light of the moon; the third, citrinitas or yellowing, unfolds the direct light of the sun in the adept's inner being, the complete union with the cosmos; and the fourth, rubedo or reddening, signals the return to earthly life in a newly spiritualized body and self. See Hamiton 1985, 5-8; Jung 1968, 333-35; Amberlain 2005, 32-33.

[2] For outlines of the stages, see Pregadio 2012a, 3; 2012a, 180; and Skar 2000, 485; Lu 2009, 79; Mozias 2020, 85.

> Human beings can reach a minor level of accomplishment to be healthy and happy and extend their years, a medium level to live long without dying, or a major level to gain liberation from material reality and ascend to the immortals. (ch. 3)

> Initially they can reverse old age and recover youth; later they can enter utmost states and transcend ordinary life. (ch. 5)

Most basic and most widely known is the healing dimension, administered either by someone outside the person in the form of acupuncture, herbs, and massages, or through the personal practice of longevity techniques—including moderation, diet, exercise, self-massages, breathing, and basic energy guiding (Kohn 2012). This allows people to integrate their *qi* with nature and cultivate its inner flow, reaching the fullness of their natural life expectancy in health and vigor. It often leads to an increase in years, a youthful appearance, and continued strength and enjoyment of life. People enhance and empower the natural patterns of life, consciously following the rhythm of yin and yang and creating harmony in themselves and their surroundings.

Longevity, second, intensifies this dimension through an increasingly subtle awareness of internal energies and their systematic modification. People identify yin and yang, water and fire in their bodies and refine them by opening circulation tracks through central meridians in close accordance with the daily and seasonal cycles. They also work with the five inner organs, enhancing their productive patterns (Wang and Bartosh 2019, ch. 15A). This level involves intensive meditation and trance training as well as more radical forms of diet and other longevity practices. It results in a bypassing of death, so that the end of the body has no impact on the continuation of the person.

Immortality, third, raises the practices to a yet higher and more transcendent level. Unlike health and longevity, it means moving beyond the natural cycles and applying the techniques in a reverse manner. To attain it, people have to transform all their *qi* into primordial *qi* and proceed to refine it to subtler levels. This finer *qi* will eventually turn into pure spirit, with which practitioners increasingly identify to become transcendent spirit people. In addition, practitioners attain supersensory powers and eventually gain residence in otherworldly realms (Kohn 2016, ch. 8).

The very same kinds of practices may be used on all three levels, albeit in different ways and with caution. Certain practices that are useful for health may be superfluous in the attainment of longevity, while some applicable for immortality may be harmful when health is the main focus. Take breathing as an example. When healing or extending life, natural deep breathing is emphasized, with the abdomen expanding on inhalation. When moving on to immortality, however, reversed breathing is advised, which means the intentional contraction of the abdomen on inhalation (Lu 1970; Kohn 2008b). Undertaking this too early or at the wrong stage in one's practice can cause complications, from dizziness to disorientation or worse.

This holds also true for sexual practices. For health, sexual activity with a partner is encouraged in moderation, with both partners reaching regular climaxes. In longevity practice, sexual activity may still be performed with a partner, but ejaculation as a loss of *qi* is avoided and sexual stimulation is used to increase the positive flow of *qi* in the body (Wile 1992). In immortality, finally, sexual practices are undertaken internally and without a partner. They serve the creation of an immortal embryo through the refinement of sexual energy into primordial *qi* and cosmic spirit (Ho 2018). Going beyond nature, immortality practitioners are not interested in creating harmony and balance, but strive to overcome the natural tendencies of the bodymind and actively lessen or even relinquish earthly existence in favor of cosmic and heavenly states.

Diets are another case in point. Chinese medicinal diets use ordinary ingredients and recipes, focusing strongly on rice, beans, and vegetables as well as meat, tofu, and other forms of protein. They require a conscious adaptation to seasonal patterns and the application of warming or cooling foods, spices, herbs, depending on the patient's condition. Eating on the longevity level utilizes the same principles and is still grain-based, but involves the abstention from heavy meats and fats as well as from strong substances such as alcohol, garlic, and onions. Practitioners are encouraged to eat lightly and in small portions, matching the seasons and always conscious of their internal *qi*. Contrary to this, immortality practice is to "avoid grain" (*bigu* 辟穀). Here practitioners eliminate ordinary foodstuffs and increasingly rely on herbal and mineral supplements. Their goal is the refinement of *qi* to a level where food intake is completely replaced by the conscious absorption of *qi* through breath, leading to a fundamental transformation of the physical constitution (Arthur 2006; Kohn 2010a).

The cultivation system of internal alchemy is commonly described in terms of refining essence (*jing* 精) to energy (*qi* 氣), energy to spirit (*shen* 神), and spirit to merging with Dao (*hedao* 合道), from where adepts return to emptiness (*fanxu* 反虛).[3] Farzeen Baldrian-Hussein identifies this process with the three levels of accomplishment and links them further with the purification of inner nature and life-destiny (*xingming* 性命) (1984, 54; see also Zheng 2010, 35). While this holds true for later systems,[4] the Zhong-Lü texts do not describe the stages in this form. They talk about re-

---

3 For discussions of the process, see Kohn 2001, 145; 2009, 1; Furth 1999, 196; Lu 2009, 78; Needham et al. 1983, 79; Pregadio 2000, 489-90; 2012a, 3; Robinet 1989a, 317-21; 1995; Zheng 2010, 34, 40.

4 See Lu 2009, 81; Pregadio 2014b, 159; 2014c, 474; Robinet 1989a, 306.

fining physical form to energy and spirit (*Chuandao ji* 13), but more in conjunction with reverting *qi* and fluid to the elixir fields than in direct connection with the three levels of accomplishment. In addition, they speak of inner nature and life-destiny in more general and often somewhat denigrating terms, such as understanding inner nature (*Bifa*, Pref.) or wrongly focusing on cultivating it (*Chuandao ji* 2), as well as nurturing destiny or reaching the end of life (chs. 1, 2). The full system of cultivation from essence through energy to spirit and Dao as well as the specific link of inner nature and life-destiny with the alchemical process are of later origin.

The Three Vehicles

The *Daoshu* editions of the *Chuandao ji* and the *Lingbao bifa* refer to the three levels of accomplishment as the Three Vehicles (*sancheng* 三乘).[5] The latter speaks of the lesser vehicle as "good for extending the years and increasing longevity," the middle vehicle as "leading to becoming an earth immortal" (ch. 5), and the great vehicle as allowing one to "become a celestial immortal" (ch. 10), matching the three accomplishments in the *Chuandao ji*. The text further outlines "four ways of working with the minor vehicle" and "three ways of working with the middle vehicle" (ch. 4).

The Three Vehicles (*triyāna*) are originally a Buddhist concept, describing different paths to attainment. They are listening (*srāvaka*), cultivating oneself (*pratyekabuddha*), and striving for universal salvation (*bodhisattva*) (Soothill and Hudous 1937). While it is possible to see them as consecutive, they really constitute alternative approaches to enlightenment, relating to the fundamental outlook and concerns of different kinds of practitioners rather than stages of progress in a cultivation system.

This changed in Daoism. Lu Xiujing 陸修靜 (406-470), a leader of both the Celestial Masters (Tianshi 天師) and Numinous Treasure (Lingbao 靈寶) schools, adopted the notion of the Three Vehicles and used it to designate a successive ranking system of schools. He placed the Numinous Treasure school with its strong ritual and communal commitment at the top, Highest Clarity with its focus on transcendence and immortality second, and the Three Sovereigns (Sanhuang 三皇) third. This latter school, which did not survive beyond the mid-7th century, focused on political divination and proper rulership with the help of talismans and cosmic correspondences (see Steavu 2019). Lu further assigned the Celestial Masters school and various methods of healing and personal morality the position at bottom of the scheme, acknowledging them as the foundation of the entire pyramid (Ofuchi 1979, 257).

---

[5] It also features in the *Zhonghe ji* (Cleary 2003, 383-84).

In the 6th century, under pressure of political unification and the rise of the Highest Clarity school, the system was redesigned with Highest Clarity at the top and renamed the Three Caverns (*sandong* 三洞). Their central deities were joined together into one group known as the Three Pure Ones (Sanqing 三清), that is, the Daoist trinity. Named after three major heavens and still prominent today, they are presented with the Heavenly Worthy of Primordial Beginning (Highest Clarity) in the center, the Lord of the Dao (Numinous Treasure) to his left, and Lord Lao (Three Sovereigns/Celestial Masters) to his right.

The three deities further match the Three Treasures (*sanbao* 三寶) of the religion, another concept adopted from Buddhism, where it designates *buddha* (enlightenment), *dharma* (teaching), and *sangha* (community of followers). In Daoism, they are Dao, scriptures, and masters. The gods of the trinity represent the Three Treasures in the sense that the Heavenly Worthy is the creative power at the root of all existence, the Lord of Dao is the revealer of scriptures and presenter of revelations, and Lord Lao is the practical teacher, who provides instructions in various techniques and communicates most closely with humanity (Kohn 2001b, 119).

The texts associated with each cavern match this division, including central materials and so-called supplements, consisting of both revealed and humanly authored works, with a greater emphasis on technical and hagiographic materials as well as non-mainstream schools in the latter. The overall system, still used in the Daoist Canon and a part of the ordination system today (see Benn 2000), is as follows:

Cavern	School	Supplement
Perfection (Dongzhen)	Highest Clarity	Great Mystery (Taixuan)
Mystery (Dongxuan)	Numinous Treasure	Great Peace (Taiping)
Spirit (Dongshen)	Three Sovereigns	Great Clarity (Taiqing)
	Celestial Masters	Orthodox Unity (Zhengyi)

Referring to this system, Zhongli Quan says in the preface to the *Lingbao bifa,* "Presenting the combined methods of the Three Vehicles, I call this work *Lingbao bifa*, 'The Conclusive Methods of Numinous Treasure'."

In contrast, the *Chuandao ji* states that the "three levels of accomplishment—minor, medium, and major, each with their own proven effects—are entirely unlike the Three Vehicles of the Buddhist teaching, which refer to carts drawn by a ram, a deer, and an ox" (ch. 12).

This latter usage of the term is a Song-dynasty development under the auspices of the harmonization of the three teachings—Daoism, Confucianism, and Buddhism—indicating different modes of cultivation toward oneness. Thus, the *Chongyang zhenren jinguan yusuo jue*, a set of practical instructions associated with the Complete Perfection founder Wang Chongyang, outlines a visualization of an interior energy journey and says,

> Another three miles further on, there is a huge mountain. On the eastern slope of this mountain is a gray ox. This represents the energy of Lord Lao. On the western slope of the mountain, you can see a white ram. This is the energy of the sage Confucius. Then again, on the slope straight to the south, there is a yellow deer. This is the energy of the Golden Immortal of Great Awakening [the Buddha]. (18b; Kohn 1993, 176; see also Komjathy 2007)

In sum, the term Three Vehicles has three distinct usages, designating alternative approaches to spiritual attainment, successive levels of schools and practices, and systematic stages in the cultivation process.

Medicines

Another set of three stages that relates to internal alchemy appears in the Chinese classification of medicines (*yao* 藥): crude drugs serve to cure diseases, medium remedies enhance energy and enrich life, and superior compounds open the path to advanced states, including the acquisition of magical powers. As Ge Hong's *Baopuzi* says,

> Superior compounds make it possible to keep one's body at rest, prolong life, and ascend into heaven as an immortal. One may also come and go freely between heaven and earth, control all kinds of demons, grow feathers on the surface of the body, and obtain any food one desires without difficulty. (ch. 11; Ware 1966, 177)

The full system is spelled out in the *Shennong bencao jing* 神農本草 (Shennong's Materia Medica), compiled by the Highest Clarity patriarch Tao Hongjing 陶弘景 (456-536) around the year 500. This consists largely of citations from the Han-dynasty *Shennong bencao* and *Mingyi bielu* 名醫別錄 (Special Record of Famous Physicians). In certain passages, it is similar to the *Wushier bingfang* 五十二病方 (Remedies for Fifty-two Diseases; trl. Harper 1998), a formulary unearthed at Mawangdui, and also reflects the *Wuwei fang* 無為方(Formularies from Wuwei), a set of bamboo slips found in a Later Han tomb at a place called Wuwei in Gansu (Akahori 1989, 74).

Medicines here are made from organic ingredients—metal, mineral, and botanical—and used either individually in their crude form or concocted in various combinations as compounds (Pregadio 2006a, 125). Ge Hong in his *Shenxian zhuan* 神仙傳 (Biographies of Spirit Immortals; trl. Campany 2002) outlines the lives of ninety-two immortals, among whom twenty-three are using medicinal remedies: crude drugs based on pine trees such as resin, nuts, needles, and bark; a variety of fungi and tree excrescences; as well as basic minerals such mica and realgar (Needham et al. 1974, 70). These medicines have the power to prolong life to 500 or 5000 years even when taken in small doses, but do not afford transcendence (Akahori 1989, 78).

A more detailed outline of the functioning of a crude drug, which can be applied to immortality in a special form, appears in the Dunhuang manuscript *Shiliao bencao* 食療本草 (Material Medica for Dietary Therapy):

> Lotus root restores the weakened functioning of the middle heater and strengthens the spirit. It increases the overall vitality and expels the various diseases. Administration over a long period of time lightens the body weight and allows adepts to tolerate extreme cold. . . .
>
> It has a decoagulating effect on the blood. Also, it tastes good and can easily be substituted for the normal diet. Taking steamed lotus root enriches the lower heater; it improves the functioning of the intestines and the stomach. Moreover, it increases overall vitality. When taken together with honey it keeps the intestines free from worms. Some immortals do not require any food; they can reduce their body weight to such a degree that they can fly in the air. These effects are due to their eating lotus seed and root which have been dried for one thousand years. (Akahori 1989, 80)

In contrast to crude drugs, complex compounds, as first outlined in the *Wushier bingfang*, varied greatly in their preparation methods and came in the form of pills, powders, decoctions, and pastes. In the *Wuwei fang*, prescriptions are mostly powders, apparently the dominant form during the Han dynasty. In contrast, in the late-Han *Shanghan lun* 傷寒論 (On Cold-Induced Disorders; trl. Mitchell et al. 1999), prescriptions are mostly decoctions (Akahori 1989, 83). The ultimate and most potent compounds are elixirs, immortality drugs concocted from the mixture of several base ingredients following a complicated procedure.[6] They tend to appear as paste, which can then be formed into pills.

Ge Hong's *Baopuzi* lists fifty-six different elixirs with effects ranging from rejuvenation, longevity, and immortality to the acquisition of magical powers and the creation of gold (Needham et al. 1976, 90-95; Pregadio 2006a, 136). To prepare an elixir, adepts first of all have to find the necessary crude drugs to be used as base ingredients or raw materials, often rare substances that only appear in certain geographical regions. They included highly disparate and frequently poisonous substances, such as pine needles, pine resin, mushrooms, persimmons, apricot kernels, deer antlers, mother-

[6] Called "cinnabar" (*dan* 丹) after their main ingredient, they are justifiably called "elixirs." The word goes back to "the Greek *xerion*, used to describe the agent of transmutation—originally a medicinal powder for curing wounds. Jabir uses the same term, transliterated into Arabic as *al-iksir*. This word has come down to us as 'elixir,' still used for substances, especially medicines, with marvelous effects. Elixirs 'heal' the metals by adjusting their ratio of qualities, just as medicine heals the sick by adjusting the ratio of humors" (Principe 2013, 39). See also Katz 2008, 35.

of-pearl, mica, aconite, realgar, sulfur, mercury, arsenic, silver, and gold. They might also involve animal and human substances, such as sex and pituitary hormones isolated and distilled from urine—a substance called "autumn mineral" since it looked like frost in the fall (*Huainanzi*). Thus, Gu Yong 顧雍 (25 BCE) says, "Masters of methods say that by fusing cinnabar they can transform it and make yellow gold, and that for dark and muddy [concentrated] urine they can make a hard, white ice-like [crystalline] substance" (Temple 1986, 127).

For the most part, though, both in China and the West, the starting materials were mineral and the recipe included mercury and sulfur. "Steps in the process were seen as the marriage between the sulfur and the mercury, with the sulfur as the male (dry) and mercury as the female (wet), resulting in the Philosophers' Stone, the hermaphrodite,"[7] "just as male semen coagulates female blood into a fetus" (Principe 2013, 122; Eliade 1962, 48).

Elixir Concoction

The subtlety of the process necessitated that alchemists should withdraw to an uninhabited place on one of the sacred mountains with no more than three companions. It was important for that place to be secret, for any contact with commoners or, worse, disbelievers upsets the preparation. From here, alchemists underwent purification for a hundred days, bathing in water enriched with fragrant herbs, changing their diet toward fasting, abstaining from anything polluting, and practicing concentration of mind (Ware 1966, 75). As Mircea Eliade notes,

> The artisan takes the place of the Earth-Mother and it is his task to accelerate and perfect the growth of the ore. The furnaces are, as it were, a new matrix, an artificial uterus where the ore completes its gestation. Hence the infinite number of precautions, taboos, and ritual acts which accompany the smelting. (1962, 57)

Next, the concoction process commenced, a lengthy and complicated procedure that involved various chemical reaction methods, most importantly calcination, that is, heating something strongly in air, melting, or evaporating it; and distillation, a method for separation of substances, for isolating their spirit or essence, so it could be recombined with a body that results in gold or the elixir (Cobb et al. 2014, 39). Lesser techniques also included maceration, that is the soaking of fresh or dried substances in water and left standing in room temperature; circulation, also called percola-

---

7 Cobb et al. 2014, 96. See also Amberlain 2005, 21; Katz 2008, 6. 33; Tramer et al. 2007, 9-10. For a modern psychological reading, see Freeman 2014, 19.

tion or reflux, the application of a condenser over a flask to let moisture condense, rise up, and drip back; as well as extraction, substances joined in a thimble then placed in an extractor to obtain a concentrated fluid (Albertus 1974, 26).

The exact methods for each step followed specific cosmic instructions, often obtained through revelation from the gods. Placed in a cauldron coated with various luting compounds, they were surrounded by magical and protective devices to ensure the proper atmosphere for the elixir to grow. Over months or even years, the right times of firing and cooling, stirring and burying had to be observed to the minutest detail (Kohn 2009, 18).

The end result, often called the "great medicine" (*dayao* 大藥), matches what Western alchemists called the quintessence, "the fifth, underlying power of the four elements (earth, water, fire, air), active in the vegetable, animal, and mineral kingdoms" (Albertus 1974, 28), the ultimate remedy and most potent drug of all. As Bruce Moran notes,

> What they were all looking for was a super-medicine, an elixir or *aqua vitae* that could purify physical bodies of their impurities, rid the human body of disease, and prolong life. . . . This elixir was not so much a product of combining different distilled ingredients but instead the end product of a series of distillations (even of one substance only) gradually increasing in purity. The most pure substance of all (a universal medicine created by art and found nowhere in nature) had lots of names, but the one that was used most often was the fifth essence. (2005, 11-12)

The process, as also in Western spiritual alchemy,[8] was thought to imitate the growth of gold in the earth on a microcosmic scale, and accordingly followed the stages of cosmic creation as perceived at the time. Essentially the work of the alchemist occurred on three levels: the concrete concoction of the elixir for immortality, the creation of gold from base metals for personal wealth, and the replication of the cosmic processes of creation for insights into (and power over) the innermost secrets of the universe. Alchemy was, therefore, both a chemical and a mystical endeavor, which led not only to chemically induced trances and visions but also to the high spiritual states necessary for immortal transformation. Once complete, the elixir had varying effects, not only effecting immortality but also providing talismanic protection (Steavu 2019, 85). Generally, the better the raw materials and the longer and more complex the process of refinement, it seems, the stronger it was (Akahori 1989, 87).

The *Chuandao ji* describes the process of operative alchemy, using the Yellow Emperor as an example. Following the instructions of his master Guangchengzi 廣成子, described as such in the *Zhuangzi* (Roth 1997), he

---

[8] See Amberlain 2005, 23; Beebe 2014, xviii; Carty 2007, 5; Northage-Orr 2009.

utilized cinnabar, called "vermilion sand" (*zhusha* 朱砂), among the eight minerals and black lead (*heiyan* 黑鉛) among the five metals, processing them to collect mercury and silver.[9] Overcoming the obstacle that "good raw materials are hard to find and correct concoction techniques are hard to obtain," he then, matching the classical model (Robinet 2011, 61) "erected a three-storied furnace, each story nine inches in height, square on the outside and round on the inside to assemble the *qi* of the eight directions and imitate the phases of the four seasons" (ch. 9).

Refining the raw materials for three years, he reached a minor level of accomplishment and was able to "eliminate the hundred diseases." Another three years brought about a medium level, allowing life extension. After three more years, the elixir of the major level provided the ability "to lift off and ascend spontaneously, be strong in physique and with mighty arms, easily able travel a thousand or ten thousand miles" (ch. 9). The same potency applies to internal elixirs, "parallel in many ways to the spiritual alchemy of the West, which used the preparation of the philosophers' stone to stand for the process by which an individual passes through the 'death of the soul' to rebirth and spiritual perfection" (Sivin 1968, 30).

Created in installments of one hundred days rather than three years, they were much preferred and soon overshadowed external drugs. "The old alchemical writings were either reinterpreted in terms of physiologic procedures (and even religious meditation) or else dismissed as aberrations (1968, 31; Gulik 1961, 80-84). Still, as the text insists, external drugs have their place as initial energy builders, notably for "adepts who come to realization only in their later years and tend to be not very firm and stable in their root and source" (ch 9).

---

[9] The eight minerals are cinnabar, realgar, mica, malachite, sulfur, salt, saltpeter, and orpiment (Pregadio 2006a, 223). The five metals are gold, silver, lead, mercury, and copper. Their use in alchemy makes good sense. "They can all be found as natural sulfide minerals or in association with sulfide minerals, and a sulfurous odor (a vague smell of rotten eggs) can be detected when these ores are scratched or heated. All metals can be liquified under certain conditions of temperature and pressure (mercury is already a liquid), and five of the metals have the silvery appearance of mercury when molten (exceptions are gold and copper). The attraction of real sulfur for real mercury is evidence by the use of sulfur in modern mercury spill kits: sulfur sprinkled on mercury instantly changes its slippery surface to a grainy surface that can be captured. Gold acts like a mercury sponge and spontaneously forms an amalgam (as mercury alloys are called) at a rate that is impressive to witness" (Cobb et al. 2014, 44).

Core Ingredients

The central ingredients of the external elixir in the Zhong-Lü system are mercury and silver, extracted from cinnabar and lead. In the body, they are the yang dragon and the yin tiger, derived from the energies of the heart and kidneys. The main distinction is that "lead and mercury that issue from metals and minerals are inanimate" while "the materials that issue from the body are animate. Still, they can be used just like lead and mercury" (*Chuandao ji* 11). "Mercury," then, "is like the yang dragon; silver is like the yin tiger. Heart fire is like red like cinnabar; kidney water is black like lead" (ch. 9).

The latter two, moreover, are the elementary energies at the core of gestation: "Heart fire and kidney water fuse and refine into seminal florescence" (ch. 3) to form a zygote and constitute the beginning of human life. In addition, they are water and fire on a more cosmic level as defined in the *Yijing* and represented by the trigrams Kan and Li (Robinet 1989a, 313). That is to say, each individual contains the fundamental energies of universal unfolding in their deepest organs.

Just as yin and yang in the greater context of heaven and earth continue to rise and fall, ascend and descend, wax and wane, so their internal counterparts, the energies of the heart and kidneys, never cease to flow and interact with each other. The *Lingbao bifa* notes, "The heart and kidneys are like heaven and earth; *qi* and fluid are like yin and yang" (ch. 2). Also, just as yin and yang on the cosmic level are never a hundred percent pure but always contain a trace of the other deep within, so water in the body is never fully yin and fire is never fully yang, again reflecting the trigrams. The *Chuandao ji* asserts, "There is also yang contained in water and yin in *qi*" (ch. 3). This leads to a dynamic internal process:

> The kidneys are water, which also contains fire and ascends as *qi* to move toward the heart. The heart is yang, and yang fuses with yang. When it reaches its great ultimate, it generates yin. The accumulated *qi* then generates fluid, which naturally descends from the heart and reverts to the kidneys. (ch. 6)

The traces of yang within yin and vice versa, moreover, are there on the basis of essential cosmic workings, that is, they form part of a deeper and subtler level of existence and are accordingly described as "true" or "perfect" (*zhen* 真). As the *Chuandao ji* notes:

> *Qi* tends to ascend, yet it also contains perfect water. Water tends to descend, yet also contains perfect *qi*. Thus, perfect water is perfect yin and perfect *qi* is perfect yang. Perfect yang descends as it follows water. (ch. 3)

Residing dominantly in the heart and kidneys (Needham et al. 1983, 71), these pure powers of heaven and earth yet also manifest in the other organs and flow in the order of the five phases. "They keep on circulating up and down, back and forth, and as long as there is no loss or obstruction, people can extend their years" (*Chuandao ji* 3). In addition, their interaction forms the basis of the elixir:

> When fire ascends, it supports kidney *qi* and generates perfect water. Kidney water then ascends to fuse with heart fluid and generates perfect *qi*. At a minor level, this eliminates all diseases; at a major level, it serves to refine material reality and concoct the elixir. (ch. 8)

The first order of practice is thus to match the natural cycles: work with the proper alignment of the five phases and connect to the timing of the sun and the moon. This is specified in the *Lingbao bifa*:

> At any particular time when *qi* is dominant [in a certain organ], every day utilize the appropriate trigram [time], so that in relation to *qi*, you take in a lot and release only a little, then retain it with some force in the abdomen. The moment *qi* ascends from below, make sure not to let it leave; as soon as it moves in from without, immediately retain it. (ch. 1)

On this basis, adepts further proceed to isolate and extract the perfect aspects, which become alchemical ingredients and as such can be visualized in a variety of ways. The *Chuandao ji* points out,

> To facilitate yang ascending, visualize a male, a dragon, fire, heaven, clouds, a crane, the sun, a horse, smoke, mist, a carriage, a chariot, flowers, or pure *qi*. . . To facilitate yin descending, visualize a female, a tiger, water, earth, rain, a turtle, the moon, an ox, spring mud, a boat, or a leaf. (ch. 16)[10]

The most common visual aids, both in classical medicine and internal alchemy, are the dragon and tiger, primarily identified as the image (*xiang* 象) of the liver and the physical form (*xing* 形) of the lungs (Robinet 2011, 30-31). They are the core energies of perfect water and fire.

> Water grows from heart fire, a fluid that is in fact perfect water. Within this water, obscure and mysterious, the perfect dragon is deeply hidden. It does not reside in the liver, but emerges from the Li [Fire] palace [heart].
>
> Similarly, fire grows from kidney water: it is in fact perfect fire. Within this fire, blurred and indistinct, the perfect tiger is deeply hidden. It does not reside in the lungs but emerges from the Kan [Water] position [kidneys]. (ch. 8)

---

[10] For an exhaustive list of corresponding images and substances used in internal alchemy, see Needham et al. 1983, 60.

In order to gain access to the dragon and tiger as lead and mercury (Needham et al. 1976, 66; Eliade 1962, 120), the essential raw materials of the elixir, one must cut excess yin in the kidneys and eliminate excess yang in the heart. Thereby one isolates the energies at their most creative, that is, as the water of perfect oneness (*zhenyi zhi shui* 真一之水)—called *qi* of cosmic oneness in the *Lingbao bifa*—and the *qi* of rightful yang (*zhengyang zhi qi* 正陽之氣) (Baldrian-Hussein 1984, 76).

These two are core forces of gestation and renewal, representing yin (water) and yang (*qi*) as well as the most fundamental powers of the universe. Perfect oneness is Dao *in statu nascendi*, the original, non-ultimate condition of the universe at the brink of creation. Rightful—upright, proper, well aligned, or straightforward—yang signals a smooth, harmonious, and active flow, a balanced yet dynamic state of being (Kohn 2005, 12). The *Chuandao ji* notes,

> Since the liver corresponds to yang, by eliminating excess yin in the kidneys, we know that the moment the *qi* moves past the liver it turns into pure yang. Pure yang *qi* in turn contains the water of perfect oneness. Blurred, indistinct, and formless, we call this the yang dragon.
>
> Similarly, as the lungs correspond to yin, by cutting off all excess yang in the heart, we know that the moment the fluid arrives at the lungs, it turns into pure yin. Pure yin fluid in turn supports the *qi* of rightful yang. Obscure, mysterious, and invisible, we call it the yin tiger. (ch. 8)

These two are further described in terms of lead and mercury, so that "perfect *qi* hidden deep within the internal kidneys is lead" and "the water of perfect oneness within this *qi is* the perfect tiger, alternatively called silver within lead." Similarly, fluid generated in the heart on the basis of *qi* contains the *qi* of rightful yang or cinnabar, that is, the root of mercury. "Mercury is the *qi* of rightful yang within heart fluid" (ch. 10).

The method to attain these substances is nurturing primordial *qi*. It should be undertaken "at sunrise, at Gen (3 am)." The *Lingbao bifa* specifies:

> Loosen your clothing and sit in meditation to nurture your *qi*: let go off all thoughts, forget all emotions, gently undertake healing exercises, in turn bending and stretching your arms and legs three to five times, to allow the *qi* of the four limbs to rise. In this manner you can guard primordial *qi* within as it ascends to move to the heart. Swallow one or two mouthfuls of saliva, tap and rub your head and face twenty to thirty times. This way, you can expel all the bad and turbid *qi* accumulated in the course of the night. If you do this over prolonged periods, you will have a glossy complexion and amazing beauty, your muscles and flesh will be radiant and supple. (ch. 2)

A similar practice session at night, at the hour marked by Qian (9 pm), involves using the breath to move the heart fire down while pulling on to testicles to "shift the *qi* from the bladder into the kidneys." Moving up and down, practitioners fuse kidney fire with heart fire and warm their lower elixir field, thereby "to obtain the perfect *qi* of great oneness" (ch. 2).

The explanation for this timing is that yang-*qi* is at its most subtle as it rises in the early morning hours and can be enhanced through the practice of healing exercises, saliva swallowing, and self-massages. "This way one spreads the fire throughout the four limbs and nurtures primordial *qi*." On the other hand, yang-*qi* tends to scatter in the late evening and should be sustained through inhalations deep into the heart and massages of the kidney area. "This allows it to merge with kidney *qi* and lets the three fires merge into one, thereby coagulating primordial *qi*" (ch. 2).

The Immortal Embryo

Once *qi* and water are ready, they fuse in a process called the mating of dragon and tiger (*longhu jiaogou* 龍虎交媾), first mentioned in the *Cantong qi* 參同契 (The Seal of the Unity of the Three, DZ 999; trl. Pregadio 2011a).[11] The two join like the sperm of the father and blood of the mother at conception and transform into a new entity, the equivalent of a single-cell organism or zygote, in the alchemical context called the "yellow sprout" (*huangya* 黃芽) (Eskildsen 2004, 78-79). This designates the fresh, new growth of being or the incipient embryo, matching "metallic lead smelted from its core" or unoxidized bright lead in operative alchemy (Needham et al. 1976, 67; 1983, 223). Sometimes also called the mysterious pearl (*xuanzhu* 玄珠; 1983, 91), it provides the root of the elixir or great medicine and signals the transition from regressive to progressive cosmogony. As the *Chuandao ji* describes it,

> The yellow sprout is none other than the great medicine. Its raw materials fundamentally consist of the water of perfect oneness that forms a zygote by fusing with the *qi* of rightful yang. This is just like the perfect *qi* of father and mother fusing at conception, essence and blood creating first life. (ch. 10)

Once this merger is complete and the yellow sprout manifests, adepts "transfer it into the yellow court" (*huangting* 黃庭) the equivalent of the womb in gestation (Zhang 2009, 69).

---

[11] The text is ascribed to Wei Boyang 魏伯陽 of the 2nd century, but probably goes back to the 5th. It is highly obscure, combining the vision of Han cosmology with the divination of the *Yijing* and the concepts of operative or external alchemy (*waidan* 外丹). Studies include Fukui 1974; Pregadio 1995; 1996; 2012a; 2012b. The dragon and tiger appear in ch. 64 (Pregadio 2011a, 106).

> The yellow court is located below the spleen and stomach and above the bladder, north of the heart and south of the kidneys, west of the liver and east of the lungs. Clear at the top and turbid at the bottom, it bears four colors on the outside. Its size is big enough to hold two pints; its pathways connect to the eight channels. (*Chuandao ji* 10)

This matches medieval descriptions in Ge Hong's *Baopuzi* and early meditation manuals, such as the *Huangting jing* and the *Laozi zhongjing* 老子中經 (Central Scripture of Laozi, DZ 1168).[12] Here the yellow court is a divine palace in the center of the abdomen, housing the core deities and essential potencies of life. In later works of internal alchemy, on the other hand, it is an open cavity between the heart and the kidneys, a positive, non-empty void that forms the lodge of spirit and *qi* (Neswald 2009, 38).

The process of mating and impregnation is envisioned quite like the first joining of a newly-wed couple. As the *Chuandao ji* describes it, adepts imagine kidney water and heart fire as two deities: the perfect father is a young man dressed in red, the color of fire, who stands above; the perfect mother is a young woman dressed in black, the color of water, who rests below. They move toward a yellow hut where they encounter an old woman, the matchmaker, who invites them to enter the nuptial chamber where they become husband and wife. "Just as in a wedding ceremony among people, they have a great time, full of joy and delight."

After their successful union, they separate: the young man rises up while the young woman moves down, each returning to their cosmic abodes in heaven and earth. They leave their mingled essences behind: "The yellow dame holds something shaped like a mandarin orange. She throws it right into the yellow hut, where it enters a golden vessel" (ch. 16; Baldrian-Hussein 1984, 76-77).

An alternative visualization involves the dragon and tiger as actual beasts:

> See a black spark [tiger] rise up from a blazing fire and a red dragon dive down from turbulent waves. When the two beasts encounter each other, they fight, right in front of the tower pavilion. Its red gate opens wide and, in the midst of wildly raging smoke and flames, a kingly personage appears who directs the great fire to burn all the way to heaven in waves reaching up a myriad yards.
>
> After the fire reaches its highest point it starts to drop again, smoke and flames filling heaven and earth. The dragon and tiger whirl and coil around each other, then enter the golden vessel. Moving down into the yellow hut, they settle in as if in a cage or closet. (ch. 16)

---

[12] For studies of the *Huanting jing*, see Baldrian-Hussein 2004; Kroll 1996. On the *Laozi zhongjing*, see Schipper 1979; 1995. Both are discussed in Lagerwey 2004; Pregadio 2006b, 129-35.

Thus joined into one, the two energies transform into the yellow sprout, which quickly coagulates and grows to the size of a grain of rice or millet. From here, adepts nurture the sprout like a pregnant woman would an embryo, growing it over the period of ten months or three hundred days (Baldrian-Hussein 1984, 88).[13] As the *Chuandao ji* says,

> Continue the practice for a hundred days without fail, and the compound is fully potent. After two hundred days, the sagely womb is stable, and after three hundred days, the immortal embryo is fully formed. (chs. 8, 11; *Bifa* 3, 4)

These three phases of a hundred days each—contracting the 3,000 years it takes jade to reach perfection to a single year (Baldrian-Hussein 1984, 89)—are each further linked to the three accomplishments, so that the great medicine or medicine provides enhanced health and well-being, the presence of the sagely womb (*shengbao* 聖胞) affords extensive longevity, and the immortal embryo (*xiantai* 仙胎) is the gateway to transcendence.

Firing Times

The process that leads to these results is described in terms of reduction and augmentation (*youdian* 抽添) of yin and yang, lead and mercury, in close alignment with the proper firing times (*huohou* 火侯). The latter require complete control over the powerful element of fire:

> The alchemist, like the smith and like the potter before him, is a 'master of fire,' It is with fire that he controls the passage of matter from one state to another. . . That which natural heat—from the sun or the bowels of the earth—took so long to ripen, is transformed by fire at a speed hitherto undreamed of. (Eliade 1962, 79)

In Daoist internal practice, firing involves complicated cycles of heating and stimulating energy,[14] utilizing healing exercises (*daoyin* 導引), breathing practices (*huxi* 呼吸), and internal *qi*-guiding (*xingqi* 行氣) at specific hours and to different degrees, matching the cosmic and internal rhythms of yin and yang, the sun and the moon. Adepts work with different kinds of fire, "ruling (*jun* 君), subordinate (*chen* 臣), and common (*min* 民)," rendered "royal, minister, and common" by Farzeen Baldrian-Hussein (1984, 78). They "all originate from primordial yang and generate perfect

---

[13] For more on the immortal embryo, see also Ho 2018, ch.6; Hudson 2008; Lu 1979, 160-74; Mozias 2020, ch. 5; Needham et al. 1983, 84-85, 215-17; Pregadio 2006a,210-14; 2006b, 138-39and Skar 2000, 486.

[14] On the firing process, see Baldrian-Hussien 1984, 118; Eskildsen 2004, 79; Mozias 2020, 86; Needham et al. 1983, 45; Pregadio 2011a, 89; 2012a, 184; Neswald 2009, 40; Robinet 1989a, 316-17; 1995; Sivin 1976, 518; 1980, 266-97.

qi" (*Chuandao ji* 7) and are associated with the heart (ruling) and the bladder (common; *Bifa* 2) and work particularly "to refine the physical form" (*Chuandao ji* 12).

In particular, during the first stage, the *Lingbao bifa* requires practice at Li and Qian, that is, at noon and 9 pm, when dragon and tiger join and fluid reverts back to its origin in the kidneys. At Li, one should assemble the compound; at Qian, one heats and refines it—working more at assembling in winter and spring and more at refining in summer and fall (ch. 4).

During second stage, "once the holy womb is stable, match the firing times to the count of the lesser heavenly circuit: this is called the lesser heavenly circuit. Once the embryo is fully formed and perfect *qi* is generated, match the firing times to the count of the greater heavenly circuit: this is called the firing process of the greater heavenly circuit" (ch. 4).[15] That is to say, one circulates the energy through the body in close accordance with the daily and annual cycles of yin and yang. Matching the circadian rhythm, the innate, biological patterns of the body that are closely related to hormonal secretions, especially of the pineal glands (Temple 1986, 124), adepts begin at midnight and work systematically through the double-hours of the day (Baldrian-Hussein 1984, 97-98; Sivin 1976, 518). The process requires complete dedication:

> Give up all worldly activities and live in seclusion, focusing your mind on inner observation, never letting internal projections leave or external projections enter, like a woman nurturing a baby or a dragon nurturing a pearl. Even at times of eating and drinking, resting and sleeping, remain silent like a snoozing baby, unassuming as a young girl. Lest there by loss or diminishing, never even for a moment separate from Dao. (ch. 4)

More concrete practices are detailed for the Zi hour or time of the trigram Kan at midnight and for the time of the trigram Gen at 3 am. Kan marks the winter solstice, when yang begins to grow; Gen is when kidney *qi* fuses with liver *qi*. At this time, one practices a combination of stretches, breathing, and mental guiding to slowly push open the barriers along the spine and allow the *qi* to rise all the way into the head.

Not every day is the same, though, but firing varies in the course of the seasons. "Throughout the year, fire in accordance with the seasons, never losing the rhythm of Qian and Kun. Throughout the month, fire with the proper reduction and augmentation" (ch 9). Thus, for example, when liver

---

[15] The usage of lesser/major heavenly circuit (*xiao/da zhoutian* 小大周天) is not the same in each case: the former refers to the orbit of the celestial bodies in the course of time; the latter indicates the circulation of energy throughout the body. Neither matches the contemporary understanding of the terms as micro/macrocosmic orbit (see Chia 1983; Winn 2006; Komjathy 2009).

qi dominates in the spring, on the days of Jia and Yi, when wood controls earth, it is important "to raise the fire to refine spleen *qi* at the right time: use the double-hours marked by the earthly branches Chen and Xu (7-9 am/pm) as well as Chou and Wei (1-3 am/pm)" (*Bifa* 8). On other days during this season, one had best work "at Dui (6 pm) to reduce metal and sublimate lung *qi*," the yin counterpart of the liver. At all occasions, adepts should "enter the meditation chamber to inhale deeply and exhale gently, making sure the respiration is long and steady, holding the breath in for increasingly longer periods" (ch. 8).

This presentation closely echoes other works of internal alchemy, yet it is also different in significant ways. Thus, while it works with the same cosmological patterns as outlined in the beginning sections of the Zhong-Lü texts, it is nowhere near as intricate as the *Cantong qi* and other works in its wake, which speak of the firing times in terms of trigrams designating specific days of the month that match certain key phases of the moon (3rd, 8th, 15th, 16th, 23rd, and 30th), placing the most intense practice on the full moon in the middle of the month. The text also utilizes twelve hexagrams of first increasing, then decreasing yang lines to designate the months and double-hours of the day and indicating the intensity of practice. They begin with the hexagram Fu, which consists of five yin lines and one yang line, and move all the way through Qian (all yang) to Kun (all yin) to begin again.[16]

䷗ ䷒ ䷊ ䷡ ䷪ ䷀ ䷫ ䷠ ䷋ ䷓ ䷖ ䷁

The *Cantong qi* further outlines sixty hexagrams—all except Qian and Kun, Kan and Li—that are active in the course of each month, that is, two per day, one in the morning during rising yang and one in the afternoon during rising yin (Pregadio 2011a, 93-95; Baldrian-Hussein 1984, 100; Robinet 2011, 14).

The Zhong-Lü texts are also much less technical than later works on the firing times that specify numbers and distances of respiration. These include the *Zhenxian michuan huohou fa* 真仙秘傳火侯法 (Methods of Firing Times Secretly Transmitted by the Perfected Immortals, DZ 273), a text based on materials contained in the *Daoshu* and dating from the late 12th or early 13th centuries (Baldrian-Hussein in Schipper and Verellen 2004, 808), as well as the *Jindan nijin pian* 金丹泥金篇 (Mud of Gold in [Forming] the Golden Elixir; *Daoshu* 23) and the *Xiuzhen zhixuan pian* 修真指玄篇 (Pointers to the Mystery and the Cultivation of Perfection, *Daoshu* 19).

---

[16] See Pregadio 2011a, 95-99; Needham et al. 1976, 62-66; 1983, 57; Baldrian-Hussein 1984, 102-05. For later uses, see Mozias 2020, 81.

According to these, human beings take 13,500 breaths in the course of one day, each moving the *qi* forward by an inch. Practitioners extend this distance first to a foot, then to ten feet, thereby speeding up the movement of energy and intensifying its impact. They move it along the five-phases system of gestation, beginning with the kidneys and going on to the liver, spleen, lungs, heart, and their related yang organs. Working in a rhythm of twenty-four or thirty-six repetitions at a time, they also hold the breath in, up the count of 108, to increase heat in the body and raise the fire that much higher so they can retain more and more primordial *qi* (Baldrian-Hussein 1984, 91-94; see also Pregadio 2013, 28). As they do so, the energy transforms:

> Steam and nurture it without stopping. First use yin to retain yang, then use yang to refine yin. *Qi* thus turns into essence, essence turns into mercury, mercury turns into cinnabar, and cinnabar turns into the golden elixir. Once the golden elixir is produced, perfect *qi* naturally grows. Refine this *qi* into spirit and attain transcendence and liberation. (*Chuandao ji* 10)

Elixir Reversion

Another dimension of the process is the circulation of *qi* and fluid through the body in a number of different ways, called *huandan* 還丹), literally "reverted cinnabar" (Pregadio in Pregadio 2008, 498). The term goes back to operative alchemy, where it indicates "an elixir or part of an elixir prepared by cyclical transformation, such as may be brought about by repeated separation or sublimatory re-combination of mercury and sulfur, reducing cinnabar and re-forming mercuric sulfide" (Needham et al. 1983, 25).

The idea of reversion comes from the fact that cinnabar, basically a hydrothermal mineral found as rocks near volcanoes, sediments at hot springs, and sand in coatings on rock surfaces, is a mercury sulfide (HgS) that dissolves into its parts when heated, then reconstitutes itself back into cinnabar—forming the core of the alchemical process (Eliade 1962, 116). In addition, its life-giving, magical power—already activated in the paleolithic (Kohn 2017, 199)—has to do with its strong, brilliant red color commonly called vermilion and covering the range from bright orange-red to a more somber bluish tinge (Pregadio 2006a, 68). Chemically the powdered ore of mercury, cinnabar was highly toxic and had to be carefully mined in a process that was difficult, expensive, and dangerous, but believed to lead to a higher and subtler level of being (Mahdihassan 1986, 65).

The process usually consisted of more than a single reversion, though. To cite the words of Nathan Sivin,

> Cyclical transformation (*zhuan / huan*), the key process of Chinese alchemy, is essentially repeated sublimation in a hermetically sealed vessel. If we begin

> enumeration with (1) preparation of the reactants in the first cycle, or pulverization and optional additional treatment of the previous product in later cycles, the subsequent steps in one complete cycle are: (2) charging into the reaction vessel; (3) closing, hermetical sealing, and preheating to dry the lute; (4) the sublimation itself, usually after a gradual raising of the temperature; (5) cooling and opening of the reaction vessel; and (6) collection of the sublimate. (1968, 148n3)

In internal practice, as Joseph Needham notes, "the phrase *huandan* was applied by the physiological alchemists . . . to a *qi* or substance generated by techniques purposefully within the human body which would bring about a reversion of the tissues from an aging to an infantile state" (1983, 25). As such it appears, for example, in a chart showing the course of refining energy from and to the kidneys, moving up through the spine and down through the five organs, leading to a renewal and rejuvenation of internal potency (Baldrian-Hussein 1984, 140). However, in the Zhong-Lü texts, *huandan* is a process rather than a resulting energy or substance and means "reverting to the elixir field."

A definition appears in the *Jindan wenda* 金丹問答 (Questions and Answers on the Golden Elixir) by Xiao Tingzhi 蕭廷芝 (fl. 1260), a recipient of the teachings of the Southern School and best known as author of the *Dadao zhentong* 大道正統 (True Succession of the great Dao) (Boltz 1987, 219). He says: "A worthy man of the past said: '*Dan* 丹 means the elixir field (*dantian* 丹田), fluid means the fluid of the lungs. Since the fluid of the lungs reverts to the elixir field, it is called golden fluid reverting to the elixir [field]" (Fabrizio Pregadio, personal communcation).

In the Zhong-Lü texts, this reversion applies to a variety of practices:

> Reversion to the elixir field comes in various forms: minor, major, seven-based, nine-based, golden fluid, or jade fluid. There is also reversion from the lower to the upper elixir field, from the upper to the middle field, from the middle to the lower field, from yang to yin, and from yin to yang. Not only are they different in name but their timing is varied and their setting is not alike. (*Chuandao ji* 13)

The process consists of the systematic movement of *qi* and fluid through the various organs and reverting them to the elixir field, thereby increasingly refining and transmuting the self. The process is much like the official circuit of the emperor and his entourage through his realm or the course of senior divinities inspecting the continents of the world. As the *Chuandao ji* describes the relevant visualization, adepts are to envision "an officer in vermilion robes climbing on his carriage and making a full circuit" of the ten continents[17] or "covering the five sacred mountains," always beginning in the north and continuing steadily round after round, "obtaining gold and jade on his way" (ch. 16; Baldrian-Hussein 1984, 153).

Within this framework, then, minor reversion to the elixir field is the alignment of the five phases mentioned earlier, the systematic guiding of *qi* through the five organs in both the generating and control cycles, always directing the energy back to the lower field and strengthening its presence there (ch. 13), matching the level of minor accomplishment. As Wang Liping points out, the system works like a three-dimensional Taiji structure with "connecting lines from the kidneys to the bladder, forming both sides of yin and yang. After reaching the bladder, they rotate diagonally, connecting to the liver and the heart. The heart then connects to the stomach and moves on to the lungs, where there is also a rotating diagonal line" (Wang and Bartosh 2019, 325). He also notes that the Complete Perfection founder Wang Chongyang—in the wake of the Zhong-Lü texts—called this minor reversion, leading to the merging of water and fire. More specifically, the process works by using external as well as internal and cosmic forces to push *qi* to circulate through the five organs (2019, 325).

The *Lingbao bifa* further calls this "reversion to the elixir field for assembling and supplementing;" it "serves to extend the years and increase longevity, becoming what we call a human immortal." Its tangible effects include "the mouth generating sweet saliva, mental projections vanishing, emotions and desires ceasing, the bones being disease-free, spirit light manifesting in the darkness, and the eyes flashing like lightning" (ch. 3).

Next, moving on to the medium stage, major reversion to the elixir field involves the mating of dragon and tiger to form the yellow sprout as well as the ongoing reduction and augmentation of lead and mercury to produce the great medicine. In particular, it means the continued circulation of energy "into the upper field from the lower and again down into the lower field from the upper. As the *qi* rises in back and comes down in front [of the torso], the loop of circulation is fully established. This is called major reversion to the elixir field" (*Chuandao ji* 13; see Baldrian-Hussein 1984, 141).

Elixirs associated with the numbers seven and nine in operative alchemy indicate the number of recirculations of cinnabar and are accordingly called seven- or nine-times reverted or "cyclically transformed."[18] In the Zhong-Lü texts, they similarly involve a certain number of cycles, but more

---

[17] The ten continents are paradise realms or abodes of the immortals, complete with divine palaces, supernatural flora, and wondrous animals. For details, see Smith 1990; Kirkova 2016, 181.

[18] Needham et al. 1976, 141; Pregadio 1991; 2012a, 180; Spooner and Wang 1948.

importantly are internal processes based on complex numerology and activated as part of attaining a major level of accomplishment.

Thus, yin matching even numbers, "it reaches its ultimate at eight and burgeons at two," which means that in the course of the five organs, "the number two belongs to the heart and the number eight to the liver." Similarly, yang as it connects to odd numbers "is exhausted at nine and burgeons at one," so that "the number one belongs to the kidneys and the number nine to the lungs" (ch. 13)

> Daoist adepts begin by mating dragon and tiger, then assemble the *qi* of rightful yang in the heart. This *qi* matches the number seven of the heart. It revolves seven times to the middle field, then enters the lower field to nurture the immortal embryo. From here, it circulates back to the heart. For this reason, this process is called seven-based reversion to the elixir field. (ch. 13)

Along the same lines, as soon as yin has dissolved at the positions marked by the numbers two and eight, "yang can grow at nine and three" and comes to circulate "nine times to the lungs to support the heart," indicating the process of nine-based reversion. In both cases, the refined energy is stored increasingly in the middle elixir field.

Golden and Jade Fluids

A yet different variant of reversion to the elixir field involves the golden and jade fluids. As pointed out earlier, gold and jade—commonly used in funerary rituals and longevity practice to preserve the body (Eliade 1962, 114)—are the most precious among metals and minerals, the equivalent of the sun and the moon in that they represent the most intense potency of yin and yang.[19] They move in a rhythmic circuit around heaven and earth, matching internal patterns. As the *Lingbao bifa* notes,

> The *qi* of gold and jade entering deep into the earth and transforming into sweet dew, fresh springs, grasses, and trees is just like reversion of jade fluid to the elixir field. The *qi* of gold and jade coagulating in the void and becoming fortunate *qi* and auspicious vapor is just like *qi* refining physical form and material reality. (ch. 6)

In external alchemy, golden fluid (*jinye* 金液) is a liquid elixir (Mahdihassan 1957, 89; Pregadio 2012a, 167). As described in Ge Hong's *Baopuzi* (ch. 4), "potable gold" is concocted through a process of aurification by

---

[19] This thinking is quite similar to in Western alchemy. "Silver grown under the influence of the moon; the ore of gold grows under the influence of the sun. The birth of copper is explained by the influence of the planet Venus, that of iron by the influence of Mars, and that of lead by the influence of Saturn" (Eliade 1962, 49).

placing various substances, such as gold, realgar, leonite, iron alum, saltpeter, as well as lead and mercury, into a reaction vessel and heating them systematically over several months until they liquefy (Ware 1966, 89; Needham et al. 1976, 88-89). The concoction is easier than that of most other elixirs, but its efficacy is about the same (1976, 82-83; Sivin 1968, 41; see also Eliade 1962, 110).

In internal practice, golden fluid is associated with the lungs, gold being a primary metal, and thought to hold the core powers of lead and mercury. As the *Chuandao ji* notes, "It forms the womb that contains the dragon and tiger and protects their transmutation once it has been sent to the yellow court" (ch. 13). Th work here involves the rotation of kidney *qi* to the heart and thus into the lungs (Baldrian-Hussein 1984, 139, 147, 153). The *Lingbao bifa* specifies,

> What we call golden fluid is kidney *qi* ascending and fusing with heart *qi*, then steaming into the lungs. The lungs are the Flowery Canopy. From here, condense the two *qi* downward and thus obtain lung fluid, which you then store in the lower field.
>
> When you move it up from the Tail Gate, we speak of quickening the gold crystal and guiding it to the brain, there to supplement the Niwan palace. When you again move it down and guide it back to the lower field, we speak of reverting golden fluid to the elixir field.
>
> Repeatedly reverting it to the lower field and moving it up again, it comes to pervade and fill all four limbs, continuously going up and down. We call this refining the physical form through golden fluid: it matches the theory of how gold is generated in soil. (ch. 7)

Jade fluid (*yuye* 玉液), on the other hand, is a traditional term for saliva, matching other "jade" terms, such as jade juice (*yujiang* 玉漿) and jade spring (*yuquan* 玉泉), both indicating pure levels of saliva, as well as jade pond (*yuchi* 玉池) for the mouth (Needham et al. 1983, 150; Pregadio 2006a, 208). Its assembly and systematic swallowing are associated with extensive longevity: "One will live no less than three hundred years without taking any medications" (*Baopuzi* 13; Ware 1966, 223; Needham et al. 1983, 191).

In internal alchemy, the *Lingbao bifa*, matching this as well as earlier works (Maspero 1981, 378), describes jade fluid in terms of the collection and swallowing of saliva through systematic breathing (Baldrian-Hussein 1984, 139). The practice is to be undertaken in a remote and secure place, free from the impact of ordinary people. First, adepts burn incense and sit in meditation, letting go of all thoughts while allowing internal fire to rise.

> At Gen [3 am], quicken the gold crystal and guide it to the top of the head, then briefly lift the head and stretch the neck, to feel the *qi* flow through the

> throat like fire. See it in front of your head, then lower the head and bend the neck, curl the tongue back to press against the upper palate.
>
> You should have clear and pure water in your mouth, tasting like sweet incense. Above it pushes into the gate of the head; below it flows through the hundred arteries. Naturally in your nose you smell a kind of perfect incense and on your tongue you taste a wondrous flavor.
>
> Swallow without rinsing and move it back to the yellow court: this is what we call reverting jade fluid to the elixir field. (ch. 6)

Beyond these, related methods also involve moving *qi* from yin to yang and vice versa to isolate the water of cosmic oneness and the *qi* of rightful yang. In addition, adepts transfer *qi* from the lower to the upper field, then drip it into the middle field, stoke the fire, and circulate it back to the lower field. They reverse the course of the five phases and engage the three fields in mutual exchange. This is how "they refine the physical form into *qi* and refine *qi* into spirit," allowing the latter "to exit through the celestial gate to leave behind the ordinary bodily shell, enter the line of sages, and attain a rank among the immortals" (ch. 13).

Chapter Five

Key Practices

As part of the three stages and various major processes, adepts work with a certain number of key practices that allow them to enhance personal health and effect cultivation refinement. They can be divided into five groups, working with breath, body, *qi*, mind, and universe. Breathing exercises are primarily embryo respiration, a subtle way of drawing in energy from the universe that moves beyond the normal respiratory organs. Physical practices involve specific body movements, bends and stretches, contractions and releases, notably pulling the elbows back while pushing the head forward to put pressure on certain points of the spine to move vital energy upward.

The same upward move is also attained through concentrated *qi*-guiding, which in this context comes in the two highly technical methods of the river carriage in its various modifications and a technique described as "full saturation" and linked with the 63rd hexagram of the *Yijing*. Mental practice here means visualization and inner observation. Visualization involves the intentional imagination of specific images and scenes to facilitate various internal activities, such as the mating of dragon and tiger. Inner Observation, unlike in most medieval works, is a more formless, nonaction-based internal awareness that allows the alchemical process to unfold on its own.

All this culminates in specific practices of transcendence and liberation, which sees the energy of the five organs recover their primary nature and the three yang powers assemble at the top of the head. From here, adepts release the immortal embryo into the universe and attain ascension to the heavens of the immortals.

Breath Practice

The primary form of breath practice in the Zhong-Lü system is embryo respiration (*taixi* 胎息), a subtle form of breathing which leads to a state where, "instead of being supported by a mother's body, adepts are nourished in the womb of the universe. . . . Primordial union has been reestablished, and the practitioner partakes of the unlimited supply of original, primordial, ever-circulating *qi*" (Jackowicz 2006, 82-83; Kohn 2012, 78).

As a practice, it is mentioned first in Ge Hong's *Baopuzi,* which emphasizes that the proper circulation of *qi* through the breath eliminates the hundred diseases and makes people immune to fire and water, hunger and thirst. "The most important thing is simply to breathe like an embryo. He who can do this will inhale and exhale as if still in the womb, without using nose or mouth" (ch. 8; Ware 1966, 139; Needham et al. 1983, 143).[1]

In the context of Highest Clarity, embryo respiration is described in the *Shenxian shiqi jin'gui miaolu* 神仙食氣金櫃妙錄 (Wondrous Record of the Golden Casket on the Spirit Immortals' Practice of Eating *Qi*, DZ 836; trl. Kohn 2012, 79-94), allegedly by Master Jingli 京里 or Jinghei 京黑 of the 4th century (Kohn 2012, 74). It says, "To practice embryo respiration, you no longer use the mouth and nose, but learn to breathe like the embryo in the womb, thereby to attain Dao" (8a; Kohn 2012, 85). The *Han Wudi waizhuan* 漢武帝外傳 (Outer Record of the Han Emperor Wu, DZ 293) of the 5th century specifies related techniques and speaks of it in terms of holding the breath and swallowing saliva to create internal ways of nourishment (Kohn 2008b, 129).

A number of works on breathing in the Tang dynasty mention it (for a list, see Despeux in Pregadio 2008, 953-54). Among then, the *Taixi koujue* 胎息口訣 (Oral Instructions on Embryo Respiration), contained in the early-Song encyclopedia *Yunji qiqian* 雲笈七籤 (Seven Tablets in a Satchel of the Clouds, ch. 58), provides a definition:

> As long as the embryo is in the womb of the mother, its mouth is filled with a kind of mud, and respiration does not penetrate here. It is through through the navel that it receives *qi* and nourishment for its physical form. Thus it arrives at its completion and we know that the navel is the gate of destiny. (58. 12a; Needham et al. 1983, 145)

Cultivation of Dao, it goes on, means to learn how to "breathe like the embryo in the mother's womb," thereby to "revert to the origin and regenerate primary vitality" (1983, 146).

In terms of practice, the *Taishang yangsheng taixi qi jing* 太上養生胎息氣經 (Highest Scripture on Nourishing Life Through Embryo Respiration and *Qi*, DZ 819) prescribes that the practice should be undertaken at midnight by breathing slowly and subtly, holding the breath, as well as gathering saliva (Kohn 2008b, 85). "Contract your nose and make the *qi* return, going up to the head and sinking down inside the mouth. There it can transform into jade spring [refined saliva]. From here, pull the *qi* to the root of the tongue, swallow, and send it off . . . to guide it into the elixir field" (3b-4a; Jackowicz 2006, 85).

---

[1] See also Baldrian-Hussein 1990, 180; Engelhardt 2000, 77; Eskildsen 1998; 2007, 34, 46; Mozias 2020, 187-90; Pregadio and Skar 2000, 468.

The *Huanzhen xiansheng fu neiqi juefa* 幻真先生服內氣訣法 (Master Huanzhen's Method Instructions on How to Absorb Internal Qi, DZ 828; trl. Kohn 2012, 234-50) of the late Tang places embryo respiration in its last section and says:

> First click the teeth thirty-six times. Turn the head to right and left. Stretch the neck forward like a turtle. Then to begin embryo respiration, fill the throat and swallow the *qi*. Repeat three times.
>
> Keep the mouth closed, let the tongue move about inside and out, rubbing the gums to produce saliva. Let it fill the mouth and mentally flow it upward to the center of the head, then swallow it. This supplements the Niwan palace above. The Niwan is the center of the head. Below it, the *qi* moistens the five organs. As Laozi said: "Sweet rain moistens the myriad beings." In the same way, embryo fluid moistens the five organs. (13a]

The Zhong-Lü texts similarly place the practice in the early morning hours and describe it as beginning with clicking the teeth, calming the mind, and centering the spirit (Baldrian-Hussein 1984, 75, 171). In the early stages associated with "inhaling much and exhaling little" (*Chuandao ji* 16), thereby to accumulate *qi* in the body, its full practice should be undertaken "only after the immortal embryo is present, when perfect *qi* is generated. Once perfect *qi* is generated, one naturally activates embryo respiration. Through this one can refine *qi*, and by refining turn it into spirit" (ch. 15)

Another dimension, also mentioned in the *Taixi qijing* involves using internal breath to guide *qi* into the organs in accordance with the productive sequence of the five phases, "each breath dispersing or cooling the *qi* in the preceding organ and tonifying or heating it in the following" (5b-7b; Despeux 2006, 55; Kohn 2012, 75). The Zhong-Lü texts pick up on this, outlining a system of breathing through the five organs in conjunction with the correct timing of month and day (Baldrian-Hussein 1984, 167-69).

In internal alchemy today, embryo respiration is described in terms of "breathing through the pores of the entire body, having them imitate the breathing inside the mother's womb" (Wang and Bartosh 2019, 121). This is a way of opening and closing the pores to absorb cosmic energy while allowing natural breathing to become slower and subtler, working with the organs and matching the appropriate times of day.

> Count the frequency of the heartbeat while inhaling, for example, eight times; then again, when you exhale, the heart should also beat eight times. Keep on counting and make sure they are both synchronized. Once there is synchronization, you can feel the pores open and close simultaneously, totally matching the rhythm of the heart. This cultivation method is required according to the *Lingbao bifa*. (2019, 70)

Energy Activation

The most basic method to activate internal energy is contracting the yang barrier (*le yangguan* 勒陽關), defined as "tightening the abdomen" (*Bifa* 4) and used throughout the process. "Always on inhalation slightly lift up the anus and contract the front genitals and lower abdomen, so the *qi* keeps on rising into the lower field" (Wang and Bartosh 2019, 207). Not unlike the three locks in yoga—at the perineum, abdomen, and throat—the yang barrier represents the power to close off the body and prevent leakage of energy. It can be tightened or released as needed. The *Lingbao bifa* says,

> To assemble [the medicine] at this time [of Qian], one must guard spirit consciousness deep within, keep the breath flowing smoothly through the nostrils, and hold the belly and abdomen gently contracted. Should the navel and kidney area feel too hot, gently release and ease the contraction; if they are not warm at all, increase it. Let them gradually get hot, then keep them steady, relax the intention and release the will until they fill both Qian and Kun. This is called contracting the yang barrier to refine the cinnabar medicine. (ch. 4; see also *Chuandao ji* 7)

Another key practice to get the internal energy moving also involves bends and stretches along the lines of healing exercises. It is called pulling back the elbows, literally "elbows behind" or "behind the elbows" (*chouhou* 肘後), a term that in early medieval literature means "close at hand" and is applied to precious books or manuals (Pregadio in Pregadio 2008, 443, 945). In internal alchemy, it designates a particular method of moving *qi*, described in some detail in the *Lingbao bifa*. Ideally working in the early morning hours, right before "kidney *qi* fuses with liver *qi*," adepts begin by entering the quiet chamber, loosening their clothing, making their hands into fists, and sitting cross-legged. The text then instructs,

> Mentally push down into the liver area of your abdomen, thereby forcing the *qi* to ascend through the body. Then push the chest forward and slightly bend the head back to close off the Double Barrier at the Narrow Strait near the neck.
>
> Next, pull the elbows back once or twice like leaves of a door, stretch from the waist, and feel a hot rush like fire ascending from the Tail Gate, rising up from the waist [through the spine] and pressing against the Narrow Strait.
>
> Be careful not to break through the barrier, but at this moment use the extremely hot *qi* to gradually, little by little, open the Narrow Strait, letting the *qi* flow past it.
>
> Next, lift up your face and create tension at the back of your skull to close the upper barrier [Jade Pillow]. Be careful not to break through it, but be aware of the extremely hot *qi* as it gradually, little by little, pushes it open and flows into the head, there to supplement the Niwan and the ocean of marrow

> [in the brain]. This will make the body resistant to cold and heat; it is the foundation of long life.[2] (ch. 5)

From here, adepts again push the chest forward and stretch from the waist to put pressure on the midpoint of the spine at the Narrow Strait. They "bend and stretch a few times" until "no more fire rises from the waist." After this, they sit in quiet meditation, gently observing the internal processes unfold naturally.

The method serves to reduce lead and increase mercury, and is commonly described in terms of quickening, literally "flying," the gold crystal (*fei jinjing* 飛金晶), a primary form of the golden fluid (Wang and Bartosh 2019, 267). It is closely related to reversion to the elixir field in that adepts release the refined energy to flow down along the front of the body and gather it in the lower elixir field, thus establishing a full circuit (Baldrian-Hussein 1984, 113, 136). As the *Lingbao bifa* notes,

> Pull the elbows back, pull golden fluid up, and guide it to the brain, then let it descend again from there to the lower field: this is called reversion to the elixir field. Next move it up again along the front and let it flow widely to fill the four limbs, moving from bottom to top: this is called refining the physical form. (ch. 7; *Chuandao ji* 12)

Thus matches, as the *Chuandao ji* notes, the practice of "reverting essence to nourish the brain" (*huanjing bunao* 還精補腦; ch. 11), originally a method in sexual cultivation or the bedchamber arts (*fangzhong shu* 房中術). Based on the theory that both brain and semen were expressions of vital essence and that one could supplement and support the other, it involved the prevention of ejaculation during intercourse by either holding the penis or pressing the perineum with the index and middle fingers of the left hand, while grinding the teeth and mentally pushing the aroused energy up along the spine and into the brain.[3] Already mentioned in the Han, it appears in Ge Hong's *Baopuzi* as a key way to enhance vigor and attain extended longevity (chs. 5, 6; Ware 1966, 103, 122).

In internal alchemy, it lost its primary sexual connotation and became a solo practice (Pregadio and Skar 2000, 469). Here it means "making the *qi* spiral up the spine and down the chest, blending the fire and water of the

---

[2] A similar outline also appears in the Complete Perfection manual *Dadan zhizhi* (1.12ab). See Eskildsen 2004, 84-85; Komjathy 2014a, 137.

[3] Despeux in Pregadio 2008, 524-25. See also Baldrian-Hussein 1984, 109; Engelhardt 2000, 99; Goldin 2006; Harper 1998; Hudson 2008, 418-24; Kohn 2008b, 10; Maspero 1981, 522-29; Mozias 2020, 9-10; Needham et al. 1983, 197-201; Van Gulik 1950, chs. 6-7; Wile 1992, 46-50.

body, and eventually causing the spirit to crystallize in the lower elixir field" (Winn 2006, 167). Its modern equivalent, the microcosmic orbit, utilizes the Governing and Conception Vessels for the same purpose, creating "a transitional pathway for *qi*-flow between external and internal sexual alchemy, between cultivating post-natal and pre-natal *qi*" (2006, 168; 2009, 196; see also Komjathy 2009; Chia 1983).

In some variants, the practice also required external pressure in addition to the contraction of the abdomen. Thus, the *Lingbao bifa*, as part of the work with primordial *qi* prescribes that adepts "deeply inhale and pull on the external kidneys [testicles]," thereby "shifting the *qi* from the bladder into the kidneys" and warming the lower elixir field (ch. 2). Matching this, Wang Liping recommends sitting on a rolled-up towel to put pressure on the perineum.

> To activate the heavenly circuit, the leakage of the Magpie Bridge in the mouth should be sealed [by pressing the tongue against the upper palate] as much as that of its lower counterpart in the rear genital area, also called Magpie Bridge. This is best done by sitting tightly on the perineum and mentally sealing the three genital orifices. (Wang and Bartosh 2019, 35)

> Contract the lower field until you start to feel something in the front genital area, some sort of movement. Start to inhale, lift up the anus, contract the front genitals, and focus the *qi* in the lower abdomen. The purpose of doing all this at the same time is to seal the three lower yin orifices, which allows the lower field to become fuller. Think of a way to let the breath seal the lower three yin orifices, and you will no longer need a towel. (2019, 245)

The River Carriage

Quickening the gold crystal by pulling back the elbows closely connects to, and in some passages (e. g., *Chuandao ji* 11) is identical with, a dynamic process known as the river carriage (*heche* 河車) (Neswald 2009, 41-42; Mozias 2020, 193-95). The term appears first in the *Cantong qi* in the context of water being the core axis of Dao. Here the river carriage is the symbol of the north, representing lead (Pregadio 2011a, 78). In internal alchemy, it appears as the flow of the primary energy of the kidneys, associated with the north and with water, through the organs and elixir fields (Needham et al. 1983, 225). The *Chuandao ji* says, "The river carriage arises in the rightful water of the northern direction. The kidneys contain perfect *qi*: the rightful *qi* generated from this is called the river carriage" (ch. 12).

It further explains the term by noting that "'carriage' indicates the idea of transportation, while 'river' expresses the perceptible manifestation of much yin" and insists that it never stops moving through all the different reservoirs, peaks, and palaces of the body.

> Up and down, forward and back, it carries loads in the eight jasper [pools] and drives with speed through the four oceans. Ascending toward heaven, it enters Kunlun [head] above; fully saturated there, it rushes to the phoenix towers [kidneys] below. Carrying primordial yang, it goes directly into the Li palace; transporting perfect *qi*, it meanders back to the office of long life. Coming and going throughout the nine provinces, it never stops even for an instant; moving all around the three peaks, it never halts for a moment. (ch. 12)[4]

The carriage here is a real yet cosmic conveyance, "an object that matches the image of heaven and earth in its cover and chassis while its rotating wheels are like the sun and the moon" (ch. 12). It is depicted as such in the *Neijing tu* (see below), with a boy and a girl working a wheeled device near the bottom of the spine (Komjathy 2009, 70-71). The caption calls it "the mysterious yin-yang treadmill." The poem reads,

> Repeatedly, constantly, it is peddled in cycles;
> When the mechanism revolves, the water flows east.
> The water, ten-thousand fathoms deep, is clear to the very bottom;
> A sweet spring bubbles up, rising to the summit of Southern Mountain.

Louis Komjathy (2009, 70), as well as Eva Wong (2000, 95), translate *heche* as "waterwheel." Moving away from the image of the chariot, central to the Daoist vision, this is yet technically correct, since the device is indeed a "water-raising machine" (Needham et al. 1983, 60) and the word *che is*

[4] This echoes the description of the water carriage (*shuiche* 水車) by the Confucian thinker Zhu Xi 朱熹 (1130-1200) as "a machine in ceaseless revolution for days, months, and years, endlessly turning and revolving" (Needham et al. 1965, 359), linking it to the fundamental functioning of the cosmos.

often used to mean "wheel" or "machine" rather than carriage, as for example in *fanche* 翻車, the "square-pellet chain-pump" (1983, 225; 1965, 339).

The waterwheel, also called by its Arabic name *noria*, was probably invented in India (1965, 361; Habib 2000).[5] A "peripheral pot wheel," it appears in China in the Han dynasty, consisting of one or several double-rimmed wheels, "with buckets, pots, or bamboo tubes attached to the circumference, collecting water at the bottom and discharging it at the top" (Needham et al. 1965, 356). The wheels, moreover, are suspended from a framework, with their lower ends in the river. Often covered by a platform, they are powered either by the current or, more commonly, by animal or human force, as shown in the illustration below (Yannopoulos et al. 2015, 5037, based on Landels 1981, 238).

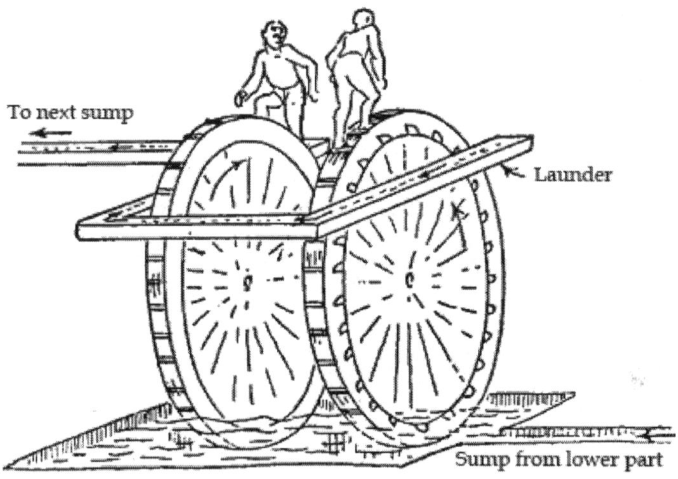

The waterwheel played an important role in Chinese agriculture and engineering, and served as the forerunner of the Chinese steam engine, described by Wang Chen of the 14th century:

> A place beside a rushing torrent is selected, and a vertical shaft is set up in a framework with two horizontal wheels, so that the lower one is rotated by the force of the water. The upper one is connected by a driving-belt to a smaller wheel in front of it, which bear an eccentric lug. Then all as one, following the turning of the driving-wheel, the connecting-rod attached to the eccentric lug pushes and pulls both the rocking roller and levers to its left and right, which

---

[5] It is the successor of the stone-age *shaduf*, a horizontal pole on an axis that seesaws back and forth to lift up water (Yannopoulos et al. 2015, 5034), mentioned in the *Zhuangzi* as a "well sweep" (ch. 12; Watson 1968, 134).

> assure the transmission of the motion to the piston-rod. Thus this is pushed back and forth, operating the furnace bellows. (Temple 1986, 65)

This device was used "to provide fully automated continuous airblasts for metallurgical operations," just as the waterwheel enabled the ongoing flow of water from the river into the fields and the river carriage provided the raw power of the never-ceasing circulation of *qi* throughout the body.

This, as the *Chuandao ji* points out, happens in three major modes, matching the three levels of accomplishment. The most basic or minor mode is "reversing the flow of the five phases" in preparation for the "mating of dragon and tiger to transform into the yellow sprout." The second, major mode, is "quickening the gold crystal by pulling back the elbows and reverting it into the Niwan," thereby to "reduce lead and augment mercury and produce the great medicine." The third, called the "purple" mode, involves "transporting the spirit to enter the physical organism. Thus, one merges with time and flows along; transforming into a sage and leaving the ordinary behind, one become a feathered guest" (ch. 12).

Beyond all this, the river carriage works in ordinary people, albeit not as focused or intentionally. Here, it can be in the "broken mode," the emotions rampant, the mind scattered, the body exhausted; in the "messenger mode," the intention moving through the body to combat illness and disease; or in the "thunder mode," a state of mental stillness with "yin and yang fully fused, water and fire in the same place," a state and practice also known as full saturation (*Chuandao ji* 12).

Full Saturation

"Full saturation" literally means "already complete" (*jiji* 既濟). This is the name of the next-to-last hexagram of the *Yijing* (no. 63), which consists of the two trigrams Kan and Li, i. e., water over fire (Wilhelm 1950, 244; Sung 1971, 268). A development of *tai* 泰, "peace" (no. 11)—earth over water (Bertrand 2019, 154)—it stands in contrast to *weiji* 未濟, "not yet complete," the last hexagram (no. 64), which consists of fire over water.

That is to say, in the system of the *Yijing*, the last hexagram signals the transition to the next cycle of cosmic and personal unfolding, and it accordingly ends on a note of balance but not stability (Wang 2012, 68). Fire over water, as the text has it, is "the image of the condition before transition." Richard Wilhelm comments, "When fire, which by nature flames upward, is above, and water, which flows downward, is below, their effects take opposite directions and remain unrelated" (1950, 249). In "already complete," on the other hand, the image suggested is a kettle of water hanging over a fire, so that "the two elements stand in relation and thus generate energy."

The hexagram signals that the transition from confusion to order is complete and perfect equilibrium has been attained (1950, 244-45).

In internal alchemy, the term has two usages. Most simply, it indicates the completion of a certain aspect of practice. For example, as *qi* circulates, "ascending toward heaven, it enters Kunlun [in the head] above; fully saturated [*jiji*] there, it rushes to the phoenix towers [kidneys] below" (*Chuandao ji* 12). On a more complex level, the term refers to a meditation practice of filling the mouth with saliva, the body with *qi*, and the mind with harmony (Baldrian-Hussein 1984, 87). It means relaxing into the natural flow and attaining fullness of energy, signaling the attainment of smooth reversion to the elixir field.

Saturation means opening to the internal equilibrium of water and fire, which "serves to extend the years and increase longevity, becoming what we call a human immortal" (*Bifa* 3; *Chuandao ji* 14). It allows adepts to "recognize whether the inner scenery is perfect or fleeting while sitting in oblivion" (*Bifa* pref.) and is aided by various visualizations:

> See clouds and thunder descend while smoke and flames ascend. See variegated flowers raining from heaven or a fresh breeze and auspicious *qi* ascend from the palace chambers. Maybe imagine immortal ladies and jade maidens riding multicolored phoenixes and fine steeds, arriving from the clear empyrean. See them offer a golden dish filled with jade dew and frosty liquor to the kingly personage below. This is how to use visualization to revert golden fluid to the elixir field as well as to attain full saturation. (*Chuandao ji* 16)

The *Lingbao bifa* further links the practice of full saturation with the method of "incinerating the body" (*fenshen* 焚身). A technical, energy-based way of getting rid of the last remnants of socially constructed identity and emotional complexes, it also serves to eliminate the three deathbringers (*sanshi* 三尸)—supernatural parasites that make people sick and cause them to die so they can feast on their corpse (see Kohn 2015a). It goes back to the practice of guiding internal heat to specific areas in the body to eliminate diseases or demonic influences (Baldrian-Hussein 1984, 160).

It begins by sitting in meditation, then closing the eyes and visualizing a wheel of fire in the lower elixir field, then moving it throughout the torso by "letting the *qi* rise both front and back at the same time" (1984, 161).

> Heat Qian [the back] before noon by quickening the gold crystal; heat Kun [the front] after noon by contracting the yang barrier. To heat Qian, move from bottom to top, guiding the *qi* up both in front and back. Do this for three or five days in winter and summer, then practice the methods of full saturation. Make sure not to overdo, but let the golden elixir be rich and glossy, then swallow the fire used to incinerate the body. (*Bifa* 7, 9; *Chuandao ji* 7)

From here, adepts imagine that they "roam throughout heaven and earth, seeing the entire space filled with raging flames. Eventually the fire ends and all becomes clear and cool, and you realize there are no longer any beings" (*Bifa* 9). The body, moreover, is envisioned as an embattled country that needs to be transformed back into the peaceful land of the pure physical form. As the *Chuandao ji* says,

> To be victorious in war, one must have a strong military. To keep the people at peace, one must have a prosperous country. The military here is the primordial *qi*. Troops on the inside dissolve the yin of the material form; troops on the outside capture the *qi* of heaven and earth.
>
> The country here is the body. If the body matches the perceptible image, its resources are sufficient and it always has a surplus; if it is free from the [constraints of the] physical form, it is firm and stable and never suffers lack.
>
> The myriad gates always open, there is not even one mishap of loss; not even one horse [untamed thought] roaming wildly, there are many, many gains. Moving in front or along the back, primordial *qi* constantly refines material reality and incinerates the body; flowing above or below, it always nurtures yang and dissolves yin. (ch. 14)

Visualization

Images and imaginary scenes such as these are part of visualization (*cunxiang* 存想), a meditation practice that pervades all forms of Daoism,[6] and is practiced in a quiet chamber or oratory (*jingshi* 靜室; see Yoshikawa 1987) with no distractions. As the *Lingbao bifa* says,

> To begin, select an auspicious spot and set up a quiet chamber, then kneel and bow and burn incense. Sit cross-legged with a straight back, loosen your hair and clothing, make your hands into fists, and focus on the spirit as you calm your mind and close your eyes. (ch. 9)

Once concentrated and at peace, adepts move on to engage in the active, intentional use of imagery to transform mind and emotions. As in visualization practice elsewhere, they work variously: with colors or colored energies imagined to pervade parts of the body; with static objects, such as a vase, a diagram, a landscape, or the statue of a deity; or with an entire sequence of activities and events, almost in movie fashion, either for detached viewing or active engagement. Since the brain does not distinguish outside stimuli from imagined ones, visualization is a powerful tool for ac-

---

[6] See Eskildsen 2015; Huang 2012, ch.1; Kirkova 2016, 223; Pregadio 2006b; Robinet 1989b; 1993.

cessing the subconscious mind to retrain brain mechanisms and transform emotional reactions.[7]

Images (*xiang* 象), moreover, are a primary way of communicating with the right hemisphere of the brain, the internal function that opens human beings to the cosmic flow.[8] Thus, when Harvard University brain anatomist Jill Bolte Taylor suffered a hemorrhage in her left hemisphere in 1996 and lost its function, she found that "all concepts of time and space evaporated, leaving me instead feeling open-ended, enormous, and expansive" (2009, 68; Kohn 2016, 207-08). Thinking in images and resting in the eternal now, her entire self-concept shifted toward fluidity and energetic presence. She says,

> My left hemisphere had been trained to perceive myself as a solid, separate from others. Now, released from that restrictive circuitry, my right hemisphere relished in its attachment to the eternal flow. I was no longer isolated and alone. My soul was as big as the universe and frolicked with glee in a boundless sea. (Taylor 2009, 69)

Daoists utilize images and visualization to open toward this fluid and flowing state. As the *Chuandao ji* says, masters of old noticed that:

> The mind was like a monkey and the intention like a wild horse—never staying or stopping. They worried that people would get enticed by things and lose their will to practice, so they set up images in nothingness to prevent people's ears form hearing, their eyes from seeing, their mind from going crazy, and their intention from getting distracted. (ch. 16)

Images in this context are more than mere pictures or representations. Part of the greater cosmos, they are perceptible manifestations (Baldrian-Hussein 1984, 225) of fundamental truth and subliminal universal patterns, that is, what Susan Huang discusses in terms of the "true form" (*zhenxing* 真形; 2012, 8). Midway between formlessness and forms, they represent an intermediary world, fluctuating between the primordial and the created, between the inner and the outer realms (Huang 2012, 9; Robinet 1989b, 160; 2011, 26). "Visible, but lying outside the material world, images place themselves between the formless principle and the material entities" (2011, 28), occupying "a third space" between "psychological reality and outer factuality" (Robinet 1989b, 160).

---

[7] Kohn 2008c, 128; 2016, 152. For more on visualization and the brain, see Begley 2007, 9, 151-52; Ratey 2002, 147; Samuels and Samuels 1975, 56-63.

[8] Kohn 2016, 84; Bygott 2014, 31; Mathers 2014, 65; Steavu 2019, 62; Zheng 2010, 46, 50.

Cosmologically, images are part of the abstract structure underlying nature and the universe. According to the *Lingbao bifa*, when Dao first divided, numbers emerged; when it unfolded, images arose; when it separated into different realms, domains settled; and when it dispersed, material reality came about (ch. 8). Part of the primary function of life, images are neither logical nor linear; they are subtler and more expressive than language, names, or forms.

As the *Xici* says, the sage ruler Fuxi "established images to express his thought, which cannot be entirely expressed in words" (Robinet 2011, 28). Words convey a rough idea, images give it imaginary shape, thought grasps it, and eventually it is made real and becomes present (*cun* 存). The potent structures at the root of creation become real to adepts through visualization practice, as they utilize images to bridge the gap "between the unspeakable message of intuition, the inexpressible vision of totality, and the deficiency of discourse" (2011, 29).

The earliest documented visualization involved bringing colors and thus cosmic *qi* into the five organs. It is described in the *Taiping jing shengjun bizhi* 太平經聖君秘旨 (Secret Instructions of the Holy Lord on the Scripture of Great Peace, DZ 1102), a short redaction of meditation methods of the *Taiping jing* 太平經 (Scripture of Great Peace; trl. Hendrischke 2006), the first revealed Daoist scripture known from the literature (Kohn 1989a, 130; 2016, 155). A second dimension appears in the understanding that the various organs and energy centers of the body are the home of divinities, commonly known as body gods, documented in the *Baopuzi* as well as in the meditation manuals *Huangting jing* and *Laozi zhongjing*.

While the gods here tend to be static and the emphasis is on keeping them stable within the body, in the Highest Clarity tradition, starting in the mid-4th century, visualization expands to include dynamic movement. Practitioners, like shamans of old, travel ecstatically around the far reaches of the earth and rise up into the heavens of the immortals while colored energies and deities arrive on clouds and enter the adept's body through the mouth to nurture the organs (Robinet 1989b; 1993; see also Eskildsen 2007, 31). For example, the *Dadong zhenjing* 大洞真經 (Perfect Scripture of Great Pervasion, DZ 6) says,

> Think of a five-colored purple cloud entering your body through the Niwan palace. Inhale it with your breath and swallow it with your saliva twelve times, then allow it coalesce into the body of a divinity. Surrounded by a vaporous ring and a luminous wheel of five colors, radiating purple and white, the divinity rests in the light. He spreads downward throughout your entire body, distributing his *qi* all the way to the nine orifices and assembling it at the tip of your tongue. (6.13b-14a; Pregadio 2006a, 211-12)

Along the same lines, the Zhong-Lü texts present a number of images and visualizations to facilitate the activation of internal processes, working with objects, animals, colors, deities, and more. However, they are not the ultimate, which is the attainment of emptiness and oneness. As the *Chuandao ji* has it, "Abandoning all thoughts and being free from imaginations is a state of perfect cognition: perfect cognition signals perfect emptiness" (ch. 16). Once the alchemical processes are fully functioning, then, adepts should stop working with visualization and switch to inner observation.

Inner Observation

Inner observation (*neiguan* 內觀) in the Zhong-Lü texts is an advanced method of meditation, a way of "exchanging yin and yang to be undertaken when one is ready to change from an ordinary to immortal being" (*Chuandao ji* 16; Baldrian-Hussein 1984, 178; Zheng 2010, 52). Unlike in other alchemical techniques, "there are no fixed hours or seasons, no particular methods or rules." Sitting "in a remote and quite chamber, day and night upright with hands folded," adepts let go of all structure, intention, and activity, instead allowing the natural processes to reach their fullness while increasingly "coming to recognize yang spirit and chase out all yin ghosts" (*Chuandao ji* 16). The *Lingbao bifa* says,

> Carefully select a hidden dwelling, so you can properly practice inner observation. First complete three bows, then keep your body stable, not letting it rise too high. Sit up straight, neither bending nor stretching. Close your eyes and calm your mind. Once you reach ultimate stillness and move to the prime, your self and body feel as if up in the air, spirit and *qi* floating about, hard to contain or control.
>
> Silently continue with inner observation, and there will be bright light instead of darkness. You see mountains and rivers glorious and beautiful, towers and pavilions so very fine. Purple *qi* and red radiance divide and spread all around. Auspicious phoenixes and colorful peacocks, their voices clear as reeds, a marvelous landscape rich and luxurious. One can say it is the perfect place within a gourd, a new world within a grotto heaven.
>
> As you follow it along, you are present naturally: in deep inner darkness no longer aware that there are things tied to the world of dust. In moments of perfect void, your *qi* keeps on transforming spontaneously, and there is no more need for methods relying on specific timing. (ch. 10)

In other words, inner observation consists of stabilizing the body and focusing the mind in complete stillness, then letting the internal processes take over, leading to the arising of an inner light and the experience of ecstatic visions of otherworldly regions.

In this usage, the texts differ from medieval works where inner observation refers to the active, conscious introspection of body and mind in favor of a more Dao-based perception, akin to—and historically connected to—Buddhist sources of the Tiantai 天台 school that use *guan* 觀 to translate *vipasyanā*, insight meditation, and connect it with *zhi* 止, *samatha* or cessation (Kohn 1989b, 195-96; 2010b, 40).

Insight meditation or mindfulness in general involves an openness to all sorts of sensory stimuli and encourages a sense of free-flowing awareness with detached observation. It usually begins with the recognition of physical sensations and subtle events in the body and means paying attention to reactions occurring to outside stimuli, recognizing but not evaluating them. Often associated with notions of deeper understanding or wisdom, it encourages the appreciation of life as flow and lets practitioners see body and self as unstable, ever-changing energetic entities (Kohn 2010b, 4).

The *locus classicus* for its adaptation in medieval Daoism is the *Neiguan jing* 內觀經 (Scripture of Inner Observation, DZ 641; trl. Kohn 1989b, 203-22; 2010b, 179-87). Dated to the late 7th century, it is revealed by Lord Lao and outlines various ways of observing the internal workings of body and mind, adding detailed definitions of mental aspects. It first presents the various spiritual forces that assemble in the course of pregnancy to form the human organism, then describes major body gods in the different parts and psychological forces in the organs. After defining key terms in this context, the text encourages adepts to step back from sensory involvement and "inwardly observe the arising of the six states of consciousness," leading to a state where the mind is empty, open, free, and at peace, thus allowing adepts "to keep always pure and calm" so that "Dao can come to stay" (Kohn 1989b, 215, 219).

In the same mode, inner observation also appears in modern usage. Thus, Wang Liping, links it variously to visualization along the lines of the *Huangting jing* and defines it as "reverse looking" or "turning the vision inward," which opens "the deep structures of the body and the scenery within" to inspection (Wang and Bartosh 2019, 69, 356, 374). More specifically, adepts sit with spine straight and teeth lightly touching, then breathe slowly and softly while focusing their attention on the lower elixir field. Switching it upward to activate the Heavenly [Third] Eye point, they allow a light to arise in the head, then shift their pupils to gaze inward and move systematically through the body, observing and breathing along with all the different organs (2019, 374-78).

The methods associated with inner observation in the Zhong-Lü texts have little to do with this. Rather, the practice they describe is more like "sitting in oblivion" (*zuowang* 坐忘), which in fact they often mention right next to inner observation (*Chuandao ji* 16). Sitting in oblivion is a formless, non-conceptual meditation that releases the hold of the self and allows adepts to "relish nonbeing, emptiness, and cosmic vastness" (2019, 184). Formally undertaken in a seated position, it requires a stable physical alignment—legs crossed or folded, back straight but light, stomach empty, head drawn upward, eyes holding a relaxed gaze, tongue touching the roof of the mouth, hands resting comfortably in the lap, and the breath flowing gently and in complete silence (Kohn 2010b, 15; 2015b, 162).

The stability of the body allows the release of mind and self, the forgetting and dropping away of concerns, considerations, and conceptions. This is clear already from the classical passage in the *Zhuangzi*, where Yan Hui 顏回 reports to Confucius that he has managed to forget benevolence and righteousness as well as rites and music, then claims to have forgotten everything: letting go of limbs and physical structure, perception and intellect, as well as physical form and knowledge, he opened to great pervasion (*datong* 大通) (ch. 6; Watson 1968, 90; Kohn 2010b, 7, 17; 2015, 162).

The resulting state, closely matching the ideal in the Zhong-Lü texts, is further outlined in a speech by Vast Concealment (Hongmeng 鴻蒙) to Cloud Chief (Yunjiang 雲將) in the *Zhuangzi*:

> Just take the position of nonaction and all things unfold naturally. Let your body and limbs fall away, expel perception and intellect, leave relations and things behind in oblivion. Become mystically one with the immense and boundless, release your mind and free your spirit.
>
> Be silent and without an active spirit soul, and the ten thousand things will each return to their root. Each return to their root and rest in unknowing—dark, obscure, chaotic: they remain like this for the rest of their days.
>
> However, the moment you try to know this state, you have already effected a separation from it. Don't ask its name, don't measure its foundation—it's the spontaneous life of each being. (ch. 11; Watson 1968, 122; Kohn 2010b, 20)

The Highest Clarity patriarch Sima Chengzhen 司馬承禎 (647-735) expands on this in his *Zuowang lun* 坐忘論 (Discourse on Sitting in Oblivion, DZ 1036; trl. Kohn 2010b, 137-58), outlining oblivion as a complex system of meditation that also integrated inner observation. Here adepts begin by controlling their mind, then move on to revise the way they see themselves and the world, occupying a position of "perfect observation" (*zhenguan* 真觀).

Moving on from here, they reach a state of "great serenity" or the "stability of cosmic peace" (*taiding* 泰定), a level of mental immersion that allows them to participate in cosmic harmony while resting in deep oblivion, open to the flow of cosmic power in great pervasion (Kohn 2010b, 96; 2015, 176). This matches the instructions in the *Chuandao ji*: "To practice Dao and diminish every day, enter the realm of the invisible and inaudible, and use particular methods less and less" (ch. 16).

From here, adepts can "attain Dao" (*dedao* 得道), the title of Sima Chengzhen's last section. Moving beyond all ordinary limitations, one becomes a spirit person—"spirit and inner nature empty and fused into one, the organism no longer changing or decaying, the physical form merged with Dao." Then one can "pass freely in and out of the spaceless" and reach for immortality (Kohn 2010b, 156).

Attaining Primordiality

The full realization of Dao involves a complete realignment of internal energies and structural patterns toward a more primordial state. As Steven Jackowicz says when discussing the medieval practice of the absorption of *qi* (*fuqi* 服氣),

> The practice leads to being permeated by cosmic *qi* and transformed into an integral aspect of the universe. The individual's nature is reoriented to be in perfect alignment with the whole, attaining an immanent return to the primordial state. . . .
>
> Aligned perfectly with the whole, the mechanics of the body are restructured to match the greater workings of all things, and practitioners are no longer scavengers in the phenomenal world who eat and defecate. Rather, they are as intact a part of the system as the rivers and mountains. They are one with the Dao, and thus infinitely fulfilled. (2006, 88-89)

The key, then, is the reorganizing or "retooling of the mechanism of the practitioner's body into something more than mere human." The Zhong-Lü texts describe this in terms of "the five qi move to the prime" (*wuqi chaoyuan* 五氣朝元) and "the three yang gather at the top of the head" (*sanyang juding* 三陽聚頂). They call this "a method of the major level of accomplishment unique to the perfected and immortals, matching the core workings deeply hidden in heaven and earth" (*Chuandao ji* 15).

They further define the five *qi* in close relation to the five emperors of the phases, that is, the energies of the inner organs as they relate to the pure powers of the cosmos. "Move to" translates the word *chao* 朝, which literally means "attending audience with" (Baldrian-Hussein 1984, 174), while the "prime" is the original state of the universe—the "great prime" (*taiyuan* 太元, *Bifa* 3) or "perfect prime" (*zhenyuan* 真元, *Chuandao ji* 2) that divided to form great beginning. The *Chuandao ji* provides an appropriate visualization:

> Imagine cranes leaving their nest, dragons exiting from their lair, the five emperors going to audience with heaven, five-colored clouds rising up, dancing red phoenixes soaring through the turquoise sky, or ascending along the celestial thoroughfare as if in a dream while celestial flowers fall in profusion and immortal music fills the air. A golden radiance flows along as one enters the

> palace hall; variegated flowers float as one goes into the place. This is how to use visualization in moving to the prime.[9] (ch. 16)

In addition, the text outlines the process in terms of the transformation of the *qi* of the five organs:

> Transmuting the golden elixir in the yellow court, one refines yang spirit in all five *qi*. Thus, green *qi* surges up in the liver, white *qi* issues from the lungs, a red radiance manifests in the heart, black *qi* moves up from the kidneys, and a yellow color comes out from the spleen. (ch. 14; see also *Bifa* 8)

Wang Liping provides further details, citing a commentary to the *Chang qingjing jing* 常清靜經 (Scripture of Constant Clarity and Stillness, DZ 620), which links the recovery of the prime to emotions and psychological agents.[10] For example,

> When you are empty of all joy, the spirit soul stabilizes.
> Once it is stable,
> The *qi* of the Green Emperor of the east moves to the prime.
>
> When you are empty of all anger, the material soul stabilizes.
> Once it is stable,
> The *qi* of the White Emperor of the west moves to the prime.
> (Wang and Bartosh 2019, 61)

Similarly, adepts are to empty themselves of all sadness to stabilize spirit, so that the Red Emperor of the south moves to the prime, of all happiness to stabilize essence for the Black Emperor of the north, and of all desires to stabilize intention for the Yellow Emperor of the center (2019, 61-62). Wang Liping further specifies that the practice to be undertaken at this stage is the intentional closing of the sensory organs, the orifices that serve as the channels of *qi* from the organs to the outside world.

Once adepts do this and rest in emptiness, "the intention stays in the spleen and the five phases recover their center. . . . Water and fire assist each other as they are located in the heart and kidneys. kidney *qi* rises,

---

[9] The term "prime" is also used to designate the elixir fields, i. e., upper, middle and lower (e. g., *Bifa* 5, *Chuandao ji* 13).

[10] I have not been able to find this commentary in any Daoist collection. It appears online under the title *Qingjing jing zhujie* 清靜經註解 (Commentary and Explanation of the Scripture of Clarity and Stillness), with the relevant passage found in Section 11, "Xukong pin" 虛空品 (On Emptiness). Websites include: www.xw.qq.com/cmsid/20150806023598;www.rufodao.qq.com/a/20150806/023598.htm; www.read01.com/yO2egQx.html#.XvhBsuhKjIU.

heart fire sinks, going back and forth, to eventually return to the Wuji [Non-Ultimate] position above earth," that is to the state of pre-creation primordiality (Wang and Bartosh 2019, 202).

The original passage in the main body of the *Chang qingjing jing* similarly emphasizes the importance of emptiness and links its internal attainment to the practice of observation and great serenity. It says,

> Observe emptiness and see that it is indeed empty—
> Yet there is also nothing that is empty.
> Observe nonbeing and see that it is indeed nonbeing—
> Yet there is also nothing that is not there.
> Constantly serene, yet there is ultimately no serenity.
> How would desires arise?
> Desires not arising, there is perfect stillness.
> (Kohn 1993, 27; see also Komjathy 2008b; Wong 1992)

Rather than perfect stillness, however, in internal alchemy, the state of primordiality is seen as smooth, unhindered circulation (*Bifa* 3). As the *Chuandao ji* says, "The five *qi* move to the prime and the three yang gather at the top of the head. The masters of old would describe this as golden essence moving down to enter the elixir field, then moving up again to refine the body and give it a golden hue" (ch. 11).

The ongoing circulation purifies adepts of all remnants of yin and creates an entity of pure yang. "Using yang to refine yin, adepts make sure yin does not emerge; using *qi* to nurture spirit, they make sure spirit does not scatter. In this way, their five *qi* move to the prime" (ch. 4). This, moreover, constitutes the completion of the immortal embryo. "It is the hour to transcend the ordinary body, the day when the golden elixir is fully mature" (ch. 14). The recovery of primordiality, then, opens the refinement of the physical form into *qi* and thus the transformation into a spirit immortal (ch. 1; *Bifa* 8).

Another aspect of the process is the gathering of the three yang at the top of the head. According to the Zhong-Lü texts, they are "the yang within yang, the yang within yin, and the yang within yin and yang," defined as the pure energy of the kidneys, heart, and yellow court (*Chuandao ji* 15). It also notes,

> The yang in the yin of the lower prime [elixir field] is completely free from yin: it ascends to gather in the spirit palace. The yang in the yang of the central prime no longer generates yang: it ascends and gathers in the spirit palace. The great medicine in the yellow court is devoid of yin and consists entirely of pure yang: it, tohuio, ascends to gather in the spirit palace. Thus, the five fluids move to the lower prime, the five *qi* move to the middle prime, and the three yang move to the upper prime. (ch. 14)

In a different variant, the *Chuandao ji* (ch. 12)—as well as the *Xishan qunxian huizhen ji* (*Daoshu* 38; Baldrian-Hussein 1984, 171-72)—calls the three yang the "three flowers" (*sanhua* 三華). The commentary to the *Chang qingjing jing* uses the same term and describes them as manifestations of pure spirit resting in the major centers of the body.

> When spirit is empty and rests in the lower burner,
> In essence arises a flower of lead.
> When spirit is empty and rests in the middle burner,
> In *qi* appears a flower of mercury.
> When spirit is empty and rests in the upper burner
> In spirit arises a flower of gold.
> Then the three flowers gather at the top of the head.
> (Wang and Bartosh 2019, 61)

In either case, the qualifying factor is the overriding purity of yang (Eskildsen 2006, 374). As the *Chuandao ji* asserts, "Those of pure yang without any yin are immortals" (ch. 1), beings of subtlety and light able to ascend far beyond ordinary life.

Transcendence and Liberation

The ultimate goal of internal alchemy is the complete transcendence of worldly existence and the liberation from all forms of life and death. Thus the last section of the *Lingbao bifa* is entitled "Transcendence, Liberation, and Multilocation" (*chaotuo fenxing* 超脫分形; Baldrian-Hussein 1984, 184). More specifically, the text says, "Transcendence means to go beyond the ordinary body and enter the sagely ranks; liberation means to leave behind the common womb and emerge as an immortal child" (ch. 18). This level of attainment is open only to spirit or celestial immortals (*Chuandao ji* 1) and occurs after the correct alignment with primordiality, reached from a state of "perfect emptiness," that is, of deep oblivion in the trance of inner observation. Once here, "one can connect to the perfected, undergo immortal transformation, and escape from the dark crossing, gradually attaining transcendence and liberation" (ch. 16).

The transition, moreover, is the result of the refinement of energy: "In *qi*, there is another *qi*; refining this *qi* into spirit, one can attain transcendence and liberation" (chs. 10, 11). This, in turn, means having the choice of living extensively on earth, "keeping the spirit merged with the physical form" or whirling out of it all and "ascending to the immortals, wandering afar to the isles of Penglai" (chs. 14, 17; Eskildsen 2009, 89; Baldrian-Hussein 1984, 191). Once spirit has attained full maturity and the purity of yang, it can travel limitless distances: "The immortal embryo starts to fly off, and an auspicious light pervades the chamber" (ch. 18).

At the same time, "adepts gain psychic powers, such as the abilities to see things in remote locations, to know the future, and to read minds. They no longer dream in their sleep and can no longer fall into bad rebirths" (Eskildsen 2009, 91), but are free to ecstatically travel to the otherworld and visit the paradises of the immortals. As the *Chuandao ji* says,

> Sitting in oblivion or practicing inner observation, one wanders far to the realm of Huaxu and visits the lands of the spirit immortals. Full of women and music, with splendid towers and terraces, variegated and colorful, beautiful and extraordinary, they are like nothing at all like the human world. (ch. 18)

This leads to a charmed existence, both here and in the beyond.

> After attaining transcendence and liberation, one is always enveloped by a radiant vapor and surrounded by auspicious *qi*. Wondrous flower petals fall like rain from heaven, and mysterious cranes come to visit.
>
> A fabulous fragrance spreads as jade maidens descend to present celestial writs and purple summons. Once concluded, one dresses in an immortal cap and gown and takes hold of various other regalia. Banner-baring majestic beings line up in front and behind, right and left, too many to count.
>
> They escort one formally to the purple office on the isles of Penglai, where one has audience with the Perfect Lord of Great Tenuity. He orders one's name and place of origin to be entered into the heavenly ledgers. (ch. 18; also *Bifa* 10)

This description matches other accounts of transcendence in internal alchemy. Adepts enter a state of deep absorption, so that the embryonic spirit can detach from the *qi* circulating in the body, manifesting in various supernatural sensory experiences such as seeing a shower of heavenly blossoms, smelling divine perfumes, or entering a high pagoda (Despeux and Kohn 2003, 240). Going beyond the Zhong-Lü system, other texts in additional describe the opening of a hole at the top of the head for the spirit to exit and enter, outline the manifestation of a heavenly light at the time of transcendence, or present the various voyages of the spirit and its training in more detail (Eskildsen 2009, 90; Despeux and Kohn 2003, 240).

On the other hand, the Zhong-Lü texts are quite specific in their description of the physical effects of the practice during the three major stages. The last chapter of the *Chuandao ji* focuses on this and is accordingly called "Confirmation Experiences" (*chengyan* 證驗) or "Signs of Proof" (Eskildsen 2001). It echoes effects already described in the *Cantong qi*:

> White hair turns black again, lost teeth regrow, old men become young studs, and old women revert to being gentle maidens. . . . Your body will feel light, and you can travel long distances in an instant, step into fire without getting burnt, jump into water without getting wet. You have control over life and

> death and are always happy and free from worry. (Pregadio 2011a, 81-82; Ho 2018, 125)

During the first stage, the effects are mainly physical. Even in a hundred days, all sorts of conditions including chronic ailments—high blood pressure, cardiac ailments, sexual dysfunction, indigestion, insomnia, and colds—are resolved. One is free from disease and experiences strong vigor, the body naturally straight and erect, the muscles and joints supple and open. The lower elixir field starts to produce heat and the channels open, leading to an overall increase in body temperature as well as the activation of the genital areas: men have spontaneous erections while women experience waves of sexual desire (Ho 2018, 4, 101-02).

The Zhong-Lü texts further claim that first "the heart meridian opens so that there is sweet fluid in the mouth," then there is rumbling in the abdomen, followed by the elimination of "small ailments or minor discomforts in the six viscera and four limbs" without the need for medication. Next, "the elixir fields warm up spontaneously, the complexion is clear and luscious, and the eyes see a spirit light even if in a dark room" (*Chuandao ji* 18; *Bifa* 1-2, 5). Overall, one no longer loses essence involuntarily and experiences pervasive well-being. "This serves to extend the years and increase longevity, becoming what we call a human immortal" (*Bifa* 3).

On the second level, further mental and spiritual changes occur, notably an "increase in wisdom, mental concentration, and precision of thinking." Adepts have "profound understanding, deep insight, and mystical experiences" (Ho 2018, 5-6). The senses are sharpened, perception is subtler, and the body attains an ever more youthful appearance. Entropy is reversed, so that teeth and hair regrow, recovering their original coloring. Reduced hearing or eyesight are restored, the complexion becomes fresh and childlike, and there is an overall lightness of the body (Ho 2018, 5). As the *Lingbao bifa* says,

> Your eyes are brilliant like dots of lacquer, your flesh is like coagulated fat. Fresh hair grows anew, wrinkles come to fill out, all signs of old age vanish. Forever you gain a youthful look, and your eyes are so sharp they can spot an autumn hair at a hundred paces. All over your body all sorts of old scars and marksnaturally go away; you are free from all tears, mucus, snot, and sweat. The sagely elixir produces a good flavor in your mouth; the fluid of pure life force pervades you with a lovely fragrance. (chs. 6, 8; *Chuandao ji* 18)

The third and highest stage, finally, leads to four distinct physical effects. As Chung-tao Ho describes them,

> First is the ability to fast or "abstain from grains" (*bigu* 辟穀) for prolonged periods. After three months of practice, practitioners should have so much

> energy in their bodies that they no longer feel hungry. Deeply absorbed in fetal breathing, they can let their digestive system stop operating.
>
> Second is the ability to live without sleep, which appears at six or seven months. The yang spirit being in a state of perfection, there are no more yin aspects in the body, which can function without getting tired or requiring sleep.
>
> Another effect is the ability to stop the heart beat in a state not unlike suspended animation. Due to continued absorption in embryo respiration, after eight or nine months, practitioners will no longer breathe through the nose or mouth nor will they have a pulse or heartbeat. Instead, they exchange spirit with the greater universe through the pores.
>
> Last but not least is the emergence of the six supernatural powers (*liutong* 六通): unlimited vision, the ability to understand all, multilocation, knowledge of past and future, mind-reading, and clear spiritual awareness. (2018, 120; see also Eskildsen 2004, 120)

The Zhong-Lü texts closely match this description. Thus, the *Chuandao ji* notes,

> Spirit and material souls no longer wander about, and there is no more need for sleep and dreams. Spirit luscious and essence strong, one functions equally well night and day. One's body entirely made up of yang essence, the spirit residence is strong and stable, the four limbs no longer fear cold and heat, and one no longer thinks of life and death as opposites. . . .
>
> One can shift shape and location at will. One's secret powers fully developed, one starts to look like an immortal. Like a tree of jade, one consists of strange bones and issues a golden glow. Wherever one goes, any place one stays, there are always spirit helpers that naturally appear and report for service; quickly and easily summoned, they fulfill your every wish. (ch. 18; *Bifa* 7)

Translation

Notes on Translation

> According to Danyangzi 丹陽子 (1123-1183), internal alchemy is nothing but metaphors. To him, it is nothing really new except that it uses a special language that aims at disrupting ordinary thinking by tearing apart the hardened knots, the solid barriers. Eventually this language will soften the mind in exactly the same way as the body has been relaxed previously by the various techniques of respiration. (Robinet 1989a, 301)

Linguistic Polysemy

"Alchemical masters face the universal problem of transmitting and translating the unspeakable into words" (Robinet 2011, 17). To bridge this gap, to help adepts learn about cultivation while also "preventing improper people from adapting and possibly abusing it, they employ highly obscure language and use many images and analogies" (Lu 2009, 79). As a result, they resort to a language that leaves space for silence while opening multiple levels of meaning.

The tradition is fundamentally esoteric, which means that much of its deeper mysteries must remain secret and cannot be explained in distinct, open language. "It is a major characteristic of internal alchemy to be paradoxical: the system needs to be transmitted yet also kept mysterious" (Ho 2018, 17). "Masters feared that their essential concepts and core theories might fall into the wrong hands or would not be passed on properly to later generations, and thus used written documents only as supplementary aids, often expressing themselves in poetry" and various other elliptical, enigmatic, and obscure ways (2018, 8). "There are poems, diagrams and charts, paradoxes, contradictions, the koans of Chan, philosophical essays full of playful dialectic, and most of all, the polysemy contained in all the images and words" (Robinet 1989a, 307). Fabrizio Pregadio describes it as follows,

> Alchemical language lends itself to two main functions. The first is the description of alchemical ideas and practices in the strict sense. The second is the illustration of metaphysical and cosmological doctrines, many of whose features can be expressed by means of alchemical symbolism and vocabulary.
>
> When the symbolic usage of the language prevails over the literal one (as it does in the *Cantong qi*), the alchemical terms connote in the first place formless principles, and the material entities or phenomena literally denoted by those terms are seen as instances of those principles. (2011a, 53)

The task of the aspiring alchemist, then, is to engage completely with the practice and become part of its unique expression. Michael Winn calls this the "deep grammar of *qi*-patterns," activated in personal cultivation and through interaction with the master. "Its language consists of *qi*-channels and fields in the human body perceived as resonating spheres of sensation, feeling, and spiritual qualities. Alchemy requires close observation of these natural body processes, and sometimes employs images of the seasons, color, sound, or direction as its symbols" (2009, 183).

Already the Quanzhen master Chen Zhixu 陳致虛, better known as Shangyangzi 上陽子 (1289-ca. 1335), made the distinction between "the way that establishes a discourse," including both words and practices, and "mind-to-mind transmission," which involves a close personal relationship and sincere growth of intuitive potential (Robinet 2011, 18). Still, discourse forms an essential stepping stone in this growth process, and alchemical discourse is based strongly on polysemy, analogy, and metaphors (Pregadio 2011a, 54).

For example, depending on the context, dragon and tiger may denote the *qi* of the liver and the lungs, or they may indicate spirit and *qi*. "The change in function reveals a change in the level of meaning, which again corresponds to a change in the level of consciousness" (Robinet 1989a, 310). Similarly, "the vibration of the color red may be used to activate the phase fire, the physical heart, its passions, the direction south, the planet Mars, and more"—or even all of these at the same time (Winn 2009, 183).

Another key feature is the ubiquitous use of the binary system and images of the *Yijing* to overcome the inherent opposition between language and silence, between concrete outer reality and subtle internal processes (Robinet 1989b, 307).

> Alchemists play with the binary system in a manner reminiscent of the illusionist—they let it proceed in a stunning manner, showing all its aspects—and whoever follows them along in their ways and byways, turns and returns, will be truly dazzled.
>
> Equivalents are superimposed on one another, contradicting and confusing; pairs cross and join one another; opposing and similar principles move in opposite directions; there are alternations; complements, contrasts, all kinds of different logical levels are unceasingly changing in their relationships from one moment to the next.
>
> Principles bring each other forth in one instant and destroy each other in the next; values are established and at once reversed; terms are used in one definite sense now and mean something entirely different in the next moment; they switch instantly from one level to the next, while the same principles are superimposed on different levels at the same time. (1989b, 308)

The discourse of internal alchemy is never linear, its "development is never continuous: disruptions of thought and language are applied constantly, and consciously. While the discourse is descriptive, it deliberately moves from one to another plane of perspective, leaps from one to another state of the work, from the part to the whole, and vice versa" (Robinet 2011, 32). The way alchemists describe their system tends to be repetitive, dismembered, and fragmented. In the middle of explaining a particular procedure, they "suddenly open a vision of the final accomplishment;" while outlining a specific stage, they "go back to summarizing what has already been said, repeat and expand the old discourse" (2011, 17, 33). It is thus futile to expect a systematic, linear, logical, or even structured treatment of the material.

This certainly holds true for the Zhong-Lü texts. They are systematic outlines only to a certain degree. For example, in actual practice the river carriage in the *Chuandao ji* (ch. 12) does not come after reduction and augmentation (ch. 11) or before reversion to the elixir field (ch. 13). Rather, all three describe ways of working with internal energy, and each refers to the three stages or levels of accomplishment set out in the beginning. Similarly, in the midst of highly detailed practice instructions, the *Lingbao bifa* time and again reverts back to cosmological theory and the description of the dynamic cycles of the sun and the moon.

Still, and despite of all this, alchemical "authors insist that there is a task to be accomplished in successive stages, that the world is to be created, that there is a set process to follow" (Robinet 1989b, 322). That is, the works make sense, and the Zhong-Lü texts more so than many others. Both provide section headings and move from the more cosmological to the more practical, ending with an overview of levels and experiences. They also start with simple definitions, then get increasingly complex and focus more on advanced stages and methods as they go along.

Specific Terms

As regards terminology, I have experimented with various English phrases and selected the one that seemed most appropriate for this group of texts. Thus, to distinguish different ways of referring to a primordial, pre-creation state, I have used "fundamental" or "basic" for *ben* 本, "origin" for *yuan* 原, "source" for *yuan* 源, and "prime" for *yuan* 元. The original nature of the cosmos as well as the quality of the potent ingredients and the ultimate state of attainment is commonly called *zhen* 真, literally "real," "true," or "genuine." I have opted for the rendition "perfect" for the main reason that the opposite of real, true, or genuine is artificial, false, or fake—and the created world in Daoism is none of these things. It is, however, quite imperfect, and perfection, both as original potentiality and ultimate state, is a core value of the system.

To express the functioning of the universe the texts use the term *ji* 機, literally "mechanism," a term preferred by Fabrizio Pregadio. Following Eva Wong, I render it "inner workings," since this conveys a sense of dynamic that is organic rather than mechanic. The process of cosmic unfolding, moreover, is *zaohua* 造化 or "creative transformations." They work through the ascent and descent (*shengxiang* 升降) of yin and yang as well as the rising and setting (*chumo* 出沒) of the sun and the moon. More specifically, the process functions by each force in turn generating (*sheng* 生), burgeoning (*sheng* 盛), reaching dominance (*wang* 旺), and declining (*shuai* 衰).

Practitioners of internal alchemy are named variously in the text. The most basic are Daoist followers, literally "those who love Dao" (*haodao zhe* 好道者), followed by the more commonly used Daoist adepts or "knights who venerate Dao" (*fengdao zhi shi* 豐道之士). Once they are seriously practicing "cultivation with dedication" (*xiuchi* 修持), they have every chance to become "advanced adepts" (*dashi* 達士).

The factor that makes this progress possible, moreover, is that human beings are made up of different energetic potencies, the most elementary of which is pure animal vitality or life force (*ling* 靈), a term often translated "numen" or "numinous." Next comes "essence" (*jing* 精), manifest in semen in men and menstrual blood in women, and the root of reproduction and gestation. *Qi* 氣, vital energy, is the most general of the forces, often matched with fluid (*ye* 液), which can come in yin or yang form, golden or jade. In practice, the two contain their opposite, so that *qi* is refined into the water of perfect oneness (*zhenyi zhi shui* 真一之水) and fluid brings forth the *qi* of rightful yang (*zhengyang zhi qi* 正陽之氣).[1] If left untended, on the other hand, the two devolve into body secretions (*jin* 津), defined as mucus, tears, phlegm, saliva, and sweat.

Beyond all these, spirit (*shen* 神) is the most subtle and powerful form on energy. It is the root of consciousness and leads to a variety of mental functions, the most basic of which are elementary recognition (*shi* 識) and straightforward knowing (*zhi* 知). More complex are comprehension (*da* 達) and realization (*wu* 悟), while imagination (*xiang* 想) and visualization (*cun* 存) signal its focused application.

Within this set up, human beings have a tendency to waste and scatter (*haosan* 耗散) or release and lose (*zoushi* 走失) their vital energy and hea-

---

[1] The word *zheng* 正 means "upright," "straight," "correct," "proper." It denotes the way things function in perfect harmony and excellent alignment. I use "rightful" to describe this state.

ven-given potentials. To remedy this, masters have provided general methods (*fa* 法) and specific techniques (*shu* 術) to train body and mind.

The most fundamental practice, then, involves getting the different forces to work together smoothly, make them interact (*jiao* 交), exchange (*huan* 換), fuse (*he* 合), or mate (*jiaogou* 交媾). Reversing (*fan* 反) or inverting (*diandao* 顛倒) the natural patterns of flow, they establish reversion (*huan* 還) in set cycles (*zhou* 周) or loops (*huan* 環).

From there, they work on the cinnabar or elixir medicine (*danyao* 丹藥), often called the "great medicine" (*dayao* 大藥). They collect the raw materials (*yaocai* 藥材) and assemble the medicine (*caiyao* 採藥), in turn gathering (*ju* 聚), heating (*shao* 燒), refining (*lian* 煉), reducing (*you* 油), augmenting (*dian* 添), and cleansing (*muyu* 沐浴).

As part of this process, which also involves stoking the fire (*jinhuo* 進火) in accordance with the correct firing times (*huohou* 火候), adepts establish a sagely womb (*shengtai* 聖胎) and give rise to an embyonic spark or zygote (*taibao* 胞胎), which eventually grows into the immortal embryo, literally "womb immortal" (*taixian* 胎仙). All the while, they see various changes in their body and mind, signs of proof that the practice is working and they are doing it correctly. These are generally called experiential effects (*yan* 驗) or, more specifically effectual experiences (*gongyan* 功驗) or confirmation experiences (*zhengyan* 證驗).

It all serves to overcome ordinary life (*fan* 凡), leave the world of dust (*zhenshi* 塵世) behind and attain transcendence and liberation (*zhaotuo* 超脫).

Text One[1]

Zhong-Lü Chuandao ji

1. Perfected and Immortals

Lü asked: In human life, what ways are there so one can be healthy without getting sick, remain young without growing old, and continue to live without dying?

Zhong replied: Human life comes about when father and mother engage in intercourse, and their two *qi* fuse together, so essence [semen] and blood form a zygote, which evolves from the state of great antecedence into that of great material reality. As yin nurtures and yang grows, *qi* transforms in gestation and after three hundred days the physical form is complete. The light of the life force enters the physical organism, and the child is ready to part from the mother.

From the state of the great immaculate onward, there are ascent and descent [of *qi*]. Through them, the infant grows like a yellow sprout. After 5,000 days [13.5 years], his *qi* is fully viable and the correct count comes to eight-one. Reaching the age of fifteen, he is a young man. At this time, his *qi* is half yang within yin, just like the light of the sun rising in the east. From here on, people tend to release and lose primordial yang, waste and scatter perfect *qi*. As their *qi* weakens, they suffer sickness, old age, death, and ultimate destruction.

Their whole life stupid and ignorant, they keep on diminishing the light of their life force. Their entire lifetime violent and obstructive, they continue to reduce the count of their years. For this reason, in any future lives their bodies are distinct in rank, their life expectancy is long or short.

---

[1] The text is translated, with some recourse to the previous rendition by Eva Wong (2000), on the basis of its edition in the Daoist Canon (DZ 263, chs. 14-16). While it also appears in the *Daoshu* (chs. 39-41), its version is heavily abridged and lacks section divisions and chapter headings. In addition, it only contains about half the dialog and shortens the questions and answers it does present, in some cases conflating two into one, while yet retaining most of the diction and the core teachings. It has no significant additions, but starts its presentation by noting that "Master Lü in studying Dao had worked already with over seventy masters when he finally encountered Master Zhongli." In addition, it uses a few variant expressions, such as counting time in 10-day weeks (*xun* 旬) rather than hundreds of days (*ri* 日) and speaking of "vehicles" rather than "accomplishments."

Once born, they perish again; once gone, they are born again. Cycle after cycle they do not realize this; life after life they keep on sinking lower.

Eventually they lose their human form and are born among other species, leak their life force and incarnate in different shells. Their root nature of utmost perfection no longer part of humanity, they are mired in the relentless cycle of reincarnation and rebirth, forever without any chance of liberation. However, if they encounter a perfected immortal or utmost person, he can help them to dissolve their sins, take them out of animal forms, and restore them to life in a human body.

Even while stuck in delusion and disease, stupidity and ignorance, if they manage to accumulate good deeds for hundreds of eons, they can ascend back to the blessed land [of human life], albeit while suffering hunger and cold, oppression and afflictions. If they steadily pursue the ascent to immortality, they can gradually become whole and complete again, albeit while living among slaves and servants, humble and despised. Should they, on the other hand, again commit the same sins as before, like being stuck in place or walking in a circle, they are bound to once more fall into the relentless cycle of reincarnation and rebirth.

Lü asked: I have been born in the Middle Kingdom and am fortunate enough to live in a time of great peace. I have sufficient clothing and food and am not yet old in years. Still, I love health and hate disease, desire life and fear death. Today, as I am facing you, my venerable teacher, I repeatedly bow and offer my respects. Thinking of the immense affairs of life and death, may I dare ask that you show me the principles of how never to get sick or die and give some teaching pointers to this humble seeker?

Zhong replied: If people in this life want to avoid falling into the cycle of reincarnation and rebirth and never come to life in the body or shell of another species, they must overcome sickness, old age, death, and suffering. Making sure that their head reaches up to the sky and their feet stand firmly on the earth, always supporting yin and embracing yang is the best way of being human. Being human, to make sure they do not become ghosts, they must cultivate themselves to attain immortality, and once they have reached it, they must continue to practice to attain ascent into heaven.

Lü asked: When people die, they become ghosts. Those whose Dao is accomplished become immortals. Immortals are of one kind. What must one do to attain ascent into heaven as such?

Zhong replied: There is more than one kind of immortal. Those of pure yin without any yang are ghosts. Those of pure yang without any yin are immortals. Those who have a mixture of yin and yang are human beings. Only humans have the opportunity to become either ghosts or immortals. If they fail to practice cultivation in their youth, give in to emotions and let their intention run wild, they will get sick and die, thus turning into ghosts.

Knowing this and cultivating refinement, you can transcend ordinary life and enter the ranks of the sages, be liberated from material reality and become an immortal. Immortals come in five ranks; methods lead to three levels of accomplishment. The dedication to cultivation depends on the person, and the merit attained depends on one's allotment.

Lü asked: What are the three levels of accomplishment and the five ranks?

Zhong replied: The three levels of accomplishment based on various methods are minor, medium, and major. The five ranks of immortals are ghost, human, earth, spirit, and celestial. They are all immortals. Ghost immortals do not leave the realm of ghosts; human immortals do not leave the realm of humanity; earth immortals do not leave the realm of earth; spirit immortals do not leave the realm of spirit; and celestial immortals do not leave the realm of heaven.

Lü asked: What, then, are ghost immortals?[2]

Zhong replied: Ghost immortals are the lowest among the five ranks. Having attained transcendence and liberation in the realm of yin [the dead], their spirit and image are not bright. They have no family names in the [registers of the] ghost hills, no personal names in the [ledgers of the] three mountains. Although not part of the cycle of reincarnation and rebirth, they yet cannot return to [the blessed isles of] Penglai and Yingzhou. With no place to call home, in the end they again entrust themselves to a womb for shelter [are reborn].

Lü asked: What techniques and do people undertake and what kind of merit do they need to end up as ghost immortals?

Zhong replied: People dedicated to cultivation often start out not realizing the great Dao, yet want to accomplish it quickly. They make their physical form like a withered tree, their mind like dead ashes, keeping their spirit consciousness contained within and their will unified, never letting it scatter.

In deep stability [*samadhi*], their yin spirit emerges, so they become ghosts of plain life force rather than immortals of pure yang. Since their will remains firmly unified and their yin life force never scatters, they are called ghost immortals. Although classified as immortals, they are really ghosts. In the past as much as today, many followers of the Buddha have applied a lot of merit and ended up like this, saying that they "attained Dao." How ridiculous is that!

Lü asked: What are human immortals?

Zhong replied: Human immortals are the second lowest among the five ranks. They are adepts of the cultivation of perfection who do not realize the nature of the great Dao. Among all its different ways, they pick one

[2] The part on ghost immortals is also translated in Eskildsen 2006, 376-77.

method; among all its different methods, they choose one technique. Then, with sincere mind and earnest will, they do not budge from it until the end of their days. As a result, their energies of the five phases interact wrongly and go awry, making their physical form and material reality excessively firm. They only manage to become immune to the eight wayward influences, allowing them be mostly healthy and rarely ill. Thus they are called human immortals.

Lü asked: What techniques do people undertake and what kind of merit do they need to become human immortals?

Zhong replied: People dedicated to cultivation, they start out by hearing of the great Dao. But since their sins weigh heavy and their good fortune is thin, all kinds of demonic attacks and hardships alter their initial mind, and they can only reach a minor level of accomplishment. Although they gain merit based on the right methods, they are unable to modify and budge from them as long as they live, never changing with the four seasons.

They may abstain from the five flavors, but have no clue about the six *qi*. They may forget the seven emotions, but have no clue about the ten precepts. Some practice rinsing and swallowing [saliva], yet dismiss those who do breathing exercises as being wrong; others assemble and supplement [*qi*], yet ridicule those who meditate in clarity and stillness as being foolish.

Some like to match other beings to steal the *qi* of heaven and earth, yet refuse to abstain from grains; others like to practice visualization to assemble the essence of the sun and the moon, but refuse to undertake healing exercises. Some sit in solitude and hold their breath, never knowing how to follow the natural flow.

Others bend their body and labor their physical form, never considering to work with nonaction. To assemble yin, some obtain women's *qi*, not understanding that this is entirely different from drawing in the golden turtle [testicles]; to nourish yang, others suckle at women's breasts, completely unaware that this is different from refining the elixir.

Their many kinds of operations and investigations are impossible to count: they all represent some way of practice, but are no match for the great Dao. Limiting themselves to a single method or technique within the great Dao, such adepts gain the merit of living healthy and happy for extended years, but that is all: thus, they are called human immortals.

Among them there is yet another type, who are happy for a short while and vexed in the long term. Lacking diligence in their work, they use the wrong times and mix up the days, then on the contrary get sick and diseased, unable to extend their years. This actually happens quite often in the world.

Lü asked: What, now, are earth immortals?'

Zhong replied: Earth immortals stand midway between heaven and earth. Although endowed with the potential to become spirit immortals, they do not realize the nature of the great Dao and stop with methods of the minor level. Never able to see real merit, they get to live a very long life in this world and do not die as humans.

Lü asked: How do earth immortals practice?

Zhong replied: They start out by working with the principles of the continuous ascent and descent [of *qi*] through heaven and earth and work with the correct count of the waxing and waning of the sun and the moon. Within their lifetime, they apply years and months; within each day, they work with double-hours and segments. First they must properly recognize dragon and tiger, then learn to match Kan [Water] and Li [Fire]. They need to know the difference between a pure spring and turbid water and properly distinguish the energy and phasing of morning and evening. They must perceive perfect oneness, examine the two forces [yin-yang], rank the three powers [heaven, earth, humanity], distinguish the four images [yin-yang, yin-yin, yang-yin, yang-yang], differentiate the five cycles [phases], determine the six *qi* [weather patterns], gather the seven treasures [of the body], balance the eight trigrams, and pace the nine continents. Inverting the direction of the five phases, they must transfer the *qi* [from the child] to the mother and move the fluid from husband to wife. Reverting *qi* to the three fields, they heat the cinnabar medicine and settle it firmly in the lower field. Thus, they refine their physical form to the point where they can stay in the world and live long without dying. Spirited immortals of the earth, they are called earth immortals.

Lü asked: What are spirit immortals?

Zhong replied: Spirit immortals are earth immortals who reject living in the world of dust and continue their work without stopping, so their bones and joints are well linked. Reducing lead and augmenting mercury, their golden essence refines at the top of their head and their jade fluid reverts to the elixir field. As they thus refine their physical form into *qi*, the five *qi* move to the prime and the three yang gather at the top of the head. When their work is complete, they forget their physical form and the immortal embryo naturally transforms. Their yin all gone, their yang is utterly pure, and beyond this body they have yet another body. Liberated from material reality, they ascend to the immortals; transcending ordinary existence, they enter the ranks of the sages. Completely vanquishing the world of dust, they return to the three mountains [of Penglai]. Thus they are called spirit immortals.

Lü asked: What, then, are celestial immortals?

Zhong replied: Earth immortals who no longer want to live in the world of dust and continue their work without stopping attain transcendence and liberation and thus become spirit immortals. Earth immortals who reject living on the three isles of the blessed and instead spread Dao among humanity, gain great merits in Dao, and guide the people to practice, eventually accumulate sufficient merit and receive a celestial invitation to join the grotto heavens, are called celestial immortals. Those among them who reject living in the grotto heavens, come to work as judges and officials among the immortal administration. The lowest among them serve as officials in the administration of water; those of middle rank are officials of earth; the highest are officials of heaven. If they accumulate great merit in heaven and earth, doing great deeds in the past as much as today, they rise through the ranks of office, working their way through all thirty-six grotto heavens, moving on to the eighty-one yang heavens, and from there reach the realm of emptiness, nonbeing, and spontaneity of the Three Clarities.

Lü asked: I certainly have no interest in pursuing the state of a ghost immortal, and I do not dare to hope for that of celestial immortal. So, may I please learn more about the methods leading to the rank of human, earth, and spirit immortal?

Zhong replied: Human immortals never go beyond the methods of the minor level; earth immortals never reach more than the methods of the medium level; and spirit immortals do not exceed the methods of the major level. Although counted as three levels of accomplishments, they are in fact one. It is possible to use any method to pursue Dao; Dao is really not hard to reach. Using Dao to pursue immortality, immortality, too, becomes easy.

Lü asked: Adepts in the past as much as today who nurture life-destiny all pursue long life and hope for ascent to the immortals. Why is it then that some never make it?

Zhong replied: Typically, their methods do not match Dao: they listen to a lot of teachings and try hard to comprehend them, but tend to get stuck in minor, sectarian methods. This makes it impossible for them to avoid sickness and disease, death and demise. Just like those who claim to practice deliverance from the corpse, but all they do is confuse and delude the common people! They promote and praise each other, never getting a chance to learn of the great Dao. They may be of sincere mind and earnest will and practice with dedication for a long time, yet in the end they never see any merit and inevitably enter into the realm beneath the [Yellow] Springs. How sad!

2. The Great Dao

Lü asked: What is the great Dao?

Zhong replied: The great Dao has neither form nor name, asks no questions and gives no answers. It is so great it has no outside, so small it has not inside. None can ever fully know it, none can ever fully practice it.

Lü asked: Advanced adepts in the past as much as today usually start out by studying Dao, then get hold of it, attain it, and eventually realize it fully. Once they get there, they leave the world of dust behind and enter [the isles of] Penglai, ascend into the grotto heavens, reach the heavens of pure yang, and move into the Three Clarities. All these are masters who have realized Dao. Now, you, my venerable teacher, say that Dao cannot be known or practiced. So, what is the secret about Dao?

Zhong replied: I have no secrets about Dao. Many of those praised as Daoist adepts are Daoist followers in name only. When taught about the great Dao, they have no sincere mind, or if they have a sincere mind, they lack an earnest will. They set out to do something in the morning and abandon it by evening, sit down to do something and forget it as soon as they stand up. They may start out with painstaking diligence, but soon lapse into indulgent laziness. For this reason, I say that the great Dao is hard to know and difficult to practice.

Lü asked: Why exactly is the great Dao hard to know and difficult to practice?

Zhong replied: Using minor, sectarian methods, it is easy to gain some merit, but the tendency is to desire too much too soon. Passing these methods on from one to another, practitioners never gain full realization as long as they live; following the current fashion of the common world, they end up destroying their access to the great Dao.

There are those who fast and observe the precepts, abstain from grains, assemble *qi*, swallow saliva, leave the family, eliminate flavors, sit in absorption, abstain from speaking, practice visualization, gather yin, absorb *qi*, maintain purity, still the mind, eliminate entanglements, open the top of the head, withdraw the turtle [testicles], eliminate physical labor, study the scriptures, heat and refine [the elixir], hold the breath, exercise, control the breath, gather and supplement [*qi*], give donations, perform sacrifices, aide and rescue others, live in the mountains, study inner nature, remain unmoving, work with dedication, and so on and so forth.

The list of minor, sectarian methods is endless, going as far as working with the efflorescence of the sun and the moon, the *qi* of heaven and earth, the thoughts in their minds and imaginations in their intention, the hope to refine cinnabar sand, the bending of the body and laboring of the physical form—all in search of transcendence and liberation and usually putting in lots of effort with little to show for, quite possibly inviting an attack of disease. By practicing perfect embryo respiration, cutting off all thoughts, and forgetting all words, it is possible to nurture inner nature. Containing perfect *qi* in great oneness, keeping the golden lance from drooping, and making the yellow river flow backward are lower-level methods for nurturing life-destiny. Making the physical form like a withered tree and the mind like dead ashes are minor techniques of gathering spirit.

How hard all those Daoist adepts in the past as much as today work their minds, how persistently they apply their intention! Swallowing saliva to use as a medicine, how can they ever reach creative transformation? Gathering *qi* to use as cinnabar, how can they ever stop the process? Identifying the liver as the dragon and the lungs as the tiger, how can they ever attain cosmic fusion? Recognizing Kan as lead and Li as mercury, how can they ever attain reduction and augmentation?

Pouring and watering all through the four seasons, they expect to grow the yellow sprout. Concentrating their intention, never letting it scatter, they desire to pursue the great medicine. Throughout, they mistake the years, use the wrong the months, mix up the days, and confuse the double-hours. Without comprehending the true root of the five phases, how can they ever know the three powers in their creative transformations?

Seeking out the branches and plucking the leaves, they delude themselves and lead their successors astray. All this causes the great Dao to get further away every day, get forever more distant. Weird and extreme practices arise and turn into common fashion, as practitioners increasingly lose sight of the original intention of the ancestral teachers and move away from the doctrines of Dao and virtue, the teachings transmitted carefully from mouth to ear.

As they then present instructions to their ignorant disciples, passing their systems on to the next generation, they inevitably condemn them to enter into the realm beneath the [Yellow] Springs and cause people to become cold-hearted. They all want to explicate and spread the great Dao, but being in the world, their sins weigh heavy, and their good fortune is thin. They do not trust the core workings of heaven, placing instead great value on wealth and belittling life-destiny. Thus, they are bound to turn into ghosts.

Lü asked: Now that I understand all about the minor, sectarian methods, what can you tell me about the great Dao?

Zhong replied: Dao originally is beyond all questions, and questions originally have no answers. When perfect prime divided and great simplicity scattered, "Dao generated the One; the One generated the two, and the two generated the three" [*Daode jing* 42]. The One is substance, the two are function, and the three represent the creative transformations. Substance and function do not go beyond yin and yang, and all creative transformations are caused by mutual mating. Above, middle, and below are the three powers: heaven, earth, and humanity together constitute the one Dao. Dao generated the two *qi*, which generated the three powers. They generated the five phases, which in turn generated the myriad beings.

Among the myriad beings the one with the most life force and the most noble is the human. Only human beings can penetrate the principle of the myriad beings, fully explore their own inner nature. Doing so, they arrive at a clear perception of life-destiny. Fulfilling their destiny and protecting their life, they attain harmony with Dao. Then they can be as firm and stable as heaven and earth and live just as long!

Lü asked: Living eternally means continuing for thousands of years without limit. People's optimal life expectancy is about a hundred years, and those making it to seventy are rare. Why is Dao so close to heaven and so far from humanity?

Zhong replied: Dao is never far from humanity; it is human beings who move away from Dao. They are away from Dao because they do not know the right methods to nurture their life-destiny. They do not know the right methods because at the lowest level they do not understand proper timing. They do not understand proper timing because they do not comprehend the core workings of heaven and earth.

3. Heaven and Earth

Lü asked: May I please learn about what you call the core workings of heaven and earth?

Zhong replied: The core workings of heaven and earth indicate how the great Dao of heaven and earth revolves and functions. Moving up and down, coming and going, it works without slackening and thus can live forever, remaining always firm and stable. Its secrets are not lightly revealed to human beings.

Lü asked: What exactly are the so-called core workings of heaven and earth in relation to Dao? How do their orbits and cycles first start? How can we see their effects?

Zhong replied: Once the great Dao divided, there was physical form; once there was physical form, there was correct count. Heaven attained the Dao of Qian and relies on the number one as its substance. Light and clear, it resides above, functioning through yang. Earth attained the Dao of Kun and relies on the number two as its substance. Heavy and turbid, it resides below, functioning through yin. Yang moves up while yin moves down; they interact and fuse. As they function through Qian and Kun, they never deviate from Dao. They start according to the seasons; their effects manifest in the days.

Lü asked: I understand that heaven attains the way of Qian and functions through yang. But if yang dominantly ascends, how can it interact with earth? Earth attains the way of Kun and functions through yin. But if it dominantly descends, how can it interact with heaven? If heaven and earth do not interact, how can yin and yang come to fuse? If yin and yang do not fuse, how can Qian and Kun function properly? If they do not function properly, even though one may know the season of their start and the day of their effect, how can the great Dao be attained?

Zhong replied: In the way of heaven, Qian is substance and yang is function; it accumulates *qi* above. In the way of earth, Kun is substance and yin is function; it accumulates water below. So heaven can work according to Dao, it has Qian connect to Kun.

The first time they connect, they generate their oldest son, Zhen [Thunder]. The second time, they generate their middle son, Kan [Water]. The third time, they generate their youngest son, Gen [Mountain]. Thus, through the interaction of heaven with earth, of Qian connecting to Kun, they generate the three yang.

So earth can work according to Dao, it has Kun connect to Qian. The first time they connect, they generate their oldest daughter, Xun [Wind]. The second time, they generate their middle daughter, Li [Fire]. The third time, they generate their youngest daughter, Dui [Lake]. Thus, through the interaction of earth with heaven, of Kun connecting to Qian, they generate the three yin.

As the three yang interact and fuse with the three yin, the myriad beings grow; as the three yin interact and fuse with the three yang, the myriad beings mature. Thus, the interaction and fusion of heaven and earth have their origin in the connection of Qian and Kun and from there revolve and move along with Dao.

As Qian and Kun connect to each other, they generate the six *qi*. As the six *qi* interact and fuse, they divide into the five phases. The five phases in turn interact and fuse to generate and mature the myriad beings. Qian follows its path and moves down: once its threefold connection [to Kun] is finished, yang ascends again. Thus, the yin contained in the yang also returns to heaven. Similarly, Kun follows its path and moves up: once its threefold connection [to Qian] is finished, yin descends again. Thus, the yang contained in the yin also returns to earth.

Now, there is yin contained in yang. This yin never dissolves and is known as perfect yin. Once perfect yin reaches heaven, it follows yang and starts to grow, then again descends from heaven. How can there not be yang in yin? Similarly, there is yang contained in yin. This yang never perishes and is known as perfect yang. Once perfect yang reaches earth, it follows yin and starts to grow, then again ascends from earth. How can there not be yin in yang? Yin within yang never dissolves and again returns to earth; yang within yin never perishes and again returns to heaven. Circulating back and forth, they revolve around each other without ever stopping. Their fusion and interaction never loses Dao, so they can can live forever, remaining always firm and stable.

Lü asked: Heaven and earth in their core workings revolve along with Dao and thereby live forever, which is the ultimate effect of their activities and functioning. Only human beings, although they possess the inherent nature of being smart and bright, have the ability to rest their minds in clarity and stillness. Desiring to venerate and practice the great Dao, they can reach a minor level of accomplishment to be healthy and happy and extend their years, a medium level to live long without dying, or a major level to gain liberation from material reality and ascend to the immortals.

How can one work with these functions, learn to revolve along with the great Dao and pattern one's movements on the core workings of heaven to attain a state where one can live forever, remaining always firm and stable, existing permanently for vast kalpas?

Zhong replied: The great Dao has no form, only when others attained it did forms come about; it has no name, only when others came into being did names come about. When heaven and earth attain it, it manifests as the Dao of Qian and Kun; when the sun and the moon attain it, it manifests as the Dao of yin and yang. When human beings attain it, it manifests in official life as the Dao of ruler and minister, in private residences as the Dao of in husband and wife, in villages as the Dao of seniors and juniors, in social circles as the Dao of friends and acquaintances, and in the family as the Dao of father and son.

Looking at this from the outside, it becomes clear that they all have their own Dao. Thus, when father and mother interact, the father being yang advances first while yin follows behind; perfect *qi* receives perfect water, heart fire and kidney water fuse and refine into seminal florescence. Once this emerges, if the yin of the mother advances first, her water drips into a place of no further use; if her yang moves first, her blood settles near the palace [womb]. Then essence and blood form a zygote, which encompasses perfect *qi* and in due course enters the palace of mother and child.

Over a succession of days and strings of months, perfect *qi* becomes a human being. This is just like heaven and earth moving along with Dao, Qian and Kun connecting and generating the three yin and three yang. Perfect *qi* is yang; perfect water is yin. Yet there is also yang contained in water and yin in *qi*. *Qi* tends to ascend, yet it also contains perfect water. Water tends to descend, yet also contains perfect *qi*. Thus, perfect water is perfect yin and perfect *qi* is perfect yang.

Perfect yang descends as it follows water. Behaving like Qian connecting to Kun, it creates Zhen above, Kan in the middle, and Gen below. Matching this to the human body and taking the center as the baseline, it moves down from the top, making Zhen the liver, Kan the kidneys, and Gen the bladder.

Perfect yin ascends as it follows *qi*. Behaving like Kun connecting to Qian, it creates Xun below, Li in the middle, and Dui above. Matching this to the human body and taking the center as the baseline, it moves up from the bottom making Xun the gallbladder, Li the heart, and Dui the lungs.

Once its physical form and image are fully prepared and the correct count is reached, it leaves the mother. After birth, primordial yang resides in the kidneys and there generates perfect *qi*. Perfect *qi* moves to the heart and there generates perfect fluid. This in turn reverts back to the prime. It keeps on moving up and down, back and forth.

As long as there is no loss or obstruction, people can extend their years. If they know the proper timing without fail and observe the right measure of reduction and augmentation, they naturally live long. If they work hard without slackening, maintain dedicated cultivation without stopping, their yin will be all gone and their yang utterly pure, allowing them to transcend ordinary existence and enter the ranks of the sages.

These are the principles of the deep creativity of the core workings of heaven, information that has never been transmitted in the past or today. Now, if people are confident in their mind and free from indecision, regard fame and profit as restrictive chains, see love and compassion as plundering enemies, abhor the suffering of sickness and disease and fear the hardships of death and destruction, want to prevent losing their human body to be born in a different shell and worry thinning out their life force and being born among other species, they must maintain a strong will toward clarity and stillness, stabilize their root source, and never let primordial yang be lost or perfect *qi* scatter.

Then *qi* will be abundant and the spirit soul free from yin; yang will be strong and the material soul full of *qi*. Ascending and descending in proper rhythm, people in this fashion never go beyond heaven and earth; waxing and waning in right alternation, they come and go matching the sun and the moon.

4. The Sun and the Moon

Lü asked: Now that I roughly know about the principles of heaven and earth, what impact do the orbits and interactions of the sun and the moon have on humanity? May I please hear about this?

Zhong replied: The great Dao has no form but it generates and nurtures heaven and earth. The great Dao has no name, but it revolves and moves the sun and the moon. The sun and the moon are the essence of great yin and great yang. They structure the patterns of the interaction of heaven and earth; they support the efforts involved in the generation and maturation of the myriad beings. They rise and set in the east and west to differentiate day and night. They come and go in the south and north to determine heat and cold.

Night and day never stop, heat and cold continuously succeed each other. Within their dark portion [lit. material soul], their bright part [lit. spirit soul] arises; from the center of this bright part in due course the dark portion again takes root. Their waxing and waning occur at regular times, never losing the correct count of Qian and Kun. They come and go in the proper measure, never failing the periodic changes of heaven and earth.

Lü asked: How exactly do they rise and set in the east and west to differentiate day and night?

Zhong replied: When murky chaos first divided, the dark and the yellow took up their positions. Heaven and earth took shape and in their physical form looked like an egg. Within the six harmonies they were round like a ball. Then the sun and the moon began to rise and set, revolving by moving alternatively up toward heaven and down toward earth. Moving up and down, east and west, their course is an every-turning wheel. The sun rises in the east and moves west—before it sets, it is day. It rises in the east and moves west—before it rises, it is night. Thus, the rising and setting of the sun determine day and night.

The rising and setting of the moon are different from those of the sun. It supports its dark portion in the west and receives its bright part to the east. It radiates brightly during the night but hides its brightness during the day. As the days go on, it works during different double-hours, either rising or setting, usually going from west to east.

When at first its bright part emerges in its dark portion, it looks like a bent bow; early in the night it shines brightly in the west. Next, within its dark portion, its bright part grows to occupy half: it reaches its first quarter and early in the night it shines brightly in the south. In the next phase, the bright part completely covers the dark portion and it faces the sun; early in the night it shines brightly in the east.

Next, within its bright part, the dark portion resurfaces and it looks like a broken mirror; early in the day its bright part hides in the west. Next, within its bright part, its dark portion grows to occupy half: it reaches its last quarter; in the day its bright part hides in the south. From here the dark portion completely covers the bright part and it faces away from the sun; early in the day its bright part hides in the east. Thus, the rising and setting of the moon in their own way differentiate day and night.

Lü asked: How do their coming and going in north and south determine heat and cold?

Zhong replied: After the winter solstice, the sun rises sometime in the first 50 units after the Chen hour [7-9 am] and sets sometime in the last 50 units of the Shen hour [3-5 pm]. It rises and sets from south to north until it reaches the summer solstice.

After the summer solstice, the sun rises sometime in the first 50 units of the Yin hour [3-5 am] and sets sometime in the last 50 units of the Xu hour [7-9 pm]. It rises and sets from north to south until it again reaches the winter solstice.

Going from south to north, as winter turns into summer, cold becomes heat. Going from north to south, as summer turns into winter, heat becomes cold. Accordingly the days in the summer are as long as the nights in the winter; the days in the winter are as long as the nights in the summer.

After the winter solstice, the moon rises in the north and moves south: this matches the sun in the summer. After the summer solstice, it rises in the south and moves north: this matches the sun in the winter. Thus, the comings and goings of the sun and the moon determine the manifestation of heat and cold.

Lü asked: The core workings of heaven and earth involve the continuous ascent and descent of yin and yang, which perfectly match human activities with no major distinction. How, then, do the rising and setting, coming and going of the sun and the moon, their interaction and orbits compare to human beings?

Zhong replied: The core workings of heaven and earth depend on the continuous ascent and descent of yin and yang. Alternating ascending and descending, they generate each other as they each reach their great ultimate. They mutually generate and mature each other, forever cycling through and beginning anew. Never losing Dao, they can live forever.

Adepts of cultivation, if they pattern themselves on heaven and earth, can attain live long without dying. As they match the orbits of the sun and the moon, the interaction of their coming and going, if they stop when the moon receives the bright part of the sun, they change yin into yang, so that their yin is all gone and their yang is utterly pure. Using lunar florescence to become radiant and pure, they can eliminate their dark portions and shine forth like the sun, illuminating all above and below. At this time, if they further continue to refine themselves, they can use *qi* to mature spirit, be liberated from material reality and ascend to the immortals. Refinement is thus the attainment of pure yang.

Lü asked: For Daoist adepts who cultivate perfection, which comes first in their work, applying the principles of yin and yang ascending and descending through heaven and earth or initiating the rhythmical interaction of solar essence and lunar florescence?

Zhong replied: They should start by imitating the core workings of heaven. Applying the principles of the continuous ascent and descent of yin and yang, they fuse perfect water and perfect fire into oneness, refine them to form the great medicine, and settle it firmly in their elixir field. Thus, they will not die for vast kalpas and can live as long as heaven and earth. If they do not want to keep on living in the world of dust, they should not stop in their work, but apply the interaction of the sun and the moon. Using yang to refine yin, they make sure yin does not emerge; using *qi* to nurture spirit, they make sure spirit does not scatter. In this way, their five *qi* move to the prime and their three [yang] flowers gather at the top of the head. Abandoning the currents of ordinary living, they joyfully return to the three isles [of the blessed].

Lü asked: Effectual experiences like these come about thoroughly and promptly. It seems the biggest thing to worry about is not matching the proper time.

Zhong replied: That is correct. Yin and yang keep on ascending and descending through heaven and earth: they cycle through one interaction in the course of a year. The essence and efflorescence of the sun and the moon keep on coming and going: they cycle through one interaction in the course of a month. *Qi* and fluid of the human body, in their turn, cycle through one interaction in the course of one day and one night.

5. The Four Levels of Time

Lü asked: May I please ask about the specific interactions of the sun and the moon between heaven and earth in the course of years, months, days, and hours?

Zhong replied: Time overall comes in four levels. Human life lasts about one hundred years. From age one to thirty is the time of youth and strength; from thirty to sixty is the time of growth and maturity; from sixty to ninety is the time of old age and infirmity; and from ninety to a hundred or a hundred and twenty s the time of decline and demise. This is how time works in the human body: it is the first level.

Now, twelve double-hours make up one day; five days make one base-week [lit., phase]; three base-weeks make one *qi*-period; three *qi*-periods make one division; two divisions made one season. The seasons consist of spring, summer, fall, and winter.

During spring, yang grows to half fullness within yin and the weather changes from cold to warm—this defines spring. During summer, yang reaches fullness within yang and the weather changes from warm to hot—this defines summer. During fall, yin grows to half fullness within yang and the weather turns from hot to cool—this defines fall. During winter, yin reaches fullness within yin and the weather turns from cool to cold—this defines winter. This is how time works in a year: it is the second level.

Now, the lower pitch pipes generate tube semitones, and the higher tubes generate pitched sounds. One month has thirty days, which equals 360 double-hours, 3000 segments, and 180,000 units. While the moon waxes from new moon to its first quarter, yang grows to half fullness within yin. While it waxes from its first quarter to full moon, yang reaches fullness within yang. When it wanes from full moon to its last quarter, yin grows to half fullness within yang. When it waxes from its last quarter to darkness, yin reaches fullness within yin. This is called how time works in a month: it is the third level.

Sixty units make one segment, eight segments and twenty units [500 units] make one double-hour, and one and a half double-hours mark one trigram [three-hour point]. In space, the trigrams determine the eight directions; in time, they divide into four key positions.

That is, from the Zi [11 pm–1 am] to the Mao hour [5-7 am], yang grows to half fullness within yin, that is, minor yang arises within major yin. From the Mao to the Wu hour [11 am-1 pm], yang reaches fullness within yang, that is, major yang arises within minor yang. From the Wu to the You hour [5-7 pm], yin grows to half fullness within yang, that is, minor yin arises within major yang. From the You to the Zi hour, yin reaches fullness within yin, that is, major yin arises within pure minor yin. This is called the time how time works in a day: it is the fourth level.

The proper time of the human body is hard to attain and easy to lose. The months within the year are fast to pass and slow to come. The double-hours of the day are elusive like lightning and swift like raging flames. Days accumulate and turn into months; months accumulate and turn into years. The months of the year slip by and fall away; personal years move along swiftly. Desiring fame and pursuing profit lead the mind astray without reprieve; loving children and coddling grandchildren causes the continued arising of care and emotion. When one finally thinks to turn the mind back toward Dao, one has to wrangle with old age and declining *qi*. Like snow in the spring and flowers in the fall, one only has moments of time left; like evening sun and full moon, one follows an impermanent, fleeting light.

Dao followers find it hard to attain the proper time of the human body. Throughout gorgeous mountains and enticing scenery, multi-colored plants exude deluding fragrance; in pavilions perched over rivers and edifices on dangerous cliffs, soft breezes delight the intention. They invite leisurely talks during moonlit nights and drinking with friends during snow-bound days. All these are lascivious pleasures without end that chisel away at our limited time. When one finally thinks to turn the mind back toward Dao, the body is riddled with sickness and disease. Like being in a shipwreck before rescue, who would not be filled with a yearning for salvation? Like sitting in a leaking house about to cave in, who would abandon the intention toward renewed cultivation?

Daoist adepts often pass their youth in vain pursuits. Before the rooster has even crowed, they leave their house, anxious that they might be late. When the city's drums are heard widely [at sunset], they return to their house, complaining that is too soon. Avarice and madness, competition and eagerness barely pause; foolish imaginings and pervasive worries never stop! Their houses are full of gold and jade, but how does that help them to ward off disease? Their vision is focused on children and grandchildren, but how does that let them exchange rather than lose their *qi*? Night and day never stop. People of the world don't realize that! Daoist adepts thus should cherish the time of each day.

Lü asked: The different levels of the human body, year, month, and day are manifestations of time. You, my venerable teacher, have said that the proper time of the human body is hard to attain, while that of each day should be cherished. Why is that?

Zhong replied: Daoist adepts have a hard time practicing in their youth. Were they to cultivate it with dedication while young, when their root is firm and their primordial *qi* still whole, they would find it easy to see success. Within even a mere thousand days, they could reach a major level of accomplishment. They also have a hard time in their middle years. Practicing in middle age, they first have to supplement their *qi* to reach a basic level of fullness, then apply themselves thoroughly to pursue success. Initially they can reverse old age and recover youth; later they can enter utmost states and transcend ordinary life.

Daoist adepts often do not realize this in their youth and refuse to reflect on it during middle age. Only if pursued by hardship and disasters do they finally settle their minds in clarity and stillness; only when suffering sickness and disease do they place their will on the invisible and inaudible. For those practicing in their later years, we first discuss saving and preserving [*qi*], then talk about supplementing and increasing it. Practicing in this manner, they gradually reach a minor level of accomplishment, from which, by accumulating more merit, they get to the medium level. Again accumulating more merit, they can reverse old age and recover their youth.

Refining their physical form, they can stay on in the world, but their five *qi* cannot move to the prime and their three yang have a hard time gathering at the top of the head. They lack the karmic conditions to gain liberation from material reality and ascend to the immortals. This is what I mean when I say that the proper time of the human body is hard to attain.

Lü asked: I see: the proper time of the human body is difficult to know and hard to attain. But what about cherishing the time of each day?

Zhong replied: One day in human life is the same as one month for the sun and the moon or one year for heaven and earth. After the great Dao generated and raised heaven and earth, they took up their separate positions above and below, 84,000 miles apart. After the winter solstice, yang begins to ascend from earth. Each *qi*-period or fifteen days, it advances 7,000 miles, and after 180 days arrives in heaven [sky] above. Reaching its great ultimate, it generates yin. After the summer solstice, yin beings to descend from the sky. Each *qi*-period or fifteen days, it advances 7,000 miles, and after 180 days arrives at the earth below. Reaching its great ultimate, it again generates yang. The cycle renews continuously and their circulation never stops. Since they never lose Dao, they can live forever.

The orbits and revolutions of the sun and the moon give shape to days and months as they each cover a distance of 840 miles. After the new moon, nine [yang] arises in six [yin]. Each day, in the course of twelve double-hours, from its dark portion [lit. material soul] the bright part [lit. spirit soul] advances seventy miles, so by day fifteen, after 180 double-hours, it reaches 840. After the full moon, six arises in nine. Each day, in the course of twelve double-hours, from its bright part the dark portion advances seventy miles, so by day fifteen, after 180 double-hours, it reaches 840. The cycle renews continuously and their circulation never stops. Since they never lose Dao, they can remain strong and stable.

The great Dao supports and nurtures the myriad beings, among whom humans are the most spiritual and noble. The heart and kidneys in the human body are 8.4 inches from each other. Between them yin and yang keep ascending and descending, no different from heaven and earth. Fluid arises from *qi*; *qi* emerges from fluid. *Qi* and fluid generate each other along the very same path as the sun and the moon.

Heaven and earth connect through Qian and Kun, and yin and yang keep ascending and descending between them, cycling through one interaction in the course of one year. Since they never lose Dao, one year is always followed by another. The sun and the moon in alteration generate their bright parts and dark portions, their essence and efflorescence constantly coming and going. They cycle through one interaction in the course of one month. Since they never lose Dao, one month is always followed by another.

In human beings, similar interaction and fusion occur once in the course of a day and night. Unaware of the correct time of this fusion, they have no method to assemble and collect [*qi*]. At the times of diminishing [*qi*], they do not know how to supplement it; at the time of increasing [*qi*], they do not understand how to contain it. When yin is in fusion, they do not realize that they should nurture yang; when yang is active, they do not understand that they should refine yin. If over a month, they do not realize the proper times of diminishing and increasing, they cannot possibly practice correctly in the course of a day.

Also, every year that passes means one year less; every day that passes means one day less. Subject to wind, lying down in dampness, exposed to heat, and wading through cold, they have no chance to dedicate themselves to cultivation. Coddling their hearts, they incur diseases, thus wasting their best years and ending up with nothing left to do but sit up and wait for death.

Lü asked: I think it is not that Daoist adepts do not know that, if they waste their best years and let the months slip by, they will find their body riddled with sickness and disease and eventually end in death. Rather, they do not know the right methods of cultivation and the correct times of serious practice. Thus, they mistake the times of the fusion of yin and yang and do not match the rhythm of the hours and months.

Zhong replied: The human body works with years; years work with months; months work with days; and days work with hours. The energies of the five organs rise and decline over specific months; they advance and withdraw over certain days; and they interact and fuse in the course of particular hours. They revolve in five degrees and their *qi* transfers in six phases. Making sure that metal, wood, water, fire, and earth each take their turn without fail, that east, west, south, north, and center undergo generation and maturation in accordance with the right numbers, they refine essence to generate perfect *qi*, refine *qi* to fuse with yang spirit, and refine spirit to become one with the great Dao.

6. The Five Phases

Lü asked: The *qi* of the five organs are metal, wood, water, fire, and earth; the positions of the five phases are east, south, west, north, and center. This being so, how do they achieve mutual generation and maturation? What is the timing of their interaction and fusion? What is the best time to assemble and collect them? Please teach me about this.

Zhong replied: After the great Dao divided and generated heaven and earth, they again split and set up emperors in the five directions. Thus, the Green Emperor of the east is the ruler of spring, when yang arises from yin and the myriad beings are born. The Red Emperor of the south is the ruler of summer, when yang generates yang and the myriad beings grow. The White Emperor of the west is the ruler of fall, when yin arises from yang and the myriad beings reach maturation. The Black Emperor of the north is the ruler of winter, when yin generates yin and the myriad beings die.

Within the ninety days of each of these four seasons, the last eighteen are ruled by the Yellow Emperor [of the center]. In spring, he assists the work of the Green Emperor and finalizes generation. In summer, he regulates the work of the Red Emperor and enhances growth. In fall, he enhances the work of the White Emperor and arranges proper positions. In winter, he tightens the work of the Black Emperor and issues severe injunctions. The five emperors divide their rule, each governing for seventy-two days, making a total of 360 days or one year, consistently aiding heaven and earth and moving along with Dao.

The children of the Green Emperor are [the earthly stems] Jia and Yi: they belong to the east and the phase wood. The children of the Red Emperor are Bing and Ding: they belong to the south and the phase fire. The children of the Yellow Emperor are Wu and Ji: they belong to the center and the phase earth. The children of the White Emperor are Geng and Xin: they belong to the west and the phase metal. The children of the Black Emperor are Ren and Gui: they belong to the north and the phase water. They become apparent as images during the seasons: wood as the green dragon, fire as the red bird, earth as the hooked line [Gouchen], metal as the white tiger, and water as the Dark Warrior [lit. tortoise].

They also become apparent in living beings over the seasons. Thus, when Yi fuses with Geng in spring, there are elm trees; green will take on a white tint, embodying the colors of metal and wood. When Xin fuses with Bing in fall, there are dates; white will take on a red tint, embodying the colors of metal and fire. When Ji fuses with Geng in late summer and early fall, there is squash; green will take on a yellow tint, embodying the colors of earth and wood. When Ding fuses with Ren in summer, there are mulberry trees; red will take on a black tint, embodying the colors of water and fire. When Gui fuses with Wu in winter, there are mandarin oranges; black will take on a yellow tint, embodying the colors of water and earth. This is visible pattern among many different species, all manifesting the interaction and fusion of the five emperors in the seasons and throughout all created beings. They are too many to count.

Lü asked: So this is how the five phases work over the seasons. How do they function in human beings?

Zhong replied: In human beings, the head is round and the feet are square: the image of heaven and earth. The continuous ascent and descent of yin and yang match their core workings. The kidneys are water, the heart is fire, the liver is wood, the lungs are metal, and the spleen is earth. In the system of mutual generation among the five phases, water generates wood, wood generates fire, fire generates earth, earth generates metal, and metal generates water. The generating phase is the mother, the one being generated is the child.

In the system of mutual control of the five phases, water controls fire, fire controls metal, metal controls wood, wood controls earth, and earth controls water. The controlling phase is the husband, the one being controlled is the wife. Looking at it in terms of mother and child, kidney *qi* generates liver *qi*, liver *qi* generates heart *qi*, heart *qi* generates spleen *qi*, spleen *qi* generates lung *qi*, and lung *qi* generates kidney *qi*.

Looking at it in terms of husband and wife, kidney *qi* controls heart *qi*, heart *qi* controls lung *qi*, lung *qi* controls liver *qi*, liver *qi* controls spleen *qi*, and spleen *qi* controls kidney *qi*.

In other words, the kidneys are the husband of the heart, the mother of the liver, the wife of the spleen, and the child of the lungs. The liver is the husband of the spleen, the mother of the heart, the wife of the lungs, and the child of the kidneys. The heart is the husband of the lungs, the mother of the spleen, the wife of the kidneys, and the child of the liver. The lungs are the husband of the liver, the mother of the kidneys, the wife of the heart, and the child of the spleen. The spleen is the husband of the kidneys, the mother of the lungs, the wife of the liver, and the child of the heart.

The heart manifests on the inside in the blood vessels, on the outside in the complexion. It uses the tongue as its sensory gateway. It is controlled by the kidneys and exerts impact on by the lungs, relating to them in the mode of husband and wife. Receiving liver *qi*, it burgeons; encountering spleen [*qi*], it decreases, relating to them in the mode of mother and child.

The kidneys manifest on the inside in the bones, on the outside in overall appearance. They use the ears as their sensory gateway. They are controlled by the spleen and exert impact on the heart, relating to them in the mode of husband and wife. Receiving lung *qi*, they burgeon; encountering liver [*qi*], they decrease, relating to them in the mode of mother and child.

The liver manifests on the inside in the muscles, on the outside in the nails. It uses the eyes as its sensory gateway. It is controlled by the lungs and exerts impact on the spleen, relating to them in the mode of husband and wife. Receiving kidney *qi*, it burgeons; encountering heart [*qi*], it decreases, relating to them as in the mode of mother and child.

The lungs manifest on the inside in the skin, on the outside in the body hair. They use the nostrils as their sensory gateway. They are controlled by the heart and exert impact on the liver, relating to them in the mode of husband and wife. Receiving spleen, they burgeon; encountering kidney [*qi*], they decrease, relating to them in the mode of mother and child.

The spleen manifests on the inside in the organs, where it summarily nurtures the heart, kidneys, liver, and lungs. On the outside, it matches the flesh. It uses the lips and mouth as its sensory gateway, and determines the coming and going of the breath. It is controlled by the liver and exrts impact on the kidneys, relating to them in the mode of husband and wife. Receiving heart *qi*, it burgeons; encountering lung [*qi*], it decreases, relating to them in the mode of mother and child.

Such are the workings of five phases within human beings, either generating or controlling each other and transferring *qi* along the lines of husband and wife or mother and child. All decline and dominance happen this way.

Lü asked: The heart being fire, how can one get this fire to descend? The kidneys being water, how can one get this water to ascend? The spleen being earth, and earth occupying the center, when it receives fire, it burgeons, but is it also controlled by water from below? The lungs being metal, and metal occupying the high position, when they receive fire, they diminish, but can their *qi* also be generated by water?

When the organs are in the cycle of mutual generation, they transfer *qi* to each other yet are at a distance. When they control each other, they get close yet have a hard time shifting along. So, how can we best deal with the process of mutual diminishing and control?

Zhong replied: The five phases always return to the source, guided and pulled by the *qi* of cosmic oneness. Primordial yang ascends and generates perfect water; through creative transformation perfect water generates perfect *qi*; through creative transformation perfect *qi* generates yang spirit. From the beginning, as soon as the five phases assume their positions, they interact alternating in the mode of husband and wife.

Thus, the kidneys are water; they contain metal, which originally generates water. In practice, it is essential to recognize the metal within water. Water is originally tamed by earth, so when assembling the medicine, it is essential to get earth to return to water. The dragon is the image of the liver; the tiger is the physical form of the lungs. The dragon, being yang, emerges from the Li palace; the tiger, being yin, arises in the Kan position.

When the five phases follow their natural course, *qi* is transferred from mother [to child]. The period between Zi [midnight] and Wu [noon] is accordingly when one can generated yang within yang. When the five phases invert, fluid flows from husband to wife. The period between Wu and Zi is accordingly when one can refine yang within yin. If it does not get any yang, yin cannot mature. Eventually, there is no more yin and one will not die. If it does not get any yin, yang cannot grow. Eventually, yin is eliminated and one can live long.

Lü asked: The five phases take their origin from the *qi* of cosmic oneness of yin and yang. What exactly is this *qi* of cosmic oneness?

Zhong replied: The *qi* of cosmic oneness appears when father and mother have intercourse; through creative transformation their essence and blood turns into physical form. During gestation, the kidneys generate the spleen, the spleen generates the liver, the liver generates the lungs, the lungs generate the heart, the heart generates the small intestine, the small intestine generates the large intestine, the large intestine generates the gallbladder, the gallbladder generates the stomach, and the stomach generates the bladder.

In this process, yin takes essence and blood and transforms them into physical form while yang emerges at the moment when life first begins, a single spark of primordial yang settling in the two kidneys. Now, the kidneys are water, which contains fire and ascends as *qi* to move to the heart. The heart is yang, and yang fuses with yang. When it reaches its great ultimate, it again generates yin. The accumulated *qi* then generates fluid, which naturally descends from the heart and reverts to the kidneys.

The liver is originally the mother of the heart and the child of the kidneys; it transfers kidney *qi* to the heart. The lungs are originally the wife of the heart and the mother of the kidneys; they transfer heart fluid to the kidneys. *Qi* and fluid in the body keep on ascending and descending just like yin and yang between heaven and earth. Liver and lungs transfer *qi* just like the sun and the moon keep on coming and going.

The five phases are a way to express their rhythm. As regards their interaction and fusion, generation and maturation, they all originate from primordial yang, the *qi* of cosmic oneness. *Qi* generates from fluid; fluid generates from *qi*. The kidneys are the root of *qi*; the heart is the source of fluid. If adepts keep the root of their life force firm and stable, vaguely and indistinctly, perfect water will naturally grow within *qi*. If they keep the source of the heart clear and pure, obscurely and mysteriously, perfect fire will naturally grow within fluid. From the fire they know how to collect the perfect dragon; from the water they know how to obtain the perfect tiger. Next, dragon and tiger mate and transform into the yellow sprout, which transforms further into the great medicine. This is called the golden elixir. Once the golden elixir is produced, they can become spirit immortals.

Lü asked: I see. Once the golden elixir is produced, one gains liberation from material reality and can ascend to the immortals to take up residence on the ten continents. But what is the yellow sprout?

Zhong replied: It is none other than the perfect dragon and the perfect tiger.

Lü asked: And what are this dragon and tiger?

Zhong replied: The dragon here is not the liver, but the dragon of pure yang. It arises in perfect water at the Li palace. The tiger here is not the lungs, but the tiger of perfect yin. It arises in perfect fire at the Kan position.

7. Water and Fire

Lü asked: People who want to live long need to refine and produce the golden elixir. To refine the golden elixir, they first need to assemble the yellow sprout. To obtain the yellow sprout, they must get hold of the dragon and tiger. You have said that the perfect dragon emerges from the Li palace and the perfect tiger is generated in the Kan position. Li and Kan contain water and fire. What exactly is this water and fire?

Zhong replied: Water in the human body manifests in the four oceans, five lakes, nine rivers, and three islands. Flowery pond, nephrite pond, phoenix pond, celestial pond, jade pond, chaos pond, primordial pool, lofty garden, spirit water, golden wave, jasper fluid, jade spring, yang cream, white snow—these are some of the many names and appellations for it, too numerous to list completely.

Fire in the human body manifests in ruling, subordinate, and common fire. All three originate from primordial yang and generate perfect *qi*. If perfect *qi* holds together, there is health; if it is weak, sickness arises. If people waste and scatter perfect *qi*, release and lose primordial yang, it will soon be all gone. When pure yin is all that's left, primordial spirit leaves the body, and there is death.

Lü asked: In the human body, then, there is a spark of primordial yang that promotes the three forms of fire. Since they arise within a multiplicity of water and a host of yin forces, they are easy to scatter and hard to kindle. A state of weak yang and burgeoning yin, little fire and much water causes people to decline and age rapidly, making it impossible for them to attain long life. What can one do about this?

Zhong replied: The heart is the ocean of blood; the kidneys are the ocean of *qi*; the brain is the ocean of marrow; and the spleen and stomach are the ocean of grain. They are the four oceans. The five organs each have their own fluid, located in their respective positions of east, west, south, north, and center. They are the five lakes. The small intestine is twenty-four feet long and meanders in nine bends. They are the nine rivers. Its lowest section, moreover, is known as the primordial pool.

The top of the head is called the upper island; the heart is the middle island; and the kidneys are the lower island. The three islands are also described as root, source, and lofty garden. The flowery pond is beneath the yellow court; the nephrite pond emerges in front of the cinnabar tower. The chaos pond connects to the jade capital above; the celestial pond bubbles up right in the inner courtyard. The phoenix pond sits between the heart and the lungs; the jade pond is inside the lips and teeth.

Spirit water is generated from *qi*, while golden waves drip down from heaven. Where the red dragon resides, there naturally arise the jasper fluid and jade spring. After the embryo is formed, white snow and yang cream appear. When they start to drip down, one gets them to burgeon with rich fluid and strong flames. This is first called jade fluid, then golden fluid; both can be reverted to the elixir field. Working with reduction and augmentation in proper measure, one can properly bathe [the embryo].

Doing so first in the middle field, then the lower field, adepts can refine the physical form. Then the jade medicine and the golden flower turn into a body of yellow and white; rich liquor and sweet dew refine into a substance of extraordinary fragrance. Such are the benefits of managing water efficiently.

When common fire ascends, it supports kidney *qi* and generates perfect water. Kidney water then ascends to fuse with heart fluid and generates perfect *qi*. At a minor level, this eliminates all diseases; at a major level, it serves to refine material reality and heat the elixir. Quickening the celestial orbits, fire arises and one can incinerate the body; contracting the yang barrier, one can revert the cinnabar medicine to the prime. From here one should arrange things in the system of the nine continents to nurture yang spirit; incinerate the entanglements of the three deathbringers to eliminate the yin ghosts. Moving up, push through the three barriers; moving down, dissolve the seven material souls. Refine the physical form into *qi* and become light and lofty as if flying. Refine *qi* into spirit and gain liberation from the womb like a cicada [shedding its shell]. These are the benefits of managing fire efficiently.

Lü asked: Earlier I heard in your instructions that the greatest affliction is a state of too little fire and too much water, which causes people to rapidly age and decline. Next I listened to your lofty discourse describing the effectual experiences of water and fire. Ultimately, how do they transform, and what can one do to increase of what there is little and strengthen what is weak?

Zhong replied: Working in the rhythm of two and eight, yin dissolves; through three and nine, yang is enhanced. The bright, red golden elixir can thereby be completed. Working through seven cycles and nine circulations, the immortal embryo develops naturally. Perfect *qi* resides in the heart, which is the source of all fluid. Primordial yang resides in the kidneys, which form the ocean of *qi*. The bladder houses common fire, but with common fire alone it cannot function. Rather, it must also store secretions and fluids. If people do not comprehend the core workings of heaven, they can never fathom the mysterious principles. Daoist adepts then have a hard time transmuting [*qi*] and will not be able to avoid sickness, disease, and death.

Lü asked: So, when you speak of transmutation, you mean the ability to enhance yang and dissolve yin. How exactly can one produce the golden elixir and get the immortal embryo to develop naturally?

Zhong replied: The heart and kidneys in the human body are 8.4 inches apart, matching the distance between the positions of heaven and earth. *Qi* and fluid each reach their great ultimate and generate each other, matching the interaction and fusion of yin and yang. One day has twelve double-hours, matching the twelve months of the year.

The heart generates fluid, however, it does not do spontaneously. Rather, it needs fluid descending from the lungs, which the heart then transfers. Fluid follows the mode of husband and wife, moving first up then down. When it returns to the lower field, we speak of the wife returning to the husband's palace.

The kidneys generate *qi*, however, they do not do so spontaneously. Rather, they need *qi* ascending from the gallbladder, which the kidneys then transfer. *Qi* follows the mode of mother and child, moving first down then up. When it moves to the prime in the center [middle field], we speak of the husband returning to the wife's chamber.

Liver *qi* guides kidney *qi*, moving first down then up all the way to the heart. The heart is fire. When the two *qi* interact, steam suffuses the lungs. When lung fluid descends to the heart, it issues from there and we say that the heart generates fluid. This fluid generated in the heart, if never allowed to disperse or scatter, becomes perfect water.

Lung fluid transfers to heart fluid, moving first up then down all the way to the kidneys. The kidneys are water. When the two waters interact, they inundate the bladder. Bladder *qi* then ascends to the kidneys and gives rise to kidneys *qi*. This *qi* generated in the kidneys, if never allowed to dissolve or be destroyed, becomes perfect fire.

Perfect fire arises from water. Blurred and indistinct, it appears as a substance: look at it and do not see it; grab for it and do not catch it [*Daode jing* 14]. Perfected water arises from fire. Obscure and mysterious, it appears as an essence: see it but do not grasp it, grasp it, yet cannot make it go.

Lü asked: The kidneys are water. *Qi* generated from water is called perfect fire. So, what substance is there in this fire? The heart is fire. Fluid generated from fire is called perfect water. What essence is there in this water? The substance in the fire, the essence in the water have no form or shape to pursue. If one pursues them, they are hard to obtain. And once obtained, how should one apply them?

Zhong replied: All the highest sages and accomplished Dao-masters of the past as much as today have never worked without these two. They fuse and transform into the yellow sprout; following the correct count, the [immortal] embryo develops fully and they can they produce the great medicine. These two, then, are none other than the perfect dragon and the perfect tiger.

8. Dragon and Tiger[3]

Lü asked: The dragon is originally the image of the liver, while the tiger is the physical form of the lungs. This being so, a fluid is generated in the midst of heart fire. This fluid is in fact perfect water. Within this water, obscure and mysterious, the perfect dragon is deeply hidden. Thus, the dragon does not reside in the liver, but emerges from the Li palace. How is this so?

Similarly, fire is generated in the midst of kidney water. This fire is in fact perfect fire. Within this fire, blurred and indistinct, the perfect tiger is deeply hidden. Thus, the tiger does not reside in the lungs but emerges from the Kan position. How does that happen?

Zhong replied: The dragon is a being of yang. It flies up and soars into heaven, and when it howls, clouds arise. In charge of moisture, it benefits the myriad beings. Among images, it is the green dragon; among the directions, it is Jia and Yi [east]; among the [five] substances, it is wood; among the seasons, it is spring; among the virtues, it is benevolence; among the trigrams, it is Zhen; among the five organs of the human body, it is the liver.

The tiger is a being of yin. It runs around on the earth, and when it roars, wind blows. In control of mountains, it awes and controls the hun-

3 This section is also translated in Pregadio 2019, 61-67.

dred beasts. Among images, it is the white tiger; among the directions, it is Geng and Xin [west]; among the [five] substances, it is metal; among the seasons, it is fall; among the virtues, it is righteousness; among the trigrams, it is Dui; among the five organs, it is the lungs.

Now, the liver is yang, yet it resides in a position of yin. For this reason, kidney *qi* transfers to liver *qi*: following the mode of mother and child, water generates wood. When kidney *qi* is sufficient, liver *qi* is generated, and once this happens, it is possible to eliminate excess yin in the kidneys and allow the *qi* of pure yang to ascend.

Similarly, the lungs are yin, yet they reside in a position of yang. For this reason, heart fluid transfers to lung fluid: following the mode of husband and wife, fire controls metal. When heart fluid reaches the lungs, lung fluid is generated, and once this happens, it is possible to eliminate all excess yang in the heart and allow the fluid of pure yin to descend.

Since the liver corresponds to yang, it eliminates excess yin in the kidneys. Therefore, we know that the moment the *qi* passes through the liver, it turns into pure yang. Pure yang *qi* in turn contains the water of perfect oneness. Blurred and indistinct, it is formless. We call it the yang dragon. Similarly, as the lungs correspond to yin, they cut off excess yang in the heart. Therefore, we know that the moment the fluid passes through the lungs, it turns into pure yin. Pure yin fluid in turn supports the *qi* of rightful yang. Obscure and mysterious, it is invisible. We call it the yin tiger.

Qi ascends while fluid descends, but normally they cannot fuse. However, when the water of perfect oneness in the *qi* encounters fluid, they fuse with each other. When the *qi* of rightful yang in the fluid encounters *qi*, they spontaneously gather. During the transmission process, if adepts apply specific methods to control it, they can prevent kidney *qi* from being released and lost and assemble the water of perfect oneness. Similarly, they can make sure that heart fluid does not disperse and scatter, and assemble the *qi* of rightful yang from it. When mother and child meet, they long for and take care of each other.

Within a day, the medicine grows to the size of a grain of rice. If adepts continue the practice for a hundred days without fail, the medicine is fully potent. After two hundred days, the sagely womb is stable; and after three hundred days, the immortal embryo is fully formed. "In physical form like a pellet or pill, it has the color of a mandarin orange" [*Baopuzi* 6]. We call this the cinnabar medicine. As it rests permanently in the lower field, one can maintain the physical form and stay on earth, living on and on for vast kalpas. This is what we call an earth immortal.

Lü asked: Kidney water generates *qi*, which contains the water of perfect oneness. This is called the yin tiger. When the tiger encounters fluid, they join. heart fire generates fluid, which contains the *qi* of rightful yang. This is called the yang dragon. When the dragon encounters *qi*, they fuse.

Things of the same kind gather together while beings of different types separate—such is the principle of nature.

This means that, when *qi* is generated, fluid descends. But does the water of perfect oneness within *qi* not always follow fluid and descend to the five organs? When fluid is generated, *qi* ascends. But does the *qi* of rightful yang within fluid not always follow *qi* and ascend to the twelve-storied tower? If perfect water descends as it follows fluid, the tiger cannot interact with the dragon. If perfect yang ascends following *qi*, the dragon cannot fuse with the tiger. If the two do not fuse, how can one obtain the yellow sprout? And without the yellow sprout, how can one ever obtain the great medicine?

Zhong replied: When kidney *qi* is generated, it is like great yang [the sun] rising over the ocean: mist and dew cannot overshadow its light. When fluid descends, it is like a falling curtain: how can it be strong enough to overcome *qi*? And if *qi* is strong, the water of perfect oneness naturally burgeons. When heart fluid is generated, it is like stern heaven [cold climate] killing living beings: all wailing and crying cannot combat this cold. *Qi* ascends like a feathered fan: how can it be strong enough to overcome fluid? And if fluid is abundant, the *qi* of rightful yang is either strong or weak, a state yet to be determined.

Lü asked: *Qi* and water grow at specific times. At certain times *qi* is generated; if it is strong, the water of perfect oneness burgeons. At other times fluid is generated; if if burgeons, the *qi* of rightful yang also flourishes. But I still do not understand what exactly is meant by burgeoning and decline.

Zhong replied: Kidney *qi* disperses and scatters easily, and it is hard to obtain the perfect tiger. Heart fluid accumulates and gathers with difficulty, and it is easy to lose the perfect dragon. The myriad scrolls of elixir scriptures in their various discourses and explanations never go beyond yin and yang, and the things we call yin and yang, whether subtle or gross, are none other than dragon and tiger. Only one or two in ten thousand Daoist adepts are really in the know. Most listen a lot and read widely so that, although they may understand the principles of dragon and tiger, they do not really comprehend the timing of their mating or know the right methods of assembling and collecting [the ingredients]. For this reason, advanced adepts in the past as much as today, though they may dedicate themselves to cultivation until their hair turns white, only reach a minor level of accomplishment. They may continue the generations and extend their years, but will never even hear of transcendence and liberation. This is because they never manage to get dragon and tiger to mate, thus failing to assemble the yellow sprout and produce the cinnabar medicine.

9. The Cinnabar Medicine

Lü asked: I now understand the principles of the dragon and tiger, but may I please learn what exactly you call the great medicine of the golden elixir [cinnabar]?

Zhong replied: A medicine is something that cures disease. Now, disease comes in three forms [suffering, old age, death]. Subject to wind, lying down in dampness, exposed to heat, and wading through cold, going to extremes in labor and leisure, losing all rhythm in hunger and satiation, continuously ailing in one way or another: this is suffering, and suffering is the disease of the seasons.

Next, refusing to dedicate themselves to cultivation and instead indulging in emotions and letting the intention run wild, scattering and losing primordial yang, dispersing and diminishing perfect *qi*, with increasing years getting dry and desiccated: this is old age, and old age is the disease of the years.

Third, *qi* all gone, the physical organism hollow, the spirit soul dissolved, and the spirit drummed out, all tones reduced to a single sound, the four limbs without a ruler, the body lying still and decaying in the ground in the wilderness: this is death, and death is the disease of human life.

The reason why there is the disease of the seasons is that spring, summer, fall, and winter revolve through states of cold, heat, warmth, and coolness. Yang in excess and yin in deficiency require a cure through cooling; yin in excess and yang in deficiency require a cure through warming. Old people are cold a lot, while youngsters tend to be hot; obese people have too much saliva, while rich folks have too much accumulation. In males, disease grows from *qi*; in females, afflictions originate in blood.

To cure, one must supplement what is empty, release what is full, protect what is weak, and reduce what is excessive. For minor cases, there are acupuncture and moxibustion; for major ones, there are herbal remedies and medicines. Continuously ailing and suffering from the disease of the seasons, people rely on learned adepts and respected physicians, manage their diet in accordance with the disease, and thereby gain a modicum of healing.

However, what can be done about the disease of old age? How can one cure the disease of death? Skilled physicians of old could irrigate the colon and enhance the flesh, but none was able to smooth out facial wrinkles and restore a youthful complexion. Skilled physicians of old could perform head surgery and mend broken limbs, but none was able to preserve the body to remain in the world and attain long life.

Lü asked: Continuous ailments and the disease of the seasons can be cured by respected physicians and efficacious medicines. But how can one cure the disease of ongoing decline and aging years, the hardship of exhausted *qi* and limited life-destiny? Are there medicines for that?

Zhong replied: Now, disease comes in three forms. The disease of the seasons can be cured with medicines made from grasses and trees. Those of human life and of the years can be cured with two medicines, the internal and external elixir.

Lü asked: What, then, is the external elixir?

Zhong replied: In antiquity, when the Lord of Highest Prime transmitted Dao to humanity, he outlined the principles of the continuous ascent and descent [of *qi*] through heaven and earth, the patterns of the sun and the moon coming and going. From that came elixir scriptures that filled the world and allowed people to learn about the great Dao.

For example, Guangchengzi [Master of Vast Completion] taught the Yellow Emperor, who practiced according to his methods in his spare time from governing, yet for the longest time never saw any success. Guangchengzi then told him that the heart and kidneys contained perfect *qi* and perfect water and that *qi* and water held perfect yin and perfect yang, and taught him to fuse them into the great medicine. He also pointed out that they are just like the precious ores hidden among metals and minerals and outlined how to use the materials deep inside Mount Kongtong to refine the great elixir.

Among the eight minerals use only cinnabar [lit. vermilion sand], and from this collect mercury. Among the five metals use only black lead, and from this collect silver. Mercury is like the yang dragon; silver is like the yin tiger. Heart fire is like red like cinnabar [lit. sand]; kidney water is black like lead. Throughout the year, fire them in accordance with the seasons, never losing the rhythm of Qian and Kun. Throughout the month, fire them with the proper reduction and augmentation, naturally matching civil and martial divisions.

Erect a three-storied furnace, each story nine inches in height, square on the outside and round on the inside. It assembles the *qi* of the eight directions and imitates the phases of the four seasons. Reflecting the image of a golden cauldron, it harbors lead and mercury: it is no different from the lungs with their fluid. The main ingredient is sulfur, which combines with the numinous sand: it is just like the yellow dame.

After three years, adepts reach a minor level of accomplishment: taking the elixir, they can eliminate the hundred diseases. After six years, they reach a medium level: taking the elixir, they can extend their years. After nine years, they reach a major level: taking the elixir, they can lift off and ascend spontaneously. Strong in physique and with mighty arms, they easily travel a thousand or ten thousand miles. Although they cannot move on to Penglai, they can remain among humanity earth for vast kalpas without dying.

Lü asked: Throughout history many practitioners have refined the elixir but only a few have seen success. Why is that?

Zhong replied: There are three cases when practitioners fail to complete the elixir. They cannot tell whether the raw materials are genuine or fake and they they have no clue about the proper firing times for reduction and augmentation. They take precious ores and scatter them in the flames of the fire, thus burning them to dust and ashes, and also fail to observe the proper timing and confuse the days, so in the end do not succeed. This is the first case.

They may have good-quality raw materials, but they do not know the proper firing times. Or they may know the proper firing times, but lack the right raw materials. The two do not match up and in the end they do not succeed. This is the second case.

They may have good-quality raw materials and also work with the proper firing times, in the course of the year making no mistakes about the months, in the course of the month never getting the days wrong. Adding and decreasing according to the right count, advancing and withdrawing at the right times, the *qi* is sufficient and the elixir gets completed. However, then they are not ready to work with it externally, and the mysterious crane flies off into the void. They never get the chance to ingest the elixir and in the end they do not succeed. This is the third case.

Now, the raw materials are originally substances solidified from the marvelous *qi* of heaven and earth; the firing times are unique arts of attaining Dao developed through the dedicated cultivation of spirit immortals. In the age of the Three Sovereigns, the Yellow Emperor refined the elixir, completing it upon ninefold circulation. In the wake of the five emperors, Chaos Prime [Lord Lao] refined the elixir, completing it in the course of three years.

Then it came to the Warring States period, when murderous *qi* polluted the air, floating corpses filled the wilderness, and there was no way for substances to receive the marvelous *qi* of heaven and earth. As a result, there were no proper raw materials in the world. Those who knew the right methods fled into mountains and valleys to escape from suffering, old age, and death. Whatever elixir techniques and immortality methods they recorded on bamboo and silk have long since been lost and destroyed and are no longer available in the world.

Had there been proper raw materials in the world of dust, the First Emperor of Qin would not have sought them out in the isles of the ocean. Had there been correct elixir techniques in the world of grime, Wei Boyang would not have had to consult the *Yijing*. Instead, there were numerous oral transmissions and strong convictions, which deluded later seekers and led them astray, ruined many tens of thousands of families but did not lead to even single successful completion. Looking for the elixir on the outside, therefore, is entirely futile.

Lü asked: The principles of the external elixir go back to Guangchengzi. Applying its internal system in accordance with the methods and rules it is possible to complete it successfully over nine years. Still, good raw materials are hard to find, correct concoction techniques are hard to obtain, and ultimately one manages to lift off flying but cannot transcend ordinary life, enter the ranks of the sages, and return to the ten continents. So, may I please learn more about the internal medicine?

Zhong replied: Do not dismiss external medicines as totally useless. Daoist adepts who come to realization only in their later years tend to be not very firm and stable in their root and source. The kidneys are the root of *qi*; if the root is not deep, the leaves cannot flourish. The heart is the source of fluid; if the source is not clear, the current cannot be long. They, therefore, must make use of the five metals and eight minerals over accumulated days and many months to refine them into the three substances.

The three substances each come in three levels, making a total of nine. Together they are called the great elixir of dragon and tiger. They help to bind perfect *qi*, making it possible to refine the physical form, remain in the world, and become as light as if flying. If one then continues to cultivate the internal system, is aware of the right timing of [*qi*] interaction and fusion, and knows the correct methods of assembling and collecting, the immortal embryo is soon produced. Then a day will come when one can attain transcendence and liberation.

Some people never realize this and hold on to the external elixir. Cooking it over fire for many days, they take it in the desire to ascend to the celestial realm—it really is ridiculous! Rather than pursuing the source of external medicines, adepts should examine the principles of the internal elixir. Its raw materials emerge from the heart and kidneys—every one has them. They originate with heaven and earth, clearly visible every day. The firing times work according to the rhythm of the coming and going of the sun and moon, and match the pattern of the intercourse of husband and wife. In due course, the immortal embryo grows from perfect *qi*. In this *qi*, there is another *qi*, like a dragon nurturing a pearl. When the great medicine is complete, yang spirit emerges. Beyond the human body, there appears another body, like a cicada shedding its skin. The internal medicine originates from the fusion of dragon and tiger and their turning into the yellow sprout. When this is mature, it divides into lead and mercury.

10. Lead and Mercury

Lü asked: The internal medicine is nothing but dragon and tiger. The tiger emerges from the Kan palace and is essentially water within *qi*. The dragon emerges from the Li palace and is essentially *qi* within water. Mercury collected from cinnabar in the external medicine is just like the yang dragon; silver collected from lead is like the yin tiger.

Lead and mercury being external, why is it that the dragon and tiger mate and transform into the yellow sprout, and the yellow sprout grows to divide into lead and mercury? In other words, what is meant by lead and mercury in the context of the internal medicine?

Zhong replied: That which encompasses the material of celestial oneness, the master of the five metals, is black lead. Lead generates silver; it is the mother of silver. That which stimulates the *qi* of great yang [sun], the master of the host of minerals, is cinnabar. Cinnabar generates mercury; mercury is the child of cinnabar. It is difficult to collect silver from lead and mercury from cinnabar. When silver and mercury fuse, they naturally amalgamate into precious ore. These are the fundamental principles of lead and mercury as evident externally.

Now, when we speak of the internal system, they manifest in the human body. Commentaries and treatises in the past as much as today differ vastly in their description, offering all kinds of theories about their mystery and wonder. Basically, at the moment when father and mother engage in intercourse, essence and blood fuse and engender perfect *qi*, then settle this substance in the mother's palace of pure yin while storing the spirit in a place where yin and yang are as yet undifferentiated. After three hundred days the embryo is complete; after 5,000 days, the *qi* is fully viable.

In terms of the five phases, since the human body fundamentally consists of essence and blood, water is primary. In terms of the five organs, since essence and blood create physical form and image, the kidneys come first. Kidney water contains the perfect *qi* of father and mother, first received at conception. This perfect *qi* is hidden deep within the internal kidneys [testes]: it is lead. The kidneys generate *qi*, and the water of perfect oneness within this *qi* we call the perfect tiger.

Alternatively we also speak of it as silver within lead. Kidney *qi* transfers to liver *qi*, and from there moves into heart *qi*. At the heart *qi* reaches its great ultimate and generates fluid. This fluid contains the *qi* of rightful yang; what we call cinnabar is none other than heart fluid. Mercury, then, is the *qi* of rightful yang within heart fluid. Accumulate *qi* and fluid to form a zygote, then transfer it into the yellow court. Stoking the fire without fail, the immortal embryo develops naturally. This matches the amalgamation of silver within lead and mercury, their forging into precious ore.

Lü asked: Among the five metals, silver emerges from lead; among the eight minerals, mercury issues from cinnabar. Placing them into a cauldron or vessel, they fuse into a medicine or remedy. Mercury naturally turns into cinnabar, and silver spontaneously becomes precious ore.

However, when it comes to lead in the human body, how does one collect the silver? How does one get mercury out of cinnabar? How does mercury again produce cinnabar? And how does silver turn into precious ore?

Zhong replied: Lead originates when the perfect *qi* of father and mother fuse into one; utterly pure, it does not separate. After the physical form is complete, it is stored in the kidneys. The two kidneys match each other and together push the *qi* to ascend: this is the *qi* of primordial yang. This *qi*, moreover, contains water, which is called the water of perfect oneness. The water follows the *qi* on its upward movement, so that whenever the *qi* stops, the water also stops; whenever the *qi* scatters, the water also scatters. Like mother and child, they never separate.

Many advanced practitioners are only aware of the *qi* and never notice the water. The process of taking the water of perfect oneness and fusing it with the *qi* of rightful yang is described as dragon and tiger mating and turning into the yellow sprout. The yellow sprout is none other than the great medicine. Its raw materials fundamentally consist of the water of perfect oneness that forms a zygote by joining the *qi* of rightful yang. This is just like the perfect *qi* of father and mother fusing at conception, essence and blood creating the first zygote.

After it develops for three hundred days, the embryo is complete and its *qi* fully viable. When the physical form is ready, spirit arrives, and the infant separates from the mother. Although outside her physical form, they remain energetically fused—their fusion allows one physical form to generate another.

In Daoist adepts, kidney *qi* interacts with heart *qi* so that the water of perfect oneness within the *qi* supports and carries the *qi* of rightful yang. When *qi* interacts with water, they create a zygote that looks like a grain of millet. Steam and nurture it without stopping. First use yin to retain yang, then use yang to refine yin. *Qi* thus turns into essence, essence turns into mercury, mercury turns into cinnabar, and cinnabar turns into the golden elixir. Once the golden elixir is produced, perfect *qi* naturally grows. Refine this *qi* into spirit and attain transcendence and liberation. Transform into a fiery dragon to leave the dark road [of ordinary life] behind; stride upon a mysterious crane to fly off to the isles of Penglai.

Lü asked: When one physical form interacts with another, the two fuse and generate another physical form; when one *qi* merges with another, the two fuse and generate another *qi*. The correct count of this process does not exceed three hundred days, then the new physical form separates. After that, there are males and females with different physical endowments. Why, then, are they the same with regard to the color and consistency of cinnabar sand?

Zhong replied: When father and mother join in their physical form, the essence of the father advances first and the blood of the mother follows behind. If the blood is enveloped by the semen, they form a female. In a female, yang is inside and yin is outside. As the image of the mother, blood is on the outside.

If the blood of the mother advances first and the essence of the father follows behind, the essence is enveloped by the blood and they form a male. In a male, yin is inside and yang is outside. The image of the father, essence is on the outside.

What we call blood in this context is originally generated by the heart, but it contains no *qi* of rightful yang; essence in contrast is originally generated by the kidneys, and it does contain *qi* of rightful yang. This *qi* of rightful yang is the foundation of mercury. When it fuses with the water of perfect oneness and enters the yellow court, mercury uses lead to heat up and steam while lead uses mercury to fire and boil. If lead never obtains any mercury it cannot develop the water of perfect oneness. If mercury never gets any lead, it cannot turn into the *qi* of pure yang.

Lü asked: Lead in the kidneys generates the *qi* of primordial yang, and this *qi* contains the water of perfect oneness: one may look at it but cannot see it. As lead connects with mercury, mercury generates the *qi* of rightful yang. When this is heated and refined through lead, the generated *qi* burgeons and issues the water of perfect oneness, enabling it to ascend.

Now, mercury is originally the *qi* of rightful yang; it fuses with the water of perfect oneness. Together they form a zygote and transfer it into the yellow court. This process is none other than the mating of dragon and tiger, yin and yang ceasing together. Using lead to heat up and steam them, won't there be too much yin? Won't perfect yang scatter? How, then, can one complete the great medicine and generate *qi* within *qi*?

Zhong replied: When kidney *qi* joins heart *qi*, it reaches its ultimate and generates fluid. This fluid contains the *qi* of rightful yang, which in due course fuses with the water of perfect oneness. This process we call the mating of dragon and tiger. Each day you obtain a quantity the size of a grain of millet, called the great medicine or golden elixir. Protect it and send it into the yellow court.

The yellow court is located below the spleen and stomach and above the bladder, north of the heart and south of the kidneys, west of the liver and east of the lungs. Clear at the top and turbid at the bottom, it bears four colors on the outside. Its size is big enough to hold two pints; its pathways connect to the eight channels.

The medicine thus obtained stays here day and night. If adepts assemble the medicine but do not stoke the fire properly, it will disperse, unable to remain in place. Similarly, if they stoke the fire without first assembling the medicine, the yang within yin will escape. They can then only issue kidney *qi* to warm the prime below.

To assemble the medicine at the right time and stoke the fire in the proper count, adepts must obtain *qi* from lead. Then they stoke the fire to make sure the great medicine is firm and stable and settles firmly in the lower field. This is called the method of selection and supplementation.

If they next refine mercury to supplement the elixir field, they can extend their years and increase longevity, becoming an earth immortal. If they assemble the medicine and use it to reduce primordial lead, they can work with quickening the gold crystal by pulling back the elbows. Once they have reduced lead, they must augment mercury.

If they do not augment mercury and only revert essence upward to nourish the brain, how can they ever generate perfect *qi*? If perfect *qi* is not generated, how can yang spirit ever be fully formed? To augment mercury adepts must reduce lead. If they do not reduce lead and later proceed to refine mercury to supplement the elixir field, how they you ever turn it into cinnabar? And without cinnabar, how can they ever produce the golden elixir?

11. Reduction and Augmentation

Lü asked: To assemble the medicine, one must work with the water contained in the *qi*; to stoke the fire, one must rely on the *qi* within the lead. Ultimately it is necessary to reduce lead to complete the great medicine. Only by increasing mercury can one supplement the elixir field. What then, may I ask, is the principle behind reduction and augmentation?

Zhong replied: In the old days, the highest sages transmitted Dao to humanity, but because the people of high antiquity were pure and simple, dim and unknowing, they could not really understand the great Dao. Thus, the sages pointed to heaven and earth modeling the patterns of the continuous ascent and descent of yin and yang, causing the different *qi* of warm, cool, hot, and cold to change and thus creating seasonal time.

Ever since the correct count [of days] in one year was established, heaven and earth have maintained their cycle, always starting anew. Never losing Dao, they can live forever. Never concerned that human beings do not know this, they have continued to demonstrate the great principles, containing them in each aspect of life. For example, there are the principles of the coming and going of the sun and the moon in their essence and florescence as well as the times of the waxing and waning of the new, full, and half moon: all rising and setting regularly without fail.

Ever since the correct count [of days] in one month became viable, the sun and the moon have revolved around each other without stopping. Never losing Dao, they can live forever. Inevitably when cold goes heat comes, when heat goes cold comes—still the people of the world do not realize the pattern of the continuous ascent and descent of [*qi* through] heaven and earth.

When the moon is full it returns to being new, when it is new it again returns to being full—still the people of the world are not aware of the principle of coming and going of the sun and the moon. Lascivious intentions without end chisel away at their limited time. Wealth and nobility, luxury and splendor come and go like tiny sparks in floating dreams, while love and caring create a host of vexations that ultimately accumulate burdens for lives to come.

Always chasing entertainment in song and music, they soon face suffering and frustration; savoring fame and fortune, their ruddy complexion slips away. Greedy for material goods, hankering after ever more stuff, they speak of eternal life lasting ten thousand eons. Loving their children and attached to their grandchildren, they expect to continue their family as long as the world. Avaricious and crazed without stopping, they have delusions of long life, all the time dispersing and scattering primordial yang, releasing and losing perfect *qi*. Only when hideous diseases tie up their body does the day come when they curb their mind. Only when the great limitation [of death] approaches their head does the time arrive when they stop their bad habits.

The perfect immortals and highest sages take pity on people being stuck in the endless wheel of reincarnation and repeatedly falling into misery. They deeply desire for them to understand and realize the great Dao and attain a life as long as that of heaven and earth, the sun and the moon. Thus, they first explicate the principles of the continuous ascent and descent of yin and yang through heaven and earth; then they illustrate the principles of the coming and going of the sun and the moon in their essence and florescence.

Still, people do not comprehend the core workings of heaven and are unable to fathom their mystery and wonder. So, the sages liken internal to external medicines, explain inanimate through animate substances. Metals and minerals are inanimate and constitute external medicines; *qi* and fluid are animate and constitute internal ones. What is big are heaven and earth, what is bright are the sun and the moon, what is external are metals and minerals, and what is internal are *qi* and fluid. Once isolated, they must be augmented; once augmented, they must be reduced.

The principle of reduction and augmentation is at the root of all creative transformations. For example, after the winter solstice, yang ascends from earth, and the earth reduces its yin. As great yin is reduced, it becomes partial yin; at the same time minor yang is augmented and becomes yang brightness. Next, as partial yin is reduced further, it becomes minor yin; at the same time yang brightness is augmented further and becomes great yang. If this were not the case, cold would not turn into warmth nor warmth into heat.

Similarly, after the summer solstice, yin descends from heaven, and heaven reduces its yang. As great yang is reduced, it becomes yang brightness; at the same time minor yin is augmented and becomes partial yin. Next, as yang brightness is reduced further, it becomes minor yang; at the same time partial yin is augmented further and becomes great yin. If this was not the case, heat would not turn into coolness nor coolness into cold. Thus, yin and yang ascending and descending through heaven and earth and turning into the six *qi* are experiences due to reduction and augmentation.

Similarly the moon receives the bright part [lit. spirit soul] of the sun, and the sun transforms the dark portion [lit. material soul] of the moon. For the first fifteen days [of the month], the moon reduces its dark portion while the sun augments its bright part. Once its essence and florescence are completely full, its light radiates brightly above and below. If this were not the case, there would be no initial generation and transformation into the first quarter moon nor would the latter change into the full moon. Then again, the moon reverts to yin darkness, and the sun contains its yang essence.

Over the last fifteen days [of the month], the sun reduces its bright part while the moon augments its dark portion. Once its radiant glow is gone, its yin darkness is complete. If this were not the case, there would be no transformation into the last quarter moon nor would the latter change into the darkness of the new moon. Thus, the sun and the moon coming and going and transforming the nine [yang] and six [yin] are experiences due to reduction and augmentation.

People of the world do not comprehend the core workings of heaven and are unable to fathom their mystery and wonder. Thus, the perfect immortals and highest sages latch onto the fact that people in their hearts love to be free from disease and live long, and talk about refining metals and minerals into the great elixir. They use people's deep desires for yellow gold and white silver, and talk about transmuting lead and mercury into precious ore.

Their original intention is to make the people of the world realize the great principles: that by using inanimate metals and minerals, working with the proper firing times without fail, and reducing and augmenting to the correct count, they can extend their years and increase their longevity. They can also use animate materials in the human body, such as the *qi* of rightful yang and the water of perfect oneness.

Knowing the right time of their interaction and fusion and understanding the correct methods of isolation and collection, they can accumulate their days and extend their months. In *qi*, there is another *qi*; refining this *qi* into spirit, one can attain transcendence and liberation. In the past as much as today, these are hard to attain.

Both among humanity and in heaven, only a few have realized them, understanding that they must dedicate their will and mind fully to cultivation and completely eliminate all extraneous affairs. To imitate the eternal existence of heaven and earth, the sun and the moon, they stay firmly away from all erroneous paths and settle their mind fully on Dao. This, then, is the theory of the external medicine.

In the past as much as today, many sages and wise man have explicated this theory and taught it in the world. Still, the people of the world do not realize it. Cheating themselves and deceiving others, they lose the original intention of the teachers of old. They collect mercury from cinnabar, then infuse it into lead, and once the lead dominates the mercury, they transform it into tin. Not caring for their personal body or life-destiny, they madly scramble for wealth and material goods. Praising and promoting each other, they call themselves Daoist followers, yet in fact only love profit, their will focused entirely on the arts of [making more] yellow and white [gold and silver].

The former sages and highest immortals never quite managed to set up a system of transformation that matches human affinities, so they teach the theory of lead and mercury to the people, using it as an illustration of what goes on deep within. Lead and mercury that issue from metals and minerals are inanimate, yet they have the ability to transform into precious ore. The materials that issue from the body are animate and can be used just like lead and mercury. They all form part of the creative transformations, and once they start to transform creatively, they are vastly superior to any yellow or white substances.

Daoist adepts must study this thoroughly and never get stuck with the arts of the external elixir and the cinnabar stove. The lead within human beings has been there from the very beginning of heaven and earth. After great initiation, great material reality emerged, serving as the mother of the myriad beings. Following upon this, there was the great immaculate. Its substance was metal within water; its function was water within fire. It served as the ancestor of the five phases and the root of the great Dao.

Thus, to assemble the medicine, one must first augment mercury, and to do so one must reduce lead. For this reason, reduction and augmentation do not happen on the outside. From the lower field, they enter the upper field: this process is called quickening the gold crystal by pulling back the elbows, alternatively known as starting the river carriage to move the dragon and tiger. It is also called reverting essence upward to nourish the brain and thereby living long without dying.

Once lead has been reduced, mercury naturally descends from the center: it reverts from the middle to the lower field. This is when the dragon and tiger first mate and transform into the yellow sprout. The process is an inversion of the regular flow of the five phases. Through reducing lead and augmenting mercury, this process nourishes the immortal embryo, moving back and forth between the three fields. If the five phases were not inverted, dragon and tiger would not mate, the process would not move back and forth between the three fields, and the immortal embryo could never be complete in its *qi*.

Reducing lead and augmenting mercury for one hundred days allows the medicine to be fully potent; after two hundred days, the sacred womb is established; after three hundred days, the immortal embryo is fully formed and perfect *qi* is generated. Once perfect *qi* is generated, one can refine it into spirit. With the process complete, one can forget the physical form and the immortal embryo evolves of its own. This is called a spirit immortal.

Lü asked: What issues from metals and minerals are external lead and external mercury. Through systematic reduction and augmentation, they can be made into precious ore. What issues from the perfect *qi* of father and mother stored in people's kidneys is internal lead. What transforms on the basis of the medicine created through the fusion of perfect oneness and rightful yang is internal mercury. Through systematic reduction and augmentation, they can generate spirit. So, what we call perfect lead and perfect mercury—are they also subject to the process of reduction and augmentation?

Zhong replied: In the beginning adepts must use lead to obtain mercury, but it is a mistake to use lead all the way to the end. Instead, they must reduce it and enter it in the upper palace, preventing primordial *qi* from being transferred. When they then revert essence upward to enter the brain, they obtain mercury. When yin is all gone and yang is utterly pure, essence turns into cinnabar, and cinnabar turns into gold: this is pure lead.

Perfect lead is obtained from the fusion of perfect *qi* in the body. It is generated from perfect *qi*, which contains the water of perfect oneness. All five *qi* move to the prime and the three yang gather at the top of the head. The masters of old would describe this as golden essence moving down to enter the elixir field, then moving up again to refine the body and give it a golden hue.

This is none other than perfect lead moving up into the internal offices [organs] and from there issuing a white radiance. Once below, it moves up; once up, it moves down. Reverting it to the elixir field and refining the physical form is the work of the golden essence as it keeps coming and going. Once in front, it moves back; once in back, it moves forward. Incinerating the body and harmonizing the *qi*, this is the work of perfect *qi* in creative transformation. Without reduction and augmentation, its daily functioning would stop. How, then, would it be possible to have good effects from assembling the medicine and stoking the fire?

Lü asked: In the process of reduction and augmentation, how can we make sure that the up and down movements have the right measure, the forward and back pattern is without flaw?

Zhong replied: At the time of moving up, never move it down; at the time of reduction, never augment it. Moving up and down, coming and going without flaw and in minute precision: that is the power of the river carriage.

12. The River Carriage

Lü asked: What is the river carriage?

Zhong replied: Wise men of old observed how the floating clouds covering the sun produced shade and duly produced shelters; they watched how fallen leaves floating on the waves carried objects and duly produced boats; they also saw how tumbling brambles following the wind came and went, twisted and rolled without any effort of their own and duly produced carriages.

The carriage as an object matches the image of heaven and earth in its cover and chassis while its rotating wheel hubs are like the sun and the moon. Daoist adepts took inspiration from the carriage, notably its feature of moving on the earth and rolling on firm soil. Thus today there is this concept of the river carriage.

Now, the human body contains little yang and much yin, so that places named after water are exceedingly numerous. "Carriage" accordingly indicates the idea of transportation, while "river" expresses the image of much yin. Therefore, this river carriage does not move things on dry land but functions on water. Up and down, forward and back, it carries loads in the eight jasper [pools] and drives with speed through the four oceans.

Ascending toward heaven, it enters Kunlun [in the head] above; fully saturated there, it rushes to the phoenix towers [in the kidneys] below. Carrying primordial yang, it goes directly into the Li palace; transporting perfect *qi*, it meanders back to the office of long life. Coming and going throughout the nine provinces, it never stops even for an instant; moving all around the three peaks, it never stops for a moment.

Once dragon and tiger have mated, it carries the yellow dame into the yellow court; as soon as lead and mercury separate, it helps the golden lad transport them into the golden towers. A jade spring flowing through a thousand arteries, it moves for only half a segment of time and there are clear results; a golden fluid filling the entire vessel, it transports for barely more than a fraction of a segment and there is evidence of success.

If the five phases did not have this carriage for transport, they would have a hard time in their generation and maturation. If the *qi* of cosmic oneness were without it, how could it ever interact and engage with anything else? Matching the correct periods and following the right hours, one must rely on this carriage for transportation. Only then can one have the right experiences. In all affairs of nurturing yang and refining yin, one depends on it for transportation, and only then can be without error.

Before Qian and Kun were established in their purity, it was its work to get yin and yang to come and go. Before the inner universe was fully established, it was its work to get blood and *qi* to interact and flow. Moving from the outside in, it transports the pure and unadulterated *qi* of heaven and earth and guides primordial yang to the original palace. Moving from ordinary to sagely, it transports the perfect and rightful *qi* of yin and yang and supplements and refines the primordial spirit in the original body. Its work cannot be overestimated!

Lü asked: The river carriage having such wondrous functions, may I ask what its basic principles are? Ultimately residing in the human body, what things does it do? And once obtained, how should one use it?

Zhong replied: The river carriage arises in the rightful water of the northern direction. The kidneys contain perfect *qi*: the rightful *qi* generated from this is called the river carriage. Its concrete functions have rarely been taught in the past or today, since the perfect immortals kept it secret and never talked about it.

When Qian connects to Kun for the second time, they generate Kan, which is fundamentally water, and water is the essence of yin. When yang connects to this yin, yang reverses its course and carries yin as it returns home. In the process they pass Gen, Zhen, and Xun. Because yang attracts yin, it takes the yin out of the yang and transports it to Li, which is generated due to an infusion of yang. This is how the river carriage transports yin into the palace of yang.

Similarly, when Kun connects to Qian for the second time, they generate Li, which is fundamentally fire, and fire is the essence of yang. When yin connects to this yang, yin reverses its course and embraces yang as it returns home. In the process they pass Kun, Dui, and Qian. Because yin attracts yang, it takes the yang out of the yin and transports it to Kan, which is generated due to an infusion of yin. This is how the river carriage transports yang into the palace of yin.

Next, assemble the medicine in the nine palaces above and get it to move down into the yellow court. Reduce lead in the winding river below and transport it into the inner courtyard. At this point, revert jade fluid and golden fluid to the elixir field: transporting them to the right place, you can refine the physical form and make the water flow upward. Now, ruling fire and common fire start to refine the physical form: transporting them to the right place, you can heat the elixir and make the fire move down.

Next, the five *qi* move to the prime, each transported at the right time; the three flowers [yang] gather at the top of the head, each transported on the correct day. When the spirits gather, there are many demonic forces: transport perfect fire to incinerate the body and thereby eliminate the three deathbringers without a trace. When the medicine dries in the various oceans, transport misty juice to moisten it and thereby infuse water without making waves. All these are functions of the river carriage.

Lü asked: The river carriage is originally the rightful *qi* of the northern direction; it transports things without end, carrying and shifting yin and yang to make sure they each reach their completions and full production. Its functions and effects are more than one. Please, could you, venerable teacher, explain them in some more detail?

Zhong replied: The five phases run in a loop: they complete it and immediately start over. Through the technique of silently inverting their flow, one can mate dragon and tiger to transform into the yellow sprout: this is the river carriage in its minor mode. Quickening the gold crystal by pulling back the elbows and reverting it into the Niwan, one can reduce lead and augment mercury and produce the great medicine: this is great river carriage in its major mode.

Once the dragon and tiger have mated, they transform into the yellow sprout; once lead and mercury have fused, they form the great medicine. Perfect *qi* grows, the five *qi* move to the prime, the spirit of primordial yang is ready, and the three spirits transcend and move into the inner courtyard. When you complete the purple, golden elixir, your can fly off like a mysterious crane; when you achieve mercury white as jade, you can soar up like a fiery dragon.

A golden radiance of a myriad rays covers all ordinary bones with its bright glow; a fairy tree of a single trunk blossoms into a fresh flower of lustrous brilliance. One keeps entering and leaving [the world], all the while spontaneously increasing [in power]; one keeps coming and going, never encountering any obstacles. Transporting the spirit to enter the physical organism, one merges with time and flows along; transforming into a sage and leaving the ordinary behind, one become a feathered guest. This is the river carriage in its majestic [lit. purple] mode.

The appellations of these three carriage modes match the three levels of accomplishment: minor, medium, and major, each with confirmation experiences. They are entirely unlike the Three Vehicles of the Buddhist teaching, which refer to carriages drawn by ram, deer, and ox.

However, the Daoist system has three further carriage modes beyond the river carriage. Gathering fire and getting the heart to work it and the intention to send it out in order to combat illness and disease is called the messenger mode. Allow it to fully saturate the entire body from top to bottom, yin and yang fully fused, water and fire in the same place.

Remaining deeply still and manifesting sounds of thunder and lightning, this is called the thunder mode. If one's mind is run by mental projections and one's being is tethered by emotions, one is pushed by others and lets the *qi* of perfect yang scatter. Always subject to outside stimulation, one never knows a moment's rest.

Over long periods, this causes the *qi* to weaken and the physical structure to become emaciated, leading to decline and old age. It might also allow wayward [*qi*] and the five plagues into the body, severely impacting one's perfect *qi*. Since primordial yang has a hard time resisting, leading to old age, disease, and eventually death, this is called the broken mode.

Lü asked: When the five phases invert and dragon and tiger mate, the river carriage functions in its minor mode. When *qi* moves back and forth through the three fields and you quicken the gold crystal by pulling back the elbows, the river carriage is active in its major mode. How, then, does one get it to function in its majestic mode?

Zhong replied: Adepts of the cultivation of perfection after they have heard about the great Dao, must encounter an enlightened master, so they can comprehend the principles of the continuous ascent and descent [of *qi*] through heaven and earth, the correct count of the coming and going of the sun and the moon.

To begin, they match their rhythm to yin and yang; next, they learn to collect and scatter water and fire. After that, they assemble the medicine and stoke the fire, increase mercury and reduce lead: this sets up the river carriage in its minor mode.

From here, they quicken the gold crystal by pulling back the elbows and enter it into the top of the head, while allowing the great medicine to gradually mature in the yellow court. With one strike they open the three barriers and directly transcend into the inner courtyard, letting the *qi* ascend from behind and flow down in front [of the torso], supplementing above and refining below: this sets up the river carriage in its major mode.

At this point, they can revert jade fluid or golden fluid to the elixir field, which allows them to refine their physical form. After refining the physical form, they refine their *qi*; after refining their *qi*, they refine their spirit. Eventually they refine their spirit and merge with Dao, reaching a state known as full accomplishment of Dao. This allows them to leave the ordinary and enter immortality: it is the river carriage in its majestic mode.

13. Reversion to the Elixir Field

Lü asked: I do not quite dare to ask for instructions about the exact process of refining the physical form into *qi*, refining *qi* into spirit, and refining spirit to merge with Dao. However, what do you mean when you speak of reversion to the elixir [cinnabar] field?

Zhong replied: When I speak of cinnabar, I am not referring to a particular color: it is nothing like red or yellow. Nor am I referring to a particular flavor: it is nothing like sweet or blended. Rather, cinnabar is short for cinnabar or elixir field, of which there are three. The upper field is the abode of spirit; the middle field is the office of *qi*; the lower field is the region of essence. Essence generates *qi*, which resides in the middle elixir field. *Qi* generates spirit, which resides in the upper elixir field. Perfect water and perfect *qi* merge to create essence, and essence resides in the lower elixir field.

Daoist adepts all have the three elixir fields. However, as long as *qi* stays in the kidneys, it does not move to middle prime [elixir field]; as long as spirit remains in the heart, it does go beyond to the upper courtyard [elixir field]. Then the flower of essence cannot circulate and fuse with the others. In other words, although the three elixir fields are fully established in people, they have no use whatsoever.

Lü asked: Mystery within mystery: all people have life-destiny. Yet this life-destiny has no essence of its own. Thus I do not have any personal *qi*, but only the primordial yang of father and mother. Without essence and without *qi*, I do not have any personal spirit, but only the primordial spirit of father and mother. How, then, can one obtain essence, *qi*, and spirit—the so-called treasures of the three fields—and make sure they stay constantly in the three palaces, upper, middle, and lower?

Zhong replied: The kidneys generate *qi*, which contains the water of perfect oneness. As adepts cause this water to revert to the lower elixir field, essence nurtures the root of the life force and *qi* is spontaneously generated. The heart generates fluid, which contains the *qi* of rightful yang. As adepts get this *qi* to revert to the middle elixir field, *qi* nurtures the source of the life force and spirit is spontaneously generated. As they gather life force into spirit, they can merge with spirit and enter Dao. As they revert it to the upper elixir field, they can attain liberation.

Lü asked: There are three elixir fields: upper, middle, and lower. Reversion means [energies] move forward, then revert. Thus, we speak of reversion to the elixir field. May I please ask for more profound instruction and subtler details of its principles?

Zhong replied: Reversion to the elixir field comes in various forms: minor, major, seven-based, nine-based, golden and jade fluids. There is also reversion from the lower to the upper elixir field, from the upper to the middle field, from the middle to the lower field, from yang to yin, and from yin to yang. Not only are they different in name but their timing is varied and their setting is not alike.

Lü asked: What, then is minor reversion to the elixir field?

Zhong replied: Minor reversion begins in the lower prime, which is the ruler of the five organs and the root of the three fields. Water generates wood, wood generates fire, fire generates earth, earth generates metal, and metal generates water. This sequence of mutual generation never fails in its timing. As soon as one is generated, it moves on to the next that is not yet generated, matching the mutual affection between mother and child.

Similarly, fire controls metal, metal controls wood, wood controls earth, earth controls water, and water controls fire. This sequence of mutual control never loses its rhythm. As soon as one is controlled, it supplements the next that is not yet controlled, matching the interaction of husband and wife.

Qi and fluid revolve in cycles: once one is complete, they start again. From Zi [11 pm-1 am] to Wu [11 am-1 pm], yin and yang are in mutual generation; from Mao [5-7 am] to You [5-7 pm], they are in mutual constriction. Each day and night, they revert to the lower field, completing one loop. This is called minor reversion. Daoist adepts, when they assemble the medicine and stoke the fire, must focus on the lower elixir field and best start with this.

Lü asked: Now that I know about minor reversion to the elixir field, may I ask, what is its major form?

Zhong replied: Dragon and tiger mate and transform into the yellow sprout. Reducing lead and augmenting mercury, one produces the great medicine. The gold crystal arises in the palace of the Dark Warrior and perfect *qi* begins to ascend from below the mountain of Jade Capital.

Next, run the river carriage at the top of the peaks and drip jade fluid into the central crossing, then move it up into the upper field from the lower and again down into the lower field from the upper. As the *qi* rises in back and comes down in front [of the torso], the loop of circulation is fully established. This is called major reversion to the elixir field.

Daoist adepts, when their internal dragon and tiger ascend and they quicken the gold crystal to nurture their immortal embryo and generate perfect *qi*, must set up the middle elixir field and best start with this.

Lü asked: Now that I know about major reversion to the elixir field, may I ask, what are those based on seven and nine?

Zhong replied: The generation and maturation of the five phases come to fifty-five in terms of numbers. Heaven is one, earth is two, heaven is three, earth is four, heaven is five, earth is six, heaven is seven, earth is eight, heaven is nine, earth is ten. The odd numbers one, three, five, seven, and nine are yang; the even numbers two, four, six, eight, and ten are yin. Together they come to thirty.

Starting from the kidneys, water is one, fire is two, wood is three, metal is four, and earth is five: these are the numbers of the generative cycle of the five phases. Three are yang and two are yin. Similarly starting from the kidneys, water is six, fire is seven, wood is eight, metal is nine, and earth is ten: these are the numbers of the completing cycle of the five phases. Three are yin and two are yang.

The human body, too, contains the path of the generation and maturation of the five phases. Here water is the kidneys, and the kidneys match the numbers one and six. Fire is the heart, and the heart matches two and seven. Wood is the liver, and the liver matches three and eight. Metal is the lungs, and the lungs match four and nine. Earth is the spleen, and the spleen matches five and ten. Thus, each organ has both yin and yang.

Yin reaches its ultimate at eight and burgeons at two. For this reason, when the *qi* arrives at the liver, all excess yin in the kidneys is gone. When it gets to the heart, it reaches its great ultimate and generates yin. Thus, the number two belongs to the heart and the number eight to the liver. Similarly, yang is exhausted at nine and burgeons at one. For this reason, when the fluid arrives at the lungs, all excess yin in the heart is gone. When it gets to the kidneys, it reaches its ultimate and generates yang.

Thus, the number one belongs to the kidneys and the number nine to the lungs. Daoist adepts begin by mating dragon and tiger, then assemble the *qi* of rightful yang in the heart. This *qi* matches the number seven of the heart. It revolves seven times to the middle field, then enters the lower field to nurture the immortal embryo. From here, it reverts to the heart. For this reason, this process is called seven-based reversion.

Yin dissolves at the numbers two and eight. When perfect *qi* is generated and there is no more yin in the heart, it cuts off at two; when the great medicine is complete and there is no more yin in the liver, it cuts off at eight. As soon as yin has dissolved at two and eight, yang can grow at nine and three. As liver cuts off its yang, it supports the heart and liver *qi* can burgeon at three. After it reverts to the heart seven times, it also cuts off lung fluid, allowing it to circulate nine times to the lungs to support the heart. Thus, yang grows at the nine and three. This is nine-based reversion.

Lü asked: During seven-based reversion, one takes the yang of the heart and reverts it repeatedly to the heart, storing it in the middle elixir field. During nine-based revolution, one takes the yang of the lungs as originally generated in the heart and reverts it repeatedly to the heart, also storing it in the middle field. Now that I know about seven- and nine-based reversion, may I ask what is meant by reversion to the elixir field working with golden or jade fluids as well as through the interaction of the upper, middle, and lower [fields] and going back and forth between yin and yang?

Zhong replied: The wise men of old and sages of the past often called the process of moving lung fluid into the lower field reversion to the elixir field on the basis of golden [metal] fluid. They called the process of moving heart fluid into the lower field reversion to the elixir field on the basis of jade fluid. It is not that their discussions are not wondrous, but they do not exhaust the mysterious workings.

Generally, lung [*qi*] generates kidney [*qi*] just like metal generates water. If adepts infuse metal into water, how can you call that reversion to the elixir field? Kidney [*qi*] controls heart [*qi*] just like water controls fire. If practitioners infuse water into fire, how can call that reversion to the elixir field?

Golden fluid is the fluid of the lungs. It forms the womb that contains the dragon and tiger and protects their transmutation once it has been sent to the yellow court. In order to complete the great medicine, practice reduction by pulling back the elbows, thereby causing lung fluid to fly up and enter the upper palace, from where it reverts down to the middle elixir field. From here it reverts further to the lower field, which is why we speak of reverting golden fluid to the elixir field.

Jade fluid is the fluid of the kidneys, which follows primordial *qi* and ascends to move to the heart. If coagulated, it turns into golden fluid; if raised up, it fills the jade pond; if scattered, it turns into jasper blossoms; if refined, it becomes white snow.

If adepts contain it, they can move it from the middle to the lower field, where—as part of assembling the medicine—it washes and cleanses the immortal embryo. If they raise it up, they can move it from the lower field into the four limbs, where—as part of refining the physical form—it purges the dust from your bones. If they neither raise nor contain it, but revert it repeatedly, we speak reversion to the elixir field on the basis of jade fluid.

Next, when yin reaches its ultimate, it generates yang. This contains the water of perfect oneness, which follows yang and ascends: this process is called reversion to the elixir field from yin to yang. Similarly, when yang reaches its ultimate, it generates yin. This contains the *qi* of rightful yang, which follows yin and descends: this is called reversion to the elixir field from yang to yin.

To nourish the brain and refine the top of the head, adepts revert *qi* from the lower to the upper field. Allow it to reach full saturation, then pour and drip the *qi*, allowing it to revert from the upper to the middle [field]. To heat the elixir and stoke the fire, they revert it from the middle to the lower [field]; to refine matter and incinerate the body, they revert it from the lower to the middle [field].

In this manner, the five phases are inverted, the three fields are repeatedly cycled, and all engage in mutual interaction and exchange. Eventually adepts will thereby refine the physical form into *qi* and refine *qi* into spirit. First they move it from the lower to the middle field, then from the middle to the upper field, and from here they let it exit through the celestial gate. Leaving behind the ordinary bodily shell, they enter the line of sages and attain a rank among the immortals. When these three moves are compete, always moving up from below, there is not need for further reversion!

14. Refining the Physical Form

Lü asked: Now that I know about reversion to the elixir field, may I ask about the principles of refining the physical form?

Zhong replied: In human life, physical form and spirit function as outside and inside. Spirit is the master of the physical form, and the physical form is the abode of spirit. Essence contained in the physical form generates *qi*, and this *qi* in turn generates spirit.

In addition, there is mutual generation of fluid and *qi*, functioning within the physical form like mother and child. Beyond this, water generates wood, wood generates fire, fire generates earth, earth generates metal, and metal generates water. *Qi* transfers from one to the other in the mode of mother and child, while fluid functions like husband and wife. They are the manifestation of yin and yang in the physical form.

Water transforms into fluid, fluid transforms into blood, blood transforms into secretions: they are all generated when yin obtains yang. If yin and yang lose their rhythm, mucus, tears, phlegm, saliva, and sweat issue frequently. That is because yin has lost its proper generative role.

Qi transforms into essence, essence transforms into a pearl, the pearl transforms into mercury, and mercury transforms into cinnabar [lit. sand]: they all mature when yang obtains yin. If yin and yang lose their rhythm, disease, old age, death, and suffering arise. That is because yang has lost its proper role of maturation. If yin does not obtain yang, there is no generation; if yang does not obtain yin, there is no maturation.

Daoist adepts cultivate yang rather than yin, refine themselves rather than outside entities. When the human body first receives *qi* form, the perfect *qi* of father and mother stops moving, their essence and blood form a zygote, and they provide material support for it in the mother's palace of pure yin. As yin generates yin, her physical form creates a new physical form. Eventually the embryo is fully developed and its *qi* becomes viable.

Even as a six-foot body, into which he eventually grows, the person still depends entirely on yin, with only a tiny spark of primordial yang deep within. If people want to live long without dying, they must refine the physical form so it can remain in the world and continue to exist for eons after eons. If they want to transcend the ordinary and enter the ranks of the sages, they must refine the physical form into *qi* and thereby create another body beyond this body.

Lü asked: Physical form and image are essentially yin, which by nature has substance. To take this from a state of being into nonbeing, one must transform the physical form into *qi*. From there one can transcend the ordinary body and enter the ranks of the sages. This is the highest method of refinement.

Getting the physical form to retain *qi* and using *qi* to nurture the physical form leads to several attainments: on a minor level, one can live healthy and happy and extend one's years; on a major level, one can remain in the world continuously. The old one can reverse the aging process and recover youth; the young can stabilize their looks and reach extreme longevity.

360 years make up one life cycle; 26,000 cycles make up one eon; and 36,000 eons make up one vast kalpa. A vast kalpa lasts so long that no one knows the number of its years or months. To live as long as heaven and earth is confirmation experience of the refinement of the physical form. Still, may I now ask, what are the confirmation experiences of the principles of refining the physical form and the inner workings of the creative transformations?

Zhong replied: As the human being grows in physical form, it takes three hundred days for the embryo to develop fully. After birth, it takes 5,000 days for the *qi* to be viable. The average body grows to five feet, five inches, which number matches the generation and maturation of the five phases. While some are larger or smaller and do not entirely match this, they still measure in inches and feet, and their tall or short stature is in line with the overall pattern.

Above the heart there are nine layers of heaven; below the heart are nine layers of earth. The kidneys are located 8.4 inches from the heart, and the heart is 8.4 inches from the first ring of the twelve-storied tower, which in turn is 8.4 inches from the top of the head. That means, the kidneys are 25.2 inches from the top of the head. Primordial *qi* fills this area in the course of one day and one night, moving 320 times. Each time covers 25.2 inches, which comes out to eighty-one cubits.

Primordial *qi* thus matches nine times nine, the number of the continuous nature of yang, just as the space between the heart and the kidneys matches the overall distance between heaven and earth. From the kidneys to the top of the head, it is 2.5 feet, which reflects five times five, the number of the five phases and of pure yang.

Primordial *qi* leaves the body with the exhalation. Once it leaves, the protective and defensive channels flow with ease, filling with the rightful *qi* of heaven and earth that matches the cosmic fusion and follows the proper rhythm. Always coming together and separating, it is without limit and cannot be measured in cubits and feet.

Primordial *qi* enters the body with the inhalation. Once it enters, the vessels and meridians are wide open. Each time, with one exhalation and one inhalation, the perfect *qi* of the three forces of heaven, earth, and humanity comes and goes through the twelve-storied tower. One round of breathing in and out is called one breath. In the course of one day and one night, human beings take 13,500 breaths. More specifically, this means that there are 13,500 exhalations when the primordial *qi* of the self leaves from the inside; and 13,500 inhalations when the rightful *qi* of heaven and earth enters from the outside.

As long as one's root and source are strong and stable, primordial *qi* does not dissipate. Between exhalation and inhalation, one can capture the rightful *qi* of heaven and earth. Using this *qi* to refine one's own *qi*, one can spread it widely to fill the four major [energy systems]. Its pure aspects move into protective *qi* while its turbid dimensions enhance defensive *qi*, flowing freely and pervasively. Its vertical aspects join the conduits while its horizontal lines support the meridians, filling all extensively and widely. Then cold and heat cannot do any harm, labor and hardship cannot cause any mishaps. The body is light, the bones are strong, the *qi* is vigorous, and the spirit is clear: forever preserving unlimited longevity and always remaining free from aging.

However, if one's root and source are not stable, essence depletes and *qi* weakens. No *qi* dripping in from above, one's fundamental palaces cannot be nurtured below. Upon exhalation, the *qi* of heaven and earth leaves in droves, all eighty-one cubits of nine times nine primordial *qi* dissipating rapidly. No longer maintained within, *qi is* taken back by heaven and earth. Then how can one ever capture rightful *qi*? As time goes on, yin burgeons while yang declines, *qi* weakens and one gets sick. Eventually it is exhausted and one dies to fall back into the wheel of reincarnation and rebirth.

Lü asked: How, then, can one make sure that primordial *qi* is never dispersed and lost, so that one can refine the physical form? How can one capture the rightful *qi* of heaven and earth and thereby live continuously for vast kalpas?

Zhong replied: To be victorious in war, one must have a strong military. To keep the people at peace, one must have a prosperous country. The military here is the primordial *qi*. Troops on the inside dissolve the yin of the material form; troops on the outside capture the *qi* of heaven and earth. The country here is the body.

If the body matches the image, its resources are sufficient and it always has a surplus; if it is free from the [constraints of the] physical form, it is firm and stable and never suffers lack. The myriad gates always open, there is not even one mishap of loss; not even one horse [untamed thoughts] roaming wildly, there are many, many gains.

Moving in front or along the back, primordial *qi* constantly refines material reality and incinerates the body; flowing above or below, it always nurtures yang and dissolves yin. Heating Qian and Kun [back and front], it naturally follows the proper hours and times, so how can the forging of *qi* and fluid be without proper days and periods?

Refining the physical form with jade fluid, one can stride on the scaly dragon and ascend in flight while white snow fills one's flesh of dust. Refining the physical form with golden fluid, one can follow the thunder carriage and descend while a golden radiance fills one's bedchamber.

Lü asked: Now I roughly understand the principles of refining the physical form. But what, I pray, are golden and jade fluid?

Zhong replied: Upon refining the physical form with golden fluid, the bones radiate in a golden color, the body issues a golden radiance, and golden flower petals appear miraculously in the air. The five *qi* move to the prime and the three yang gather at the top of the head: it is the hour to transcend the ordinary body, the day when the golden elixir is fully mature.

Upon refining the physical form with jade fluid, the flesh is moistened with yang cream, and the physical form is like a gem tree full of jasper flowers and jade leaves. The ordinary body changes to issue rays of radiant light. One can stride on the wind, mounting it to fly off as one pleases, since the physical form is nothing but *qi*.

Daoist adepts may know the methods of reversion to the elixir field, but they will also see great effects by refining the physical form. For that, they must revert jade fluid, use it to bathe and cleanse the immortal embryo, move it upward, and with the help of their river carriage transport it to their four great [energy systems].

Start with the liver. When the liver receives is, its radiance overflows through the eyes, which shine bright like a spark of lacquer. Next move to the heart. When the heart receives it, the mouth generates a fluid of pure life force, which soon turns into white snow. From here move to the spleen. When the spleen receives it, the flesh becomes rosy like coagulated fat, and all marks and scars disappear for good.

Next come the lungs. When the lungs receive it, the nose perceives celestial fragrances and the complexion recovers a youthful appearance. Then there are the kidneys. When the kidneys receive it, the elixir returns to its original home, the ears constantly hear the sound of strings and pipes, and the hair loses any gray or white color. This is how the jade fluid refines the physical form.

Using golden fluid to refine the physical form is not like this at all. First, revert the elixir to areas not yet covered, so it spreads ruling fire everywhere: this is called full saturation. Next revert it up again, so it can battle perfect yin: this is called refining material reality.

Earth controls water. When golden fluid rests in earth, it makes the Yellow Emperor radiate widely, thus merging with great yin. Fire controls metal. When golden fluid rests in fire, it causes the red child to join the furnace, generating purple *qi*. Fire arising from water means that all yin is dissolved within yang. Transmuting the golden elixir in the yellow court, one refines yang spirit in all five *qi* [organs].

Thus, green *qi* surges up in the liver, white *qi* issues from the lungs, a red radiance manifests in the heart, black *qi* moves up from the kidneys, and a yellow color comes out from the spleen. As all five *qi* move to the central prime, they follow ruling fire and enter the inner courtyard. The yang in the yin of the lower prime is completely free from yin: it ascends to gather in the spirit palace. The yang in the yang of the central prime no longer generates yang: it ascends and gathers in the spirit palace. The great medicine in the yellow court is devoid of yin and consists entirely of pure yang: it, too, ascends to gather in the spirit palace. Thus, the five fluids move to the lower prime, the five *qi* move to the middle prime, and the three yang move to the upper prime.

Once the move to the prime is concluded, one has accumulated the full 3,000 merits. Then a crane will dance at the top of one's head, and a dragons will dance in one's body. One will hear beautiful music and see immortal petals swirl. The purple court all decked out, perfect fragrance wafts everywhere. Having accumulated the full 3,000, one is no longer a person of this world of dust. In the time it takes a stick of incense to burn out, one becomes a resident of the blessed isles of Penglai and Ying. This is called transcending the ordinary and entering the ranks of the sages, being liberated from material reality and ascending to the immortals.

15. Moving to the Prime

Lü asked: Now that I know about the principles involved in refining the physical form, may I ask what you mean by moving to the prime?

Zhong replied: Once the great medicine is complete, one works to revert jade fluid to the elixir field to bathe and cleanse the immortal embryo. Once perfect *qi* is generated it infuses the jade fluid, which then ascends and changes the bones of dust: this is called using the jade fluid to refine the physical form.

Quickening the gold crystal by pulling back the elbows, the river carriage transports it to the inner courtyard [upper elixir field]. From the upper to the middle and from the middle to the lower [field], golden fluid everts to the elixir field. Thus one refines metal dust [essence], allowing the five *qi* to move to the prime and the three yang to gather at the top of the head. This is how one refines *qi* into into spirit, which goes beyond refining the physical form and living continuously in the world.

What I call moving to the prime is known only to a few, in the past as much as today. Those who do know about it are sages and wise men who never speak of it. It is a method of the major level of accomplishment unique to the perfected and immortals, matching the unfathomable core workings deeply hidden in heaven and earth. It truly is a well-kept secret of the Three Clarities, a mysterious instruction beyond all words and images, a wondrous principle beyond any questions and answers.

I am afraid your will is not nearly sincere enough to receive this teaching, nor is your heart stable enough for me to answer this question. Speaking lightly and talking at ease increase the potential transgression of leaking the sagely core workings, so I will not speak about this further.

Lü asked: I started out by realizing that there are perfected immortals and recognized the great Dao. Next, I learned about the proper times and periods and comprehended the core workings of heaven. I discerned the perfect source of water and fire, and came to know that dragon and tiger are not generated in the liver and lungs. I explored the overarching principles of reduction and augmentation, and learned that lead and mercury are not the same as Kan and Li.

The correct count of the five phases in inverse order was covered in the instructions I received; the core workings of the three fields in their cycles were laid out before me. I gained earnest appreciation of the principles of reversion to the elixir field and refinement of the physical form; I acquired knowledge of the techniques leading to long life without dying. Still, the ground of going beyond the ordinary and entering the ranks of the sages, the Dao of being liberated from material reality and ascending to the immortals all rest with refining *qi* and moving to the prime. So, please, tell me in more detail what this means.

Zhong replied: Dao was originally without form, and the universal ground was mere simplicity. The pure above and the turbid below were fused in oneness. They reached their great ultimate and divided. Then chaos first split into heaven and earth, and east, west, south, and north arranged themselves in the five directions.

Each direction came to have its particular emperor, and each emperor had two children: one yang, the other yin. Next, the two *qi* started to generate and complete each other, dividing into the five phases. The five phases, too, came to generate and complete each other, establishing the six *qi* that come in three yin and three yang.

Seen from this perspective, it is just like when human beings are first conceived. Essence and *qi* fuse in oneness, then they separate and generate the two kidneys. The kidney on the left is the "mysterious": it ascends with *qi* and transfers it up into the liver. The kidney on the right is the "female": it follows fluid and transfers it down into the bladder.

The mysterious and the female come originally from nothingness: they turn from nonbeing into being. Since the perfect *qi* of father and mother take root in the place of pure yin, we say, "The spirit of the valley never dies; it is the gate of the mysterious and the female" [*Daode jing* 6]. It is just like the root of heaven and earth. The mysterious and the female are the two kidneys.

The five organs and six viscera are all generated from the kidneys. Among them the liver matches the phase wood: is called by the stems Jia and Yi, it is just like the Green Emperor of the east. The heart matches the phase fire: called by the stems Bing and Ding, it is just like the Red Emperor of the south. The lungs match the phase metal: called by the stems Geng and Xin, they are just like the White Emperor of the west. The spleen matches the phase earth: called by the stems Wu and Ji, it is just like the Yellow Emperor of the center. The kidneys match the phase water: called by the stems Ren and Gui, they are just like the Black Emperor of the north.

When human beings are first conceived, they have neither physical form nor image but consist only of one yin and one yang. Once the embryo is fully developed, they have intestines and stomach, and partake in the division of the six *qi* that come in three males and three females. The *qi* of cosmic oneness revolves with the five phases; the five phases revolve through the six *qi*.

So, first understand yin and yang, realizing that there is yang within yin and yin within yang. Next comprehend metal, wood, water, fire, and earth, realizing that there is fire within water, water within fire, metal within water, wood within metal, fire within wood, and earth within fire. The five constantly interact with and turn into each other, and thereby the two *qi* divide into six. In other words, the great Dao disperses into five phases.

After the winter solstice, one ray of yang is generated in the five directions on earth, signaling the overall ascent of yang. In each season, one emperor is in command, and the other four assist him. This means that once the command of spring has begun, if the Black Emperor does not relinquish his command, there is no way cold can turn into warmth. Similarly, if the Red Emperor is not ready to take over, warmth has no chance to turn into heat.

After the summer solstice, one ray of yin is generated in the five directions in heaven, signaling the overall descent of yin. Again, one emperor is in command, and the other four assist him. This means that once the command of fall has begun, if the Red Emperor does not relinquish his command, there is no way heat can turn into coolness. Similarly, if the Black Emperor is not ready to take over, coolness has no chance to turn into cold.

At the winter solstice, yang is generated on earth and its *qi* moves toward heaven. At the summer solstice, yin is generated in heaven and its *qi* moves toward earth. Daoist adepts must investigate these principles in depth. In the course of days and months, when one ray of yang is first generated, the *qi* of the five organs moves to the middle prime. When one ray of yin is first generated, the fluid of the five organs moves to the lower prime. The yang within yin, the yang within yang, and the yang in yin and yang are the three yang that move to the inner courtyard [upper yang], and the spirit of the heart returns to the heavenly palace. This is what is meant by moving to the prime.

Lü asked: When yang is generated, the five *qi* move to the middle prime. When yin is generated, the five fluids move to the lower prime. This causes the yang within yang, the yang within yin, and the yang within yin and yang to move to the upper prime. Cultivating this assiduously, how can a persistent adept with good understanding attain transcendence and liberation and leave the world of dust behind?

Zhong replied: The *qi* of primordial yang, when one yang is first generated, moves up to the middle prime: this happens in all people. The fluid generated from accumulated *qi*, when one yin is first generated, moves down to the lower prime: this happens in all people. As long as adepts work merely with this, they cannot attain transcendence and liberation.

If they want to go beyond the ordinary and enter the ranks of the sages, be liberated from material reality and ascend to the immortals, they must first mate dragon and tiger and complete the great medicine. Once it is complete, they can generate perfect *qi*. After perfect *qi* has been generated, they work with the months in the course of a year to stabilize monthly flourishing and decline. They work with the days in the course of a month to manage daily affairs. They work with the double-hours in the course of a day to stabilize hourly counts of breath. Doing so, they use yang to nourish yang until there is no more residual yin within yang. They use yang to refine yin until there is no more scattered yang within yin.

Generally, in spring the liver is dominant and the spleen is weak. In summer the heart is dominant and the lungs are weak. In the fall the lungs are dominant and the liver is weak. In winter the kidneys are dominant and the heart is weak. Since the kidneys are the root and foundation of human life, each season has a time when the spleen is strong and the kidneys are weak, which means the only organ that is diminished in all four seasons is the kidneys. This is one reason why people get sick a lot.

When Jia and Yi manage affairs in the liver, keep spleen *qi* from being inactive. When Bing and Ding manage affairs in the heart, keep lung *qi* from being inactive. When Wu and Ji manage affairs in the spleen, keep kidney *qi* from being inactive. When Geng and Xin manage affairs in the lungs, keep liver *qi* from being inactive. When Ren and Gui manage affairs in the kidneys, keep heart *qi* from being inactive.

In each case, one *qi* is strong while another is weak; one organ is dominant while another is in decline. This is another reason why people get sick a lot.

Then again, heart *qi* sprouts in the Hai hour [9-11 pm], grows in Yin [3-5am], dominates in Si [9-11 am], and weakens in Shen [3-5 pm]. Liver *qi* sprouts in Shen, grows in Hai, dominates in Yin, and weakens in Si. Lung *qi* sprouts in Yin, grows in Si, dominates in Shen, and weakens in Hai. Kidney *qi* sprouts in Si, grows in Shen, dominates in Hai, and weakens in Yin.

Spleen *qi* in spring follows the liver, in summer it follows the heart, in autumn it follows the lungs, and in winter it follows the kidneys. People do not understand how to use this system of the days and have no idea of the times when the different forms of *qi* grow and dominate, are strong or weak. That is yet another reason why they get sick a lot.

The three yang powers gather on certain days, months, and hours: then adepts can refine yang and ensure that yin is no longer generated. The three yin powers gather on certain days, months, and hours: then they can nourish yang and make sure it no longer scatters.

With the help of the *qi* of pure yang they next refine the *qi* of the five organs without stopping until each emerges in its original condition and you can lift it up into the celestial pond. First the yin in the kidneys disappears, and the nine rivers [of the intestines] are free from waves [disturbances]. Next the yin in the liver disappears, and the eight passes [orifices] are constantly closed. Then the yin in the lungs disappears, and metal joins fire in the cauldron. From here, the yin in the spleen disappears, and the jade chamber is firmly sealed.

Now perfect *qi* ascends and the four *qi* gather into one. Even if there is some golden fluid trying to descend, its little cup of water cannot overcome the raging fire. Rather, water and fire embrace and merge into one and enter the spirit palace. When this happens, adepts should stabilize breathing and practice inner observation. The intention fully at one and never scattering, their spirit consciousness becomes whole and wondrous.

In deep stillness, they will always hear music and song. Feeling that they are in a dream, they are in fact not dreaming. Deep in mental projections of emptiness and nonbeing, they see radiant scenery and amazing beings unlike anything in the ordinary world, florescence and beauty far beyond the human realm. Towers and terraces, palaces and gates glitter with turquoise tiles like floating mist. Studded with pearls and kingfisher feathers, silk and gauze adorn all, and the air is thick with a fabulous fragrance.

When there is an experience like this, we speak of transcending to the inner courtyard. These are signs that the yang spirit has gathered and reverted to the upper elixir [field]. From here, one can refine spirit into immortality and merge with the great Dao. One knock on the celestial gate, and a golden hue and radiance manifest throughout the divine body, variegated flower petals drift down and cover the entire person. One walks on air as easily as on flat ground and can cover ten thousand miles by extending an arm.

Upon reentering the original body, spirit and physical form remain completely merged and one can live as long as heaven and earth. It is possible to choose to live on in the world of dust or leave the ordinary shell and return to the ten continents [of the blessed]. In the purple halls, the residence of perfect lords of great abundance, one may adopt a new place of origin and find an appropriate new name.

Depending on the level of merit and attainment, one may even get to live on the three isles [of Penglai], but in all cases one can freely wander forever beyond the realm of wind and dust. This is what we call transcending the dust and being liberated from the ordinary.

Lü asked: Refining the physical form leads only to permanence in this world while refining *qi* allows one to ascend to the immortals. Some people today do not comprehend the mysterious core workings. Without [having assembled] the medicine, they start by practicing embryo respiration. Strongly focusing their attention on the belly, they either accumulate cold *qi* and get sick or generate vacant yang and fall ill. While they practice such cultivation with the hope of attaining long life, they are holding on to a delusion and in the end cannot avoid illness and disease.

They do not realize that only after the immortal embryo is present can perfect *qi* grow and that, once perfect *qi* is generated, embryo respiration flows naturally. Through embryo respiration one can then refine *qi*, and by refining turn it into spirit. However, to refine *qi* properly one must work with the months in the course of a year, the days in the course of a month, and the double-hours in the course of a day.

Sitting upright in the meditation chamber, one must forget all workings and eliminate all traces. At this time, then, when mind and mental projections are not yet completely gone, how should one get rid of them? Also, if erroneous imaginations have not yet stopped, if awareness and consciousness have leaks, one's will is firmly set on ascent to the immortals yet heart and spirit are not stable, what can one possibly do?

Zhong replied: Mating and fusion each have their specific time; working and holding [in cultivation] each have their unique methods. Practicing the methods in accordance with the correct time, one follows the right path to pursue Dao and with each day comes closer to attainment. It is as easy as turning the palm. Advanced adepts in the past as much as today only need to close the eyes and calm the mind to enter the sphere of the invisible and inaudible. The best way to do so is by inner observation, which naturally settles spirit and consciousness.

16. Inner Observation

Lü asked: May I now learn about the principles of inner observation?

Zhong replied: Early wise men and later sages adopted some methods of inner observation, sitting in oblivion, and visualization, and did not adopt others. They noticed that the mind was like a monkey and the intention like a wild horse—never staying or stopping. They worried that people would get enticed by things and lose their will to practice, so they set up images in nothingness to prevent people's ears from hearing, their eyes from seeing, their mind from going crazy, and their intention from getting distracted. By visualizing specific things or objects, practicing inner observation and sitting in oblivion, people would not fall into nothingness.

However, there are also followers of little learning and no understanding who have no clue about the proper times of [yin-yang] interaction and do not know the right way to practice. They tend to expect visualization alone to lead to full attainment. They think they can produce the elixir wholly by focusing their intention and assemble the medicine merely in their imagination. They inhale through the nose and exhale through the mouth, then envision the breath shaped like sun and moon or flowing in nonaction like heaven and earth, to eventually hold it in the abdomen. This is mere child's play!

Highly advanced adepts and extraordinary people, in contrast, do away completely with sitting in oblivion and visualization. They see them as obtaining wealth in a dream: how can it be useful for salvation? Or like drawing the picture of a cake in the dust: how can it satisfy hunger? To them these methods are just emptiness within emptiness, unreal like flowers in a mirror or moonlight over water. Ultimately they make it hard to complete the great work.

Despite all this, there are some methods that can be adopted. Generally it is easy to agitate the mind into splintering and hard to subdue the intention into being unified. Good days and auspicious times must be properly selected. Even if one rests in a place of clarity and purity, how can the mind function as the overall manager while the will is influenced by emotions? Time passes like a flash of lightning, illuminating an inch of darkness. An error of an instant, and one is as far from success as heaven is from earth. Even over accumulated years and many months, one will never see any effects, the mind being lost and the intention gone crazy.

Adepts may get good at seeing, but then their will gets stuck on the beauty of cinnabar and green [colors] and they never come to see greatness and florescence. They may get good at listening, but then their will focuses only on the perfect sounds of strings and flutes and they never get to hear thunder and lightning. The application of hearing and seeing is minor indeed! Compared to them, the unified mind can travel widely through the six harmonies, embracing all. So as long as you work with the right time and the right method, how can you not use visualization and inner observation to realize the goal?

Lü asked: How, then, does one practice visualization in inner observation?

Zhong replied: To facilitate yang ascending, visualize a male, a dragon, fire, heaven, clouds, a crane, the sun, a horse, smoke, mist, a carriage, a chariot, flowers, or pure *qi*. Things like these, envisioned in inner observation and visualization, are appropriate images for yang ascending.

To facilitate yin descending, visualize a female, a tiger, water, earth, rain, a turtle, the moon, an ox, a spring mud, a boat, or a leaf. Things like these, envisioned in inner observation and visualization, are appropriate images for yin descending.

The green dragon, white tiger, red bird, and the Dark Warrior have images that go with their names. The five peaks, nine rivers, four oceans, three isles, gold lad, jade maiden, river carriage, multi-storied tower, and other appellations of this kind that are too numerous to list all have images set up in nothingness to help settle mind and consciousness.

Before one has caught the fish one must not discard the trap; before one has gotten the rabbit one must not eliminate the snare [*Zhuangzi* 26]. For later carriages to be able to move, they must run in the tracks of earlier vehicles; once a great vessel is complete, it serves as the model for later pots. Thus, the methods of inner observation are a form of practice impossible to do without, but one must neither hold on to it forever nor abandon it too soon: both are unacceptable.

Abandoning all thoughts and being free from imagination is a state of perfect cognition: perfect cognition signals perfect emptiness. In a state of perfect emptiness, one can connect to the perfected, undergo immortal transformation, and escape from the dark crossing, gradually attaining transcendence and liberation. To lay a good foundation and get a solid start, proceeding toward success by advancing every day—that's an appropriate application of visualization. To practice Dao and diminish every day, entering the realm of the invisible and inaudible [*Daode jing* 48, 14], using particular methods less and less—that's all part of inner observation.

Lü asked: How can one visualize the mating of dragon and tiger and matching of yin and yang?

Zhong replied: In the beginning, to fuse yin and yang and stabilize Kan and Li, visualize nine august perfected guide a red-clad boy upward and nine august mothers guide a black-clad girl downward. See them meet in front of a yellow hut, welcomed an old woman dressed in yellow. Just as in a wedding ceremony among people, they have a great time, full of joy and delight.

Afterwards, see the girl moving further down and the boy moving further up, just like lovers separating on earth. Once this is done, see the yellow dame holding something shaped like a mandarin orange. She throws it right into the yellow hut, where it enters a golden vessel.

Now, the boy is Qian connecting to Kun, and as yang reverts to its original position, it carries yin with it, so both return to their old home. The girl is Kun connecting to Qian, and as yin reverts to its original position, it embraces yang, so both meet in their old home. Such are the images associated with the interaction of Kan and Li and the mating of yin and yang.

[For the formation of the yellow sprout], see a black spark [tiger] rise up from a blazing fire and a red dragon dive down into turbulent waves. When the two beasts encounter each other, they fight, right in front of the tower pavilion. Its red gate opens wide and, in the midst of wildly raging smoke and flames, a kingly personage appears who directs the great fire to burn all the way to heaven in waves reaching up a myriad yards. After the fire reaches its highest point it starts to drop again, smoke and flames filling heaven and earth. The dragon and tiger whirl and coil around each other, then enter the golden vessel. Moving down into the yellow hut, they settle in as if in a cage or closet. Such is the visualization of the mating of dragon and tiger and transforming into the yellow sprout.

Lü asked: Now that I know how to use inner observation and visualization with regard to the matching of yin and yang and the mating of dragon and tiger, how do you use it in stoking the fire to heat and refine the cinnabar medicine?

Zhong replied: In this case, visualize the central vessel as a tripod or a cauldron, either yellow or black, shaped like a carriage wheel. It has the green dragon on the left, the white tiger on the right, the red bird in front, and the Dark Warrior behind. On its sides are two attendants, clad in purple robes, standing with head bowed and holding jade tablets. Behind them are various servants and officers.

When the fire is lit under the vessel, a king appears clad in vermilion. He rides a red horse and descends from the air astride on a fiery cloud. He raises his whip and issues commands, shouting that the fire is too small and the flames are too feeble. The blazing flames rage wildly into the air and knock on heaven in their desire to enter. When the celestial gate does not open, the smoke and fire turn back down and revolve around the four directions.

The people, the vessel, the kingly personage, and the attendants are now engulfed in red flames, all shouting to stoke the fire even more. The water in the vessel is free from *qi* and seems to coagulate. The pearl in the water is free from darkness and seems to glow brightly. This is how to use visualization in stoking the fire to heat and refine the cinnabar medicine.

Lü asked: Are inner observation and visualization limited to assembling the medicine and stoking the fire? Or is there more? Are there other methods or ways of working?

Zhong replied: Visualize clouds and thunder descend while smoke and flames ascend. See variegated flowers raining from heaven or a fresh breeze and auspicious *qi* ascend from the palace chambers. Maybe imagine immortal ladies and jade maidens riding multicolored phoenixes and fine steeds, arriving from the clear empyrean. See them offer a golden dish filled with jade dew and frosty liquor to the kingly personage below. This is how to use visualization in reverting golden fluid to the elixir field as well as for full saturation.

Alternatively imagine dragon and tiger pulling a carriage through the fire and pushing upward through the three barriers, each guarded by soldiers and officers too many to count. Their weapons, staffs, pikes, and shields instill terror in people. First see the tiger and dragon knocking on the barriers, but they do not open. Then see a huge fire heating them, and under its impact they break down. Thus one reaches Kunlun but does not stop there, instead going all the way to the celestial pond and only then taking a rest.

Next, imagine three cranes soaring into the three heavens, a pair of butterflies entering the three palaces, the red-clad infant being lifted through the celestial gate on a five-colored cloud, or the kingly personage being carried beyond the three worlds in a golden carriage with jade wheels. This is how to use visualization in quickening the gold crystal by pulling back the elbows and running the major river carriage.

Then again, see an officer in vermilion robes climbing on his carriage and making a full circuit: from Yizhou he goes to Duizhou, Qingzhou, Xuzhou, Yangzhou, Xingzhou, Liangzhou, and Yongzhou, then begins again in Yizhou. Covering east, west, south, and north, he rests in Yuzhou for a while before again commencing his circuit. Having obtained gold and jade on his way, he completes his tasks. When the officer issues a command, all nine continents are in harmony. Always as soon as he completes a circuit, he starts again, moving on and on without end.

Alternatively see him covering the five sacred mountains, beginning with Hengshan [in the north] or going around the five lakes starting from Beizhao [in the north], carrying a celestial talisman commanding the five emperors and a royal decree summoning the five nobles. This is how to use visualization in reversion to the elixir field.

Then again, visualize pearls and jade falling to the ground, rain and dew showering living creatures, ocean tides filling the hundred rivers, yin bubbling up in a myriad whirlpools, flames rising all through heaven and earth, or smoke and mist filling the universe. This is how to use visualization in refining the physical form.

You can also imagine cranes leaving their nest, dragons exiting from their lair, the five emperors going to audience with heaven, five-colored clouds rising up, dancing red phoenixes soaring through the turquoise sky, or ascending along the celestial thoroughfare as if in a dream while celestial flowers fall in profusion and immortal music fills the air. A golden radiance flows along as one enters the palace hall; variegated flowers float as one goes into the place. This is how to use visualization in moving to the prime. Once done with this, stop working with visualization and switch to inner observation.

Lü asked: The mysterious principles of inner observation, I take it, are not like the previous methods. May I ask about them?

Zhong replied: When adepts of Daoist cultivation in the past as much as today do not comprehend the core workings of heaven, they do not understand at first how to use this method to practice. Desiring to attain transcendence and liberation quickly, they practice embryo respiration, inhaling much and exhaling little.

They think that obscuring the mind and closing the eyes is how to practice inner observation. They center themselves in a state of deep stability [*samādhi*] where they generate yin spirit, then turn into ghosts of concentrated life force rather than becoming immortals of pure yang.

The perfected immortals and highest sages, on the other hand, work by assembling the medicine, stoking the fire, reducing lead, augmenting mercury, reverting [*qi* and fluid] to the elixir field, refining the physical form, moving to the prime, and fusing with *qi*. Using painstaking phrases and detailed expressions, they provide in-depth explanations, worried that the people of the world would not understand. However, they have not dwelt much on inner observation. Essentially, what you need to know about inner observation is that it is a method of exchanging yin and yang to be undertaken when one is ready to change from an ordinary to immortal being.

Daoist adepts typically make light of the relevant instructions and rarely use them. As I have outlined above, all interactions have specific hours and seasons, just as all cultivation comes with particular methods and rules. As long as they trust the rhythm of Dao, practice the methods at the right times, never deviating even by a moment, they will see success with every passing day.

In the practice of inner observation, for one, there are no fixed hours or seasons; for another, there are no particular methods or rules. Sitting in a remote and quite chamber, day and night upright with hands folded, adepts come to recognize yang spirit and chase out all yin ghosts. Thus, Bodhidharma sat nine years gazing at a wall, then he transcended the inner courtyard; Shakyamuni remained six years in deep meditation, then he emerged from the cage of ordinary life.

Inner observation is hard to practice. First move from above to below, getting the purple river carriage to transport you to the celestial palace. The celestial palace is full of wealth and honor—who would not covet them? Coming and going, variegated florescence and vast luxury are what people never get to see yet they all want them.

Daoist adepts, sitting in clarity and stillness all day long, guarding the flow within, are usually deep in serenity and simplicity. Once their merits reach the correct count, they find joy and happiness. Towers and terraces, pearls and kingfisher feathers, women and music, pipes and flutes, precious repasts and rare delicacies, unusual plants and gorgeous flowers, scenic delights in wind and light—they all touch the eyes like bright daylight.

People who don't realize that these things are illusory think that they have really arrived in the celestial palace. They do not know that this is the inner courtyard within their own selves, but take it to be the perfect realm. So they get in there and never leave: they are stuck at the dark crossroads. Due to this, their physical form is bound to remain in the world. They can never attain liberation from material reality and become spirit immortals. They never get to the celestial palace, but remain stuck in inner observation.

Then yin ghosts and external demons latch onto them and generate images, which in turn produce mental states. We call these attacks by demonic troops. Daoist adepts can go crazy because of them, falling deep into wayward states. Some lose themselves in heretical teachings, never able to become immortal. Others let their three deathbringers and seven material souls prey on the death of others to created delight for themselves. Yet others allow their nine worms and six robbers inflict suffering on the peace of others, never able to find rest anywhere.

17. Demonic Attacks and Hardships

Lü asked: So, inner observation is used to gather yang spirit, then refine it to transcend to the inner courtyard, bubble up to exit through the celestial gate, and move on to enter the ranks of the sages. It leaves and enters with equal ease, coming and going without fail. It comes and goes smoothly, moving near and far without error.

If one wants to remain in the world, one can keep the spirit merged with the physical form. If one wants to ascend to the immortals, one can wander afar to the isles of Penglai. Once the merits reach the full count of 3,000, by practicing inner observation, one can attain transcendence and liberation.

However, what I do not understand is how yin ghosts and evil demons take control and cause Daoist adepts to fail in attaining ascent to the immortals.

Zhong replied: Many Daoist adepts start out with a sincere mind, and affection and love, fame and profit—the various affairs of the world of dust and labor—cannot change their great volition. Next they develop an earnest will, and their diligent efforts and meditative serenity—the various mental projections of clarity and emptiness—cannot alter their initial mind. Still, in their earnest will, they insist on pursing a major level of accomplishment, yet never make it beyond the medium, and if they shoot for a medium level, they never get beyond the minor.

The more they remain unaware of the great Dao, the less they understand the inner workings of heaven. Practicing minor methods, they get a lot of strange ideas. Wasting years and months, they never see any real results. In their later years they grow weak and old and eventually fall again into the relentless cycle of reincarnation and rebirth. This causes other [potential] Daoist followers to believe that eternal life is a false idea, that transcendence and liberation are just empty words.

However often they may hear of Dao, they do not develop a sincere mind; and if they have a sincere mind, they never grow an earnest will. Their mind entangled in mental projections, they get involved with things and lose their will. In the end they are unable to escape from the ten demonic attacks and the nine difficulties.

Lü asked: What, then, are the nine hardships?

Zhong replied: Before completing the great medicine, it is hard to deal with cold and heat. Thus, throughout the year, one needs clothing for the four seasons. Before perfect *qi* has been generated, there still are hunger and thirst. Thus, throughout the day, one needs food for three meals. Being afflicted by the urgency to procure clothing and food is the first hardship.

Next, previous karmic affinities and inherited burdens flow into the present life and have to be repaid. Busy with work, one tries to snatch a moment of leisure, yet remains bound by the obligation to honor one's elders. Controlled by the need to honor the parents, one can never get away. One pushes for clear leisure, but it is difficult to find a stretch of free time. Being afflicted by having to honor one's elders is the second hardship.

Next, loving spouse and children, taking care of father and mother are the cangue of affection and the harness of emotions, increasing and getting bigger every day. Always concerned about house and carriage, one has no time to rest and relax, and even if one manages to develop a mind of clarity and stillness, it is still hard to defeat the mental projections of worry and frustration. Being afflicted by the strangulating ties of affection and love is the third hardship.

Next, wealth accumulating to the tune of ten thousand properties, nobility culminating in the rank of the three dukes delude the mind so that one cannot be content for even a moment. Greed is ubiquitous, causing concerns without end. Being afflicted by the entanglements and fetters of fame and profit is the fourth hardship.

Next, in one's younger years one refuses to do serious cultivation. As a result, one's *qi* weakens and one gets sick, one's obstinate mind forever without a trace of realization. Alternatively, one is steeped in darkness and encounters disasters, one's whole life in the world nothing but suffering—a warning for later generations. Being afflicted by disasters, misfortunes, and the vicissitudes of life is the fifth hardship.

Next, seeing that life and death are great affairs, one rushes to seek out a teacher, never discriminating between genuine and fake. One may follow a teacher because he makes great arguments and is a proficient speaker or because he has a Daoist mien and hoary appearance. One starts out by claiming that one has found a spirit immortal and only after a long time understands that he was just in it for his own fame and profit. Being afflicted by tying themselves to false [lit., blind] teachers is the sixth hardship.

Next, false teachers and crazy fellow students wrongly point one into weird directions. Pursuing extraneous matters [lit., branches] and picking on minor details [lit., leaves], they achieve nothing of worth; working with lesser methods and strange ideas, they keep on giving useless pointers and instructions. They really do not know that the sun and the moon do not rise easily, yet when they rise, they are very bright, causing all who have eyes to see. They do not understand that thunder and lightning do not roar trivially, yet when they roar, they are very loud, causing all who have ears to hear. In comparison, such teachers and fellows are like the radiance of a small lamp and the croaking of frogs, chatter chatter blah blah blah—how can they ever offer anything of worth? Being afflicted by distinctions and divisions made in disputations and discussions is the seventh hardship.

Next, one does one thing in the morning and something else at night, sits down to practice then stands up to pursue another idea. One relishes the moment and hates planning long-term, starts out concerned and diligent and ends up lazy and indolent. Being afflicted by inconsistencies in will and intention is the eighth hardship.

Next, one wastes years in the course of life, months in every year, days in every month, and hours in every day. In one's younger years fame and profit never leave the mind; when old, one's children and grandchildren constantly occupy the intention. The bloom of the years is limited, and before one knows it, this year is already over and one has to attend on the next. People's affairs are without bounds, and before one knows it, today's business is already over one has to attend to tomorrow's. If one does not prepare today for tomorrow, how can one fight in old age to get back one's youth? Being afflicted by wasting years and months is the ninth hardship.

Only by assiduously avoiding these nine hardships can one properly venerate the Dao. Among them, moreover, if one fails to avoid even one or two, all one's labors will be in vain and one will never be successful.

Lü asked: Now that I understand the nine hardships, may I please learn about the ten demonic attacks?

Zhong replied: The so-called ten demonic attacks happen in three situations: in waking life, in dreams and sleep, and during inner observation.

There may be flowery attractions filling the eyes, the music of reeds and pipes filling the ears, the tongue tasting delicious foods, the nose enjoying strange fragrances, emotions and thoughts full of pleasures and delights, intention and will vast and extensive. If you encounter any of these, do not engage them but recognize them as a demonic attack of the six desires.

There may be jasper towers and bejeweled pavilions, painted pillars and carved beams, pearl-studded hangings and embroidered curtains, elegant chambers with fragrant orchids, all sorts of places full of jewels and treasures, or halls filled with gold and jade. If you encounter any of these, do not engage them but recognize them as a demonic attack of conspicuous wealth.

There may be golden bridles and valuable steeds, heavy covered sedan chairs going by, a duchy endowed with ten thousand household, officers bearing banners and flags, filling the gates with their green and purple robes, whips and tablets overflowing in the chambers. If you encounter any of these, do not engage them but recognize them as a demonic attack of the strife for honor.

There may be a light mist soaking and moisturizing, warm sunlight wide and open, violent winds and strong rains, rolling thunder and flashes of lightning, reeds and pipes sounding brightly, tears and wails indicating hurt and distress. If you encounter any of these, do not engage them but recognize them as a demonic attack of the six emotions.

There may be family members facing adversities, your clan suffering from calamities, sons and daughters suffering from sickness and disease, father and mother passing away, older or younger brothers far away from home, wives and concubines living separate. If you encounter any of these, do not engage them but recognize them as a demonic attack of love and affection.

It may feel as if one is losing the body in a fierce conflagration, dropping off a steep cliff, being stung by nasty insects, or harmed by poisonous drugs. On the road one may run into nasty brigands or criminals and die as a result. If you encounter any of these, do not engage them but recognize them as a demonic attack of affliction and hardship.

There may be the Ten Saviors, the Powers of Yang, the Three Pure Ones, the Jade Emperor, the Four Sages, the Seven Dipper Lords, the Powers of the Five Sacred Mountains, the Eight Kings. They are all majestic and dignified, fully in control, coming and going, wheeling about in the air. If you encounter any of these, do not engage them but recognize them as a demonic attack of sages and worthies.

There may be a battle field, full of soldiers, both infantry and cavalry, swords and weapons glittering like frost, spears and axes raised, bows and crossbows drawn, fighting to the death, full of amazing courage and agility. If you encounter any of these, do not engage them but recognize them as a demonic attack of swords and weapons.

There may be immortal ladies and jade maidens, lining up and practicing their arts, their music and singing filling the air, their dance colorful in variegated silks, their services skillful in their red sleeves as they offer wine in golden chalices. If you encounter any of these, do not engage them but recognize them as a demonic attack of entertainment and pleasure.

There may be beauties with charming looks and rich adornments, skillful entertainers at home in elegant settings, bodies smooth and scantily clad, who lean close to you, trembling seductively, inviting to have sex. If you encounter any of these, do not engage them but recognize them as a demonic attack of sexual attraction

These ten demonic attacks are hard not to engage with. Once adepts engage with them, they get attached, and once they are attached, they are completely hooked. If they never fully attain Dao, it is mostly because of this.

If Daoist adepts encounter these in real life [lit., outside the personal body] and neither engage with them nor get hooked on them, then their heart will not falter and their will not be shaken. If they see them in dreams and neither engage with them nor get hooked on them, then their spirit will not go astray and their observation will not scatter. If they encounter things like this during inner observation, they should check carefully how spurious or real they are and determine whether they are genuine or fake. Adepts must not go along with their waves or float off with their tides, engage with these robbers as if they were their children.

Once they kindle the perfect fire of *samadhi* to incinerate the body, with one stroke the host of demons will naturally scatter. They should use the purple river carriage to move the yang spirit within, transfer to the inner courtyard, and ascend to the celestial palace. From there they can pursue transcendence and liberation.

Quite commonly, Daoist followers in the past as much as today attain a mind of clarity and stillness, but then change their volition under the impact of mental projections and often have a hard time escaping from the ten demonic attacks and the nine hardships. They vainly claim the title of Daoist follower and in the end never get to see any real effects of attaining Dao. They may even get away from the labors of the world of dust, retreat to a remote place and obscure their traces, focusing their will on the gate of all mysteries [*Daode jing* 1]. However, they cannot completely do away with the nine hardships and still get trapped by one or two of the ten demonic attacks.

They may attain Dao to a certain degree, but either stop in the middle of the path or reach a medium or even only a minor level of accomplishment. If they attain immortality, they become human or earth immortals at best. However, if they do away completely with all hardships and demonic attacks, they are ready to have the confirmation experiences of step-by-step ascending to the immortals, properly using inner observation to harmonize the yang spirit, pointing at the sun, and returning to the three isles.

18. Confirmation Experiences

Lü asked: Everybody hates to get sick, but Daoist followers actively pursue being free from disease and remaining in good health. Everybody fears death, but Daoist followers actively wish to avoid death and attain eternal life. The people of the world relish living in the world, but Daoist followers actively desire ascending to the immortals and wandering far beyond all things. The people of the world relish living on the earth, but Daoist followers actively strive to transcend the ordinary and enter the grotto heavens.

They voluntarily submit to hardship and suffering, often remaining poor and humble, yet mentally float in clear serenity and ethereal lightness, hiding their traces in open fields and wilderness seclusion. Because they practice in isolation, they may not know whether their efforts are deep or shallow. When it comes time to change methods, they have a hard time judging whether to modify them sooner or later. So, once one has reached a minor level of achievement, what is the order of confimation experiences?

Zhong replied: If one practices seriously with an earnest will but in the end sees no success, this is not the fault of Dao but happens because Daoist adepts do not follow an enlightened teacher and receive the wrong methods. If one practices seriously with the correct methods but in the end sees no success, this is not the fault of Dao, either, but happens because Daoist adepts do not know the right timing and thus have no way to attain accomplishments.

On the other hand, if one encounters an enlightened teacher and gets the correct methods, then practices them properly and with the right timing, why should one worry about not having any confirmation experiences?

Lü asked: So, the methods you speak of, do they have a set number [of stages]? And the timing you mention, does that have key numbers?

Zhong replied: The methods come in a system of twelve:

1. Matching yin and yang
2. Gathering and dispersing water and fire
3. Mating dragon and tiger
4. Heating and refining the cinnabar medicine
5. Quickening the gold crystal by pulling back the elbows
6. Reverting jade fluid to the elixir field
7. Refining the physical form with jade fluid
8. Reverting golden fluid to the elixir field
9. Refining the physical form with golden fluid
10. Refining *qi* by moving to the prime
11. Renewing *qi* through inner observation
12. Transcendence, liberation, and multilocation[4]

As regards timing, in the course of a year, one works with the principles of the continuous ascent and descent of yin and yang through heaven and earth; in the course of a month, one works with the correct count of the coming and going of the sun and moon. Each day has four divisions, eight trigrams, ten stems, twelve branches, 100 segments, and 6,000 units.

Working with the various methods and distinguishing and dividing them correctly, from the first day onward, one has confirmation experiences in the right order until one reaches liberation from material reality and can ascend to the immortals—absolutely and without fail. Right from the start, stay away form all lascivious and wayward tendencies, while cultivating both within and without.

---

[4] These items match the headings of the *Lingbao bifa*, with sections 6 and 7 as well as 8 and 9 conflated into one, making a total of ten.

Once one has assembled the medicine and is filled with golden essence, mind and mental projections naturally dissolve and one can vanquish all yin ghosts. The heart meridian opens and there is sweet fluid in the mouth. Then yin and yang engage in battle, and time and again one can hear the sounds of wind and thunder in the abdomen. Spirit and material souls stir, and one may experience frightful states during dream and sleep.

After this, there may be some small ailments or minor discomforts in the six viscera and four limbs, but they naturally resolve without medication. The elixir fields warm up spontaneously at night as the complexion gets clear and luscious during the day and the eyes come to see a spirit light even if in a dark room.

In dreams, one is a valiant warrior whom no animal can harm or people dare to cheat. Alternatively, one carries a little babe home in arms. The golden barrier and jade lock are firmly sealed, and one no longer experiences unwarranted leakage while dreaming. With a clap of thunder, all joints and nodes are open and connected. Startled, one sweats freely from all four limbs.

Next, the jade fluid boils and bubbles, coagulating into fermented liquor, and the fluid of pure life force turns into creamy juice. Increasingly awesome and with a strong smell of sandalwood, it completely fills mouth and belly. One's bones become light and turn more into yang spirit, allowing one to move smoothly and run as fast as a horse, walking and stepping as if flying. One no longer pays any mind to the various mental projections and gets rid of all cravings and desires. Able to infuse perfect *qi* into other beings, one can heal people's ailments and diseases, while in inner observation, one illuminates all and remains free from darkness.

The pupils in the eyes become clear like dots of lacquer, facial wrinkles smooth out, and one looks forever young. Perfect *qi* gradually fills the entire body, and one feels forever satiated, needing only little food. Even if one drinks liquor without measure, one never gets intoxicated.

After that, the body appears suffused by light: spirit and *qi* are both gorgeous. The sagely elixir generates good taste while the fluid issues a pleasant fragrance. Fragrance and wondrous taste are constantly present in mouth and nose; even outsiders may be able to perceive and smell them.

Next, one's vision becomes so sharp one can see an autumn hair at a distance of hundred paces. All old scars and residual marks throughout the body disappear naturally, and one never again issues nasal mucus, tears, saliva, or sweat. Once the embryo is complete and the *qi* fully viable, moreover, one can abstain from all eating and drinking

Internal volition clear and lofty, one merges with great emptiness. All emotions and loving feelings as well as all mental projections naturally stop. Below, one eliminates the nine worms; above, one kills the three deathbringers. Spirit and material souls no longer wander about, and there is no more need for sleep and dreams. Spirit luscious and essence strong, one functions equally well night and day.

The body entirely consisting of yang essence, the spirit residence is strong and stable, the four limbs no longer fear cold and heat, and one no longer thinks of life and death as opposites. Sitting in oblivion or practicing inner observation, one wanders far off to the realm of Huaxu and visits the lands of the spirit immortals. Full of women and music, with splendid towers and terraces, variegated and colorful, beautiful and extraordinary, they are like nothing at all like the human world.

Once one has accumulated enough merits, practiced sufficiently, and fulfilled all karmic retributions, one receives perfect registration in the Three Clarities. As yin and yang continue to change and transform, one can predict the success or failure of people's affairs and can foretell disasters and misfortunes. Tired of the dust of the world striking the eyes, one silently turns away from it to practice further purification in a quiet place. Then the immortal embryo manifests as a body outside the body: one is a spirit sage.

Perfect *qi* is pure yang, and in one cry one can externalize the mercury entity. The immortal embryo duly starts to fly off, and an auspicious light pervades the chamber. Even when deeply quiet, one can hear the sounds of music. Coming face to face with ordinary people, even though they may be wealthy and of high rank, one always smells their stink of decay and sees them just as mere bones and skeletons.

Next, spirit becomes more refined, and one can shift shape and location at will. One's secret powers fully developed, one starts to look like an immortal. Like a tree of jade, one consists of strange bones and issues a golden glow. Wherever one goes, any place one stays, there are always spirit helpers that naturally appear and report for service. Quickly and easily summoned, they fulfill one's every wish.

As one practices outer observation in deep stillness, a purple haze fills the vision and a golden radiance spreads from the top of the head, enveloping the entire body. Suddenly the inside of the body transforms and a fiery dragon soars out or a mysterious crane flies up. These are signs that spirit and life force have transcended the ordinary bones and one is going beyond the flow of common existence: this is called transcendence and liberation.

After attaining transcendence and liberation, one is always enveloped by a radiant vapor and surrounded by auspicious *qi*. Wondrous flower petals fall like rain from heaven, and mysterious cranes come to visit. A fabulous fragrance spreads as jade maidens descend to present celestial writs and purple summons.

Once concluded, one dresses in an immortal cap and gown and takes hold of various other regalia. Banner-baring majestic beings line up in front and behind, right and left, too many to count. They escort one formally to return to the purple office on the isles of Penglai, where one has audience with the Perfect Lord of Great Tenuity. He orders one's name and place of origin to be entered into the heavenly ledgers. Upon examination and measuring of one's merits and behavior, one is assigned a place to live on the three isles—properly called a perfected person and immortal master.

Lü asked: Today, you, my venerable teacher, have explained to me in great detail the overarching principles of the invisible and inaudible, the mysterious core workings of heaven and earth. You have not only opened and clarified my vision and hearing, but also enhanced and beautified my essence and spirit.

For the remaining years of my life, I wish to be no longer of the same kind as the dust and dirt of the world. However, knowing does not mean I can practice efficiently, and practicing does not mean I can attain [Dao]. I am well aware that the great matters of life and death are enormous and that time and light pass swiftly. Although I understand the wondrous principles, without ever getting to practice seriously, in the end I cannot complete my merits and will be no different from those who don't know anything. May I, therefore, ask that you instruct me exactly in how to apply and use the proper timing of energy conjunction and the right methods of serious practice?

Zhong replied: For this, I have compiled the *Lingbao bifa* (Conclusive Methods of Numinous Treasure) in ten scrolls and twelve sections. It discusses each under six headings: 1. Golden Declarations; 2. Written in Jade; 3. Source of Perfection; 4. In Likeness; 5. Perfect Instructions; and 6. Dao Essentials.

It encompasses and explicates the great Dao, outlines and illustrates the Three Clarities. It outlines the continuous ascent and descent of yin and yang through heaven and earth as the dominant model and explains the overarching rules of the coming and going of the essence and florescence of the sun and the moon. In fact, it presents instructions for all five types of immortals and provides guidance for the three levels of accomplishment. You should keep it close by every single day!

Text Two[1]

Lingbao bifa

Preface

By Zhongli Quan, Yunfang, the Perfected of Rightful Yang

Dao cannot be explained or transmitted, named or recorded. Despite this, ever since high antiquity there have been quite a few who ascended to immortality and attained Dao. Offering my volition, I bowed down to wise forefathers and in my heart embraced the great Dao. Without meaning to do so, I came to raise swords and got involved with the military: the times were dangerous, and the world was in disorder.

Eventually I had to flee for my life, obscuring my traces among rivers, lakes, cliffs, and valleys. Once I was far enough away, I began to understand my inner nature and rested my heart, dedicating myself solely to clarity and purity, the invisible and inaudible. I read through numerous scriptures on elixirs, continuously asked advice from my friends in Dao and pursued the minute details of how to stop words and nourish life, the great, inexplicable Dao of perfect immortality.

When I lived in a rocky cave in the Zhongnan mountains, I received thirty scrolls of Numinous Treasure scriptures [in revelation]. Their first section, entitled *Jin'gao shu* (Book of Golden Declarations), was presented by [the Heavenly Venerable of] Primordial Beginning; their middle section, called *Yushu lu* (Records Written in Jade), was narrated by the Primordial Emperor [Lord of the Dao]; their last section, named *Zhenyuan yi* (Explanation of the Source of Perfection), was transmitted by the Highest Lord [Lao]. Altogether, they consisted of several thousand words.

I put on my clothes before dawn and ate after dusk [worked diligently], all the while pondering them widely and reflecting on them in great depth.

[1] The text is translated on the basis of its edition in the Daoist Canon (DZ 1191). Its *Daoshu* version (ch. 42)—available in the French rendition by Farzeen Baldrian-Hussein (1984)—has no section titles or secondary headings indicating revealed sources, such as "Golden Declarations" or "Written in Jade." It presents only a short summary of the preface and consistently omits the latter parts of each section. In the main body of the text, it consists of a complex mixture of omissions and additions. The translation marks parts not found in the *Daoshu* version in curved parentheses {} and gives parts added there in square brackets [], marked "DS".

Eventually I came to realize that there is yang within yin and yin within yang, which represents the basic order of the up and down movement of heaven and earth; that *qi* generates water and water generates *qi*, which represents the principle of the fusion of heart and kidneys. Present in the images of things, Dao is never far from humanity.

Matching and fusing them in the rhythm of heavenly stems like Jia and Geng, I worked with the golden elixir according to the proper standards. Reducing and augmenting based on the pattern of earthly branches like Mao and You, I followed the natural firing times without fail. Penetrating the bottom with red lead and black mercury I failed to complete the great medicine, but when I guided the golden and jade fluids to the top, I managed to revert them to the elixir field.

Moving [the *qi*] from nonbeing into being, I constantly maintained the heart of a valiant warrior. Raising it from bottom to top, I gradually entered the realm of the invisible and inaudible. Reducing lead and augmenting mercury, I managed to dissolve the two and eight yin. Renewing my bones and refining my physical form, I made the three and nine yang grow tall.

I discerned whether water and source were clear or turbid during the hours I experienced full saturation. I recognized whether the inner scenery was perfect or fleeting on the days I sat in oblivion. I found the obscure instructions of the mysterious pivot hard to express in physical form and written works, yet I was able to use the wondrous principles of Numinous Treasure to enter the ranks of the sages and transcend the ordinary. Presenting the combined methods of the Three Vehicles, I call this work *Lingbao bifa*, "The Conclusive Methods of Numinous Treasure." These sagely words of the great Dao I dare not keep to myself only, but transmit to my disciple Lü Dongbin. May he not keep it secret when he completes Dao, but hand it down to adepts of generations to come.

1. Matching Yin and Yang

Written in Jade: {The great Dao has no form: you look or listen for it and you cannot see or hear it [*Daode jing* 14]. The great Dao has no name: you measure and count it and you cannot fathom or calculate it. Then Dao generates form, and following form it establishes names. Its name is great: it is heaven and earth.} Heaven obtains the Dao of [the trigram] Qian and accumulates *qi to* cover all below; earth obtains the Dao of [the trigram] Kun and relies on material reality to support all above. Between their covering and supporting, above and below, they are 84,000 miles apart.

Since *qi* and matter cannot interact by themselves, heaven uses Qian to connect to Kun and reverts to earth, its yang carrying yin to make it ascend; earth uses Kun to connect to Qian and reverts to heaven [the sky], its yin embracing yang to let it descend. Ascending and descending in turn, they revolve in accordance with Dao. This is why heaven and earth can live forever.

Source of Perfection: Between heaven and earth, what tends to stay above is yang; thus, 42,000 miles from above to below is called the domain of yang. What tends to stay below is yin; thus, 42,000 miles from below to above is called the domain of yin. {Although these two have form and names, they still are hard to define by measure and count. Thus one year has four seasons, eight divisions, twenty-four *qi*-periods, seventy-two base weeks, 360 days, and 4320 double-hours. Twelve double-hours make one day, five days make one base week, three base weeks make one *qi*-period, three *qi*-periods make one division, two divisions made one season, and four seasons make one year.}

Each year begins at the division of the winter solstice. At this time, yang ascends from earth, and in the course of one *qi*-period or fifteen days, it reaches 7,000 miles. Three *qi*-periods make one division or forty-five days, during which yang ascends 21,000 miles. Two divisions make one season or ninety days, during which yang ascends 42,000 miles. Reaching the midpoint between heaven and earth, it touches the domain of yin. At this time, yang is halfway in the midst of yin. The weather [*qi*] changes to being warm: the time of the spring equinox has come.

Passing this, yang ascends further and enters the domain of yang. That is, having obtained all the *qi* [of earth], it keeps ascending. Moving as before for forty-five days, it comes to the beginning of summer. After another forty-five days, it reaches the division of the summer solstice, at which point it has passed through the entire 84,000 miles of distance and reached heaven [the sky]. Yang is now in the midst of yang. The weather changes to being hot, and accumulated yang begins to generate yin. Thus, a single yin grows in the midst of two yang.

This begins at the division of the summer solstice. At this time, yin descends from heaven [the sky], and in the course of one *qi*-period or fifteen days it reaches 7,000 miles. Three *qi*-periods make one division or forty-five, days, during which yin descends 21,000 miles. Two divisions make one season or ninety days, during which yin descends 42,000 miles. Reaching the midpoint between heaven and earth, it touches the domain of yang. At this time, yin is halfway in the midst of yang. The weather changes to being cool: the time of the fall equinox has come.

Passing this, yin descends further and enters the domain of yin. That is, having obtained all the *qi* of heaven, it keeps descending. Moving as before for forty-five days, it comes to the beginning of winter. After another forty-five days, it reaches the division of the winter solstice, at which point it has passed through the entire 84,000 miles of distance and reached earth. Yin is now in the midst of yin. The weather changes to being cold, and accumulated yin begins to generate yang. Thus, a single yang grows in the midst of two yin [the trigram Kan].

At the winter solstice, the one yang again begins to ascend, moving as before without stopping. Completing one revolution, the two forces begin yet again, without ever losing their way. The winter solstice is when yang begins to grow; it ascends to revert back to heaven. The summer solstice is when yin begins to grow; it descends to revert back to earth.

At the summer solstice, yang has fully ascended and reached heaven: a single yin comes about. At the winter solstice, yin has fully descended and reached earth: a single yang comes about. This is why these points are called summer and winter solstice [lit., times of "coming about"]. Yang ascends and passes the spring equinox: it enters the domain of yang and leaves the domain of yin. Yin descends and passes the fall equinox: it enters the domain of yin and leaves the domain of yang. Thus they are called the spring and fall equinox [lit., times of "division"].

While yang ascends after the winter solstice, there is still some yin descending, down from above, but what yin descends is excess yin within yang. It stops at the domain of yang, where it scatters and disappears. If allowed to keep on descending and to reach its domain, it will clash with the ascending yang, and the *qi* will be eliminated.

Similarly, while yin descends after the summer solstice, there is still some yang ascending, up from below, but what yang ascends is excess yang within yin. It stops in the domain of yin, where it scatters and disappears. If allowed to keep on ascending and to reach its domain, it will clash with the descending yin, and the *qi* will be eliminated.

As yin and yang ascend and descend, in all their moving up and down, they never go beyond 84,000 miles; in all their coming and going, they never exceed 360 days. Thus by appreciating the four seasons with their weather patterns of warm, cool, cold, and hot, one can recognize yin and yang; by noting the eight divisions of yang ascending and yin descending, one can know heaven and earth. {Fathoming them based on the core workings of nature, one can get a good clue of how heaven and earth function. If one just used teachings transmitted orally to compare or measure their way, how could done ever get the right estimate or calculation and truly know them?}

In Likeness: Dao generates the myriad beings, among which heaven and earth are the greatest and human beings have the most life force. Placed separately in Dao, humans yet match heaven and earth. The heart is like heaven; the kidneys are like earth; the liver is the domain of yang; the lungs is the domain of yin. The heart and the kidneys are 8.4 inches apart, matching the distance between heaven and earth that cover and support all.

Qi in the human body is like yang; fluid it like yin. The midpoint of the double-hours Zi [11 am-1 pm] and Wu [11 pm-1 am] are like the divisions of the summer and winter solstices. Those of Mao [5-7 am] and You [5-7 pm] are like the spring and fall equinoxes. One day is like one year; the eight trigrams in one day are like the eight divisions marking annual time.

During the Zi hour, *qi* grows in the kidneys; during Mao, it reaches the liver. The liver is yang, and as *qi* is dominant here, yang ascends and enters the domain of yang. This is just like the spring equinox. During the Wu hour, *qi* reaches the heart; it accumulates and generates fluid. This is just like yang reaching heaven at the summer solstice and generating yin.

During the Wu hour, fluid grows in the heart; during You, it reaches the lungs. The lungs are yin, and as fluid abounds here, yin descends and enters the domain of yin. This is just like the fall equinox. During the Zi hour, fluid reaches the kidneys; it accumulates and generates *qi*. This is just like yin reaching earth at the winter solstice and generating yang. From here, the cycle begins again, running around in a loop for days and months, never diminishing, never ceasing. Following it, one can extend one's years.

Perfect Instructions: Only human beings can fully attain the Dao of heaven and earth. {They receive their physical form from father and mother, one body growing within another, then increasingly get away from Dao.} While still in the womb, their primordial *qi* is full but soon after, the six desires and seven emotions arise, so that they waste and scatter their primordial yang, release and lose their perfect *qi*. Even though they participate in the natural pattern of the mutual generation of *qi* and fluid, they cannot match their continuous ascent and descent through heaven and earth.

With each exhalation, primordial *qi* leaves; with each inhalation, it enters. Although people in this fashion partake of the *qi* of heaven and earth, once it has entered, they cannot retain it. On the contrary, with each exhalation they let it go again, causing heaven and earth to take back their original *qi*. Once *qi* has scattered like this, they have a hard time generating fluid. Being short on fluid, they have a hard time generating *qi*.

At any particular time when *qi* is dominant [in a certain organ], every day they should utilize the appropriate trigram, so that in relation to *qi*, they take in a lot and release only a little, then retain it with some force in their abdomen. The moment *qi* ascends from below, make sure not to let it go; as soon as it moves in from without, immediately retain it [in the abdomen]. In this manner, the two *qi* fuse: they accumulate and generate the fluid of the five organs. As they revert it to the prime [elixir field], it increases even more. {Continue the work over a succession of days; stop when you see experiential effects.} [DS: This method is a minor accomplishment of embryo respiration as developed by Bodhidharma.]

Dao Essentials: To meet the oldest children of Lord Yang, make sure much [*qi*] enters and only little leaves. {As son and daughter wrestle with each other, over time you pursue and achieve perfection.}

This means accumulated *qi* generates fluid, and accumulated fluid generates *qi*. [DS: Fluid in the midst of *qi* is fluid in the process of descending; *qi* in the midst of fluid is *qi* in the process of ascending.] It refers to the method of the mutual generation of *qi* and fluid through proper matching. You will attain this through serious practice even before one year has passed. Working consecutively for one year or three hundred days is considered one practice period. Even within ten days, you will see experiential effects.

You will eat and drink well, all your ailments and diseases dissolve completely; your head and eyes will be clear and sharp, your heart and abdomen empty and joyful. You will have much strength and little fatigue, at times hear sounds like wind and thunder in your abdomen, and experience good effects too numerous to list. [DS: Breathe calmly and stop all thoughts; sit silently all day long, focusing on mental stillness and drive out the yin spirit. This is the way of the immortals.] [End *Daoshu*, sect. 1]

Explanation: The oldest children of Lord Yang are born when Qian connects to Kun, just as *qi* ascends and moves up. The son [the trigram Zhen/Thunder] is *qi*: he ascends from the kidneys. The daughter [the trigram Xun/Wind] is fluid: she descends from the heart. They clash with each other because they keep on moving up and down. Hold the breath in to generate fluid; accumulate fluid to generate *qi*. In this manner, you mate and match the two forces. Over time, you naturally obtain perfect water.

Perfect Explanation: This is the first step of the practice. When the *qi* of ascending yang is dominant in the position of Mao and the correct trigram, inhale deeply to take in the rightful *qi* of heaven and earth; exhale gently to let hardly any of your own primordial *qi* go. As you get the two *qi* to harmonize, *qi* accumulates and generates fluid; fluid increases and generates *qi*. This is the method of matching yin and yang and setting up the mutual generation of *qi* and fluid.

2. Gathering and Dispersing Water and Fire

[DS: This explains the matching of yin and yang through embryo respiration. But how about gathering and dispersing water and fire? Master Zhongli said:]

Golden Declarations: {What we call great Dao is so high it has no above. Stretch and look up far and you can see nothing above it nor can you ever see its head. What we call great Dao is so low it has no below. Bend and look down carefully and you can see nothing below it nor can you ever see its base. Its beginning has nothing prior to it: you cannot see anything before it. Its end has nothing after it: you cannot see anything beyond it.}

In the midst of the great Dao, heaven and earth came to be; they do have the dimensions of above and below. Within their midst, moreover, yin and yang came to be; they have a beginning and end that can be expressed in correct count. As they move up and down, look up far and look down carefully, and you can estimate their core workings. As they begin and end, you can measure and count, fathom and calculate and thus appreciate their principles. Approaching it in this manner, the great Dao can be known.

Source of Perfection: From the positions of heaven and earth above and below we know what is high and low throughout the universe. From the times of yin and yang beginning and ending we know what comes first and what follows in the way of nature. Heaven and earth never deviate from the correct count; this count is fulfilled in the course of one year. Yin and yang never lose their inherent order; this order works according to the eight divisions.

At the winter solstice, yang begins to grow. At the spring equinox, there is half yang within yin. Going beyond this, there is pure yang and yin is all gone. At the summer solstice, yang reaches its great ultimate [zenith] and yin begins to grow. At the fall equinox, there is half yin within yang. Going beyond this, there is pure yin and yang is all gone. {At the winter solstice, yin reaches its great ultimate, and yang again begins to grow. They ascend and descend as before, moving up and down, always beginning and ending. They may not completely exhaust the great Dao, but they never lose its foundation.} If you want to understand the great Dao, you must take in the model of heaven and earth and closely examine the order of yin and yang.

In Likeness: {The heart and kidneys are like heaven and earth; *qi* and fluid are like yin and yang. One day is like one year. [The trigram] Gen [3 am] during the day, in terms of the year, matches the division of the beginning of spring. Qian [9 pm] matches the division of the beginning of winter. Within heaven and earth, what tends to move down is yin. Thus, the area 42,000 miles up from the bottom is called the domain of yin.}

Yang begins to grow at the winter solstice and ascends from there. At the beginning of spring, it has risen 21,000 miles into the domain of yin and has a hard time prevailing over it. {Similarly, what tends to move up is yang; thus, the area 42,000 miles down from the top is called the domain of yang.} Yin begins to grow at the summer solstice and descends from there. At the beginning of fall, it has sunk 21,000 miles into the domain of yang [being 63,000 miles from the point of origin] and has a hard time prevailing over it.

{At the beginning of summer, yang keeps on ascending, being now 63,000 miles above earth and 21,000 miles below heaven. Thus it reaches the full domain of yang, with no yin whatsoever. Similarly, at the beginning of winter, yin keeps on descending, being now 63,000 miles below heaven and 21,000 miles above earth. Thus it reaches the full domain of yin, with no yang whatsoever.}

The beginning of spring in the course of a year in the course of a day is like Gen [3 am] [DS: at the end of the Chou hour (1-3 am) and the beginning of Yin (3-5 am)]. At this time, kidney *qi* moves down into the bladder

[DS: has not yet arrived at the liver but rests in the domain of yin]. Immersed in fluid, it is subtle and weak. Thus, this is a time when yang *qi* is hard put to ascend.

The beginning of winter in the course of a year in the course of a day is like Qian [9 pm] [DS: the end of the Xu hour (7-9 pm) and the beginning of Hai (9-11 pm)]. At this time, heart fluid starts to move down, following the urge to return to the prime and again enter the kidneys. Thus, this is a time when yin abounds and yang is eliminated. [DS: There is little *qi* and much fluid.] The reason why people get sick [DS: and die early] is that their yin and yang are out of alignment, {typically yang being low and yin overwhelming. This the cause of disease.} [DS: They are unable to ascend and descend, since *qi* and fluid have dried up and cannot generate each other. Alas! When *qi* is all gone, spirit disperses: this is death.]

Perfect Instructions: When yang rises to the beginning of spring, moving up from below, within days it gets to be half yang within yin. When yin sinks to the beginning of fall, moving down from above, within days it gets to be half yin within yang. This is the natural way of heaven and earth. Only human beings let their *qi* grow feeble at Gen [3 am], not knowing the right times to nurture it. They let it scatter at Qian [9 pm], not realizing the principles of gathering it.

Day and night they let the six desires and seven emotions waste and scatter their primordial yang, preventing perfect *qi* from becoming dominant. They release and lose their perfect *qi*, preventing perfect fluid from being generated. [DS: Is this not deplorable?] {For this reason, they never attain the eternal life of heaven and earth.

Thus, the masters of old practiced collecting in the morning and covering at night, and duly managed to live for extensive periods in the world. Collecting in the morning means to gather yang up from below, then bending before stretching. Once it is present in oneself, nurture and stretch it to prevent even the smallest scattering. Covering at night means to collect fresh *qi* into oneself, always moving to the light and dispelling darkness, looking for yang within yin. Once it is present within, darken and brighten it to prevent all loss.}

Around sunrise, at Gen [3 am], nurture primordial *qi*: {do not let thoughts of fame and profit agitate your mind nor ideas of good and evil disturb your intention. Loosen your clothing and sit in meditation to nurture your *qi*: let go off all thoughts, forget all emotions, gently undertake healing exercises,} in turn bending and stretching your arms and legs three to five times, to allow the *qi* of the four limbs to rise. In this manner you can guard primordial *qi* within as it ascends to move to the office of the heart.

Swallow one or two mouthfuls of saliva, tap and rub your head and face twenty to thirty times. {This way, you can expel all the bad and turbid *qi* accumulated in the course of the night.} If you do this over prolonged periods, you will have a glossy complexion and amazing beauty, your muscles and flesh will be radiant and supple. [DS: This method is called dispersing fire or the minor refinement of the physical form.]

Similarly at sunset, at Qian [9 pm], gather primordial *qi*: enter the chamber and sit in meditation, deeply inhale and pull on the external kidneys [testicles]. By inhaling deeply you take in heart fire and move it down; by pulling on the external kidneys you shift the *qi* from the bladder into the kidneys. Moving up and down, make sure to fuse the fire of the kidney *qi* so that the three fires gather into one.

This way you can supplement and warm the lower field. If there is no fluid, keep on gathering *qi* until it generates fluid; once there is fluid, heat it up so it generates *qi*. This is called gathering the fire. It is also called obtaining the perfect *qi* of great oneness. {Like in the early morning, swallow the saliva and massage the face, alternatively bending and stretching your arms and legs a few times. This is called dispersing fire or the minor refinement of the physical form.}

Dao Essentials: {Petals disperse and leaves fall in the depth of autumn. The jade man is too lazy to climb the dangerous tower. To gather the ruler and the people in harmony, feast and receive them at the right time.}

The method here involves taking in heart *qi* and receiving bladder *qi*. Without ever letting them scatter, fuse them with kidney *qi* and connect them to the trigram Kan. Soon, in the ocean of *qi* there is newly generated *qi*. Always begin this practice at the beginning of winter; stop when you see experiential effects. If you practice seriously, this will take less than a year; a full practice cycle is one year or three hundred days. Even within ten days you should see some concrete effects: your facial complexion is radiant and glossy, your flesh and skin is whole and delightful. Your lower field feels warm and pleasant, your urine output decreases, your four limbs are light and vigorous, your essence and spirit are clear and strong. [DS: These are clear concrete effects of the practice.] [End *Daoshu*, sect. 2]

All diseases, ailments, sickness, and discomfort dissolve completely. Like this you go on for all the months of the year, never tiring in your serious practice. As you keep on working on matching yin and yang, gradually these effects will become obvious. As you become more successful, augment at Gen every day; as you keep on working with this method, working at Qian, the three primes will become active. Then it is time to stop.

Explanation: "Petals disperse and leaves fall in the depth of autumn" indicates the weakening of *qi* in the human body, the radiance of the setting sun, a state when yang *qi* has scattered and no longer rises. For this reason, the text speaks of being "too lazy to climb the dangerous tower." The tower in question is the twelve-storied tower. The heart contains ruling fire; the bladder has common fire. Breathing deeply and massaging the kidneys from the outside, one causes the heart and the outer kidney *qi* to gather and become one. Thus, it says "gather in harmony." "Feast" indicates breathing, while "receive" means massaging. Never stop doing this in the early morning: this method is by far the most fundamental of all.

Perfect Explanation: Yang *qi* is subtle at Gen [3 am]. Therefore, one must practice healing exercises, bending and stretching, swallowing the saliva and rubbing the face. This way one scatters the fire throughout the four limbs and nurtures primordial *qi*.

Yang *qi* scatters at Qian [9 pm]. For this reason, one must inhale *qi* to the heart and massage the kidneys from the outside. This allows it to merge with kidney *qi* and lets the three fires gather together and merge into one, thereby coagulating primordial *qi*. Thus the text speaks of "gathering and scattering water and fire." It causes the root to be strong and the stem to be firm.

3. Mating Dragon and Tiger

Golden Declarations: When the great prime [DS: Dao] first divided, there was great beginning. From the midst of great beginning, there arose great nonbeing. From the midst of great nonbeing, there arose great emptiness. From the midst of great emptiness, there arose the great void. From the midst of the great void, there arose great material reality.

Once there was great material reality, there was the pure and turbid material nature of heaven and earth. They were like an egg, consisting of dark and yellow colors, a single one being in the great void. {Then yang ascended to heaven, and when it reached its great ultimate, it generated yin. Enveloping yang in mysterious darkness, it began to descend. Yin descended to earth, and when it reached its great ultimate, it generated yang. Carrying yin in blurred vagueness, it ascended again. Setting up the model, since then, yin has been descending and yang ascending. Heaven and earth working in this way, they generated and completed the myriad beings.}

Source of Perfection: {Heaven is like the lid of a dish: once it gets there yang cannot rise; earth is like a grindstone: once it gets there yin cannot get in.}

At the winter solstice, yang ascends from earth, reaching heaven at the summer solstice. When it reaches its great ultimate, yin starts to grow. The reason why yin can grow is that yang originally comes from within yin and ascends from earth. Blurry and murky, vague and indistinct, water arises in *qi*: it has no form. When yang reaches heaven at the summer solstice, its accumulated *qi* turns into water. Thus we say, "Yang reaches its great ultimate, and yin starts to grow."

At the summer solstice, yin descends from heaven, reaching earth at the winter solstice. When it reaches its great ultimate, yang starts to grow. The reason why yang can grow is that yin originally comes from within yang and descends from heaven. Mysterious and dark, *qi* grows in water: it has no form. When yin reaches earth at the winter solstice, its accumulated water turns into *qi*. Thus we say, "Yin reaches its great ultimate, and yang starts to grow."

In Likeness: {The sphere of the body is like the great void. Within it, heart and kidneys are like heaven and earth, while *qi* and fluid are like yin and yang. The double-hours Zi [11 pm- 1am] and Wu [11 am-1 pm] are like winter and summer.}

Zi is Kan [midnight]: *qi* starts to grow in the kidneys. Wu is Li [noon]: water starts to grow in the heart. When the *qi* of the kidneys reaches the heart, it fuses with its *qi*, reaches its great ultimate, and generates water. This means that the generation of water comes from the *qi* that originates in the kidneys. Within *qi*, there is perfect water, which is formless. At Li noon], it reaches the heart and connects with its *qi*, reaches its great ultimate and generates water. This is the process. [DS: Is this not just like the accumulation of yang that produces yin?]

Similarly, when heart fluid [DS: born at Li and moving toward Kan] reaches the kidneys, it fuses with its water, reaches its great ultimate, and again generates *qi*. This means that the generation of *qi* comes from the water that originates in the heart. Within water, there is perfect *qi*, which is formless. At Kan [midnight], it reaches the kidneys and connects with its water, reaches its great ultimate and generates *qi*. This is the process. [DS: Is this not just like the accumulation of yin that produces yang?]

It is just like yang ascending and yin descending, each reaching their great ultimate, then mutually generating each other. Thus, that which generates yin and yang is the water hidden within yang and the *qi* contained deep within yin. [DS: They are just like the yin and yang of heaven and earth.]

Perfect Instructions: *Qi* is generated in the kidneys; it contains perfect water. Fluid is generated in the heart; it contains perfect *qi*. Perfect water and perfect *qi* are the perfect dragon and perfect tiger. {When yang reaches heaven and cannot rise any further, it reaches its great ultimate and generates yin. When yin reaches earth and cannot sink any further, it reaches its great ultimate and generates yang. This is the fundamental principle of heaven and earth.}

If human beings do not manage to function like heaven and earth, {the six desires and seven emotions will cause them to be impacted by other beings and lose their willpower,} so they waste and scatter their primordial yang, release and lose their perfect *qi*. [DS: The trigram Li matches the heart within the human body; on the outside, it corresponds to the Wu hour [noon]. Perfect yang matches primordial yang in people; on the outside, it corresponds to the sun.]

At Li [noon], when kidney *qi* reaches the heart, adepts should [DS: enter the meditation chamber, place their palms on top of each other, sit cross-legged, and straighten their body]. Consciously stabilize the spirit within, breathe softly through the nose, exhaling slowly, continuously, and uninterruptedly. Allow the saliva to fill the mouth, then swallow it down carefully, thereby guiding kidney *qi* to fuse with heart *qi*. Once the *qi* reaches its great ultimate, it generates water.

At Kan [midnight], when heart fluid reaches the kidneys and connects to kidney fluid, the two naturally fuse, reach their great ultimate, and generate *qi*. Thus, just as perfect *qi* transforms into fluid, perfect water transforms into *qi*. They effect mutual fusion, and there is perfect *qi* within fluid and perfect water within *qi*. Merging and melting into each other, they desire each other and move down: this is called the mating of dragon and tiger. If one maintains the firing times without fail, reducing and augmenting in the right order, one can nurture and complete the perfect embryo within three hundred days, thereby completing the great medicine. This is the foundation of {refining material reality, incinerating the self, moving to the prime, and attaining} transcendence and liberation.

Dao Essentials: {When the *qi* of cosmic oneness first starts its primordial circulation, perfect yang comes close to reaching the Li palace. Then you must assemble the perfect dragon and perfect tiger, bathing both with spring water from the jade pond.}

This warns against leaking primordial *qi* and releasing perfect water outside the body. If *qi* scatters, it cannot generate fluid; if fluid is insufficient, there is no perfect *qi*. And if *qi* and water do not fuse, how can one ever complete the great medicine? [DS: The water of perfect oneness that is in the kidneys fuses with the *qi* of rightful yang that is in the heart. As they join together, they give birth to a new human being. If this happens within a person, they produce a spiritual power called the internal elixir. Once it grows over three hundred days, it affords an extension of life.] Thus, each year make good use of the months and begin the work at the winter solstice; each day make good use of the double-hours, timing your work to culminate at Li [noon].

If people become Daoist adepts in later years, their root and prime are no longer firm. After having undergone decline and diminishing for many years, they no longer possess sufficient *qi*. However, even ten years of decline can be made up with a single year of dedicated effort. This is called reversion to the elixir field for assembling and supplementing. {After supplementing it a number of times, you can stop this practice which we call the full saturation of water and fire. This serves to extend the years and increase longevity, becoming what we call a human immortal. The effectual experiences are too many to list.}

Once the number of supplements is complete, the mouth generates sweet saliva, mental projections vanish, emotions and desires cease, the bones are disease-free, spirit light manifests in the darkness, and the eyes flash like lightning. [DS: All these are concrete effects of the method.] [End *Daoshu*, sect. 3]

Always begin at the winter solstice, apply the methods carefully and systematically, and within three hundred days you will be liberated through the perfect embryo and come to be an immortal.

Explanation: On the outside, the Wu hour matches Li [noon], when great yang turns into perfect yang. Within the person, the heart is the Li palace and primordial yang is the perfect dragon. The perfect tiger is the water generated from the *qi* of the kidneys; the perfect dragon is the *qi* generated from the fluid of the heart. The mouth is the jade pond; saliva is spring water.

Perfect Explanation: "When the *qi* of cosmic oneness first starts its primordial circulation," means to start at the winter solstice, which is the month matching the Zi hour. "Perfect yang comes close to reaching the Li palace" means to work at Li [noon] as the key period of practice: it is the Wu hour. The "perfect dragon" is the *qi* generated in heart fluid; the "perfect tiger" is the water generated in kidney *qi*. When water and *qi* fuse, we call it the mating of dragon and tiger.

4. Heating and Refining the Cinnabar Medicine

Golden Declarations: {Heaven and earth are the physical form of the great Dao; yin and yang are its *qi*.} Cold and hot, warm and cool are *qi* in physical form. Clouds and mist, rain and dew are images of *qi*. When earth [yang] *qi* ascends, it soars and forms clouds; when they scatter, there is rain. When heaven [yin] *qi* descends, it disperses and turns into mist, coagulates and turns into dew.

When too much yin accumulates, dew becomes rain, frost, and snow; when too much yang accumulates, mist becomes vapor, clouds, and fog. When yang is suppressed within yin, yang *qi* cannot ascend: it knocks and pounds and generates thunder and lightning. When yin *qi* is suppressed within yang, it coagulates and solidifies and generates hail and sleet. [DS: Thus, the brightness of yang disperses and becomes thunder; the *qi* of yin is agitated and turns into wind.] When yin and yang do not harmonize, they oppose each other and generate flashes of lightning and thunder. When they do not match, they interact wildly and generate rainbows and sky coloring.

Similarly, when perfect yang accumulates, it forms spirit, which appears beautifully in the stars and planets of the sky. When perfect yin accumulates it forms physical form, which appears majestically in the soils and stones on earth. The greatest among the stars and planets are the sun and the moon. The most precious among the soils and stones are gold and jade.

Thus, the physical forms yin and yang take are the sun and the moon above, gold and jade below.

Source of Perfection: {When yin does not obtain yang, there is no generation; when yang does not obtain yin, there is no completion.} When yang accumulates, spirit appears beautifully in the sky, most importantly in the sun and the moon. Manifestations of perfect yang, they need to obtain perfect yin, so both can complete each other. When yin accumulates, physical form appears majestically on earth, most preciously in gold and jade. Manifestations of perfect yin, they need to obtain perfect yang, so both can generate each other.

In Likeness: Perfect yang is like the perfect *qi* in heart fluid; perfect yin is like the perfect water in kidney *qi*. If perfect water does not obtain perfect *qi*, there is no generation; if perfect *qi* does not obtain perfect water, there is no maturation. At Li [noon], perfect water and perfect *qi* fuse in harmony above the heart and below the lungs, just like mother and child cherishing each other, husband and wife loving each other.

From Li [noon], they move on to Dui [6 pm]. At this time, yin is dominant and yang is weak. This is just like the last quarter of the moon or when gold and jade are hidden in darkness: one cannot use them. The sun and the moon use yin to complete yang; when their count [of days] is sufficient, they generate light. Gold and jade use yang to complete yin; when their *qi* is sufficient, they become precious ore.

Gold and jade become precious ore because their *qi* is sufficient and they advance yang. The sun and the moon generate light because their count is sufficient and they receive the bright part [lit., spirit soul]. [DS: This just like the accumulation of *qi* in the human body that produces fluid at Li [noon]. The moment when the fluid reverts to the lower prime and before it moves into the domain of *qi* is just like the moon in its last quarter when it no longer partakes of the bright part or like gold and jade that do not emit yang [light] from their surface.] Thus, at Qian [9 pm], one must stoke the fire to refine yang in alignment with the correct count [of the days]. The more one augments the fire, the longer more yang is refined and the closer one comes to eternal life.

Perfect Instructions: At Li [noon], when dragon and tiger mate, one can assemble the medicine. At Qian [9 pm], *qi* and fluid are ready to revert to the prime. They appear above the bladder and below the stomach, in front of the kidneys and behind the navel, left of the liver and right of the lungs, right of the small intestine and left of the large intestine. At this time, spleen *qi* is dominant and lung *qi* is abundant, heart *qi* is in abeyance and liver *qi* is weak.

Perfect *qi* fundamentally comes from the fusion of yang *qi*; when yang *qi* is weak, perfect *qi* has nothing it can cherish and will disperse despite one's efforts. To assemble [the medicine] at this time [of Qian], one must guard spirit consciousness deep within, keep the breath flowing smoothly through the nostrils, and hold the belly and abdomen gently contracted. Should the navel and kidney area feel too hot, gently release and ease the contraction; if they are not warm enough, increase it.

Let them gradually get hot, then keep them steady, relax the intention and release the will until they fill both Qian and Kun. This is called contracting the yang barrier to refine the cinnabar medicine. Do not let the *qi* move upward but keep perfect water stable, pervading the spleen palace. Breathe in and out systematically, moving it into the office of destiny and yellow court areas. Once *qi* and water have undergone this creative transformation, they will turn into essence, which becomes a pearl. The pearl in due course transforms into mercury, which turns into [cinnabar] sand. Cinnabar sand transforms into gold: thus we call it the golden elixir. This work is not minor.

Dao Essentials: {To assemble the medicine, you must rely on the jade rabbit. To come close to it you must work with the yellow dame. Wait until you can see them in Yong continent, then offer them a stanza of the Song of Yang.}

This is about the daily applications needed to assemble the medicine, a work undertaken in later years to restore wholeness, supplementing all at once ten [years' worth] of diminishing [energy]. {This method is called refining mercury to restore the elixir field.} Once the correct count has been reached, stop doing it every day. Typically, assemble the medicine at Li [noon], then heat and refine it at Qian [9 pm] by contracting the yang barrier. In spring and winter practice much assembling and little refining: one round at Qian and two rounds at Li is most efficient. In fall and summer, practice little assembling and much refining: one round at Li and two rounds at Qian is most efficient.

{Matching the dominant *qi* throughout the months of the year, the work of assembling and refining will be most effective. In this way one can extend one's years in this world and become a human immortal. Once the correct count supplementation is reached and you start to see experiential effects, increase your efforts, always working carefully and systematically.} When assembling the medicine, after one hundred days it is fully potent; after two hundred days the holy womb is stable; after three hundred days perfect *qi* is generated and the immortal embryo is fully formed.

Once the medicine is fully potent, stoke the fire according to the correct count: this is called the proper firing times. Once the holy womb is stable, match the firing times to the count of the lesser heavenly circuit: this is called the lesser heavenly circuit. Once the embryo is fully formed and perfect *qi* is generated, match the firing times to the count of the greater heavenly circuit: this is called the firing process of the greater heavenly circuit.

{Assemble the medicine, then mate dragon and tiger; refine them, then stoke the fire: this is how you enter Dao.}

Give up all worldly activities and live in seclusion, focusing your mind on inner observation, never letting internal projections leave or external projections enter, like {a woman nurturing a baby or} a dragon nurturing a pearl. Even at times of eating and drinking, resting and sleeping, remain silent like a snoozing baby, unassuming as a young girl. Lest there by loss or diminishing, never even for a moment separate from Dao. (End *Daoshu*, sect. 4)

Explanation: The medicine is the perfect *qi* of the heart, the rabbit is the perfect water of the kidneys, and the yellow dame is the perfect fluid of the spleen. Join *qi* and water in harmony and move them into the yellow court. The Yong continent corresponds to the trigram Qian, while contracting the yang barrier means tightening the abdomen.

The above present four ways of working with the minor vehicle as part of becoming immortal. The middle scroll presents three ways of working with the middle vehicle to attain eternal life and no death.

5. Quickening the Gold Crystal by Pulling Back the Elbows[2]

Golden Declarations: As yin and yang ascend and descend, they never go beyond the inside of heaven and earth. As the sun and the moon revolve and circulate, they always remain on their outside. Rising and setting in the east and west, they divide day and night; coming and going in the north and south, they determine heat and cold. Day and night never stop; heat and cold always follow each other. Accumulated days become a month; accumulated months become a year.

As the months accumulate days, the moon first contains its bright section [lit., spirit soul] within its dark part [lit., material soul, i. e., it forms the waxing half moon], then contains its dark part within its bright section [forms the waning half moon]. As the years accumulate months, the sun gives rise to tones from pitches; then it gives rise to pitches from tones [yin and yang alternating each half year]. The continued revolution and circulation of the sun and the moon constitute the core workings of heaven and earth: they never leave the correct count of Qian and Kun. Although the myriad beings are generated and completed by yin and yang, their continued creative transformation rests with the sun and the moon.

Source of Perfection: The physical form of heaven and earth is like an egg. Within the six harmonies, its center is round like a pearl. As the sun and the moon rise and set, they circulate: one up above the sky, the other down below the earth. Up and down, east and west, they move around like

---

[2] The *Daoshu* version omits the entire first part of Section 5.

flying wheels. Rising in the east and setting in the west, the sun follows the way of yang; waxing in the west and waning in the east, the moon follows the way of yin.

In the course of one day, they divide day and night. After the winter solstice, the sun rises from south to north; after the summer solstice, it rises from north to south. The nights in winter are thus as long as the days in summer; the nights in summer are as long as the days in winter. In the course of one year, it determines heat and cold. The shape of the sun and the moon is perfectly round, measuring 840 miles in diameter. Four feet make one pace, and 360 paces make one mile.

Now, eight segments and twenty units make one double-hour, and twelve double-hours make one day. One month has thirty days, which is 360 double-hours, 3,000 segments, or 18,000 units. Generally, yang works with the trigram Qian: it counts by nine. Yin works with the trigram Kun: it counts by six.

The bright section of the moon grows in its dark part. Starting at new moon, it follows the number nine and does not match the number six. Thus it takes three days before this occurs. One cycle of day and night lasts a hundred segments and sixty units; in this period, the bright section growing in the dark part advances seventy miles, so that in the course of six days and nights, it moves 420 miles. At this point the bright section in the dark part is half way and we speak of the first quarter moon [lit., upper hanging string].

Over the next six days and nights, it advances a further 420 miles, making its total progress 840. Now the bright section in the dark part is full, that is, yang completely fills the domain of yin and we speak of the full moon. Beginning on the 16th day, the dark part grows in the bright section. In the course of one day and night, that is a hundred double-hours and sixty units, it advances seventy miles, so that in the course of six days and nights, it moves 420 miles. At this point, the dark part in the bright section is half way and we speak of the last quarter moon [lower hanging string].

Over the following six days and nights, it advances a 420 miles more, making its total progress 840 miles. Now the dark part in the bright section is full, that is, yin completely fills the domain of yang. There is still a tiny remnant of light in the moon, that is, the six have not fully exhausted the nine. Thus it takes three more days for the dark part of the moon to fill it completely; then we speak of the new moon.

After the waxing moon, nine rises within six. Before the new moon, six rises within nine. The count never stops and continues to give rise to periods of time. Accumulated days make a month. [Start *Daoshu*, sect. 5]

Accumulated months make a year. In terms of the months, this means that they match the six pitches and the six tones. Counting by six and filling six different positions makes a total of thirty-six: this is the number of the completion of yin.

In terms of the days, this means that five days make one base-week and seventy-two base-weeks [360 days] represent the number eight by nine, close to nine-squared, which is the number of ascending yang. If this number then fills the six positions, we get six by nine, which makes fifty-four: this is the number of the completion of yang.

One six plus one nine added, moreover, make fifteen, and fifteen is the number of one *qi*-period. The twenty-four *qi*-periods function according to the eight divisions, matching the proper times of yin and yang ascending and descending. Also, one six multiplied by one nine is fifty-four, which is divisible by four and thus matches the four seasons and corresponds to them. One season contains ninety days, and four times ninety is 360. So change based on yang matches the number 216 [Qian, 4 x 54], while change based on yin matches 144 [Kun, 4 x 36]. Added together, they make 360, the number of one complete heavenly circuit.

In Likeness: Yin and yang ascending and descending within heaven and earth work just like fusing heart fluid and kidney *qi.* The sun and the moon revolving and circulating outside of heaven and earth work just like quickening the gold crystal by pulling back the elbows. Their mutual interaction is just like stoking the fire by increasing and dampening. Yang ascends and yin descends: this is no different than the movements of the bright sections and dark parts of the sun and the moon. The sun going and the moon coming: this is no different from the activities of the *qi* and fluid of the heart and kidneys.

{After the winter solstice, the sun rises at the position Yi and sets at Geng, creating a day of forty segments. It moves from south to north in a rhythm of nine days. It grows in the east and declines in the west, advancing for sixty units, so that by the time of the spring equinox day and night are equal in length. By the summer solstice, the days are sixty segments long. After the summer solstice, the sun rises at the position Jia and sets at Xin, so that the days are sixty segments long. It moves from north to south in a rhythm of nine days. It grows in the east and declines in the west, withdrawing for sixty units, so that by the time of the fall equinox day and night are equal in length. By the winter solstice, the days are again forty segments long.

Day and night, units and segments move according to their own standard, forward and back, advancing and retreating. Moving from south to north, once the moon begins to wax, after three days, the bright section grows in the dark part, reaching equal level after six days. Six more days into the cycle, the bright section is complete: this applies the number nine. After the full moon, the dark part grows in the bright section, reaching equal level after six days. Six more days into the cycle, the dark part is complete: this applies the number six.}

The summer solstice within the year matches the 16th day of the lunar cycle. {We work with the cultivation method every day at Li [noon] because} it matches the Wu hour in human beings. The winter solstice within the year matches the day of the new moon in the lunar cycle. {We work with the cultivation method every day at Kan [midnight] because} it matches the Zi hour in human beings.

The order of yin and yang ascending and descending throughout heaven and earth, the principles of the bright sections and dark parts of the sun and the moon coming and going all follow specific number patterns and work in a precise order of interaction. Their revolution and circulation never fail. How could the *qi* and fluid of the heart and kidneys in human beings, the spirit and material souls in their liver and lungs, their daily function having divisions and order, be any more or less in their annual and monthly rhythms?

Perfect Instructions: At Kan, Yang begins to grow. {This happens in the middle of the Zi hour [midnight]. Without beginning or end,} at Gen [3 am], kidney *qi* fuses with liver *qi*. Before this happens, in your quiet chamber loosen your clothing, make your hands into fists, and sit cross-legged. Mentally push down into the liver area in your abdomen, thereby forcing the *qi* to ascend through the body. Push the chest forward and slightly bend the head back to close off the Double Barrier of the Narrow Strait at the neck.

Next, pull the elbows back once or twice like leaves of a door, stretch from the waist and feel a hot rush like fire ascending from the Tail Gate, rising up from the waist [through the spine] and pressing against the Narrow Strait. Be careful not to break through the barrier, but at this moment use the extremely hot *qi* to gradually, little by little, open the Narrow Strait, letting the *qi* flow past it.

From here lift up your face and create tension at the back of your skull, thereby closing the Upper Barrier. Be careful not to break through it, but be aware of the extremely hot *qi* as it gradually, little by little, pushes it open and flows into the head, there to supplement the Niwan and the ocean of marrow. This will make the body resistant to cold and heat; it is the foundation of long life.

Next, use the methods of reversion to the elixir field and, as before, push your chest forward and stretch from the waist to close the Narrow Strait. Bend and stretch it a few times, and when no more fire rises from the waist, practice quiet sitting and inner observation. Repeat this procedure several times, allowing the fire to rise in rhythm. Begin the practice at the Chou hour [1-3 am] and stop at the end of Yin [3-5 am]. This method is called quickening the gold crystal by pulling back the elbows. It is also known as reducing lead since it causes the *qi* in the kidneys to generate liver *qi*.

Now, the spine in the human body consists of twenty-four vertebrae [lit., divisions]. The bottom three sit right opposite the kidneys. The top three are called the Heavenly Pillar, while the area above them is known as the Jade Capital. Below the Heavenly Pillar and above the vertebrae opposite the kidneys, that is, above the Tail Gate, there are eighteen vertebrae. The central one among them is called the Double Barrier: there are nine above and nine below it.

Within a hundred days one should be able to flow through all eighteen and let the *qi* enter the Niwan. This practice must be undertaken right at the time of first yang, at Kan [midnight]. [DS: It is essential to begin this practice at Gen [3 am]. From here, the golden essence flies until Xun [9 am], when it is complete.] This is called quickening the gold crystal by pulling back the elbows.

At Li [noon], assemble the medicine; at Qian [9 pm], stoke the fire {to heat them}. This is how you contract the yang barrier. [DS: Starting at the winter solstice] and practicing for a hundred days, the gold crystal enters the brain. Just knock once at the three barriers and it directly enters the upper palace of Niwan. Begin at Kan and stop at Gen [DS: Gen to Zhen].

From Li onward, assemble the medicine, causing the *qi* of the heart and kidneys to fuse and liver *qi* to spontaneously generate heart *qi*. As these two *qi* turn into pure yang, the yin of the two eights dissolves. The combined *qi* next condenses and fills the lungs. {As you get this lung fluid to descend, it comes to harbor perfect *qi*. Over a few days,} this grows to the size of a grain of millet, which you then enter into the yellow court. This we call the raw material of the inner elixir. Practice for a hundred days without fail, and the medicine is fully potent.

To assemble the medicine at Li, practice inner observation at the proper time and keep circulating *qi* to increase its essence and fine consistency. Always stoke the fire at Qian and contract the yang barrier. Begin the practice at Dui and end at Qian. Practice like this for a hundred days, using the flying gold crystal. Sit in meditation from Kan to Zhen [DS: Gen to Xun], then stop.

When you assemble the medicine at Li as described above, {and seriously practice from Kun to Qian} for two [DS: three] hundred days without fail, the immortal embryo will form. Practice the method of contracting the yang barrier from Kun to Qian, then stop. Another hundred days should suffice. The Niwan will be full and firm, {you can reverse aging and return to youth, no longer being at all like ordinary people. Once the medicine is assembled and the immortal embryo is fully formed, perfect *qi* is generated continuously, your body is like an elastic ball, your complexion is rosy like an orange. You are forever safe in your elixir field and attain the state of an earth immortal.

Once you practice seriously for three hundred days you finish assembling the medicine at Li, firmly contract the yang barrier at Kun and start reverting jade fluid to the elixir field. Begin this at the winter solstice and keep on practicing, and within three hundred days the embryo will be fully formed, the *qi* sufficient, the internal elixir complete, and perfect *qi* generated.} As you practice this method, the five phases will invert and the three fields turn upside down. Before you start the practice, first make sure to match yin and yang, so that *qi* and fluid generate each other smoothly. {Stop when you see experiential effects.}

Next, collect and disperse water and fire to make sure root and source are strong and stable, *qi* flows freely, and fluid is clear. Stop when you see experiential effects. From here, mate dragon and tiger, {heat the medicine and refine the elixir} and keep supplementing reversion to the elixir field {to fully distill lead and mercury. Stop when you see concrete effects. Supplement it once for every ten times you diminish, making sure to count correctly and allowing *qi* and fluid to generate each other. Stop when you see concrete effects.

Practicing seriously to bring it up to the head is a method of the lesser vehicle, good for extending the years and increasing longevity. Make sure to supplement it fully and feel strong and stable. Stop when you see experiential effects.} [DS: This is called a minor level of accomplishment.]

When you select a month within the year to start, begin at the division of the winter solstice; when you select a day within the month, begin on a Jiazi day; when you select a time within the day, begin at Kan [Gen], Li, or Qian. These are the best times to start.

{For the first hundred days each, practice from Kan to Gen [12-3 am], then from Dui to Qian [6-9 pm]. For the second hundred days, practice from Kan to Zhen [12-6 am], then from Kun to Qian [3-9 pm].} [DS: Practice for three hundred days from Gen to Xun [3-9 am] and from Kun to Qian, and you will have completed a medium accomplishment.}

During this work, stay in a secluded chamber and quiet dwelling, {away from your wife and daughters, far from the noises of dogs and chickens,} [DS: where your eyes do not see and your ears do not hear], with no noxious odors entering your nostrils, or the five flavors touching your palate. Cut off all seven emotions and six desires, {keep food and drink to a minimum, and be careful to regulate heat and cold.} Even during sleep and rest be very careful not to lose your concentration.

If you do not practice diligently, {you will have a hard time completing this way. But if you practice well for three hundred days, you are sure to experience the concrete effects as described.} [DS: you will not attain immortality and can only delay death.]

Perfect Explanation: This is the method of the three primes. It includes quickening the gold crystal {at Kan,} that is, reverting *qi* from the lower to the upper field; assembling the medicine {at Li}, that is, reverting it from the lower to the middle field; and contracting the yang barrier {at Qian}, that is, reverting it from the middle to the lower field. {The system is also called the mutual reversion of the three fields.} [End *Daoshu*, sect. 5]

Dao Essentials: Working days and months in accordance with the trigrams, squat and rise over several days to open the barriers. Striving to join the meeting in Yang continent, the fire of the sixth palace fills the golden field.

Explanation: "Using days and months in accordance with the trigrams" means that the time when yang first grows in the course of a day is the Zi hour, while in the course of the year it is the winter solstice. Such is the day to select within the month, the double-hour to select within the day. "Squat and rise" means practice as described above.

"Over several days" indicates the period of a hundred days. "Open the barriers" means first open the middle barrier, than open the upper barrier. Next is the line, "striving to join the meeting in Yang continent." Here Yang continent signals the heart in people, the Wu hour during the day, and Li among the trigrams, while "meeting" refers to the interaction of perfect yin and perfect yang, in other words, assembling the medicine.

Qian, moreover, is the "sixth palace," while "fire" indicates *qi*. Contract the yang barrier and gather the *qi*, thereby to turn lung *qi* into gold, which then flows down into the elixir field near the kidneys. Thus it says, "Fire fills the golden field." It means to contract the yang barrier at Qian and gather the fire in the lower elixir field.

Perfect Explanation: "Using days and months in accordance with the trigrams" indicates the winter solstice and the Jia-Zi hour. "Squat and rise over several days to open the barriers" means to squat over the abdomen, so *qi* can rise in the body as fire, leading to an opening of the barrier within a hundred days, from Kan to Gen. This is the method of quickening the gold crystal. The "meeting in Yang continent" means to assemble the medicine at Li through the interaction of yin and yang. "The fire of the sixth palace fills the elixir field" indicates that one contracts the yang barrier at Qian, and collects lung *qi* in the lower field from Dui to Qian.

The far south road leads up a steep mountain. Ascending through the body, *qi* passes the three barriers. As you move toward the meeting in Yang continent, fight like the younger daughter heating up heaven.

Explanation: The "far south" means that the sage hides his intention in the middle son, who is none other than the trigram Kan. Gen is the mountain, and the mountain is strong. Quicken the gold crystal and get it to Xun, then stop. The second hundred days are a minor achievement, culminating when the *qi*, "ascending through the body passes the three barriers and moves toward the meeting in Yang continent." This is just like explained before.

"Fight on like the younger daughter heating up heaven" speaks of the trigram Dui. Contract the yang barrier at Qian, then stop. Move from Ke continent to Xu continent, raising the *qi* as if drawn by an ox cart. If you want to join the happy assembly on the ninth continent, begin with fire in the southwest and enter it into Yong continent.

Explanation: Gen continent is the trigram Gen. Xu continent is the trigram Xun. Start quickening the gold crystal at Gen and stop when you get to Xun. In the phrase, "drawn by an ox cart," the cart is yang and the ox is yin. It talks about getting the one *qi* from the Narrow Strait to the Niwan. The ninth continent here signals the heart in people and the Wu hour during the day. It is the previously established garden of ingredients. The southwest is the trigram Kun. Yong continent is the trigram Qian. Contract the yang barrier from Kun to Qian, then stop. This is what happens during the third hundred days of the minor achievement.

Perfect Explanation: This speaks about the work to be done during the third hundred days, explaining the method of quickening the gold crystal. Start at Gen and end at Xun. The happy assembly on the ninth continent indicates assembling the medicine as described earlier. Contract the yang barrier from Kun to Qian. [Start *Daoshu*]

All this is about how to use the days and work with the three primes. Quickening the gold crystal, enter it into the brain by reverting *qi* upward from the lower to the upper field. Assemble the medicine by reverting *qi* from the upper to the middle field, then heat it by reverting it downward from the middle to the lower field. This is how to work with the three primes. They are methods of the middle vehicle that lead to becoming an earth immortal. Stop when you see experiential effects.

For example, in your dreams, you see lots of startling and scary things [DS: Your sleep will be restless]. Should your four limbs or six viscera feel unwell, they easily get better without medication. Even with eyes closed and in a dark chamber, you see a bright light all around you, enveloping your body. Your golden barrier and jade lock are firm, strong, and stable; you never have wet emissions in your dreams. With a clap of thunder, the *qi* pushes through joints and vertebrae [lit., barriers and divisions].

[DS: Your complexion is clear, your elixir fields are at ease, and all mental projections naturally dissolve.] In your dreams you feel like you are holding a tiny infant or like you are soaring off in flight. The eight wayward forms of *qi* no longer affect you, {all mental projections naturally dissolve, you are free from all emotions and desires, and during inner observation all is bright and not dark. During the day your spirit is naturally clear and refined; at night your elixir field is spontaneously warm. These experiential effects indicate the successful completion of the medicine. Once they are properly present, keep on working carefully and systematically.} After three hundred days, the immortal embryo is fully formed and you can move on to the next level.

6. Reverting Jade Fluid to the Elixir Field & Refining the Physical Form with Jade Fluid

Written in Jade: {Perfect yin and perfect yang generate and complete each other.} Above, accumulated yang produces spirit; within spirit there are physical forms that shine in the sky: they are the sun and the moon. Below, accumulated yin produces physical form; within it are those that shine in the earth: they are gold and jade.

{In their material reality, gold and jade are hidden in the beautiful *qi* of mountains and rivers. When they float to the surface, their radiance is just as bright as that of the sun and the moon. When grasses and trees receive them, they become auspicious; when birds and beasts take them in, they turn into exceptional species.}

Source of Perfection: Yang ascends to heaven [sky]; once it reaches its great ultimate, it generates yin. If yin is deficient, yang is in excess, thus accumulated yang generates spirit. Yin descends to earth; once it reaches its great ultimate, it generates yang. If yang is deficient, yin is in excess, thus accumulated yin generates physical form. Above, spirit forms the sun and the moon; below, physical form manifests in gold and jade.

{Perfect yang contains spirit; perfect yin contains the blueprint of all physical forms. When their *qi* fuse, above and below irradiate each other, their light filling heaven and earth. This is why gold and jade can be so precious, and this is good. From this we know that when the *qi* of gold and jade coagulates in the void, it becomes fortunate *qi* and auspicious vapor. When this enters into the earth, it transforms into sweet dew, fresh springs, grasses, and trees. When human beings take it in, they become valiant and noble; when birds and beasts obtain it, they become extraordinary and marvelous.}

Thus, the material reality that is gold and jade, even though it is through physical form based on accumulated yin, deep within contains the *qi* of perfect yang. The two also closely respond to the sun and the moon, created from spirit on the basis of accumulated yang. They are none other than perfect yang shooting down from the sky and coagulating into precious ore.

In Likeness: [DS: The *qi* of the kidneys is like the moon; their fluid matches gold. The *qi* of the heart is like the sun; its fluid matches jade.} Accumulated yin producing physical form and containing perfect yang, thus forming gold and jade, is just like gold and jade in the body, which in turn are just like assembling the medicine and containing perfect *qi* to form the immortal embryo.

{The *qi* of gold and jade entering deep into the earth and transforming into sweet dew, fresh springs, grasses, and trees is just like reverting jade fluid. The *qi* of gold and jade coagulating in the void and becoming fortunate *qi* and auspicious vapor is just like *qi* refining physical form and material reality.}

When the *qi* of gold and jade pushes into the sky, it follows yang ascending and moves up; when it enters into the earth, it follows yin descending and reverts downward. Thus it moves up and down in the wake of yin and yang, passing through the four direction and the four seasons.

{Similarly one reverts fluid to the elixir fields, allowing the *qi* to refine physical form and material reality. Just like the four seasons wax and wane, there are changes in the course of every single day.}

Perfect Instructions: {To see experiential effects during assembling and supplementing, select a month within the year, a day within the month, and an hour within the day. These are the three functions of time. After a hundred days, the medicine is fully potent. After two hundred days, the sagely womb is stable. After three hundred days, perfect *qi* is generated and the immortal embryo is fully grown. Work carefully and systematically, augmenting it at the right moment.}

Once you have practiced for the complete count of three hundred days, start to work with the method of reversion to the elixir field to refine the physical form. Start the practice at Gen [3 am] by quickening the gold crystal and entering it into the brain; stop at Xun [9 am]. {This is called quickening the gold crystal after completing three hundred days.}

At Li [noon], assemble the medicine; at Kun [3 pm], contract the yang barrier. You can also work at Dui [6 pm] to contract the yang barrier and stop at Qian [9 pm]. Once Li arrives, increase inhalation and practice the method of swallowing [saliva] to refine the physical form.

This involves first swishing the tongue around the mouth, between the upper teeth and the palate, to collect bad and turbid secretions and swallow them. Next, curl the tip of the tongue backward to allow the mouth to fill the jade pond, then swallow it without rinsing as soon as the secretion is generated.[3]

In the three months of spring, liver *qi* dominates and spleen *qi* is weak: practice swallowing at Li [noon]. In the three months of summer, heart *qi* dominates and lung *qi* is weak: practice swallowing at Xun [9 am]. In the three months of fall, lung *qi* dominates and bladder *qi* is weak: practice

---

[3] The *Daoshu* version here adds the paragraph listed below under "Straight Explanation" (Baldrian-Hussein 1984, 254).

swallowing at Gen [3 am]. In the three months of winter, kidney *qi* dominates and heart *qi* is weak: practice swallowing at Zhen [6 am].

In the third month during all four seasons, spleen *qi* dominates and kidney *qi* is weak. Since kidney *qi* is the root and source of human vitality, {there are times of decline and weakness in each of the four seasons,} and the last eighteen days of the three months of each of the four seasons, practice swallowing at Dui [6 pm], working as described above. Only in the fall do not work at Dui but instead start at Gen [3 am] for your efforts. Follow the above saliva method and work as described to swallow it.

{If no secretion is generated in the jade pond between your teeth and molars, use the tongue to fill the space up and down and close off the jade pond, pull in the two cheeks and use empty saliva for your practice. Even if you only work with breath *qi*, this still contains water.}

Practice swallowing *qi* like this for one year, working with thirty-six to forty-nine repetitions. The following year, increase the number of repetitions to eighty-one; and the year after that, move on to 181. You will soon see experiential effects: this is none other than the method of reverting jade fluid to the elixir field. Practice it diligently for just three years and you should be able to moisturize your elixir fields, bathe the immortal embryo, and vastly increase your perfect *qi*.

As you practice like this, using the method of reverting jade fluid to the elixir field, within three hundred days you can completely nurture your inner elixir, allowing perfect *qi* to be generated widely. At Gen, quicken the gold crystal and knock on the three barriers: then you can easily reach the Niwan above.

{Continue working with the method of reverting jade fluid to the elixir field and allow the golden water to drip down from the top of the head, moving it into the yellow court, where the gold transforms into the elixir and is duly called the golden elixir.}

To practice the method of reverting jade fluid to the elixir field set yourself up in deep secrecy and a hidden dwelling, using a place where ordinary people never go. Burn incense, set up a matted platform, and sit cross-legged. Later squat and rise, becoming aware of the fire rising. Then sit upright and let go of all thoughts, forget all emotions, and practice inner observation.

{Purposefully, at Gen, quicken the gold crystal and guide it to the top of the head, then briefly lift the head and stretch the neck, to feel the *qi* flow though the throat like fire. See it right in front of your head, then lower the head and bend the neck, curl the tongue back to press against the upper palate. You should have clear and pure water in your mouth, tasting like sweet incense. Above, it pushes into the gate of the head; below, it flows through the hundred arteries.

Naturally in your nose you smell a kind of perfect incense and on your tongue you taste a wondrous flavor. Swallow without rinsing and revert it to the yellow court: this is what we call reverting jade fluid to the elixir field. In spring, summer, fall, and winter never mind the exact time or period, just practice after you have quickened the gold crystal and guided it to the brain. On the next level, practice this method in accordance with the proper times, beginning at Gen and ending at Xun. In the evening when you work to contract the yang barrier, start at Dui and end at Qian.

Always work according to this method, carefully and systematically following the above outline and you will be successful. You will reach a state where you can continue to live in the world in your refined form, live long and never die. However, you will not yet be able to attain transcendence and liberation.

Dao Essentials: To understand how to obtain the root and stem of the five phases, you need to know spring, summer, fall, and winter. Over time you drink many cups of jasper liquor, get drunk and return to the lunar palace for easy wandering.

Explanation: "To understand how to obtain the root and stem of the five phases" means to invert the generating and control cycles of the five phases and use the different times marked by the trigrams to undertake saliva practice. "You need to know spring, summer, fall, and winter" means to adjust your practice to the periods and seasons. "Jasper liquor" is jade fluid; the "lunar palace" is the elixir field; "get drunk and return" means to swallow a lot.

Before Fusang starts getting bright in the east, move it up the back and swallow it down the front without stopping. Ride the wild horse and float freely through space-time with the elder son reach Yang continent.

Explanation: "Before Fusang starts getting bright in the east" indicates the time before sunrise. This happens at Gen [3 am]. "Move it up the back" means quickening the gold crystal. "Swallow it down the front" refers to reverting jade fluid to the elixir field. "Ride the wild horse" means to let the fire rise and refine the physical form with jade fluid. "Float freely through space-time" means pervading and filling the four limbs. "With the elder son" indicates Zhen [6 am]; "reach Yang continent" indicates the time of Li. That is to say, the practice of using jade fluid to refine the physical form should begin at the time marked by Zhen and end at Li.

7. Reverting Golden Fluid to the Elixir Field & Refining the Physical Form with Golden Fluid

Golden Declarations: Accumulated yang produces spirit; within spirit, there is physical form. One appears first as the sun; the other appears first as the moon. Accumulated yin produces physical form; within physical form, there is spirit. One first appears first in gold; the other appears first in jade.

{The light of the sun and the moon waxes and wanes in the wake of yin and yang. They generate light in accordance with the correct count, at the foundation of which lie Qian and Kun. The *qi* of gold and jade rise and sink in the wake of yin and yang. They bring forth *qi* in accordance with the right times, at the foundation of which lie heaven and earth.}

Source of Perfection: The light of the sun and the moon, after they rise, works with the number nine; before they set, it works with the number six. Six and nine are the numbers of Qian and Kun. The *qi* of gold and jade ascend during spring and summer and descend in fall and winter: in moving up and down, they match the timing of heaven and earth. {Gold grows from jade, jade grows from minerals, minerals grow from the soil: they are physical form manifesting below. The sun contains a golden bird; the moon houses a jade rabbit. The moon depends on the bright part of the sun to produce light: they are spirit manifesting above.}

In Likeness: The sun and the moon are like *qi*: kidney *qi* is like the moon, while heart *qi* is like the sun. Gold and jade are like fluid: kidney fluid is like gold; heart fluid is like jade. What we call jade fluid is kidney *qi* ascending up to the heart where it merges with heart *qi*. The two *qi* fuse and move past the twelve-storied tower.

As you close your mouth and prevent them from leaving, secretions will fill the jade pond. When you swallow this, we speak of reverting jade fluid to the elixir field. {When you move it up, we speak of refining the physical form through jade fluid. This fluid originally comes from the kidneys and is generated in the heart. It is just like the theory of soil generating minerals and minerals generating jade.}[4]

What we call golden fluid is kidney *qi* ascending and fusing with heart *qi*, then steaming into the lungs. The lungs are the Flowery Canopy. From here, condense the two *qi* downward and thus obtain lung fluid, which you then store in the lower field. When you move it up from the Tail Gate, we speak of quickening the gold crystal and guiding it to the brain, there to supplement the Niwan palace. When you again move it down and guide it

[4] The *Daoshu* version of Section 7 is quite different in formulation and structure from the text in the *Daozang*. Its first part is very close to the beginning of the previous section, which is why Baldrian-Hussein elects not to translate it (1984, 260).

back to the lower field, we speak of reverting golden fluid to the elixir field. Repeatedly reverting it to the lower field and moving it up again, it comes to pervade and fill all four limbs, continuously going up and down. We call this refining the physical form through golden fluid: it matches the theory of how gold is generated in soil.

If you want to refine the physical form and quicken the gold crystal, start by setting yourself up in a quiet chamber. Block out the wind and the sun, widely burn incense, and chant the following secret formula to invoke the highest sages of the Three Clarities:

> I sincerely pray
> That I may live long in this world,
> Solely practice the great Dao,
> And widely disseminate it among the people.
> But first I must myself
> Practice the methods of refining the physical form.
> Thereby, I pray, let me
> No longer fear heat and cold,
> Live without grain and food,
> And roam freely beyond yin and yang.

Once you conclude this incantation, practice swallowing.

Perfect Instructions: The Tail Gate point on the spine in the back of the body is called the lower barrier, the Narrow Strait is called the middle barrier, and the back of the brain [the Jade Pillow] is called the upper barrier. When you first quicken the gold crystal to push through the three barriers, the ki*dneys are like earth and the heart is like heaven. When you reach the top of the head above, it is like getting to the nine heavens.

{To refine the physical form through jade fluid, move it from the heart to the top of the head to enter the nine heavens. In three hundred days, the great medicine is complete, the immortal embryo is fully formed, and perfect *qi* is generated. Moving it up along the front is the old way of refining the physical form through jade fluid; moving it up along the back is the old way of quickening the gold crystal. Both the gold crystal and the jade fluid are efficacious practices that will lead to experiential effects.

Always start at Kan [midnight]. Once you have moved it up along the back all the way to the top of the head, use your hands to gently cover your ears and practice inner observation as prescribed, subtly gather oral secretions and press your tongue against the tooth barrier to close the jade pond from below. Wait until the secretions from the upper palace have sunk down, then swallow. After completing one swallow, guide it up again. Finish the practice at Gen [3 am].}

During spring and winter, swallow once after two rounds of upward guiding; in fall and summer, swallow once after five rounds. Counting each swallow, limit the total number in the fall and summer to fifty; in spring and winter to a hundred. Swallow *qi* down the back, then guide it up the front of the body to fill the entire head and face, the four limbs, the five fingers. Stop when the *qi* is abundant everywhere, then start again, ending at Li [noon]. This method of swallowing and guiding the saliva up the back is called reverting golden fluid to the elixir field. Moving it down the back and guiding it up the front is called refining the body with golden fluid. Start at Gen [3 am] and refine until Li [noon], then stop. At Dui [6 pm] work on contracting the yang barrier, practicing until Qian [9 pm], then stop.

Guiding it up along the back to reach the top of the head, moving from top to bottom, is called reverting golden fluid to the elixir field. Guiding the *qi* of the golden elixir up the front, moving from bottom to top, is called refining the physical form through golden fluid. Your body and complexion will be be like a jade tree or golden flower. Using this method of reverting golden fluid to the elixir field and guiding the *qi* up both in front and back before it reaches the lower prime is called raising the fire to incinerate the body. Using the method of refining the physical form through golden fluid and guiding the *qi* up both in front and back is twofold incineration of the body. As you practice at this level, always work carefully and diligently with an earnest will and never slacken in your efforts. Then you will see the right experiential effects.

Dao Essentials: Move it up the back all through the night, then cover your ears, match the times to drink golden fluid. Join a banquet on Qing Contintent and go to live there. The sun in the west, you still hear the songs of yang.

Explanation: "Move it up the back all through the night, then cover your ears" indicates the practice of reverting golden fluid to the elixir field. It means to start by pulling the elbows back to quicken the gold crystal, then knock once on the three barriers. As the *qi* starts to move up, quickly use both hands to cover your ears, since the ears are the gate of the kidney waves. The worry is that kidney *qi* leaks outside and does not enter into the brain.

"Match the times to drink golden fluid" means that once you are aware that the *qi* has entered the brain, you work according to the methods described earlier. Tip the head and bend the neck, curl the tip of the tongue back to press against the upper palate, and invite sweet water to flow. This will have the extraordinary experiential effect of tasting sweet like pure honey. Begin at Gen by quickening the gold crystal and swallowing it once, work until Zhen, then stop. "Qing continent" is Zhen.

"The sun in the west" indicates the time of the trigram Dui. "You still hear the songs of yang" indicates to work on contracting the yang barrier beginning at Dui and ending at Qian. At this point, there is no need to assemble the medicine any further.

Drink and work all through the night, then let the fire rise, move it up the front and lift it along the back to incinerate the body. Although there is no need to adhere to a particular year and month, still each day there is Qian and Kun.

Explanation: This formula describes the method of refining the physical form through the golden fluid. "Drink and work all through the night, then let the fire rise" indicates to refine the physical form through golden fluid using the methods described earlier. Practicing it at the time of the trigram Gen serves to get the fire to rise.

"Move it up the front and lift it along the back" means quickening the gold crystal and getting the fire to rise. Generally, when using the method of refining the physical form through jade fluid, one first moves the gold crystal up the back and guides it to the top of the head, then reverts the elixir downward to move it up again the front to refine the physical form. This is not the same as the method of refining the physical form through golden fluid. Quickening the gold crystal and getting the fire to rise, one first moves *qi* up the front to refine the physical form. Letting it rise both front and back at the same time is called "incinerating the body."

Letting the fire rise and reverting [fluid] to the elixir field should be done with proper augmentation and reduction in accordance with the number patterns of the four seasons. In this method, "there is no need to adhere to a particular year and month," but one should concentrate the mind carefully and systematically and as much as possible live in seclusion and hide one's traces. "Still each day there is Qian and Kun" means to heat Qian before noon and Kun after noon. In terms of the front and back of the human body, the belly and abdomen are Kun, while the back and spine are Qian. To heat Qian before noon, quicken the gold crystal by pulling back the elbows, moving the *qi* up the front and refining the physical form. To heat Kun after noon, contract the yang barrier beginning at Dui [6 pm] and ending at Qian [9 pm].

Direct Explanation: Golden fluid is lung fluid. If you allow it to harbor dragon and tiger and guide it to the lower field, the great medicine will be complete. Thus we call it golden fluid. Pull the elbows back, pull it up, and guide it to the brain, then let it descend again from there to the lower field: this is called reverting to the elixir field. Next move it up again along the front and let it flow widely to fill the four limbs, moving from bottom to top: this is called refining the physical form. It is also called refining the physical form and complete the *qi*.

You will soon see experiential effects of refining the physical form and reverting jade fluid to the elixir field. Once they are properly present, make sure to work carefully and systematically. Rest in seclusion and burn incense properly when practicing this method. Reverting golden fluid to the elixir field is followed immediately by refining the body and contracting the yang barrier. After doing this over a year, you are ready to incinerate the body. Incinerating the body means to refine the physical form before Kan.

In terms of the front and back of the human body, the belly and abdomen are Kun while the back and spine are Qian. To incinerate the body, heat Qian [the back] before noon by quickening the gold crystal; heat Kun [the front] after noon by contracting the yang barrier. To heat Qian, move from bottom to top, guiding the *qi* up both in front and back. Do this for three or five days in winter and summer, then also practice the methods of full saturation. Make sure not to overdo, but let the golden elixir be rich and glossy, then swallow the fire used for body incineration. Stop when you see experiential effects.

Your will within is clear and lofty, as if merged with great emptiness. Your spirit soul and spirit no longer wander about and you cease all dreaming. Your yang essence is whole throughout your physical structure, your spirit residence is firm and stable. Throughout the four seasons you have no fear of cold and heat. Your spirit is selective, transforms with ease, and functions beautifully. When you meet ordinary people, even if they are rich and noble, you just smell their stink of decay, knowing you are far superior to their simple bones and common joints.

When your work is complete, secretly receive the three verses and transform into perfect yang. You can then predict the disasters and good fortune of human affairs, the state of their spirit and life force. Although your eyes may be defiled by common dust, your mind is free from the myriad projections and your *qi* is full and complete. Your mouth no longer requires any drink, and a marvelous *qi* oozes out of you in golden complexion. You immortal flesh is like jade blossoms, and in any place you visit or stay, people will think that a divine being has appeared. Anything you call upon or summon will happen right as you intend. Full of perfect *qi* and pure yang, you can dry out all outward mercury. All these manifest after you revert golden fluid to the elixir field. Such are the experiential effects of refining the physical form through golden fluid.

The above describes three ways of the middle vehicle, the rank of earth immortal.

8. Refining *Qi* by Moving to the Prime

{**Golden Declarations:** When the *qi* of cosmic oneness first divided, the great Dao assumed physical form and separated into two advancing and controlling forces. Once the two forces were settled in their domains, the great Dao assumed names and divided into the five emperors. The five emperors rule over different regions, each protecting one direction; the five directions have different *qi*, each protecting one child.

The child of the Green Emperor belongs to the positions Jia and Yi; he matches the perfect heavenly *qi* of the number nine and the power of wood.

The child of the Red Emperor belongs to the positions Bing and Ding, he matches the perfect heavenly *qi* of the number three and the power of fire.

The child of the White Emperor belongs to the positions Geng and Xin, he matches the perfect heavenly *qi* of the number seven and the power of metal.

The child of the Black Emperor belongs to the positions Ren and Gui, he matches the perfect heavenly *qi* of the number five and the virtue of water.

The child of the Yellow Emperor belongs to the positions Wu and Ji, he matches the perfect heavenly *qi* of the number one and the virtue of earth.

The *qi* of cosmic oneness generated perfect oneness, and perfect oneness came forth from earth. Therefore, the myriad beings are generated and completed on earth and the five phases are generated and completed through oneness. The Dao of perfect prime in all its aspects comes from the *qi* of cosmic oneness.}

Written in Jade: One, three, five, seven, and nine emerged as numbers when Dao divided. Metal, wood, water, fire, and earth emerged as images when Dao unfolded. {East, west, south, north, and center emerged as directions when Dao split. Green, white, red, yellow, and black emerged as material realities when Dao dispersed.

All numbers are bound to return to a state of no numbers; all images are bound to return to a state of no images. All directions bound to return to a state of no directions; all material reality is bound to return to a state of no material reality. If Dao had wanted to have no numbers, it would never have divided and there would be no numbers. If Dao had wanted to have no images, it would never have unfolded and there would be no images. If Dao had wanted to have no directions, it would never have split and there would be no directions. If Dao had wanted to have no material reality, it would never have dispersed and there would be no material reality.}

A state with no numbers is the source of Dao. A state with no images is the foundation of Dao. A state with no directions is the perfection of Dao. A state with no material reality is the wonder of Dao.

Source of Perfection: {Once the source of Dao divided, it sank down from the root and flowed into the branches. To awaken to its perfection you must follow its perfection and cultivate it, making sure internal perfection and external perfection match spontaneously. To understand its wonder you must follow its wonder and recreate it, making sure that internal wonder and external wonder match spontaneously.

When heaven and earth first attained the perfection of Dao, their perfection did not match: they could not avoid having directions. When heaven and earth first attained the wonder of Dao, their wonder did not match: they could not avoid having material reality. Once there is material reality, there are images one can pursue. Once there are directions, there are underlying numbers one can calculate.

Between heaven and earth as much as among the myriad beings, the most noble is the human. Human beings have the ability to pursue the images of heaven and earth and can accordingly know their material reality in the form of *qi* and water. They can calculate the numbers of heaven and earth and can accordingly known their positions in terms of distance and closeness. Looked at from this point of view, Dao is really not all that far removed from human beings.} [DS: Among the images of heaven and earth, I know *qi* and water; among their numbers, I know near and far. Given this, how could Dao ever be far removed?]

In Likeness: Heaven and earth having five emperors is like human beings having five organs. The Green Emperor has [the heavenly stems] Jia and Yi and manages wood. [DS: The Green Emperor matches wood; his heavenly stems are Jia and Yi.] Jia is yang and Yi is yin. They are like the *qi* and fluid of the liver.

The Black Emperor has Ren and Gui and manages water. Ren is yang and Gui is yin. They are like the *qi* and fluid of the kidneys.

The Yellow Emperor has Wu and Ji and manages earth. Wu is yang and Ji is yin. They are like the *qi* and fluid of the spleen.

The Red Emperor has Bing and Ding and manages fire. Bing is yang and Ding is yin. They are like the *qi* and fluid of the heart.

The White Emperor has Geng and Xin and manages metal. Geng is yang and Xin is yin. They are like the *qi* and fluid of the lungs.

{The seasons of spring, summer, fall, and winter are not the same, so that the heart, lungs, liver, and kidneys dominate in different months.}

Perfect Instructions: In the three months of spring, liver *qi* dominates. It does so because the perfect *qi* of father and mother, following the heavenly cycle, has come to reside in the liver. On days of Jia and Yi, wood controls earth: to raise the fire to refine spleen *qi* at the right time, use the double-hours marked by the earthly branches Chen [7-9 am], Xu [7-9 pm], Chou [1-3 am], and Wei [1-3 pm].

On other days, at Dui [6 pm], reduce metal to sublimate lung *qi*. If you cannot practice during this time, you will lessen your success. Similarly at Kan [midnight], in due accordance with the methods, raise the fire to refine kidney *qi*. At Zhen [6 am], enter the meditation chamber to inhale deeply and exhale gently, making sure the respiration is long and steady, holding it in for increasingly longer periods. Reaching one thousand in numbers is a good measure.

At that point, practice inner observation as prescribed [DS: working on the liver]. Focus your mind deeply and close your eyes. A green radiance will naturally appear. Slowly and gradually let it rise through the body and enter the Niwan, practicing from Yin [3-5 am] to Chen [7-9 am] to reach culmination at Zhen.

In the three months of summer, heart *qi* dominates. It does so because the perfect *qi* of father and mother, following the heavenly cycle, has come to reside in the heart. On days of Bing and Ding, fire controls metal: to raise the fire to refine lung *qi* at the right time, work at Dui.

On other days, at Kan [midnight], reduce water to sublimate kidney *qi*. If you cannot practice during this time, you will lessen your success. Similarly at Zhen [6am], in due accordance with the methods, raise the fire to refine liver *qi*. At Li [noon], enter the meditation chamber to practice seriously as described above. A red radiance will naturally appear. Slowly and gradually let it rise through the body and enter the Niwan, working from Si [9-11 am] to Wei [1-3 pm] to reach culmination at Li.

In the three months of fall, lung *qi* dominates. It does so because the perfect *qi* of father and mother, following the heavenly cycle, has come to reside in the lungs. On days of Geng and Xin, metal controls wood: to raise the fire to refine liver *qi* at the right time, work at Zhen [6 am].

On other days, at Li [noon[, reduce fire to sublimate heart *qi*. If you cannot practice during this time, you will lessen your success. Similarly at Xun [9 am], in due accordance with the methods, raise the fire to refine spleen *qi*. At Dui [6 pm], enter the meditation chamber to practice seriously as described above. A white radiance will naturally appear. Slowly and gradually let it rise through the body and enter the Niwan, from Shen [3-5 pm] to Xu [7-9 pm] to reach culmination at Dui.

In the three months of winter, kidney *qi* dominates. It does so because the perfect *qi* of father and mother, following the heavenly cycle, has come to reside in the kidneys. On days of Ren and Gui, water controls fire: to raise the fire to refine heart *qi* at the right time, work at Li [noon].

On other days, in the double-hours marked by the earthly branches Chen, Xu, Chou, and Wei, reduce earth to sublimate spleen *qi*. If you cannot practice during this time, you will lessen your success. Similarly at Dui [6 pm], in due accordance with the methods, raise the fire to refine lung *qi*. At Kan [midnight], enter the meditation chamber to practice seriously as described above. A black radiance will naturally appear. Slowly and gradually let it rise through the body and enter the Niwan, from Hai [9-11 pm] to Chou [1-3am] to reach culmination at Kan.

As you refine the liver in the spring, after a thousand rounds of breathing, a green *qi* emerges. However, in the last eighteen days of spring, do not practice as described. Instead, focus on stabilizing the breath as your main technique, all day long sitting in stillness to nurture the spleen and refine your perfect *qi*. At Kan, you can raise the fire to refine the kidneys rather than sublimating their perfect *qi*.

As you refine the heart in the summer, after a thousand rounds of breathing, a red *qi* emerges. However, in the last eighteen days of summer, do not practice as described. Instead, focus on stabilizing the breath as your main technique, all day long sitting in stillness to nurture and refine as above. At Zhen, you can raise the fire as described earlier.

As you refine the lungs in the fall, after a thousand rounds of breathing, a white *qi* emerges. However, in the last eighteen days of fall, do not practice as described. Instead, focus on stabilizing the breath as your main technique, all day long sitting in stillness to nurture and refine as above. At Xun, you can raise the fire as described earlier.

As you refine the kidneys in the winter, after a thousand rounds of breathing, a black *qi* emerges. However, in the last eighteen days of winter, do not practice as described. Instead, focus on stabilizing the breath as your main technique, all day long sitting in stillness to nurture and refine as above. At Dui, you can raise the fire as described earlier.

Eventually a yellow *qi* will radiate forth. Silently observe it pervading the myriad ways, covering and enveloping your entire body. As you stabilize the breath, make sure you don't retain it forcefully or hold it tightly. Rather, breathe softly and barely noticeably, working without strain, gently moving from being into nonbeing, and letting it find stability on its own.

To assemble the medicine, swallow saliva, make your hands into fists, and keep the heart very stable, thus preventing the perfect *qi* from scattering. Always when you enter the chamber, close the door, resting there alone, hidden, and still. {Stay far away from chickens and dogs, women and children as well as from all repugnant and defiling things. Carefully open a small aperture to let in light, so you can distinguish things. Never let the wind or the sun disturb the *qi* or sounds appear on your right and left.

Your goal is to turn the mind into dead ashes and stop all thinking, completely let go of all affairs and entanglements. Deeply focused and serene both within and without, never let even one object affect your intention.} Then yang spirit can gather and perfect *qi* coagulate. You will again look like an infant as if yet unformed. [DS: Keep your ears free from hearing: as soon as they hear anything, spirit and *qi* are disturbed and scatter. Any rotting smells or sensory attractions not only affect the *qi* but also impact the spirit.]

Day and night burn incense, bend your knees to worship and kowtow, invoking first heaven, then the celestial immortals, and third the immortals of earth. Bow three times to complete the sequence. Then sit in stillness and forget all about the core workings of the world.

To practice as described in this method, you must first work with the techniques previously described and see their experiential effects. If you only undertake devotions as your main practice, I'm afraid you are wasting your effort and in the end do not reach completion but stop at cultivating yin powers and the material soul, turning into a ghost immortal.

Dao Essentials: {Never, as you practice according to these methods, put a deadline on it in terms of year, month, or day. Work according to the methods as previously described. Stop when you see experiential effects. When the appropriate *qi* appears naturally, keep on working carefully and systematically without slackening, giving up on all outside affairs and focusing your entire intention on the work in the chamber, estimating the right times and periods. You can have two young boys of pure yang as helpers or work with the servants of your house, having them go back and forth for you.}

After you do this for a thousand days, you can realize the *qi* of cosmic oneness. If you work one day to do the work of ten, already after a hundred days you can see some results. After five hundred days, your *qi* is complete and you can practice inner observation, gather the yang spirit, and enter the heavenly palaces. {Refine spirit to merge with Dao, join the sages, and go beyond the ordinary. The effects of refining *qi* include a sense of the body as being extremely light, the ability to move about as if floating, a cinnabar radiance pervading the bones, and a marvelous fragrance filling the inner chamber. From here, in deep stillness, practice external observation, to find that a purple haze fills your eyes. Looking down from the top of the head, you find a golden radiance spreading through your physical structure. Various strange and obscure effects testify to your advanced state. They are too numerous to list.}

9. Renewing *Qi* through Inner Observation

Golden Declarations: The great Dao originally has no substance, but abides in *qi*. It is so big that it has no outside, and no being can fathom it. The great Dao originally has no function, but circulates through beings. It is so deep it has no measure, and no principle can penetrate it.

Only when we speak of Dao on the basis of substance does it first have the distinction of inside and outside. Only when we speak of it in terms of function does it first have the foundation of observing and seeing. Observing within and not looking without, nothing on the outside is not penetrated while the inside is fully understood. Observing spirit and not looking at the physical form, nothing in the physical form is not known while spirit is clearly seen.

Source of Perfection: Observing the myriad beings with a focused mind, one realizes that one cannot say there are too many. Letting the *qi* of cosmic oneness be disturbed by the myriad beings, one realizes that one cannot say there is not enough. When the *qi* of cosmic oneness returns to the focused mind, it can no longer be snatched up by various beings. When the focused mind flows with the *qi* of cosmic oneness, the *qi* can no longer be used as a servant by various phenomena [using *fa* in the sense of *dharma* rather than method].

When the source of the mind is clear and penetrating, it illuminates the myriad beings, yet does not know them as separate entities. When the force of *qi* is firm and strong, it activates the myriad impulses in a single breath, yet does not know them as particular phenomena. As all beings originate from no-beings, one can recover their original state in the form of images. Since all phenomena originate from no-phenomena, one can realize perfection completely and spontaneously.

In Likeness: {Images generate physical forms, then names are established in their wake. Once there are names, one can calculate their numbers. Once there are numbers, one can comprehend their principles. Generally, the sphere high above is empty and vacant, like no being ever conceived. It is just like the cultivation of refinement in human beings, with divisions and structures to be followed without fail, a systematic order that leads to completion and success.}

Pulsating and harmonizing *qi* coagulates, never to scatter. A perfect inner nature of utmost emptiness, a state of nonaction of tranquil blandness, allow spirit to merge with Dao and open the return to cosmic so-being. At this moment, no mind becomes mind, {so how can one speak of going along with beings? No beings become beings, so how can one speak of applying specific methods? Resting in perfect happiness,} one no longer knows one's body. Thus, {gradually merging with the Dao of nonaction,} one enters the realm of the invisible and inaudible. {One becomes someone who enters the ranks of the sages and goes beyond the ordinary.}

Perfect Instructions: This method of merging with Dao quite matches the frequently discussed principles of visualization and is similar to Chan monks entering *samādhi*. To begin, select an auspicious spot and set up a meditation chamber, then kneel and bow and burn incense. Sit cross-legged with a straight back, loosen your hair and clothing, make your hands into fists, and focus on the spirit as you calm your mind and close your eyes. Before the Wu [noon] hour, subtly move *qi* up within the body, raising the fire to refine the *qi*. After the Wu hour, carefully gather the *qi* within the body, gathering the fire to refine the elixir. Never mind whether day or night, keep your spirit clear and your *qi* collected, and you will naturally feel joyful and happy. While sitting, if you hear any sounds, don't listen to them; if you see any sights, don't acknowledge them. All perceived objects and mental projections will scatter spontaneously, but if you acknowledge them, they quickly turn into demonic obstacles.

If a demonic obstacle appears, do not delay, but quickly face it head on. Slightly round the body and once rounded, stretch from the hip. After that, open the chest and bend forward, no longer stretching from the hip. For a short time, raise the fire both in front and behind, pushing it up high while remaining immovable: this is called incinerating the body. As this fire rises, the demonic obstacles naturally scatter outside the body, and wayward yin [*qi*] can no longer enter your sphere. Repeat this two or three times. [End *Daoshu*, sect. 9]

After that, imagine yourself roaming throughout heaven and earth, seeing the entire space filled with raging flames. Eventually the fire ends and all becomes clear and cool, and you realize there are no longer any beings. You only see carriages and horses, singing and dancing, pavilions and canopies, flowing silk and gauze, wealth and nobility in great splendor. People and animals are frolicking joyfully, forming into troops and saluting you on your way.

You ascend on a five-colored cloud and climb into the heavenly realm. Once you get there, you see towers and terraces decked out with kingfisher feathers, courtyards and residences spread pall-mall. Precious pearls, gold and jade fill the earth without measure; flowers and fruits, ponds and pavilions are everywhere, too many to count. A wondrous and strange fragrance rises from the four directions and the sounds of entertaining music are wild and variegated. Guests and friends fill the seats, close to each other like water and dry land, all laughing and chattering away, jointly relishing the blessing of great peace. Taking various precious objects, they mutually give and receive them. At this moment, even though you are free from yin ghosts and demonic troops, still you are not yet able to recognize this as a good thing.

Generally, people who cultivate perfection give up and do away with outside affairs; they prefer and relish solitude and serenity. They hide their traces among regions of rivers and lakes, obscure themselves among companions of recluses and avoiders. They cut of all thoughts and forget all emotions, observe various precepts in their ascending and moving, for long periods undergoing labor and toil. Eventually they are lifted above the sordid bustle of life and one bright morning find their work successful and their methods complete, looking around to see all bathed in great splendor. They do not identify this as a demonic apparition but believe they have really reached the heavenly palace, never realizing that they need to transcend the ordinary womb and find the heavenly palace right within the top of their own head.

Then they develop cravings and desires, acknowledge this as a precious realm and never work on the methods of final transcendence and liberation. In the end they remain stuck within the body, their yang spirit never leaves and their immortal embryo does not transform. Practitioners like these are called masters who have emerged from the dark thoroughfare. They are spirit immortals tied to the earth, who can live long without dying but will never be completely liberated from material reality and ascend to the immortals, return to the three isles of the blessed, and become real celestials. How pitiful is that! Students, make sure to understand that, although the attainment of transcendence and liberation is hard, you cannot avoid making the effort!

Dao Essentials: If you do not do this, you will eventually perish.

10. Transcendence, Liberation, and Multilocation[5]

Golden Declarations: Dao is originally latent: if you speak in terms of presence, it is not Dao; Dao is originally empty: if you speak in terms of fullness, it is not Dao. Without structure, questions and answers are impossible; without cosmic images, seeing and hearing are impossible.

You may think of Dao as being mysterious and subtle, yet ideas of mystery and subtlety never leave the limitations of questions and answers. You may think of it as being invisible and inaudible, yet ideas of the invisible and inaudible never leave the limitations of seeing and hearing. None of them ever gets close to Dao, and you will never know just exactly what and how Dao is.

Written in Jade: All that arrives has a beginning, yet you will never know the beginning of the great Dao. Whatever leaves has an end, yet you will never know the end of the great Dao. Why is that? Above the highest of the high, there is still something further, yet you will never know whether or not above the great Dao there is any limit. Below the deepest of the deep, there is still something further, yet you will never know whether or not below the great Dao there is any ultimate. Everlasting and unfathomable, we call it Dao. Although beings may obtain it and get listed in levels and ranks, the Dao of nonaction can never be fully penetrated.

Perfect Instructions: Transcendence means to go beyond the ordinary body and enter the sagely ranks; liberation means to leave behind the common womb and become an immortal. They happen when spirit enters the womb of *qi*, *qi* is complete, and inner nature is perfect. For this, one's former merits must be in good order and one should see experiential effects being properly present. Set yourself up in a chamber of clarity and stillness, so you can enter the realm of the invisible and inaudible. Practice inner observation to acknowledge the yang spirit, then kindle the fire and subdue the demonic, incinerate the body and gather the *qi*. Let perfect *qi* ascend to the heavenly palace, so that all within your shell is clear and still, then fully realize there is not a single thing.

Carefully select a hidden dwelling, so you can properly practice inner observation. First complete three bows, then keep your body stable, not

---

5 The *Daoshu* version of Section 10 has only two short paragraphs. They are marked with "Also in DS."

letting it rise too high. Sit up straight, not bending or stretching. Close your eyes and calm your mind. Once you reach ultimate stillness and move to the prime, your self and body feel as if up in the air. Spirit and *qi* are floating about, hard to contain or control.

Silently continue with inner observation, and there will be bright light instead of darkness. You see mountains and rivers glorious and beautiful, towers and pavilions so very fine. Purple *qi* and red radiance divide and spread all around. Auspicious phoenixes and colorful peacocks, their voices clear as reeds, populate a marvelous landscape, rich and luxurious. One can say it is the perfect place within a gourd, a new world within a grotto heaven. As you follow it along, you are there quite naturally: in deep inner darkness no longer aware that there are things tied to the world of dust. In moments of perfect void, your *qi* keeps on transforming spontaneously, and there is no more need for methods that work with specific timing.

First see a green *qi* emerge from the east: ocarinas and reed music fill the air, carriages with horses, covered in banners and standards, line up to the left and right, in front and behind—you don't know how many. Next, see a red *qi* emerge from the south, a white *qi* from the west, a black *qi* from the north, and a yellow *qi* from the center. The five *qi* connect and coagulate, forming a multi-colored cloud, tunes and music create variegated sound, and a joyful *qi* pervades all. Jade lads and jade maidens come to support your self. You may stride upon a fiery dragon, travel on a mysterious crane, travel on a multi-colored phoenix, or ride a fierce tiger—soaring up into the void, moving up from below.

The places you pass are full of magnificent towers and terraces, too many to list. There are many spirit servants, officials, and runners, too many to describe. Whenever you reach a certain place, myriads of female entertainers come to play, and the palace attendants line up to pay their respects to you as if to an emperor among the people. As soon as the sages and wise men arrive, look to your side: there is no body.

From here, stride upon your carriage and ride up further until you come to a big gate, with soldiers and guards so majestic and fierce they cannot be vanquished. To your right and left, in front and behind, there are official attendants and female entertainers, fulfilling desires without end. In the end, you cannot get past the gate, so you turn your axle and canopy around and move back from above to below, again entering your old dwelling place. Experiences like these, independent of their number, are ways for the harmonized spirit to leave the physical shell.

Over several days again ripen in purity, then ascend to reach the heavenly palace and descend to return to your old dwelling, moving up and down without obstacle or obstruction. Then, as you move up quite naturally, you can climb the seven-layered precious pagoda or ascend the three-storied jasper tower. Start slowly, then move up layer by layer, until you reach the top of the seventh, but never look down, lest the spirit is startled, sticks to the body, and refuses to emerge.

Once you get to the highest of the seven layers, close our eyes and leap free. As if asleep, feel that beyond your body of flesh there is another body. In this, you have the physical form of an infant, your flesh and skin clear and bright, your spirit radiant and clear. As you look back at your old body, you already can't see it anymore: all you see is like a mass of dirt, like a withered tree. You hate its myriad issues and suddenly you can't get away fast enough and start your far-off journey.

If the spirit emerges before it is fully ripened, to fully bind and coagulate the sagely *qi*, you must come back into your original body repeatedly, going out and coming back, emerging and entering. To go on your far-off journey, begin with one step, then two; move on to one mile, then two. Over several days ripen in purity, so that you become like a strong warrior with mighty arms. Then you can move off, a thousand or ten thousand miles, seeing your physical form and spirit getting stronger and bigger, your valor and *qi* strong and stable.

After that, you can rest your bones among the famous mountains and great rivers, coming and going beyond the ordinary world, no longer the companion of common kinds and ranks. Or you can travel widely and receive heavenly writings, ride a divine bird, stride on a phoenix, leap on a tiger, or harness a dragon. Moving east or west, you enter the purple offices and first see the Perfect Lord of Great Tenuity, then come to reside on the isles below. If you wish, you can ascend to the grotto heavens or turn around to transmit the Dao and its various practices to the people. Receiving heavenly writings and ascending to the grotto heavens, you become a celestial immortal.

Only a few today and in the past have managed to succeed in practicing this method. Most have wanted to rush the practice before their merits were complete. For this reason, I have provided these instructions. As long as the experiential effects of the practice are not yet evident, stick to sitting in quiet meditation, especially if you want to pursue transcendence and liberation.

[Also in DS: As long as the yin life force is not scattered fully, if spirit emerges, it will turn you into a ghost immortal. People will be unable to see your physical form, and you will be forced to keep on coming and going, never having a place of return. Eventually you again entrust yourself to a womb and are caught in the shell of a human body, once more becoming a man. Also, if you are not fully ready to emerge and enter, go out and come back without the proper technique, you may go and try to come back but cannot get back into your original body. Then your spirit and spirit soul don't know where they are and you end up like Buddhist followers dying in meditation or Daoist practitioners undertaking deliverance through the corpse.]

Thus, to practice this way, you must first make sure all the experiential effects are properly present, then select a good spot and erect a meditation hut. Remain far away from all things dirty and defiling, avoid all stinky and evil *qi*, all sounds of coming and going, all attractions of women and children. Not only will they tarnish your perfect *qi*, but your spirit also hates them.

[Also in DS: Emerge once and again enter, but once you have entered, don't emerge again. Then your physical form and spirit can both be wondrous, and you can live as long as heaven and earth, never dying for kalpas eternal. After having entered, emerge again, then, once you have emerged, don't come back. In this manner, you can liberate yourself from the physical form like a cicada shedding its skin, fly up to the gods, and join the sages. You can completely transcend the ordinary and liberate yourself from the common, become a perfected and immortal. Permanently residing beyond the dust and wind of this world, you live on the three isles and ten continents.]

Dao Essentials: Unless you follow these methods completely, you will perish and stop to exist. The above presents the third gate of the great vehicle, becoming a celestial immortal.

Bibliography

Akahori, Akira. 1989. "Drug Taking and Immortality." In *Taoist Meditation and Longevity Techniques*, edited by Livia Kohn, 71-96. Ann Arbor: University of Michigan, Center for Chinese Studies.

Albertus, Frater. 1974. *The Alchemist's Handbook: Manual for Practical Laboratory Alchemy*. New York: Samuel Weiser.

Allan, Sarah. 1991. *The Shape of the Turtle: Myth, Art, and Cosmos in Early China*. Albany: State University of New York Press.

Ambelain, Robert. 2005. *Spiritual Alchemy: The Inner Path*. Translated by Piers A. Vaughan. http://www.alchemystudy.com

Andersen, Poul. 1990a. "The Practice of *Bugang*." *Cahiers d'Extrême-Asie* 5:15-53.

_____. 1990b. "Guideline to the Eight Trigrams." *Occasional Papers* 6:13-30.

_____. 1996. "Taoist Talismans and the History of the Tianxin Tradition." *Acta Orientalia* 57:141-52.

Ang, Isabelle. 1997. "Le culte de Lü Dongbin sous les Song du Sud." *Journal Asiatique* 285:473-507.

Arthur, Shawn. 2006. "Life without Grains: *Bigu* and the Daoist Body." In *Daoist Body Cultivation*, edited by Livia Kohn, 91-122. Magdalena, NM: Three Pines Press.

Baldrian-Hussein, Farzeen. 1984. *Procédés secrets du joyau magique*. Paris: Les Deux Océans.

_____. 1985. "Yüeh-yang and Lü Tung-pin's *Chin-yüan ch'un*: A Sung Alchemical Poem." In *Religion und Philosophie in Ostasien: Festschrift für Hans Steininger*, edited by. G. Naundorf et al., 19-31. Würzburg: Königshausen and Neumann.

_____. 1986. "Lü Tung-pin in Northern Sung Literature." *Cahiers d'Extrême-Asie* 2:133-70.

_____. 1990. "Inner Alchemy: Notes on the Origin and the Use of the Term *neidan*." *Cahiers d'Extrême-Asie* 5:163-90.

_____. 2004. "The *Book of the yellow court*: A Lost Song Commentary of the 12th Century." *Cahiers d'Extrême-Asie* 14:187-226.

Bauer, Wolfgang. 1956. "Der Herr vom gelben Stein." *Oriens Extremus* 3: 137-52.

Beebe, John. 2014. "Foreword." In *Alchemy and Psychotherapy: Post-Jungian Perspectives*, edited by Dale Mathers, xvii-xx. London: Routledge.

Begley, Sharon, ed. 2007. *Train Your Mind to Change Your Brain*. New York: Ballentine.

Belmonte, Juan Antonio. 2010. "Finding Our Place in the Cosmos: The Role of Astronomy in Ancient Cultures." *Journal of Cosmology* 9:2052-62.

Benn, Charles. 2000. "Daoist Ordination and *Zhai* Rituals." In *Daoism Handbook*, edited by Livia Kohn, 309-38. Leiden: Brill.

Bensky, Dan, and John O'Connor. 1984. *Acupuncture: A Comprehensive Text*. New York: Eastland Press.

Bertrand, Cristina. 2019. *Yi Jing: Inner Transformation – The Nonagram*. Miami Beach: Cristina Bertrand LLC.

Bertschinger, Richard. 2018. *A Record of the Assembled Immortals and Gathered Perfected of the Western Hills*. London: Singing Dragon.

Birrell, Anne. 1993. *Chinese Mythology: An Introduction*. Baltimore: Johns Hopkins University Press.

Bodde, Derk. 1991. *Chinese Thought, Society, and Science: The Intellectual and Social Background of Science and Technology in Pre-modern China*. Honolulu: University of Hawaii Press.

Bokenkamp, Stephen R. 2007. "What Daoist Body?" In *Purposes, Means and Convictions in Daoism: A Berlin Symposium*, edited by Florian C. Reiter, 131-50. Wiesbaden: Harrassowitz.

Bol, Peter. 2001. "Whither the Emperor: Emperor Huizong, the New Policiies, and the Tang-Song Transition." *Journal of Song and Yuan Studies* 31:103-34.

Boltz, Judith M. 1987. *A Survey of Taoist Literature: Tenth to Seventeenth Centuries*. Berkeley: University of California, China Research Monograph 32.

Brashier, Kenneth. 1996. "Han Thanatology and the Division of 'Souls.'" *Early China* 21:125-58.

Brindley, Erica F., Paul R. Goldin, and Esther S. Klein. 2013. "A Philosophical Translation of the *Heng Xian*." *Dao: A Journal of Comparative Philosophy* 12.2:145-51.

Bumbacher, Stephan Peter. 2001. "Zu den Körpergottheiten im chinesischen Taoismus." In *Noch eine Chance für die Religionsphänomenologie?*, edited by D. Peoli-Olgiati, A. Michaels, and F. Stolz, 151-72. Frankfurt: Peter Lang.

Bygott, Catherine. 2014. "Mysterium Coniunctionis: Fabric of Life." In *Alchemy and Psychotherapy: Post-Jungian Perspectives*, edited by Dale Mathers, 27-43. London: Routledge.

Cammann, Schuyler. 1961. "The Magic Square of Three in Old Chinese Philosophy and Religion." *History of Religions* 1:37-80.

_____. 1990. "The Eight Trigrams: Variants and Their Uses." *History of Religions* 29:301-17.

_____. 1991. "Chinese Hexagrams, Trigrams, and the Binary System." *Proceedings of the American Philosophical Society* 135.4:576-89.

Campany, Robert Ford. 2002. *To Live As Long As Heaven and Earth: A Translation and Study of Ge Hong's Traditions of Divine Transcendents*. Berkeley: University of California Press.

Capitanio, Joshua. 2013. "Health, Illness, and the Body in Buddhist and Daoist Self-Cultivation." In *Brahman and Dao: Comparative Studies in Indian and Chinese Philosophy and Religion*, edited by Ithamar Theodor and Zhihua Yao, 181-92. New York: Lexington Books.

Carty, Donald Gordon, et al. 2007. *The Emerald Tablet and the Alchemy of Spiritual Transformation*. Atlanta: Personal Development Institute.

Cedzich, Ursula-Angelika. 2001. "Corpse Deliverance, Substitute Bodies, Name Change, and Feigned Death: Aspects of Metamorphosis and Immortality in Early Medieval China." *Journal of Chinese Religions* 29:1-68.

Ch'en, Kenneth. 1973. *The Chinese Transformation of Buddhism*. Princeton, Princeton University Press.

Chan, Alan L. K. 2011. "Harmony as Contested Metaphor and Conceptions of Rightness (Yi) in Early Confucian Ethics." In *How Should One Live: Comparing Ethics in Ancient China and Greco-Roman Antiquity*, edited by R. A. H. King and Dennis R. Schilling, 37-62. Boston: DeGruyter.

Chan, Shirley. 2014. "Oneness: Reading the 'All Things Flow in Form' (*Fanwu liuxing*) of the Shanghai Museum Bamboo Texts." *Journal of Chinese Philosophy* 41.

Chan, Wing-tsit. 1963. *A Source Book in Chinese Philosophy*. Princeton: Princeton University Press.

Chang, Wonsuk. 2009. "Reflections on Time and Related Ideas in the *Yijing*." *Journal of Chinese Philosophy* 59.2:216-29.

Chao, Shin-yi. 2009. "Summoning the Thunder Generals: Internal Alchemy in the Thunder Rites." In *Internal Alchemy: Self, Society, and the Quest for Immortality*, edited by Livia Kohn and Robin R. Wang, 105-21. Magdalena, NM: Three Pines Press.

_____. 2011. *Daoist Rituals, State Religion, and Popular Practices: Zhenwu Worship from Song to Ming* (960-1644). London: Routledge.

Chen, Ellen Marie. 1974. "Tao as the Great Mother and the Influence of Motherly Love in the Shaping of Chinese Philosophy." *History of Religions* 14:51-65.

Chen, Shih-chuan. 1972. "How to Form a Hexagram and Consult the *I Ching*." *Journal of the American Oriental Society* 92.2:237-49.

Cheng, Chung-ying. 1989. "On Harmony as Transformation: Pradigms from the *I-ching*." *Journal of Chinese Philosophy* 16: 125-58.

_____. 1996. "*Zhouyi* and Philosophy of *Wei* (Positions)." *Extreme-Orient, Extreme-Occident* 18: 149–76.

_____. 2006a. "Toward Constructing a Dialectics of Harmonization: Harmony and Conflict in Chinese Philosophy." *Journal of Chinese Philosophy* 33, Supplemen: 25–59.

_____. 2006b. "Philosophy of the *Yijing*: Insights into Taiji and Dao as Wisdom of Life." *Journal of Chinese Philosophy* 33,3: 323–33.

_____. 2011. "Interpreting Paradigm of Change in Chinese Philosophy." *Journal of Chinese Philosophy* 38.3: 339–67.

Cherniak, Susan. 1994. "Book Culture and Textual Transmission in Sun China." *Harvard Journal of Asiatic Studies* 54:5-125.

Chia, Lucille. 1996. "The Development of the Jianyang Book Trade, Song-Yuan." *Late Imperial China* 17.1:10-48.

_____. 2003. "*Mashaben*: Commercial Publishing in Jianyang from the Song to the Ming." In *The Song-Yuan-Ming Transition in Chinese History*, edited by Paul Jakov Smith and Richard von Glahn, 284-328. Cambridge, Mass.: Harvard University Asia Center.

Chia, Mantak. 1983. *Awaken Healing Energy of the Tao*. Santa Fe: Aurora Press.

Clart, Philip. 2009. "The Eight Immortals between Daoism and Popular Religion: Evidence from a New Spirit-Written Scripture." In *Foundations of Daoist Ritual: A Berlin Symposium*, edited by Florian C. Reiter, 84-106. Wiesbaden: Harrassowitz.

Cleary, Thomas. 1984. *The Flower Ornament Scripture*. Boston: Shambhala.

_____. 1992. *The Secret of the Golden Flower: The Classic Chinese Book of Life*. San Francisco: Harper.

_____. 1997. *Opening the Dragon Gate: The Making of a Modern Taoist Wizard*. By Chen Kaiguo and Zheng Shunchao. Tokyo: Tuttle.

_____. 2003. *The Taoist Classics, Volume Two*. Boulder: Shambhala.

Cobb, Cathy, Monty L. Fetterolf, and Harold Goldwhite. 2014. *The Chemistry of Alchemy: From Dragon's Blood to Donkey Dung—How Chemistry Was Forged*. New York: Prometheus Books.

Cook, Constance. A., and Zhao Lu. 2017. *Stalk Divination: A Newly Discovered Alternative to the I Ching*. New York: Oxford University Press.

Cook, Scott Bradley. 2012. *The Bamboo Texts of Gudian: A Study and Complete Translation*. Ithaca: Cornell University Press.

Davis, Edward L. 2001. *Society and the Supernatural in Sung China*. Honolulu: University of Hawaii Press.

Davis, Richard L. 2004. *Historical Records of the Five Dynasties*. New York: Columbia University Press.

Deng, Kent G. 2013. "Demystifying Growth and Development in North Song China, 960-1127." *Working Papers* 178/13. www.eprints.lse.ac.uk/50969/

Despeux, Catherine. 2005. "Visual Representations of the Body in Chinese Medical and Daoist Texts from the Song to the Qing." *Asian Medicine: Tradition and Modernity* 1:10-52

_____. 2006. "The Six Healing Breaths." In *Daoist Body Cultivation*, edited by Livia Kohn, 37-67. Magdalena, NM: Three Pines Press.

_____. 2012. *Taoïsme et connaissance de soi: La carte et la culture de la perfection (Xiuzhen tu)*. Paris: Guy Trédaniel.

_____. 2019. *Taoism and Self-Knowledge: The Chart for the Cultivation of Perfection* (*Xiuzhen tu*), Translated by J. E. E. Pettit. Leiden: Brill.

_____, and Livia Kohn. 2003. *Women in Daoism*. Cambridge, Mass.: Three Pines Press.

Drexler, Monika. 1994. *Daoistische Schriftmagie: Interpretationen zu den fu im Daozang*. Stuttgart: Franz Steiner, Münchener Ostasiatische Studien, 68.

Ebrey, Patricia B. 2000. "Taoism and Art at the Court of Song Huizong." In *Daoism and the Arts of China*, edited by Stephen Little and Shawn Eichman, 95-111. Berkeley: University of California Press.

_____, and Maggie Bickford, eds. 2006. *Emperor Huizong and Late Northern Song China*. Cambridge, Mass.: Harvard University Asia Center.

Edwards, Ronald A. 2013. "Redefining Industrial Revolution: Song China and England." Paper Presented at "Lessons from History" Conference at Lingnan University, Hong Kong. economicdynamics.org/meetpapers/2013/paper_351.pdf

Eliade, Mircea. 1962. *The Forge and the Crucible: The Origins and Structures of Alchemy*. Chicago: University of Chicago Press.

Elvin, Mark. 1971. *The State, Printing, and the Spread of Scientific and Technological Knowledge in China, 950-1350*. Moscow: Nauka Publishing House.

_____. 1973. *The Pattern of the Chinese Past*. Stanford: Stanford University Press.

Emerson, John. 1996. "Yang Chu's Discovery of the Body." *Philosophy East & West* 46.4:533-66.

Engelhardt, Ute. 2000. "Longevity Techniques and Chinese Medicine." In *Daoism Handbook*, edited by Livia Kohn, 74-108. Leiden: Brill.

Eskildsen, Stephen. 1989. "The Beliefs and Practices of Early Ch'üan-chen Taoism." M.A. Thesis, University of British Columbia, Vancouver.

_____. 1998. *Asceticism in Early Taoist Religion*. Albany: State University of New York Press.

_____. 2001. "Seeking Signs of Proof: Visions and Other Trance Phenomena in Early Quanzhen Taoism." *Journal of Chinese Religions* 29:139-60.

_____. 2004. *The Teachings and Practices of the Early Quanzhen Taoist Masters*. Albany: State University of New York Press.

_____. 2006. “Emergency Death Meditations for Internal Alchemists.” *T’oung Pao* 92:373-409.

_____. 2007. “Mystical Ascent and Out-of-Body Experience in Medieval Daoism.” *Journal of Chinese Religions* 35:29-55.

_____. 2008. “Do Immortals Kill?: The Controversy Surrounding Lü Dongbin.” *Journal of Daoist Studies* 1:28-66.

_____. 2009a. “*Neidan* Methods for Opening the Gate of Heaven.” In *Internal Alchemy: Self, Society, and the Quest for Immortality*, edited by Livia Kohn and Robin R. Wang, 87-104. Magdalena, NM: Three Pines Press.

_____. 2009b. “Death, Immortality, and Spirit Liberation in Northern Song Daoism: The Hagiographical Accounts of Zhao Daoyi.” In *The People and the Dao: New Studies in Chinese Religions in Honour or Daniel L. Overmyer*, edited by Philip Clart and Paul Crowe, 389-418. St. Augustin/Nettetal: Steyler Verlag, Monumenta Serica Monograph LX.

_____. 2015. *Daoism, Meditation, and the Wonders of Serenity: From the Latter Han Dynasty (25-220) to the Tang Dynasty (618-907)*. Albany: State University of New York Press.

Fairbank, John King. 1992. *China: A New History*. Cambridge, Mass.: Belknap Press of Harvard Unversity.

Forke, Alfred. 1925. *The World Conception of the Chinese, Their Astronomical, Cosmological, and Physico-Philosophical Speculations*. London: Arthur Probsthain.

Freeman, David. 2014. “The Stone That the Builders Rejected.” In *Alchemy and Psychotherapy: Post-Jungian Perspectives*, edited by Dale Mathers, 15-26. London: Routledge.

Freemantle, Francisca, and Chögyam Trungpa. 1974. *The Tibetan Book of the Dead*. Berkeley: Shambhala.

Fukui Kojun. 1974. “A Study of *Chou-i Ts’an-t’ung-ch’i*.” *Acta Asiatica* 27:19-32.

Furth, Charlotte. 1999. *A Flourishing Yin: Gender in China’s Medical History, 960-1665*. Berkeley: University of California Press.

Geiger, Heinrich. 2013. “Sign, Image, and Language in the Book of Changes (*Yijing*).” *Frontiers of Philosophy in China* 8.4:607-23.

Gernet, Jacques. 1962. *Daily Life in China at the Eve of the Mongol Invasion.* Stanford: Stanford University Press.

Girardot, Norman. 1985. “Behaving Cosmogonically in Early Taoism.” In *Cosmogony and Ethical Order: New Studies in Comparative Ethics*, edited by Robin W. Lovin and Frank E. Reynolds, 67-97. Chicago: University of Chicago Press.

_____. 2008 [1983]. *Myth and Meaning in Early Taoism: The Theme of Chaos (Hundun)*. Dunedin, Fla.: Three Pines Press.

Glahn, Richard von. 2003. "Towns and Temples: Urban Growth and Decline in the Yangzi Delta, 1100-1400." In *The Song-Yuan-Ming Transition in Chinese History*, edited by Paul Jakov Smith and Richard von Glahn, 176-211. Cambridge, Mass.: Harvard University Asia Center.

Goldin, Paul R.2006. "The Cultural and Religious Background of Sexual Vampirism in Ancient China." *Theology and Sexuality* 12.3:285-307.

Goodrich, Charles. 1925. *The Invention of Printing in China and Its Spread Westward.* New York: Ronald Press.

Graham, A. C. 1960. *The Book of Lieh-tzu*. London: A. Murray.

_____. 1986. *Yin-Yang and the Nature of Correlative Thinking*. Singapore: The Institute for East Asian Philosophies.

_____. 1989. *Disputers of the Tao: Philosophical Argument in Ancient China*. La Salle, Ill.: Open Court Publishing Company.

Gu, Ming Dong. 2005. "The *Zhouyi* (Book of Changes) as an Open Classic: A Semiotic Analysis of Its System of Representation." *Philosophy East and West* 55.2:257-82.

Gulik, Robert H. van. 1961. *Sexual Life in Ancient China*. Leiden: E. Brill.

Habib, Irfan. 2000. "Joseph Needham and the History of Indian Technology." *Indian Journal of History of Science* 35.3:245-74.

Hamilton, Nigel. 1985. *The Alchemical Process of Transformation*. www.sufismus.ch/assets/files/omega_dream/alchemy_e.pdf

Harper, Donald. 1985. "A Chinese Demonography of the Third Century B.C." *Harvard Journal of Asiatic Studies* 45:459-98.

_____. 1994. "Resurrection in Warring States Popular Religion." *Taoist Resources* 5.2:13-28.

_____. 1998. *Early Chinese Medical Manuscripts: The Mawangdui Medical Manuscripts*. London: Wellcome Asian Medical Monographs.

Harrington, Michael. 2016. "Principle and Place: Complementary Concepts in Confucian *Yijing* Commentary." *Philosophy East and West* 66.3:861-82.

Hawes, Colin S. C. 2005. *The Social Circulation of Poetry in the Mid-Northern Song*. Albany: State University of New York Press.

Hawkes, David. 1981. "Quanzhen Plays and Quanzhen Masters." *Bulletin d'Ecole Française d'Extrême Orient* 69:153-170.

Henderson, John B. 1984. *The Development and Decline of Chinese Cosmology*. New York: Columbia University Press.

Hendrischke, Barbara. 2006. *The Scripture on Great Peace: The Taiping jing and the Beginnings of Daoism*. Berkeley: University of California Press.

_____, and Benjamin Penny. 1996. "*The 180 Precepts Spoken by Lord Lao*: A Translation and Textual Study." *Taoist Resources* 6.2:17-29.

Hervout, Yves, ed. 1986. *A Sung Bibliography, Bibliographie des Sung*. Hong Kong: The Chinese University Press.

Ho, Chung-tao. 2018. *Internal Alchemy for Everyone*. St. Petersburg, Fla.: Three Pines Press.

Homann, Rolf. 1971. *Die wichtigsten Körpergottheiten im Huang-t'ing-ching*. Göppingen: Alfred Kümmerle.

_____. 1976. *Pai Wen P'ien or The Hundred Questions: A Dialogue between Two Daoists on the Macrocosmic and Microcosmic System of Correspondences*. Leiden: Brill.

Hon, Tze-ki. 2019. "Chinese Philosophy of Change (*Yijing*). In *Stanford Encyclopedia of Philosophy*. www.plato/stanford/edu.

Huang, Jane, and Michael Wurmbrand. 1987. *The Primordial Breath: Ancient Chinese Ways of Prolonging Life through Breath*. 2 vols. Torrance, Cal.: Original Books.

Huang, Shih-Shan Susan. 2010. "Daoist Imagery of Body and Cosmos, Part 1: Body Gods and Starry Travel." *Journal of Daoist Studies* 3:57-90.

_____. 2010. "Daoist Imagery of Body and Cosmos, Part 1: Body Gods and Starry Travel." *Journal of Daoist Studies* 3:57-90.

_____. 2011. "Daoist Imagery of Body and Cosmos, Part 2: Body Worms and Internal Alchemy." *Journal of Daoist Studies* 4:32-62.

_____. 2011. "Daoist Imagery of Body and Cosmos, Part 2: Body Worms and Internal Alchemy." *Journal of Daoist Studies* 4:32-62.

_____. 2012. *Picturing the True Form: Daoist Visual Culture in Traditional China*. Cambridge, Mass.: Harvard University, Center for Chinese Studies.

Hudson, Wm Clarke.2008. "Spreading the Dao, Managing Mastership and Performing Salvation: the Life and the Alchemical Teachings of Chen Zhixu." Ph. D. Diss, Indiana University, Bloomington.

Hymes, Robert P. 1986. *Statesmen and Gentlemen: The Elite of Fu-Chou, Chiang-Hsi in Northern and Southern Song*. Cambridge: Cambridge University Press.

_____. 2002. *Way and Byway: Taoism, Local Religion, and Models of Divinity in Sung and Modern China*. Berkeley: University of California Press.

_____, and Conrad Schirokauer, eds. *Ordering the World: Approaches to State and Society in Sung Dynasty China*. Berkeley: University of California Press.

Ishida, Hidemi. 1989. "Body and Mind: The Chinese Perspective." In *Taoist Meditation and Longevity Techniques*, edited by Livia Kohn, 41-70. Ann Arbor: University of Michigan, Center for Chinese Studies.

Jackowicz, Stephen. 2006. "Ingestion, Digestion, and Regestation: The Complexities of the Absorption of *Qi*." In *Daoist Body Cultivation*, edited by Livia Kohn, 68-90. Magdalena, NM: Three Pines Press.

Jarrett, Lonny S. 2003. *The Clinical Practice of Chinese Medicine*. Stockbridge, Mass.: Spirit Path Press.

Jing, Anning. 1996. "The Eight Immortals: The Transformation of T'ang and Sung Eccentrics during the Yüan Dyansty." In *Arts of the Sung and Yüan*, edited by Maxwell Hearn and Judith G. Smith, 213-30. New York: The Metropolitan Museum of Art.

Jochim, Chris. 1998. "Just Say No to "No Self" in *Zhuangzi*." In *Wandering at Ease in the Zhuangzi*, edited by Roger Ames, 34-74. Albany: State University of New York Press.

Johnson, Jerry Alan. 2014. *The Secret Teachings of Chinese Energetic Medicine: Volume 2: Energetic Alchemy, Dao Yin Therapy, Healing Qi Deviations, Spirit Pathology*. Pacific Grove: International Institute of Medical Qigong.

Jordan, David K. 1972. *Gods, Ghosts and Ancestors*. Berkeley: University of California Press.

Jullien, François. 2007. *Vital Nourishment: Departing from Happiness*. Translated by Arthur Goldhammer. New York: Zone Books.

Jung, C. G. 1968. *Psychology and Alchemy*. Princeton: Princeton University Press.

Kalinowski, Marc. 1991. *Cosmologie et divination dans la Chine ancienne. Le Compendium des Cinq Agents*. Paris: Publications de l'Ecole Française d'Extrême-Orient.

Kaptchuk, Ted J. 2000. *The Web that Has No Weaver: Understanding Chinese Medicine*. New York: Congdon & Weed.

Karcher, Stephen. 2002. *I Ching: The Classic Chinese Oracle of Change*. London: Vega.

Karetzky, Patricia Eichenbaum. 2015. "The Transformations of Zhenwu/Xuanwu." *Journal of Daoist Studies* 8:70-96.

Karlgren, Bernhard. 1946. "Legends and Cults in Ancient China." *Bulletin of the Museum of Far Eastern Antiquities* 18: 199-365.

Katz, David A. 2008. *An Illustrated History of Alchemy and Early Chemistry*. Tucson: David A. Katz.

Katz, Paul R. 1996. "Enlightened Alchemist or Immoral Immortal? The Growth of Lü Dongbin's Cult in Late Imperial China." In *Unruly Gods: Divinity and Society in China*, edited by Meir Shahar and Robert P. Weller, 70-104. Honolulu: University of Hawaii Press.

______. 1999. *Images of the Immortal: The Cult of Lü Dongbin at the Palace of Eternal Joy*. Honolulu: University of Hawaii Press.

Kirkova, Zornica. 2016. *Roaming into the Beyond: Representations of Xian Immortality in Early Chinese Verse*. Leiden: Brill

Kleeman, Terry F. 1998. *Great Perfection: Religion and Ethnicity in a Chinese Millenarian Kingdom*. Honolulu: University of Hawaii Press.

Knaul, Livia. 1981. *Leben und Legende des Ch'en T'uan*. Frankfurt: Peter Lang.

Kohn, Livia. 1988. "A Mirror of Auras: Chen Tuan on Physiognomy." *Asian Folklore Studies* 47:215-56.

_____. 1989a. "Guarding the One: Concentrative Meditation in Taoism." In *Taoist Meditation and Longevity Techniques*, edited by Livia Kohn, 123-56. Ann Arbor: University of Michigan, Center for Chinese Studies.

_____. 1989b. "Taoist Insight Meditation: The Tang Practice of *Neiguan*." In *Taoist Meditation and Longevity Techniques*, edited by Livia Kohn, 193-224. Ann Arbor: University of Michigan, Center for Chinese Studies.

_____. 1991. "Taoist Visions of the Body." *Journal of Chinese Philosophy* 18:227-52.

_____. 1993. *The Taoist Experience: An Anthology*. Albany: State University of New York Press.

_____. 1998a. "Counting Good Deeds and Days of Life: The Quantification of Fate in Medieval China." *Asiatische Studien/Etudes Asiatiques* 52:833-70.

_____. 1998b. "Steal Holy Food and Come Back as a Viper: Conceptions of Karma and Rebirth in Medieval Daoism." *Early Medieval China* 4:1-48.

_____. 1998c. *God of the Dao: Lord Lao in History and Myth*. University of Michigan, Center for Chinese Studies.

_____. 2001a. *Chen Tuan: Discussions and Translations*. Cambridge, Mass.: Three Pines Press, E-Dao Series.

_____. 2001b. *Daoism and Chinese Culture*. Cambridge, Mass.: Three Pines Press.

_____. 2004. *Cosmos and Community: The Ethical Dimension of Daoism*. Cambridge, Mass.: Three Pines Press.

_____. 2005. *Health and Long Life: The Chinese Way*. In cooperation with Stephen Jackowicz. Cambridge, Mass.: Three Pines Press.

_____. 2006. "The Subtle Body Ecstasy of Daoist Inner Alchemy." *Acta Orientalia* 59.3:325-40.

_____. 2008a [1995]. *Laughing at the Tao: Debates among Buddhists and Taoists in Medieval China*. Magdalena, NM: Three Pines Press.

_____. 2008b. *Chinese Healing Exercises: The Tradition of Daoyin*. Honolulu: University of Hawai'i Press.

_____. 2008c. *Meditation Works: In the Daoist, Buddhist, and Hindu Traditions*. Magdalena, NM: Three Pines Press.

_____. 2009. "Modes of Mutation: Restructuring the Energy Body." In *Internal Alchemy: Self, Society, and the Quest for Immortality*, edited by Livia Kohn and Robin R. Wang, 1-26. Magdalena, NM: Three Pines Press.

_____. 2010a. *Daoist Dietetics: Food for Immortality*. Dunedin, Fla.: Three Pines Press.

_____. 2010b. *Sitting in Oblivion: The Heart of Daoist Meditation*. Dunedin, Fla.: Three Pines Press.

_____. 2012. *A Source Book in Chinese Longevity*. St. Petersburg, Fla.: Three Pines Press.

_____. 2013. "The Daoist Body of Qi." In *Religion and the Subtle Body in Asia and the West: Between Mind and Body*, edited by Geoffrey Samuels and Jay Johnston, 16-32. London: Routledge.

_____. 2014. *Zhuangzi: Text and Context*. St. Petersburg, Fla.: Three Pines Press.

_____. 2015a. "Kōshin: Expelling Taoist Demons with Buddhist Means." In *Daoism in Japan: Chinese Traditions and Their Influence on Japanese Religious Culture*, edited by Jeffrey L. Richey, 148-76. New York: Routledge.

_____. 2015b. "Forget or Not Forget? The Neurophysiology of *Zuowang*." In *New Visions of the Zhuangzi*, edited by Livia Kohn, 161-79. St. Petersburg, Fla.: Three Pines Press.

_____. 2016. *Science and the Dao: From the Big Bang to Lived Perfection*. St. Petersburg, Fla.: Three Pines Press.

_____. 2017. *Pristine Affluence: Daoist Roots in the Stone Age*. St. Petersburg, Fla.: Three Pines Press.

_____. 2019. "Armored Gods: Generals, Guardians, Killers, and Protectors." *Journal of Daoist Studies* 12:35-64.

Komjathy, Louis. 2007. *Cultivating Perfection: Mysticism and Self-Transformation in Quanzhen Daoism*. Leiden: Brill.

_____. 2008a. "Mapping the Daoist Body (1): The *Neijing tu* in History." *Journal of Daoist Studies* 1:67-92.

_____. 2008b. *Handbooks for Daoist Practice*. Hong Kong: Yuen Yuen Institute.

_____. 2009. "Mapping the Daoist Body (2): The Text of the *Neijing tu*." *Journal of Daoist Studies* 2:64-108.

_____. 2014a. *The Way of Complete Perfection: A Quanzhen Daoist Anthology*. Albany: State University of New York Press.

_____. 2014b. "Sun Buer: Early Quanzhen Matriarch and the Beginnings of Female Alchemy." *Nan Nü* 16:2:171-238.

Kroll, Paul W. 1996. "Body Gods and Inner Vision: *The Scripture of the yellow court*." In *Religions of China in Practice*, edited by Donald S. Lopez Jr., 149-55. Princeton: Princeton University Press.

Kuhn, Dieter. 2009. *The Age of Confucian Rule: The Song Transformation of China*. Cambridge, Mass.: Belknap Press of Harvard Unversity.

Lagerwey, John. 2004. "Deux écrits taoïstes anciens." *Cahiers d'Extrême-Asie* 14:131-72.

Lai, T. C. 1972. *The Eight Immortals*. Hong Kong: Swinden Book Co.

Landels, J. G. 1986. *Engineering in the Ancient World*. Berkeley: University of California Press.

Larre, Claude, Isabelle Robinet, and Elisabeth Rochat de la Vallee. 1993. *Les grands traites du Huainan zi*. Paris: Editions du Cerf.

Legge, James. 1960. *The Chinese Classics, vol. 3: The Shoo King or Book of Historical Documents*. Hong Kong: Hong Kong University Press.

_____. 1967. *Li Chi, Book of Rites: An Encyclopedia of Ancient Ceremonial Usages, Religious Creeds, and Social Institutions*. Hyde Park, NY: University Books.

_____. 1970. *The Chinese Classics, vol. 4: The She King or Book of Poetry*. Hong Kong: Hong Kong University Press.

Lo, Vivienne, and Yidan Wang. 2018. "Chasing the Vermilion Bird: Late-Medieval Alchemical Transformation in the Treasure Book of Ilkhan on Chinese Science and Techniques." In *Imagining Chinese Medicine,* edited by Vivienne Lo et al., 291-304. Leiden: Brill.

Loon, Piet van der. 1984. *Taoist Books in the Libraries of the Sung Period: A Critical Study and Index*. London: Ithaca Press.

Lorge, Peter, ed. 2011. *Five Dynasties and Ten Kingdoms*. Hong Kong: The Chinese University Press.

Louis, Francois. 2003. "The Genesis of an Icon: The Taiji Diagram's Early History." *Harvard Journal of Asiatic Studies* 63:145-96.

Lu, Henry C. 1987. *The Yellow Emperor's Book of Acupuncture*. Blaine, Wash.: Academy of Oriental Heritage.

Lu, Kuan-yü. 1970. *Taoist Yoga: Alchemy and Immortality*. London: Rider.

Lu, Xichen. 2009. "The Southern School: Cultivating Mind and Inner Nature." In *Internal Alchemy: Self, Society, and the Quest for Immortality*, edited by Livia Kohn and Robin R. Wang, 73-86. Magdalena, NM: Three Pines Press.

Maciocia, Giovanni. 1989. *The Foundations of Chinese Medicine: A Comprehensive Text for Acupuncturists and Herbalists*. New York: Churchill Livingstone.

Mahdihassan, S. 1957. "Alchemy and Its Connection with Astrology, Pharmacy, Magic, and Metallurgy." *Janus* 46.

_____. 1986. "History of Cinnabar as Drug: The Natural Substance and the Synthetic Product." *Indian Journal of History of Science* 22.1:63-70.

Major, John S. 1984. "The Five Phases, Magic Squares, and Schematic Cosmography." In *Explorations in Early Chinese Cosmology*, edited by Henry Rosemont, 133-66. Chico, Calif.: Scholars Press.

_____. 1986. "New Light on the Dark Warrior." *Journal of Chinese Religions* 13/14: 65-87.

_____. 1993. *Heaven and Earth in Early Han Thought: Chapters Three, Four, and Five of the Huainanzi*. Albany: State University of New York Press.

_____, Sarah A. Queen, Andrew S. Meyer, and Harold D. Roth. 2010. *The Huainanzi: A Guide to the Theory and Practice of Government in Early Han China*. New York: Columbia University Press.

Maspero, Henri. 1981. *Taoism and Chinese Religion*. Translated by Frank Kierman. Amherst: University of Massachusetts Press.

Mathers, Carola. 2014. "The Queen and the Servant." In *Alchemy and Psychotherapy: Post-Jungian Perspectives*, edited by Dale Mathers, 65-79. London: Routledge.

McRae, John R. 1983. *The Northern School and the Formation of Early Ch'an Buddhism*. Honolulu: Hawaii University Press.

Meulenbeld, Mark. 2015. *Demonic Warfare: Daoism Territorial* NetworkEnes *and the History of the Ming Novel*. Honolulu: University of Hawaii Press.

Mitchell, Craig, Feng Ye and Nigel Wiseman. 1999. *Shang Han Lun: On Cold Damage*. Brookline, Mass.: Paradigm Publications.

Miyakawa, Hisayuki. 1979. "Local Cults around Mount Lu at the Time of Sun En's Rebellion." In *Facets of Taoism*, edited by Holmes Welch and Anna Seidel, 83-102. New Haven, Conn.: Yale University Press.

Moeller, Hans-Georg. 2015. "Parodoxes of Health and Power in the *Zhuangzi*." In *New Visions of the Zhuangzi*, edited by Livia Kohn, 70-81. St. Petersburg, Fla.: Three Pines Press.

Mollier, Christine. 1997. "La méthode de l'empereur du nord du Mont Fengdu: une tradition exorciste du taoïsme médiévale." *T'oung Pao* 83:329-85.

Moran, Bruce T. 2005. *Distilling Knowledge: Alchemy, Chemistry, and the Scientific Revolution*. Cambridge, Mass.: Harvard University Press.

Morgan, Evan. 1934. *Tao, the Great Luminant*. Shanghai: Kelly and Walsh.

Mostern, Ruth. 2011. *Dividing the Realm in Order to Govern: The Spatial Organization of the Song State*. Cambridge, Mass.: Harvard University Asia Center.

Mote, Frederick W. 1989. *Intellectual Foundation of China*. New York: McGraw-Hill.

Mozias, Ilia. 2020. *The Literati Path to Immortality: The Alchemical Teachings of Lu Xixing*. St. Petersburg, Fla.: Three Pines Press.

Munakata, Kiyohiko. 1983. "Images of Nature: Concepts of *Lei* and *Kan-Lei* in Early Chinese Art Theory." In *Theories of the Arts in China*, edited by Susan Bush and Christian Murck, ch. 3. Princeton: Princeton University Press.

Needham, Joseph. 1965. *Time and Eastern Man*. Glasgow: Royal Anthropological Institute of Great Britain and Ireland.

_____. 1981. *Science in Traditional China*. Cambridge, Mass.: Harvard University Press.

_____ et al. 1956. *Science and Civilisation in China*, vol. II: *History of Scientific Thought*. Cambridge: Cambridge University Press.

_____. 1958. *Science and Civilisation in China*, vol. III: *Mathematics and the Sciences of the Heavens and the Earth*. Cambridge: Cambridge University Press.

_____. 1965. *Science and Civilisation in China*, vol. IV.2: *Physics and Physical Technology—Mechanical Engineering*. Cambridge: Cambridge University Press.

_____. 1973. *Science and Civilisation in China*, vol. V.1: *Chemistry and Chemical Technology—Spagyrical Discovery and Invention*. Cambridge: Cambridge University Press.

_____. 1974. *Science and Civilisation in China*, vol. V: Chemistry and Chemical Technology, Pt.2: *Spagyrical Discovery and Invention—Magistries of Gold and Immortality*. Cambridge: Cambridge University Press.

_____. 1976. *Science and Civilisation in China*, vol. V: Chemistry and Chemical Technology, Pt. 3: *Spagyrical Discovery and Invention—Historical Survey from Cinnabar Elixirs to Synthetic Insulin*. Cambridge: Cambridge University Press.

_____. 1983. *Science and Civilisation in China*, vol. V: Chemistry and Chemical Technology, Pt. 5: *Spagyrical Discovery and Invention—Physiological Alchemy*. Cambridge: Cambridge University Press

Nelson, Eric S. 2011. "The *Yijing* and Philosophy: From Leibniz to Derrida." *Journal of Chinese Philosophy* 38.3: 377–96.

_____. 2016. "Chung-ying Cheng: Creativity, Onto-Generative Hermeneutics, and the *Yijing*. *Journal of Chinese Philosophy* 43.1-2:124-35.

Neswald, Sara Elaine. 2009. "Internal Landscapes." In *Internal Alchemy: Self, Society, and the Quest for Immortality*, edited by Livia Kohn and Robin R. Wang, 27-53. Magdalena, NM: Three Pines Press.

Ni, Maoshing. 1995. *The Yellow Emperor's Classic of Medicine*. Boston: Shambhala.

Nickerson, Peter. 1994. "Shamans, Demons, Diviners, and Taoists: Conflict and Assimilation in Medieval Chinese Ritual Practice." *Taoist Resources* 5.1:41-66.

_____. 2000. "The Southern Celestial Masters." In *Daoism Handbook*, edited by Livia Kohn, 256-82. Leiden: Brill.

Nielsen, Bent. 2014. "Cycles and Sequences of the Eight Trigrams." *Journal of Chinese Philosophy* 41.1-2::130-47.

Nienhauser, William H. 1986. *The Indiana Companion to Traditional Chinese Literature*. Bloomington: Indiana University Press.

Northage-Orr, Althea. 2009. "Western Parallels: The Esoteric Teachings of Hermeticism." In *Internal Alchemy: Self, Society, and the Quest for Immortality*, edited by Livia Kohn and Robin R. Wang, 217-40. Magdalena, NM: Three Pines Press.

Nylan, Michael. 1992. *The Shifting Center: The Original 'Great Plan' and Later Readings*. St. Augustin/Nettetal: Styler Verlag.

_____. 2014. *The Five "Confucian" Classics.* New Haven, Conn.: Yale University Press.

Ofuchi Ninji. 1979. "The Formation of the Taoist Canon." In *Facets of Taoism*, edited by Holmes Welch and Anna Seidel, 253-68. New Haven, Conn.: Yale University Press.

Pankenier, David W. 2013. *Astrology and Cosmology in Early China: Conforming Earth to Heaven*. Cambridge: Cambridge University Press.

Penny, Benjamin. 1996. "Buddhism and Daoism in *The 180 Precepts Spoken by Lord Lao*." *Taoist Resources* 6.2:1-16.

Pomeranz, Kenneth.2000. *The Great Divergence: China, Europe, and the Making of the Modern World Economy*. Princeton: Princeton University Press.

Porkert, Manfred. 1974. *The Theoretical Foundations of Chinese Medicine*. Cambridge, Mass.: MIT Press.

Pregadio, Fabrizio. 1991. "*The Book of the Nine Elixirs* and Its Tradition." in *Chûgoku kodai kagakushi ron*, edited by Yamada Keiji, 539-636. Kyoto: Jimbun kagaku kenkyūjo.

_____. 1995. "The Representation of Time in the *Zhouyi Cantong qi*." *Cahiers d'Extrême-Asie* 8:155-74.

_____. 1996. *Zhouyi Cantong Qi: Dal Libro dei Mutamenti all'Elisir d'Oro*. Venezia: Cafoscarina.

_____. 2000. "Elixirs and Alchemy." In *Daoism Handbook*, edited by Livia Kohn, 165-95. Leiden: Brill.

_____. 2004. "The Notion of 'Form' and the Ways of Liberation in Daoism." *Cahiers d'Extrême-Asie* 14:95-130.

_____. 2006a. *Great Clarity: Daoism and Alchemy in Early Medieval China*. Stanford: Stanford University Press.

_____. 2006b. "Early Daoist Meditation and the Origins of Inner Alchemy." In *Daoism in History: Essays in Honour of Liu Ts'un-yan*, edited by Benjamin Penny, 121-58. London: Routledge.

_____, ed. 2008. *The Encyclopedia of Taoism*. 2 vols. London: Routledge.

_____. 2011a. *The Seal of the Unity of the Three*. Vol. 1: *A Study and Translation of the Cantong qi, the Source of the Taoist Way of the Golden Elixir*. Mountain View: Golden Elixir Press.

_____. 2011b. *Wang Mu's Foundations of Internal Alchemy: The Taoist Practice of Neidan*. Mountain View: Golden Elixir Press.

_____. 2012a. *The Way of the Golden Elixir: An Introduction to Taoist Alchemy*. Mountain View: Golden Elixir Press.

_____. 2012b. *The Seal of the Unity of the Three*. Vol. 2: *Bibliographic Studies on the Cantong qi: Commentaries, Essays, and Related Works*. Mountain View: Golden Elixir Press.

_____. 2013. *Wang Jie's Commentary on the Mirror for Compounding the Medicine: A Fourteenth-Century Work on Taoist Internal Alchemy*. Mountain View: Golden Elixir Press.

_____. 2014a. *An Introduction to Daoist Alchemy*. Mountain View: Golden Elixir Press.

_____. 2014b. "Destiny, Vital Force, or Existence? On the Meanings of *Ming* in Daoist Internal Alchemy and Its Relation to *Xing* or Human Nature." *Daoism: Religion, History and Society* 6:157-218.

_____. 2014c. "Superior Virtue, Inferior Virtue: A Doctrinal Theme in the Works of Daoist Master Liu Yiming (1734-1821). *T'oung Pao* 100.4-5:460-98.

_____. 2019. *Taoist Internal Alchemy: An Anthology of Neidan Texts*. Mountain View: Golden Elixir Press.

_____, and Lowell Skar. 2000. "Inner Alchemy (*Neidan*)." In *Daoism Handbook*, edited by Livia Kohn, 464-97. Leiden: Brill.

Principe, Lawrence M. 2013. *The Secrets of Alchemy*. Chicago: University of Chicago Press.

Queen, Sarah A. 1996. *From Chronicle to Canon: The Hermeneutics of the Spring and Autumn Annals according to Tung Chung-shu*. Cambridge: Cambridge University Press.

Ratey, John J. 2002. *A User's Guide to the Brain: Perception, Attention, and the Four Theaters of the Brain*. New York: Vintage Books.

Redmond, Geoffrey, and Tze-ki Hon. 2014. *Teaching the I Ching (Book of Changes)*. New York: Oxford University Press.

Réquéna, Yves. 2012. "The Biochemistry of Internal Alchemy: Decapitating the Red Dragon." *Journal of Daoist Studies* 5:141-52.

Robinet, Isabelle. 1979. "Metamorphosis and Deliverance of the Corpse in Taoism." *History of Religions* 19:37-70.

_____. 1989a. "Original Contributions of *Neidan* to Taoism and Chinese Thought." In *Taoist Meditation and Longevity Techniques*, edited by Livia Kohn, 297-330. Ann Arbor: University of Michigan, Center for Chinese Studies.

_____. 1989b. "Visualization and Ecstatic Flight in Shangqing Taoism." In *Taoist Meditation and Longevity Techniques*, edited by Livia Kohn, 159-91. Ann Arbor: University of Michigan, Center for Chinese Studies.

_____. 1993. *Taoist Meditation: The Mao-shan Tradition of Great Purity*. Translated by Norman Girardot and Julian Pas. Albany: State University of New York Press.

_____. 1994. "Le rôle et le sens des nombres dans la cosmologie et l'alchimie taoïstes." *Extrême-Orient, Extrême-Occident* 16:93-120.

_____. 1995. *Introduction à l'alchimie interieure taoïste: De l'unité et de la multiplicité*. Paris: Editions Cerf.

_____. 2011. *The World Upside Down: Essays on Taoist Internal Alchemy*. Translated by Fabrizio Pregadio. Mountain View: Golden Elixir Press.

_____, and Paula A. Wissing. 1990. "The Place and Meaning of the Notion of *Taiji* in Taoist Sources Prior to the Ming Dynasty." *History of Religions* 29.4: 373-411.

Roth, Harold D. 1997. "The Yellow Emperor's Guru: A Narrative Analysis from *Chuang-tzu* 11." *Taoist Resources* 7.1:43-60.

Samuels, Mike, and Nancy Samuels. 1975. *Seeing with the Mind's Eye: The History, Technique, and Uses of Visualization*. New York: Random House.

Saso, Michael. 1978. "What is the Ho-t'u?" *History of Religions* 17:399-416.

_____. 1995. *The Gold Pavilion: Taoist Ways to Peace, Healing, and Long Life*. Boston: Charles E. Tuttle.

Sawyer, Ralph D. 1993. *The Seven Military Classics of Ancient China*. Boulder: Westview Press.

Schafer, Edward H. 1967. *The Vermilion Bird*. Berkeley: University of California Press.

_____. 1997. "The Scripture of the Opening of Heaven by the Most High Lord Lao." *Taoist Resources* 7.2:1-20.

Schipper, Kristofer M. 1979. "Le Calendrier de Jade: Note sur le *Laozi zhongjing*." *Nachrichten der deutschen Gesellschaft für Natur- und Völkerkunde Ostasiens* 125:75-80.

_____. 1985. "Taoist Ritual and Local Cults of the T'ang Dynasty." In *Tantric and Taoist Studies*, edited by Michel Strickmann, 3:812-34. Brussels: Institut Belge des Hautes Etudes Chinoises.

_____. 1994a. *The Taoist Body*. Translated by Karen C. Duval. Berkeley: University of California Press.

_____. 1994b. "Purity and Strangers: Shifting Boundaries in Medieval Taoism." *T'oung Pao* 80:61-81.

_____. 1995. "The Inner World of the *Lao-tzu chung-ching*." In *Time and Space in Chinese Culture*, editied by Chun-chieh Huang and Erik Zürcher, 114-31. Leiden: Brill.

_____, and Franciscus Verellen, eds. 2004. *The Taoist Canon: A Historical Companion to the Daozang*. 3 vols. Chicago: University of Chicago Press.

_____, and Hsiu-hui Wang 1986. "Progressive and Regressive Time Cycles in Taoist Ritual." In *Time, Science and Society in China and the West*, edited by J. T. Fraser, N. Lawrence, and F. C. Haber, 185-205. Amherst: University of Massachusetts Press.

Schulz, Larry J. 2011. "Structural Elements in the *Zhou Yijing* Hexagram Sequence." *Journal of Chinese Philosophy* 38.4:639-65.

Schwartz, Adam. 2018. "Between Numbers and Images: The Many Meanings of the Trigram Gen in the Early *Yijing*." *Asiatische Studien/Etudes Asiatiques* 72.4:1133-93.

Schwartz, Benjamin. 1985. *The World of Thought in Ancient China*. Cambridge, Mass: Harvard University Press.

Seem, Mark D. 1987. *Acupuncture Energetics*. Rochester, Vt.: Healing Arts Press.

Seidel, Anna. 1987. "Traces of Han Religion in Funeral Texts Found in Tombs." In *Dōkyō to shūkyō bunka* 道教と宗教文化, edited by Akizuki Kan'ei 秋月觀英, 21-57. Tokyo: Hirakawa.

Shiba, Yoshinobu. 1970. *Commerce and Society in Sung China*. Translated by Mark Elvin. Ann Arbor: University of Michigan, Center for Chinese Studies.

Sivin, Nathan. 1968. *Chinese Alchemy: Preliminary Studies*. Cambridge, Mass.: Harvard University Press.

_____. 1976. "Chinese Alchemy and the Manipulation of Time." *Isis* 67:513-27.

_____. 1980. "The Theoretical Background of Elixir Alchemy." In *Science and Civilisation in China*, edited by Joseph Needham, V.4:210-323. Cambridge: Cambridge University Press.

_____. 1995. "State, Body, and Cosmos in the Last Three Centuries B.C." *Harvard Journal of Asiatic Studies* 55.1:5-37.

Skar, Lowell. 1997. "Administering Thunder: A Thirteenth-Century Memorial Deliberating the Thunder Rites." *Cahiers d'Extrême-Asie* 9:159-202.

_____. 2000. "Ritual Movements, Deity Cults, and the Transformation of Daoism in Song and Yuan Times." In *Daoism Handbook*, edited by Livia Kohn, 413-63. Leiden: Brill.

Smith, Kidder, ed. 1990. *Sung Dynasty Uses of the I-ching*. Princeton: Princeton University Press.

Smith, Richard J. 2008, *Fathoming the Cosmos and Ordering the World: The Yijing (I-Ching, or Classic of Changes) and Its Evolution in China.* Charlottesville: University of Virginia Press.

_____. 2012. *The I Ching: A Biography.* Princeton: Princeton University Press.

Smith, Thomas E. 1990. "The Record of the Ten Continents." *Taoist Resources* 2.2:87-119.

Sommer, Deborah. 2008. "Boundaries of the *Ti* Body." *Asia Major* (3rd ser.) 21.3:293-324.

_____. 2010. "Concepts of the Body in the *Zhuangzi*." In *Experimental Essays on Zhuangzi*, edited by Victor H. Mair, 212-27. Dunedin, Fla.: Three Pines Press.

Soothill, William E., and Lewis Hudous. 1937. *A Dictionary of Chinese Buddhist Terms*. London: Kegan Paul.

Spooner, Roy C., and C. H. Wang. 1948. "The Divine Nine Turn Tan Sha Method: A Chinese Alchemical Recipe." *Isis* 38:235-42.

Staal, Julius. 1984. *Stars of Jade: Calendar Lore, Mythology, Legends and Star Stories of Ancient China*. Decatur: Writ Press.Robinet, Isabelle. 2000. "Shangqing—Highest Clarity." In *Daoism Handbook*, edited by Livia Kohn, 196-224. Leiden: Brill.

Steavu, Dominic. 2019. *The Writ of the Three Sovereigns: From Local Lore to Institutional Daoism.* Hong Kong: The Chinese University Press.

Stein, Rolf A. 1979. "Religious Taoism and Popular Religion from the Second to Seventh Centuries." In *Facets of Taoism*, edited by Holmes Welch and Anna Seidel, 53-81. New Haven, Conn.: Yale University Press.

Sung, Z. D. 1971. *The Text of Yi King: Chinese Original with English Translation*. Taipei: Chengwen.

_____. 1974. *The Symbols of Yi King or the Symbols of the Chinese Logic of Changes*. Taipei: The Prophet Press.

Swetz, Frank J. 2003. "Leibniz, the *Yijing*, and the Religious Conversion of the Chinese." *Mathematics Magazine* 76.4:276-91.

Takehiro, Teri. 1990. "The Twelve Sleep Exercises of Mount Hua." *Taoist Resources* 2.1:73-94.

Taylor, Jill Bolte. 2009. *My Stroke of Insight*. New York: Penguin-Plume.

Temple, Robert. 1986. *The Genius of China: 3,000 Years of Science, Discovery, and Invention*. New York: Simon and Schuster.

Tramer, A., R. Voltz, F. Lahmani, and J. Szczepinska-Tramer. 2007. "What Is (Was) Alchemy?" *Acta Physical Polonica* 112:5-18.

Tsui, Bartholomew P. M. 1991. *Taoist Tradition and Change: The Story of the Complete Perfection Sect in Hong Kong*. Hong Kong: Christian Study Centre on Chinese Religion and Culture.

Twitchett, Denis, John K. Fairbank, and Paul Jakov Smith, eds. 2010. *The Cambridge History of China*, Vol. 5, Part 1: *The Song Dynasty and Its Precursors, 907-1279*. Cambridge: Cambridge University Press.

Unschuld, Paul U. 2003. *Huang Di Nei Jing Su Wen: Nature, Knowledge, Imagery in an Ancient Chinese Medical Text*. Berkeley: University of California Press.

Veith, Ilza. 1972. *The Yellow Emperor's Classic of Internal Medicine*. Berkeley: University of California Press.

Verellen, Franciscus. 2019. *Imperiled Destinies: The Daoist Quest for Deliverance in Medieval China*. Cambridge, Mass.: Harvard University Asia Center.

Waley, Arthur. 1930. "Notes on Chinese Alchemy." *Bulletin of the School of Oriental and African Studies* 6.2:1-24.

_____. 1931. *The Travels of an Alchemist*. London: George Routledge & Sons.

Wang, Liping, and Mark Bartosh. 2019. *Daoist Internal Mastery*. St. Petersburg, Fla.: Three Pines Press.

Wang, Robin R. 2005a. "Zhou Dunyi's Diagram of the Supreme Ultimate Explained (*Taiji tushuo*): A Construction of the Confucian Metaphysics." *Journal of the History of Ideas* 66.3:307-23.

_____. 2005b. "Dong Zhongzhu's Transformation of Yin-Yang Theory and Contesting of Gender Identity." *Philosophy East and West* 55.3: 209-31.

_____. 2012. *Yinyang: The Way of Heaven and Earth in Chinese Thought and Culture*. Cambridge: Cambridge University Press.

Wang, Weiwen. 2019. "Lineage Construction of the Southern School: From Zhongli Quan to Liu Haichan and Zhang Boduan." *Religion* 10.3. www.mdpi.com/2077-1444/10/3/179/htm.

Wang, Zhongjiang. 2015. *Daoism Excavated: Cosmos and Humanity in Early Manuscripts*. Translated by Livia Kohn. St. Petersburg, Fla.: Three Pines Press.

Ware, James R. 1966. *Alchemy, Medicine and Religion in the China of AD 320*. Cambridge, Mass.: MIT Press.

Watson, Burton. 1968. *The Complete Works of Chuang-tzu*. New York: Columbia University Press.

Wetering, Janwillem van de. 1974. *The Empty Mirror: Experiences in a Japanese Zen Monastery*. Boston: Houghton Mifflin Company.

Wile, Douglas. 1992. *Art of the Bedchamber: The Chinese Sexual Yoga Classics Including Women's Solo Meditation Texts*. Albany: State University of New York Press.

Wilhelm, Richard. 1950. *The I Ching or Book of Changes*. Translated by Cary F. Baynes. Princeton: Princeton University Press, Bollingen Series XIX.

_____. 1962 [1929]. *The Secret of the Golden Flower*. New York: Harcourt, Brace and World.

Winn, Michael. 2006. "Transforming Sexual Energy with Water-and-Fire Alchemy." In *Daoist Body Cultivation*, edited by Livia Kohn, 151-78. Magdalena, NM: Three Pines Press.

_____. 2009. "Daoist Internal Alchemy in the West." In *Internal Alchemy: Self, Society, and the Quest for Immortality*, edited by Livia Kohn and Robin R. Wang, 181-200. Magdalena, NM: Three Pines Press.

Wiseman, Nigel. 1994. *Fundamentals of Chinese Medicine*. Brookline, MA: Paradigm Publications.

Wong, Eva. 1992. *Cultivating Stillness: A Taoist Manual for Transforming Body and Mind*. Boston: Shambhala.

_____. 2000. *The Tao of Health, Longevity, and Immortality: The Teaching of Immortals Zhong and Lü*. Boston: Shambhala.

Wu, Baolin, with Michael McBride and Vincent Wu. 2011. *The Eight Immortals' Revolving Sword of Pure Yang*. Dunedin, Fla.: Three Pines Press.

Wu, Jing-Nuan. 1993. *Ling Shu or The Spiritual Pivot*. Washington: Taoist Center.

Wu, Zhongxian, and Karin Taylor Wu. 2016. *Heavenly Stems and Earthly Branches: The Heart of Chinese Wisdom Traditions*. London: Singing Dragon.

Yang Jwing-ming. 2003. *Qigong Meditation: Embryonic Breathing*. Jamaica Plain, Mass.: Yang's Martial Arts Association Publication Center.

Yang, F. S. 1958. "A Study of the Origin of the Legend of the Eight Immortals." *Oriens Extremus* 5:1-20.

Yannopoulos, Stavros I. et al. 2015. "Evolution of Water Lifting Devices (Pumps) over the Centuries Worldwide." Water 7:5031-60. www.mdpi.com/journal/ water.

Yao, Ted. 2000. "Quanzhen—Complete Perfection." In *Daoism Handbook*, edited by Livia Kohn, 567-93. Leiden: Brill.

Yates, Frances. 1964. *Giordano Bruno and the Hermetic Tradition*. London: Routledge.

Yetts, Percifal. 1916. "The Eight Immortals." *Journal of the Royal Asiatic Society* 1916, 773-807.

_____. 1922. "More Notes on the Eight Immortals." *Journal of the Royal Asiatic Society* 1922, 397-426.

Yoshikawa Tadao 吉川忠夫. 1987. "Seishitsu kō" 靜室考. *Tōhō gakuhō* 東方學報 59: 125-62.

Yü, Ying-shih. 1987. "O Soul, Come Back: A Study of the Changing Conceptions of the Soul and Afterlife in Pre-Buddhist China." *Harvard Journal of Asiatic Studies* 47:363-95.

_____. 2016. *Chinese History and Culture*, vol. 1: *Sixth Century BCE to Seventeenth Century*. New York: Columbia University Press.

Zaccarini, Cristina. 2011. "Daoist-inspired Healing in Daily Life: Lü Dongbin and the Multifaceted Roles of Chinese Barbers." *Journal of Daoist Studies* 4:80-103.

Zhang, Guangbao. 2009. "History and Early Lineages." In *Internal Alchemy: Self, Society, and the Quest for Immortality*, edited by Livia Kohn and Robin R. Wang, 54-72. Magdalena, NM: Three Pines Press.

Zhang, Weiwen. 2019. "Lineage Construction of the Southern School: From Zhongli Quan to Liu Haichan and Zhang Boduan." *Religions* 10.179:1-19. www.mdpi.com/journal/religions; doi: 10.339.

Zheng Canshan 鄭燦山. 2010. "Daojiao neidan de sixiang leixing jiqi yiyi: Yi Tangdai Zhong-Lü *Lingbao bifa* wei lunshu hexin" 道教內丹的思想類型及其意義: 以唐代鐘呂靈寶畢法為論述核心. *Taiwan zongjiao yanjiu* 台灣宗教研究 9:29-57.

Zürcher, Erik. 1959. *The Buddhist Conquest of China: The Spread and Adaptation of Buddhism in Early Medieval China*. 2 vols. Leiden: Brill.

_____. 1980. "Buddhist Influence on Early Taoism." *T'oung Pao* 66:84-147.

_____. 1981. "Eschatology and Messianism in Early Chinese Buddhism." In *Leyden Studies in Sinology*, edited by Wilt L. Edema, 34-56. Leiden: Brill.

Index